PERSUASION

IN

SOCIETY

To Gayle and Mike—
Great friends, not just family

PERSUASION

IN

SOCIETY

HERBERT W. SIMONS
with JOANNE MORREALE and BRUCE GRONBECK

Sage Publications
International Educational and Professional Publisher
Thousand Oaks ▪ London ▪ New Delhi

For information:

Sage Publications, Inc.
2455 Teller Road
Thousand Oaks, California 91320
E-mail: order@sagepub.com

Sage Publications Ltd.
6 Bonhill Street
London EC2A 4PU
United Kingdom

Sage Publications India Pvt. Ltd.
M-32 Market
Greater Kailash I
New Delhi 110 048 India

Printed in the United States of America

Library of Congress Cataloging-in-Publication Data

Simons, Herbert W., 1935-
    Persuasion in society / by Herbert W. Simons with Joanne Morreale
and Bruce Gronbeck.
        p. cm.
    Includes bibliographical references and index.
    ISBN 0-7619-1907-4 (cloth: alk. paper)
    ISBN 0-7619-1908-2 (pbk.: alk. paper)
    1. Persuasion (Psychology)—Social aspects. 2. Persuasion (Rhetoric)
I. Morreale, Joanne, 1956- II. Gronbeck, Bruce E. III. Title.
    HM1196 .S56 2001
    303.3'42—dc21   00-012754

    02 03 04 05 10 9 8 7 6 5 4 3 2

Acquiring Editor:	Margaret H. Seawell
Editorial Assistant:	Heidi Van Middlesworth
Production Editor:	Denise Santoyo
Editorial Assistant:	Cindy Bear
Typesetter:	Marion Warren
Indexer:	Kathy Paparchontis
Cover Designer:	Ravi Balasuriya

Brief Table of Contents

Part 3: Contexts for Persuasion

Table of Contents

Part 1: Understanding Persuasion

List of Artwork in *Persuasion in Society*

CHAPTER 11

CHAPTER 12

CHAPTER 13

CHAPTER 14

CHAPTER 15

About the Author

HERBERT W. SIMONS (Ph.D., Purdue University) is Professor of Speech Communication in the School of Communications and Theater at Temple University. Web site: http:\\astro.temple.edu\~hsimons; email: hsimons@ astro. temple.edu.

A longtime campus and community activist, Simons helped found "Conscience," a civil rights and community action organization in the mid sixties; brought University and neighboring community together for a first-ever conference; repeatedly engaged supporters of the war in Vietnam in public debate; brought scholars in Communication together for Temple's annual "Discourse Analysis" conferences; cofounded the Kenneth Burke Society at the 1984 "Discourse Analysis" conference; arranged for a replica of Tiananmen Square's "Goddess of Democracy" to be placed on the Temple campus in 1989; and founded the Temple Issues Forum (TIF) in the late nineties (Web site: www.astro.temple.edu/tif). Simons is currently engaged in a TIF-based initiative to forge a "Collegetown" culture in greater Philadelphia. These and other campaign and movement activities find expression in the book.

This is Simons' second textbook on persuasion. He authored *Persuasion: Understanding, Practice, and Analysis* (1976, 1986); edited *The Rhetorical Turn: Invention and Persuasion in the Conduct of Inquiry* (1990) and *Rhetoric in the Human Sciences* (1989); and coedited *After Postmodernism: Reconstructing Ideology Critique* (with Michael Billig; 1995), *The Legacy of Kenneth Burke* (with Trevor Melia, 1989), *Form, Genre, and the Study of Political Discourse* (with A. A. Aghazarian, 1986), and *Perspectives on Communication in Social Conflicts* (with Gerald R. Miller, 1974), among others.

The recipient of four "Best Article" awards, Simons has also served on many editorial boards and has been Editor of Sage's Rhetoric and Society series. A frequent radio and TV commentator on political persuasion, Simons is a national and international guest lecturer. Recipient of a Fulbright Award, he lectured at Uppsala

University in Sweden in 1996. Simons was Research Associate at UC Berkeley and at Honolulu's East-West Center, and was Visiting Professor at Kent State University, University of Massachusetts, University of Maryland, University of Maine, and University of Washington. He received the coveted Distinguished Scholar Award from the National Communication Association in 1995.

Acknowledgments

This book has been a labor of many years. Lots of people shaped the book along the way, but Development Editor Sabra Bissette Ledent warrants special appreciation for making the book's more difficult ideas comprehensible and its many examples come alive. Acquisitions Editor Margaret H. Seawell got this project off to a great start, Nola Lynch imposed much needed order on the book, and Alison Binder did a superb job of copyediting. Mike Buckley, Stef Fritzges, and Zack Preston offered valuable editorial assistance. They, along with many others deserve my thanks, but this is not the Academy Awards and I have not just won an Oscar, so I'll close with appreciation for just two more people, my collaborators.

Joanne Morreale was a doctoral student of mine two decades ago and is currently Chair of the Communication Department at Northeastern University. I am indebted to her especially for her work on television entertainment as persuasion and for her contributions to the chapter on analyzing product advertising. Bruce Gronbeck is A. Craig Baird Professor of Rhetoric at the University of Iowa. Gronbeck's major imprint is in the chapter on political campaigns, but as with Morreale, it is difficult to pigeonhole his varied contributions. In any case, I take full responsibility for any and all errors of fact and judgment in the book.

Preface

Persuasion in Society is an integrative, comprehensive guidebook to understanding, practicing, and analyzing persuasion. It brings together the academic contributions of humanists and social scientists and adds to them the insights of professional persuaders and communication analysts. That the study of persuasion is important—indeed vital—should need little argument. Human beings are both creators and products of their societies in a never-ending cycle. In the United States, our economic system, our republican form of government, our commitments to freedom of speech and religion and to equality of opportunity, our conceptions of ourselves as a sovereign people, and even our idea of nationhood can be traced to efforts at persuasion in centuries past. Indeed, there is scarcely a cultural truism that was not at one time or another the subject of considerable controversy. What is considered true today is certain to be questioned in the future as new efforts at persuasion take the place of the old.

Understanding society, then, requires understanding persuasion. The study of persuasion also has direct, personal payoffs. A recent survey of 2,800 executives by the American Management Association asked, "What is the No. 1 need for success in business today?" The overwhelming response was "to persuade others of my value and the value of my ideas" (Story, 1997, p. 3).

Persuading others is one side of the persuasion equation; the other is responding intelligently and discerningly to the armies of message makers who compete for your attention, your agreement, your involvement, and your money. Persuasion is the engine of our market-driven global economy, say the authors of a recent article in the *American Economic Review*—its title: "One Quarter of GDP Is Persuasion" (McCloskey & Klamer, 1995).

In our increasingly smaller but more complicated world, being an intelligent consumer of persuasive messages is not easy. Take the problem of message density.

Today, many more persuasive messages are presented to us at dizzying speeds. Tons of information are available at the click of a mouse. Yet how should we process it all? How can we make wise judgments when there are so many to be made? One obvious solution for persuadees is reliance on cognitive shorthands (e.g., "Doctor knows best," "The majority must be right," and "She's too cute to turn down"). Yet when are they reliable, and when are they not? When they're not, can we "say no" to them? When we need more than cognitive shorthands, how can we best come to judgment?

Persuasion in Society is written for the would-be persuader as well as the persuadee. It assists persuaders in thinking through issues, then preparing to engage audiences, whether for a one-shot persuasive speech or a long-term campaign or movement. It likewise assists persuadees by sensitizing them to the wiles of persuaders, including the persuader's capacity to overcome audience defenses by appearing not to be attempting persuasion at all.

This book's dual perspective, its shifting between the roles of persuader and persuadee, is also designed to place ethical questions in persuasion front and center. The central ethical problem was put by Aristotle in the first systematic treatise on rhetoric (i.e., persuasion), written thousands of years ago. Persuasion, he observed, gives effectiveness to truth, but it also gives effectiveness to error, bad judgment, and deliberate falsehood.

Moreover, deception comes in degrees and is not always harmful to others. So whose perspective should we adopt as we confront persuasion's many ethical dilemmas: that of the persuader or the persuadee? (Audiences tend to be far less forgiving of persuaders than persuaders are of themselves.) My approach in repeatedly shifting between perspectives is to cause sometimes painful, but I hope illuminating, double vision.

Persuasion in Society was written for the "beginning" student of persuasion, but this is a term that fairly begs for clarification. Chances are that you began figuring out how to persuade before your first birthday. First, you cried because your belly hurt. That was biology, not persuasion. But soon you learned that if you could *act* as if your belly hurt, whether it did or not, then you could get your mother's attention, perhaps even her sympathy. That may well have been the beginning of your career as a student of persuasion—an ignoble beginning, built on deception, but a beginning nonetheless.

Well, you're a bit older at this point. Putting technicalities aside, let's call you a beginning persuasion student if this is your first persuasion course and if you are of typical college age, say 18 to 25. The persons who have studied your generation report that your attitudes toward schooling and habits of study are quite different from those of your baby boomer parents, and different still from those of my generation (Hamlin, 1998). Some important differences so far as this book is concerned are these: You like your lessons tight, succinct, and arrestingly illustrated—just like on television. You're not much for newspaper reading or even for network television news, but you respond well to the conversational style of television talk shows. As channel surfers and Internet browsers, you look for what interests you and turn off the rest. Some observers claim that you're not very critical message recipients—you're highly selective about getting entertainment but not about gathering information for a speech or term paper.

Persuasion in Society will try to meet you halfway: lively, yes, but not at the price of cutting back on a point that needs development; interesting visuals, but selected more to instruct than to entertain. Indeed, a good deal of the "teaching" that takes place in this book is around visuals. As for reports that you're not very critical message recipients, I hope that's not true, but if it is, *Persuasion in Society* should help you do better.

It is not an exaggeration to say that this book was at least 40 years in the making. My earlier text on the subject, *Persuasion: Understanding, Practice, and Analysis* (Simons, 1976/1986), has been so thoroughly reconceptualized and updated that my editor and I feel justified in calling *Persuasion in Society* a new book, rather than a revised edition of the earlier text. Some things have not changed, including my most basic convictions that persuasion is about winning beliefs, not arguments; that communicators who seek to win belief need to communicate with their audiences, not at them; and that persuasion at its best is a matter of giving and not just getting—of moving toward persuadees psychologically, recognizing that they are most likely to give you what you want if you can show them that what you propose also gives them what they want. This is the essence of my *coactive* approach to persuasion, which involves reasoning from the perspective of the other or, better still, building from common ground.

Persuasion in Society also remains focused on clear-cut instances of attempted persuasion—called *paradigm cases*—but gives increased attention to cases in which intent to persuade is not so obvious. I've become convinced, for example, that popular entertainment programming, as in television sitcoms, does more to shape American values—indeed, the media-connected *world's* values—than do sermons and editorials, political oratory, and parental advice. Yet seldom do people think of sitcoms as forms of persuasion. Also occupying a place in what I call the *gray areas* of persuasion's domain are newscasts, scientific reports, classroom teaching, and, yes, textbooks such as this one—all rendered especially credible by appearing in the guise of objectivity.

Preview of Chapters

The preview that follows highlights some of this book's distinctive features. One of those features, amply illustrated in the first chapter of Part 1, is the book's heavy reliance on stories as a pedagogical tool. Chapter 1 uses stories to address fundamental issues: What is persuasion? How is it different from other forms of communication and other forms of influence? In that persuasion deals in matters of judgment rather than certainty, how trustworthy is it? If, on some controversial issues, well-informed experts may reasonably disagree, does this mean that any persuasive argument is as good as any other? The chapter also introduces the behavioral and critical studies approaches to the study of persuasion, the one social-scientific, the other derived from the humanities. *Persuasion in Society* draws on both of these approaches, attempting to take the best from each.

In introducing basic psychological principles, Chapter 2 pulls together behavioral theory and research on the psychology of persuasion but not in an exhaustive way, as might a text devoted exclusively to the behavioral approach. Rather, the aim of the chapter is to derive principles from theory and research that have practical payoffs as guides to the practice and analysis of persuasion. Broached in Chapter 2 for purposes of illustrating the psychology of persuasion is President Clinton's handling of the Monica Lewinsky scandal. I return to this case study in subsequent chapters, focusing especially on President Clinton's speech of August 17, 1998, in which he admitted to an affair with the White House intern.

Chapter 3 moves beyond paradigm cases to begin this book's exploration of the gray areas of persuasion. Its key principle is that the same communicated message may be multimotivated, be multileveled, and have multiple effects—thus perhaps persuading and serving other communicative functions at the same time. In addition to alerting readers to persuasion's many guises and disguises, Chapter 3 raises concerns about mass persuasion's cumulative ideological effects.

Part 2 of *Persuasion in Society* develops principles of coactive persuasion that are introduced in Chapter 4. Whatever your goals as a persuader, whatever your audience and situation, says the coactive approach, you should be engaged in a process of bridging differences by moving toward the persuadee psychologically. Usually, this involves building on common ground between the two of you, but sometimes it requires that you put aside your own perspective and attempt persuasion from the perspective of the persuadee. Emphasized here is the importance of situational analysis and audience adaptation as preconditions for bridging the psychological divide between persuader and persuadee. Also introduced are ways of combining credibility and attractiveness, reason, and emotion.

The remaining chapters of Part 2 elaborate on the principles of coactive persuasion introduced in Chapter 4. Focusing on paradigm cases, as opposed to those in the gray areas of persuasion, they identify resources of communication that are available to the persuader, including those classified by Aristotle under the headings of *ethos, pathos,* and *logos.* For Aristotle, *ethos* referred to the person of the persuader as perceived by the audience. *Pathos* translates most immediately into appeals to emotion but includes incentives of every type. Indeed, there is no clear separation between *pathos* and *logos*, the apparent logic of the message, as you should see in the chapters on cognitive shorthands and on argument.

Chapter 5 identifies verbal, nonverbal, and audiovisual resources of communication that are available to the persuader. What can you do to play up a piece of news? What can you do to play it down? How can you get a friend to comply with your request? How can you turn down a friend's request without endangering the friendship? Think of these vast resources as components of a giant rhetorical tool chest, to be drawn on as the situation requires.

Chapter 6, on framing and reframing, focuses on ways that persuaders may lead persuadees to think "outside the box." Not infrequently, the same facts can be reconfigured or recontextualized; for example, a near-certain disaster reframed as an opportunity. Brought together in this chapter are behavioral research on framing effects and critical studies across a wide range of cases, from political confrontations to psychotherapy.

Chapter 7, on cognitive shorthands, performs double duty. It first draws on a popular book on persuasion, Cialdini's *Influence: Science and Practice* (1993), as a source of useful insights about how to persuade. The chapter then illustrates persuasion in the guise of objectivity by analyzing Cialdini's book as rhetorical in its own right, warranting critical scrutiny. Does rhetorical criticism detract from social science? Not according to social scientist Joseph Gusfield (1976). Rhetoric criticism makes for *better* social science, he argued. That, in any case, is the goal of Chapter 7. It aims at deepening your understanding of cognitive shorthands, rather than undoing Cialdini's basic contribution.

Chapter 8, on reasoning and evidence, focuses on how to build a case for or against a policy proposal. While Chapter 7 concentrates on the sort of snap decision making required of all of us in our fast-paced, message-dense society, Chapter 8 is about how to come to judgment and then get audiences to share that judgment on issues requiring careful thought and deliberation.

Part 3 of this book honors the differences in contexts for persuasion and examines some of the more significant ones with a view toward suggesting principles distinctive to each. The need for Part 3 should be apparent from the variety of paradigm cases identified in Chapter 1 and from the brief discussion of gray areas of persuasion. For example, when you stand up and deliver a classroom speech, there is little advanced opportunity to question those you're trying to persuade. If you're a political candidate or a product advertiser, you may have an audience of millions and a budget that enables you to test-market messages scientifically and then air them numbers of times. If you're leading a protest movement, you may not be able to pay the bus fare of the people you're bringing to city hall for an all-day demonstration. If you're in a conflict situation, you will find that you're at least as much a persuadee as a persuader. Moreover, you and your adversary may not restrict your modes of influence to persuasion alone.

Chapter 9, on going public, is about readying yourself for that moment when you present your ideas before an audience. For unprepared and overprepared speakers, it is often an unnerving experience, but this chapter provides ways to combine passion and polish. Featured in the chapter is a three-step approach to persuasive message preparation that begins with goal setting and ends with test-marketing. The chapter concludes with lessons from research on message design and on adaptation to different types of audience.

Chapter 10, on campaign planning, identifies stages and components of organized, sustained efforts at persuading others, as in campaigns to discourage teenage smoking or to encourage charitable giving. Featured in this section are guides to conducting small-scale campaigns of a sort that students can plan and execute. Chapter 10 then takes up the topic of indoctrination campaigns, ranging from the benign (e.g., campaigns designed to make good citizens of us all) to the highly controversial (e.g., recruitment campaigns by religious cults). Briefly surveyed here, too, is the role played by persuasion in public relations, particularly in crisis management campaigns.

Chapter 11 focuses on modern political campaigns, particularly those for the presidency, in which virtually nothing is left to chance. Here we see the best in persuasion that (a lot of) money can buy. We also sometimes see the excesses of rhetorical combat, as in attack advertisements that prompt false inferences when they are not fabricating outright. Chapter 11 features a tongue-in-cheek "Machiavellian Guide" to getting elected to high office, inviting readers to confront for themselves the ethical dilemmas that candidates face on a regular basis. A typical principle: Raise as much money as you can as early as you can, all the while deploring America's corrupt system of campaign financing.

Chapter 12, on product advertising, looks first at its history, identifying at each stage certain characteristic goals and strategies, then showing how they don't so much get dropped as added to by each new generation of advertisers. Today's advertising—including the so-called anti-ad—gets the lion's share of attention in the remainder of the chapter, with sections on visual persuasion in advertising and on deceptive advertising language.

Chapter 13 examines situations in which interactants shift back and forth between the roles of speaker and listener, persuader and persuadee. The chapter focuses on interpersonal conflict situations, those in which people who live together, work together, and so forth find themselves locked in a struggle over seemingly incompatible interests. It concludes on a positive note with a vision of the ideal persuasion dialogue and with case studies of productive conversation.

Chapter 14 examines another type of struggle, that waged by social movements in behalf of causes they consider just. As with interpersonal conflicts, the study of conflicts between movements and the institutions and countermovements they oppose requires exploring new principles of persuasion, different from those that apply to nonconflict situations, such as mere differences of opinion between friends. The resources available to movement leaders also stand in sharp contrast, say, to those of other campaigners.

Besides offering chapters on the one-shot message, on various forms of campaigning, on advertising, on social movements, and on persuasion in interactive situations, Part 3 pulls together in a concluding chapter questions about the ethics of persuasion. Featured in Chapter 15 is a discussion of the ethics of faculty advocacy in the college classroom. Do your professors attempt to persuade you, or do they maintain a stance of strict neutrality in the classroom, even in discussions of highly controversial issues? What should be their role? Is it the professor's job to profess, as one scribe has argued? Is it to teach you how to think, not what to think? Is neutrality impossible on controversial issues, and are those professors who claim to be "telling it like it is" really masking their own persuasive intent? Finally, you will find three appendices in this book. Appendix I pulls together theories of persuasion to provide a compendium of "how-to" principles on the science and art of persuasion. Appendix II lists tactics of persuasion appropriate to different types of audiences. Appendix III presents in one place 116 issues of ethics vs. effectiveness that were raised in the book, and invites you to revisit them.

References

Cialdini, R. B. (1993). *Influence: Science and practice* (3rd ed.). New York: HarperCollins.

Gusfield, J. (1976). The literary rhetoric of science: Comedy and pathos in drinking driver research. *American Sociological Review, 41,* 16-34.

Hamlin, S. (1998). *What makes juries listen today.* Little Falls, NJ: Glasser LegalWorks.

McCloskey, D. N., & Klamer, A. (1995). One quarter of GDP is persuasion. *American Economic Review, 85,* 191-195.

Simons, H. W. (1986). *Persuasion: Understanding, practice, and analysis.* New York: McGraw-Hill. (Original work published 1976)

Story, R. (1997). *The art of persuasive communication.* Aldershor, UK: Gower.

PART 1

UNDERSTANDING PERSUASION

"Where shall I begin, please your Majesty?" asked the White Rabbit. "Begin at the beginning," the King said gravely, "and go on till you come to the end: then stop."

—Lewis Carroll

CHAPTER 1

The Study of Persuasion

Defining Persuasion

Why Is Persuasion Important?

Studying Persuasion

Summary

Questions and Projects for Further Study

References

Investigative journalist Janet Malcolm (1999) tells the story about a defense attorney who wound up in jail for a year because she could not, or would not, tell a persuasive story in her own defense. Instead of winning an acquittal for her client, she wound up incriminating herself—or so a jury found. The prosecution convinced the jurors that the woman had crossed the line between defending a con artist and collaborating with him. Yet the woman was innocent, Malcolm insists. Indeed, she was too innocent! Had she assembled for the jurors a convincing narrative from the wholly accurate facts at her command, any jury would have acquitted her. But the woman did not believe in coherent, convincing narratives. She preferred what she thought of as the raw, objective truth—what really happened—however messy, incoherent, and unsatisfying. And so the woman, says Malcolm, was figuratively guilty of another crime: She bored her jurors to death.

In one of Plato's *Dialogues* on persuasion, the conversation turns on the question of whether rhetoric, the art of persuasion, is a corrupt art. As was his habit in the

AUTHOR'S NOTE: As an additional convenience for readers, page numbers are provided for some cites, even when not required by usual citation standards.

Dialogues, Plato (n.d./1952) has his mentor, Socrates, speak for him, while Gorgias, for whom the *Dialogue* is named, serves as the principal antagonist.

Gorgias begins the debate by observing that the ability to impress an audience is the surest path to power and influence. His student, Polus, adds that power is the greatest good. Socrates will have none of it. Rhetoric, he maintains, is an art of gulling the ignorant about the justice or injustice of a matter, without imparting any real knowledge. Rhetoric does great damage to the world by making the worse appear the better argument and allowing the guilty to go free (Smith, 1998).

Years later, Plato's student, Aristotle, would offer a defense of rhetoric (Cooper, 1932). Aristotle's response to Plato (and to Socrates) concedes the dangers of rhetoric but rejects their alleged inevitability. Rhetoric can be—indeed, often is—an instrument for giving effectiveness to truth. He adds that truth is not always easy to come by. Still, those deliberating about issues of policy have a need to come to judgment, and those brought before the court of justice have the right to defend themselves. Only philosophers such as Plato and Socrates have the luxury of suspending judgment until they have arrived at universal principles. In the meantime, ordinary citizens will need help as decision makers in assessing alternative courses of action and as persuaders in determining from among the available means of persuasion what is best said to this audience on that occasion.

Both Plato's critique of rhetoric and Aristotle's defense of it contain a good deal of wisdom, but as you might have anticipated, this book gives Aristotle the edge in the debate. To be sure, rhetoric can be used to deceive, mislead, exploit, and oppress. Clever persuaders can exploit what Aristotle called the "defects of their hearers." The innocent in Aristotle's day could be made to appear guilty by accusers doing little more than waving a bloody shirt. Imprudent actions can still be made to appear wise by use of sham arguments, known as *fallacies,* that appear reasonable on first impression but fall apart on close examination.

All this is possible, as Socrates claimed in the *Gorgias,* but it is not inevitable. Persuaders can serve the interests of their audiences at the same time as they serve their own interests; they can achieve power *with* others and not simply power *over* others. Moreover, truth does not stand on its own hind legs. If it is to serve the interests of others, it must be communicated persuasively to them.

Insufficiently appreciated by Plato was Aristotle's key insight: Persuasion deals in matters of judgment, rather than certainty. Judgment matters cannot be settled by fact alone or by sheer calculation. On controversial issues such as these, honest differences of opinion can be expected. Even experts can legitimately disagree on what the facts are, which facts are most relevant, and, most important, what should be made of them.

Asked to advise on a host of familiar personal problems, supposedly expert mental health professionals took diametrically opposed positions. Should my husband's 7-year-old daughter from his previous marriage be permitted to sleep in our bed every time she has a bad dream? asked one distraught stepmother. "You should be more tolerant of your husband's dilemma," suggested a psychologist. "It is just inappropriate for a 7-year-old daughter to be sharing the marital bed on a regular basis," said another. Should I tell my very pregnant sister living many miles away that her father has just died? asked a concerned sibling. "I strongly favor delaying telling your sister until after she delivers her baby," urged one psychologist. "If you value the closeness of your family and respect your sister, don't exclude her at this critical time," urged another (Hall, 1998, p. 7).

The psychologists offered judgments—in these cases, conflicting judgments. But just because persuasion deals in matters of judgment rather than certainty, this was not for Aristotle an invitation to impulsive or random decision making or to perpetual indecision. As Aristotle said, only philosophers have the luxury of postponing the day of reckoning.

Nor was Aristotle of the opinion that any decision was as good as any other, any argument as good as any other. As much as audiences might be taken in by clever deceivers, still truth, according to Aristotle, had a natural advantage over falsehood, and logic a natural advantage over illogic. The power of truth and logic is best appreciated when we accede to them reluctantly, as in the following case.

At an inner-city junior high school for students who had been booted out of other schools, an eighth-grade English class came to life when a student proposed that the school be put on trial for unfair rules. But the student who proposed the mock trial found himself in the role of the defense attorney for the administration, and he could not resist doing a convincing job in its behalf. Witness 1 for the prosecution was destroyed on cross-examination as he was caught overgeneralizing. No, he admitted, the milk at the school is not always spoiled. In fact, it rarely is. Witness 2 was forced to concede that the school doesn't really enforce its rule against bringing candy to class. Then the defense attorney caught the prosecution off guard by pressing an objection: The prosecution had been leading the witness. And so it went. When the deliberations were concluded, the seven student judges voted 6 to 1 for the administration (Michie, 1998).

Consider now the story of the defense attorney who wouldn't tell a convincing story in her own defense. Aristotle would have counseled her otherwise. Indeed, his own treatise on rhetoric is spiced with stories, just as this book is. Like the tales just told of the defense attorney, the mental health professionals, and the junior high school students, stories give truths their hind legs.

Defining Persuasion

1. At a college fair in Hong Kong, a Harvard representative recruits prospective graduate students skilled in science and mathematics. Never does he

claim that Harvard is best, but the one-sided information he imparts makes the case for him.

2. An ad for a soccer shoe on British TV features a white soccer star outmaneuvering two black defenders. The same company features a black soccer hero in another ad targeted to black consumers of soccer shoes.

3. On the occasion of his 30th anniversary as pastor to a conservative congregation, a minister announces that his son is gay and that he is mighty proud of him.

4. A museum in New York keeps a priceless borrowed treasure in a collection of forgeries until it can go on display. The curator assures its insurers that burglars won't know it's a "fake fake."

5. A clothing store announces its seventh "going out of business" sale.

6. A *Jerusalem Post* editorial complains about the government's new regulations governing hate speech over the Internet.

7. An undergraduate student invents what he believes is a novel excuse for turning in a late paper; his grandmother died, and he had to attend the funeral.

8. A young Chinese activist for democracy stands defiantly before a row of tanks en route to breaking up a months-long protest demonstration at Beijing's Tiananmen Square.

9. A television ad critical of a campaign opponent's prescription plan superimposes the word *rats* subliminally—that is, at a rate below the level of most viewers' conscious awareness (see Picture 1.1).

10. An embattled presidential candidate attempts to climb out from under the shadow cast by the current president. "I'm my own man," declares Al Gore in his nomination acceptance speech.

What do these widely different scenarios have in common? The central character (or characters) has a clear intent to persuade. Another shared feature is the use of communication (sermons, editorials) to accomplish that goal. Yet another is that message recipients—otherwise referred to here as receivers, audiences, or persuadees—are invited to make a choice of some sort. These paradigm cases of persuasion involve no complex admixture of motives, no masking of persuasive intent, no questions about whether they are attempts at persuasion or some other form of influence. Typically, it is clear from their contexts what sorts of practices they are and what they are designed to accomplish. For example, editorials are featured in an editorial or op-

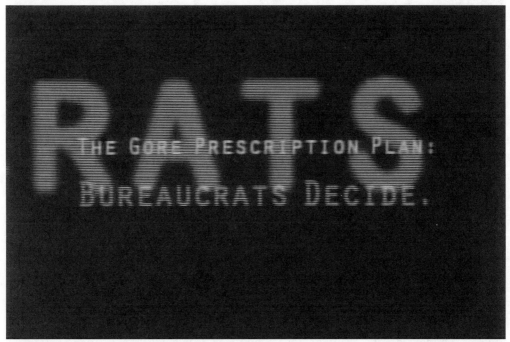

Picture 1.1. The insertion of "RATS" in this political advertisement probably backfired, but by this book's definition, it was an act of persuasion nonetheless. The ethics and effectiveness of subliminal advertising are discussed in Chapter 12.
SOURCE: Reuters/Reuters Tv/Archive Photos. Reprinted with permission.

ed section of the newspaper; sermons are usually given in places of worship by persons designated to present them. If persuasive intent is not apparent from the context, it is made obvious by what is said and by how it is said. These persuaders of the paradigm variety rely, at least in part, on linguistic or paralinguistic (languagelike) messages. Their messages clearly promote a point of view, a proposed action of some sort, or both. In general, when the term *persuasion* is used in this book, it is with the paradigm cases in mind.

This book's definition of persuasion highlights features common to the paradigm cases. Persuasion is *human communication designed to influence the autonomous judgments and actions of others.* Persuasion is a form of attempted influence in the sense that it seeks to alter the way others think, feel, or act, but it differs from other forms of influence. It is *not* the iron hand of torture, the stick-up, or other such forms of *coercion.* Nor, in its purest sense, is it the exchange of money or other such *material inducements* for actions performed by the person being influenced (see Box 1.1). Nor is it pressure to conform to the group or to the authority of the powerful.

BOX 1.1   Toy Truck: Persuasion, Inducements, Coercion

To illustrate the differences between persuasion, material inducements, and coercion, consider the following nursery school situation. Janie covets a toy truck that Reynoldo has been sitting on. Here are some of her options.

1. *Persuasion*
   a. Aren't you tired of being on that truck?
   b. That doll over there is fun. Why don't you play with it?
2. *Inducements*
   a. If you let me play on that truck, I'll play with you.
   b. I'll stop annoying you if you let me play with that truck.
3. *Coercion*
   a. If you stay on that truck, I'll stop being your friend.
   b. Get off the truck or I'll tell Mrs. S.

In her role as persuader, Janie identifies the benefits or harms from the adoption or nonadoption of a proposal but does not claim to be the agent of those consequences. In the cases of inducements and coercion, she is the agent. Inducements promise positive consequences; coercion threatens negative consequences.

Addressed as it is to autonomous, choice-making individuals, persuasion predisposes others but does not impose. It affects their sense of what is true or false, probable or improbable; their evaluations of people, events, ideas, or proposals; their private and public commitments to take this or that action; and perhaps even their basic values and ideologies. All this is done by way of communication. According to St. Augustine more than 1,500 years ago, the fully influenced persuadee

> likes what you promise, fears what you say is imminent, hates what you censure, embraces what you command, regrets whatever you build up as regrettable, rejoices at whatever you say is cause for rejoicing, sympathizes with those whose wretchedness your words bring before his very eyes, shuns those whom you admonish him to shun . . . and in whatever other ways your high eloquence can affect the minds of your hearers, bringing them not merely to know what should be done, but to do what they know should be done. (quoted in Burke, 1950/1969, p. 50)

Persuasion by this definition may succeed or fail at influencing judgments or actions, but it is still persuasion. The emphasis here is on persuasion as a *practice*. No matter what the jury's verdict, for example, the attorneys for the plaintiff and the defense are assumed to be engaged in the practice of persuasion.[1] The *core* of persuasion's "domain" consists of clear-cut attempts at persuading others (Figure 1.1).

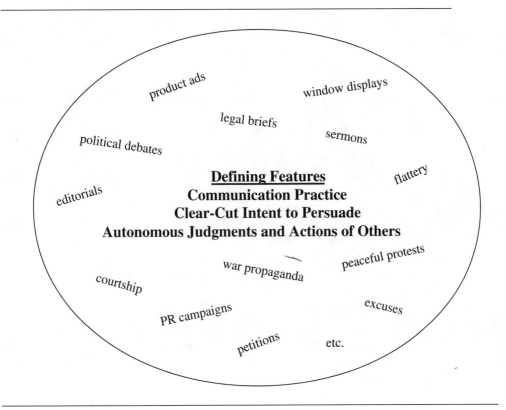

Figure 1.1. Defining Features and Core of Persuasion

The *gray* areas of persuasion are cases in which intent to persuade is not so clear. It is not always clear, for example, whether the news is being slanted deliberately or whether your teacher is knowingly promoting a point of view in the classroom. Included here as well are unintended effects of intentionally persuasive messages. Seldom are persuaders fully aware of everything they are saying and doing when communicating a message. The effects they intend are not always the effects they achieve. Combs and Nimmo (1993) have commented on the unintended effects of Barbie doll promotions (see Picture 1.2).

> Like jolly ol' Saint Nick, Barbie is a cultural icon. The doll represents something more than a plaything or diversion; combined in Barbie's face, figure, and lifestyle are a host of ideas (call them symbols) about how young girls should look, act and be. Barbie teaches young girls what growing up in American society is all about. (p. 4)

Picture 1.2. Barbie Dolls as Cultural Icons, Milan, Italy
SOURCE: Reuters/Jeff Christensen Archive Photos. Used with permission.

Some textbooks treat paradigm cases as the whole of persuasion, but this book does not. Among the cases in the gray areas of persuasion are those in which intent to influence another's judgments is masked, played down, or combined with other communicative motives. As Chapter 3 argues, our culture often neglects cases in which persuasion and expression, persuasion and information giving, and persuasion and other forms of influence are intermixed.

Why Is Persuasion Important?

Think about the last time you visited a shopping mall or even a supermarket. Virtually every object there was market tested, advertised, and merchandised to get you to buy, buy, buy. The objects in these stores do more than service your material needs; they're also symbols, especially for new generations of consumption communities in the United States and abroad. These are people who define themselves and their friends by what they wear and what music they listen to and what they watch on television (Barber, 1996). Why, for many years, was basketball star Michael Jordan (Pic-

Picture 1.3. Michael Jordan Selling Nikes, 1997
SOURCE: Reuters/Jeff Christensen Archive Photos. Used with permission.

ture 1.3) one of the most admired figures in China? Not just because some Chinese
are well versed in the intricacies of the fadeaway jump shot. Besides being a great ath-
lete, Jordan has also been a treasured brand name—a Nike celebrity who symbolizes

American-style opportunity and competitiveness (Gates, 1998). Why did the curtain that separated Eastern Europe from the West come down? One answer, the typical textbook answer, is that the Czechs and Hungarians and Poles and so forth were tired of communism and wanted democracy. Another answer is that the shopping was a lot better on the other side (Barber, 1996).

Some indication of persuasion's role in a market-driven economy is provided by these statistics:

▶ By age 20, the average American has been exposed to approximately 1 million TV commercials. Sound implausible? But that reduces down to 150 ads per day, or 20 to 25 ads for each of the 6 or so hours spent by the average American before the tube each day.[2] Of course, that doesn't count the hundreds, perhaps thousands, of persuasive messages they see or hear on a regular basis in newspapers, on billboards, over the Internet, on packages in the supermarket, and so on.[3]

▶ Fox TV boasted that $1.6 million was the average cost of a 30-second ad on Super Bowl Sunday for 1999—up 23% from NBC's $1.3 million for 1998.[4] NBC reportedly charged double its Super Bowl ad fee for 30 seconds of ad time on the last episode of *Seinfeld* (Hickey, 1998).

But the prevalence of persuasion reflects more than increased advertising, sales, and public relations. The professionals who practice persuasion—for example, lawyers, social workers, teachers, and human resource managers—have grown in numbers as well. For example, there were nearly half a million lawyers in 1991—triple what the number was just 20 years previously (*Statistical Abstracts of the United States*, 1992). That number jumped up to about 700,000 in 1998 (U.S. Bureau of Labor Statistics, 2000).

Persuasion is also the average human being's chief way of exercising influence—of making a difference—at home, among friends, in the community, and on the job. These days, lots of scientific reports show that humans are genetically programmed, environmentally conditioned, and prepackaged from childhood on. But is this the whole story? Not likely. You can make a difference as a friend, a family member, a coworker, a future professional, a community activist, and a volunteer for a charity or a political campaign.

By the time you have finished reading this book, you should be more expert as a persuader and be a more discerning, more sophisticated persuadee. Some textbooks view persuasion from the perspective of the persuader; others view it from the perspective of the persuadee. Here, both perspectives are included for three reasons.

> **BOX 1.2   How Often Do You Attempt to Deceive Others?**
>
> How often do you attempt deception? Once a month? Once a week? All the time? Do males deceive more often than females? Adults more often than children? Respondents to one survey admitted lying an average of 13 times per week (Hample, 1980). But deception, according to Hopper and Bell (1984), can include not just outright, deliberate lying but also exaggerations, tall tales, bluffs, evasions, distortions, concealments, indirectness, and—a big category— self-deceptions. With this list in mind, how often do you attempt to deceive others?

First, by learning how to assume the role of the persuader, you will become more aware, more discriminating as a consumer of persuasive messages. The next time you pick up a package of hamburger at the supermarket, ask yourself why its label says "75% lean" rather than "25% fat." What motives, what logic, what market testing prompted that labeling decision? Why does the military call its troops "freedom fighters" and their enemies "terrorists?" Why doesn't the U.S. Department of Defense call itself the Department of War (as it used to) or the Department of Offense? The answers to these questions may be obvious, but the general point is profound: We become more adept as persuadees by stepping into the shoes of persuaders.

Second, persuaders gain an edge by learning how to think, feel, and act as their intended audiences do. The packagers of hamburger didn't catch on to the "percentage of lean" idea on their own. They assumed initially that boasting about "low fat" content was the best way to market their product, but market testing on typical customers proved otherwise. Similarly, service station owners saw nothing wrong with warning customers about "credit card surcharges" until they saw their customers lured to other gas stations advertising "cash discounts." Like persuadees, persuaders benefit from practicing role reversal.

The third reason for a dual perspective bears on issues of ethics. All of us, at one time or another, have been victimized by stories that have given falsehoods *their* hind legs. Politicians have pandered to us, advertisers have gulled us with their evasions and exaggerations, and even those we've loved and trusted have, on occasion, lied to us. When it has happened to us, we have generally deplored it.

Yet like the student who concocted an obligatory funeral for his grandmother to avoid penalty for a late paper, we too may have been deceptive—but one hopes more imaginative—in offering up excuses (see Box 1.2). Like the recruiter from Harvard, we too have probably accented the positive when it has seemed advantageous. The sporting goods manufacturer that advertised one way to white soccer players and another way to blacks may have warranted our outrage, but who among us hasn't tailored our messages to different audiences? So what made the soccer shoe advertisements immoral? Are pandering, evasions, exaggerations, and even outright lying always unethical, or does the morality or immorality of deception depend on the situation? Shouldn't the curator who hid the fake fake among real fakes get credit for imaginative *and* legitimate deception?[5]

These questions may not admit of easy answers, but they are worth asking none-theless. The frequent shifting between perspectives is designed to be unsettling, en-couraging you from the outset to consider the trade-offs between winning over audi-ences by any means necessary and doing what you would want done to you and for you were *you* a member of one of those audiences.[6] Questions of ethics are raised throughout this book, and they are pulled together in a final chapter on ethics.

Studying Persuasion

A great many disciplines have something to say about persuasion; none says it all. The study of persuasion, still called rhetoric in academic circles, stood for centuries alongside politics, literature, law, and ethics as a branch of the humanities. One of the first manuscripts in recorded history could be regarded as a treatise on rhetoric: an Egyptian papyrus that contained advice on how to curry favor with important people in the pharoah's court (Gray, 1946).

But it was the Greeks, and especially Aristotle, who first systematized the study of persuasion. The method then in use remains helpful to this day; it involved learn-ing from role models and lots of practice, practice, practice. Every Athenian citizen knew Pericles' funeral oration by heart. Also well known was the legend of Demosthenes' struggle to overcome a stuttering affliction by practicing aloud with pebbles in his mouth. Athenians were familiar as well with great speeches that had been given in the deliberative assembly, in the legal tribunal, and at various sites on ceremonial occasions.

The ancient Greeks saw rhetoric through the prism of their needs to create a democratic, civil society, and their mode of communication was primarily oral. Rhe-torical scholars—called *rhetoricians*—have greatly expanded the range of their stud-ies, and they have been joined by media critics, cultural analysts, and others having a humanistic bent in a *critical studies* approach to persuasion (e.g., Cohen, 1998; Hart, 1997). Meanwhile, social scientists have been at work on persuasion using a *behav-ioral* approach to the subject matter (e.g., Allen & Preiss, 1998; Shavitt & Brock, 1994). They have been joined by applied social scientists who have developed tech-nologies of mass persuasion, as in political campaigns and product advertising, from their experience in the field. Although some textbooks on persuasion have a critical-humanistic orientation and others a social-scientific orientation, this text attempts to take the best from both. Let us look first at the behavioral approach.

The Behavioral Approach: Social-Scientific
Research on the Communication-Persuasion Matrix

Social scientists have developed an impressive array of methodologies useful in the study of persuasion, including focus group interviews, surveys, polls, and quantitative content analysis. For example, in a variation on the focus group, a group of 10 or 20 people strolling through the mall might be brought together to respond to the draft of a political speech or the *storyboard* (the scene-by-scene visual, verbal, and sound layout) of a TV commercial. Their commentary is often used to try out (*test-market*) a message. At other times, it is used in research on messages that have already been aired. A useful companion to focus groups is the moment-by-moment electronic analysis of responses to a message by *dial groups,* persons who literally turn a dial connected to a computer to register their reactions on a numerical scale of some sort (Ansolabehere & Iyengar, 1995; Jamieson, 1992).

In developing generalizations about the effectiveness of various types of persuasion, social scientists rely for the most part on research experiments conducted under carefully controlled conditions. This approach is *behavioral* in the sense of treating human judgments and actions as in some sense akin to the predictable, controllable behavior of lower-order animals in the laboratory.[7] Social scientists systematically investigate variations in source (that is, the persuader), message, medium, audience, and context—in who says what to whom, when, where, and how. These communication factors are known as *independent variables.* Determining their effects on *dependent variables* is the object of research. As McGuire (1978) has put it,

> The independent variables have to do with the communication process; these are the variables we can manipulate in order to see what happens. . . . The dependent variables . . . are the variables that we expect will change when we manipulate the independent variables. Taken together, the independent and dependent variables define what we might call the "communication-persuasion matrix." (p. 243)

Consider, by way of illustration, the following generalizations about the psychology of persuasion. Which do you think are true? Which are false? Which are so muddled or so simplistic that you simply cannot judge their veracity?

1. The best way to persuade people to stop a practice harmful to their health is to combine strong fear appeals with concrete and convincing recommendations for action.

2. It is generally effective to present both sides of an issue, making sure to indicate why you think the weight of the evidence supports your position.

3. Because opposites attract, it is generally best when using testimonials in advertisements to present sources as unlike the intended audience as possible.

4. The more you pay people to argue publicly for a position contrary to their own values, the more likely they are to change their values.

5. Very intelligent people are more likely to be persuaded upon hearing an argument than are people of very low or moderate intelligence.

6. The only rule about how to persuade is that there are no rules.

Not all the generalizations can be true, for if Rule 6 is correct, the others are not, and if any of the others are true, then Rule 6 is not.

There is something to be said for Rule 6. It could be argued that persuasion is too much an individual thing. It is too subject to variations in goals, media, contexts, audiences, and subject matter. Although persuasion may be fun to speculate about, it is impossible to generalize about with any degree of reliability. Many humanists subscribe to Rule 6. Rule 6 is probably wrong, however, or at least in need of modification. Although there are no ironclad rules that apply to all individuals in all situations, it is possible to formulate general *guidelines* for persuaders that typically apply. Often, it is necessary to factor in variations in goals, media, audiences, and the like in formulating generalizations. For example, Rule 1 is generally on target, except that people with low self-esteem tend to become overwhelmed by strong fear appeals—at least until they are repeatedly assured that help for their problem is truly available. Especially for them, clear, specific, and optimistic instruction on how, when, and where to take action is essential (Leventhal, 1970).

For reasons that will be discussed in subsequent chapters, Rule 2 is generally accurate, at least as applied to intelligent, well-educated audiences, especially those who are undecided or in disagreement with your position. Rule 3 should probably be marked false. Sources perceived as similar to their audiences tend to be regarded as far more attractive (e.g., likable, friendly, and warm) than sources seen as dissimilar. Rule 4 is generally false, and for reasons that may seem counterintuitive (see Chapter 2). Rule 5 is generally false as well; moderately intelligent people tend to be most persuadable.

But experiments testing for the effects of the independent variables in Rules 1 through 5 do not always yield the same results. Life is complicated, and persuasion is especially so. Fortunately, a statistical technique called *meta-analysis* can be used to compare studies of the same or similar variables and to reconcile apparent inconsistencies (Allen & Preiss, 1998). Ensuing chapters summarize findings from a number of these meta-analyses and report on social-scientific theories that attempt to make sense of behavioral research findings and guide the search for new knowledge.

The Critical Studies Approach:
Case Studies and "Genre-alizations"

Although the behavioral approach treats persuasion as a science, the critical studies approach treats it as an art, one that requires attention to the distinctive features of each persuasive message. Any *critic* of persuasion, then, must first take a careful reading of the message (or messages), looking also at the context in which it was presented. Then and only then can a critic assess the message—perhaps its artistry or its logic or its ethics or social consequences. If study of the case seems to suggest something more general about persuasion, the critic or analyst (these terms are used interchangeably) might comment on that as well. Indeed, some case studies are designed to illustrate the value of one theory (e.g., Farrell, 1993) or perhaps to cast doubt on the utility of another (e.g., Simons, 1996). Just as behavioral research and theory are interlinked, so critical case studies inform rhetorical theory and are informed by it. Here are two examples of the critical studies approach at work.

Catalog Description

> COM 390R Seminar in Contemporary Rhetorical Criticism. May be repeated for credit when topics vary. Semester topics have included dramatistic criticism, content analysis, and methodologies for movement studies. Prerequisite: Upper-Division Standing.

Hart (1997) analyzed this seemingly ordinary message to make two points. First, we are all experts of a sort on persuasion, having been exposed each day to a sea of rhetoric. As voracious consumers of messages, we develop *implicit* knowledge of their hidden meanings, undisclosed motives, and subtle strategies. We know, says Hart, that this is a catalog description; we would recognize it anywhere and be able to distinguish it from a chili recipe or a love letter or the lyrics to a rock song. We know, too, that descriptions such as these aren't always trustworthy. The prose bears the marks of having been funneled through a bureaucracy. Before signing up for COM 390R, perhaps we ought to check with peers or with the instructor who will actually teach the course.

Hart's (1997) second point is that even so simple a message repays close examination. For example, a good deal about persuasion can be learned by attending to its style, says Hart. For one thing, the course description is telegraphic: Incomplete sentences and abnormal punctuation patterns suggest a hurried, businesslike tone, a message totally uninterested in wooing its reader. So, too, are its reasoning patterns telegraphic. Concepts such as "seminar," "credit," and "prerequisite" are never explained. The language is also formidable: excessive use of jargon, polysyllabic words, and opaque phrases (e.g., COM 390R).

Also revealing is what is not found in the text. Nobody runs or jumps here. No *doing* has been done. The absence of verbs suggests institutionalization, hardly what one would expect from what is essentially a piece of advertising. But this is a special sort of advertising, advertising without adjectives. And much else is missing. There are no extended examples to help the reader see what the course will be like, no powerful imagery to sustain the student's visions of wonder while standing in the registration line, no personal disclosure by the author to build identification with the reader. It is almost as if this message did not care about its reader, or, for that matter, even care about itself. It does nothing to invite or entice or intrigue. (Hart, 1997, pp. 26-27)[8]

The Political Campaign Film

Documentaries are types of rhetoric often disguised as purely informative reports or descriptions (Gronbeck, 1978; Morreale, 1991a, 1991b). Morreale has focused on one such genre, the political campaign film. She began by analyzing *A New Beginning*, a campaign documentary produced for the reelection campaign of Ronald Reagan in 1984 and remains the standard for campaign films (Morreale, 1991a). She went on to examine the entire corpus of presidential campaign videos, identifying overarching patterns as well as distinctive characteristics (Morreale, 1991b). She found not only that these videos trade on the newsy aura of documentary but also that they promote in the guise of entertainment. Unlike oratory, the campaign film can provide visual "proof" of a candidate's alleged virtues, combining visuals with words and music. Yet she argues, the political campaign film "serves more to subvert than to extend democratic processes that are based on informed and reasoned dialogue" (1991b, p. 188). In the film, there is more freedom to mislead than there is in the speech.

The campaign video *A New Beginning* opens conventionally with the date of Reagan's inauguration shown on a black screen as he begins his oath of office (Figure 1.2). Although the inauguration itself is sequential, the interspersed visual images have no overtly logical relationship to the words that are being spoken. The aim of the scene, says Morreale (1991b), is to create a mood, tone, or feeling that will contribute to the overall positive impression the viewer takes away from it (p. 193).

Morreale (1991b) adds that the voice and figure of Ronald Reagan "contain" the other images in this scene. His image "surrounds those of ordinary America and Americans; his voice conjures those images, and, ultimately, he explains their significance: 'Yes, it was quite a day, a new beginning.' This refers to both the inauguration and the image of Americans beginning a new day, which are cross-cut within it." The favorable connotations of a new day are transferred to Ronald Reagan. "Reagan is imbued with the positive qualities of traditional America—its fecundity, beauty, optimism, hope" (p. 194).

Figure 1.2. Clips from the opening of *A New Beginning,* 1984. Reagan's swearing-in ceremony is intercut by scenes of "new beginnings," and sandwiched between shots of the Capitol and the White House.

Between the rigorous experimentation of the behavioral approach and the probing insights of the attentive critic, the study of persuasion will enrich your understanding of both how to persuade and how to look and listen as persuadees. In so doing, it helps reveal the underlying dynamics of persuasion and contributes to your knowledge of how society functions. The behavioral approach yields broad generalizations, whereas criticism's focus on a small number of texts restricts its range of available insights, yet the two are in many ways complementary. Says Hart (1997), "What the critic gives up in *scope* is offset by the *power* of insight made available" (p. 25). Moreover, behavioral research can test and confirm generalizations suggested by critical studies. Indeed, the power of the visual was confirmed in an experimental study (Simons, Stewart, & Harvey, 1989) comparing the effects of differing network treatments of *A New Beginning*. The major finding was that a scathing preview of the film by NBC correspondents could not undo the power of its images and might well have enhanced the film's effectiveness by increasing viewer attentiveness.

For another example of image making at a political convention, see Box 1.3.

Summary

Persuasion, a communication practice, is intended to influence the judgments and actions of others but always by giving them the power of decision. Thus, persuasion predisposes but does not impose. In paradigm cases, the intent to persuade is clearcut; in the gray areas of persuasion, it is not. Although in this text, persuasion may sometimes be treated as an effect, whether intended or not, for the most part, it is referred to as a practice. Thus, persuasion is defined as *communication designed to influence the autonomous judgments and actions of others.*

Persuasion is of vital importance in any society but especially in a democratic, market-driven society. In an age of global economics and increasing democratization, it may be only a slight exaggeration to say that one fourth of the world's GDP is persuasion.

Your most immediate interests in persuasion are probably in mastering the art and science of persuading and in becoming a more savvy persuadee. For these purposes, *Persuasion in Society* shifts back and forth between the perspectives of persuader and persuadee. It does so as well to prompt thoughtful consideration of the ethics of persuasion. Should we be forgiving ourselves as persuaders for practices we would condemn as persuadees?

The study of persuasion benefits from its being a branch of the humanities (here known as *rhetoric*) and of the social sciences. The former brings together rhetorical scholars (rhetoricians), media analysts, and other close "readers" of persuasive acts and artifacts in a critical studies approach to the study of persuasion. From these critical analyses may come assessments of a persuader's rhetorical artistry, logic, or ethics. Criticism is also tied to theory building and theory testing, usually about objects of the type—or genre—being analyzed. Thus, critical studies can lead to what is punningly referred to here as "genre-alizations" about persuasion.

Much of what is known about how to persuade derives from experiments. These consist of testing hypotheses about what works under controlled conditions. Subjected to systematic investigation are variations in source, message, medium, audience, and context—in "who says what to whom, when, where and how." Determining the effects of these independent variables on message recipients' judgments and actions is the object of the research. Behavioral research of this type is linked to social-scientific theory in the same way that criticism both informs, and is guided by, rhetorical theory.

Persuasion in Society features a *coactive* approach to the practice of persuasion. The central image is one of bridging differences; persuaders move toward persuadees psychologically in hopes that persuadees will be moved toward acceptance of their ideas or proposals for action.

Questions and Projects for Further Study

1. In your opinion, can pictures argue?
2. How would you define persuasion? Which of the following cases would you include, and which would you exclude?
   a. The blizzard persuaded me to go indoors.
   b. The puppy's sad look persuaded me to surrender choice pieces of filet mignon.
   c. The full moon persuaded us to make rapturous love.
   d. On seeing the hat on a passerby, I was persuaded to buy one just like it.
   e. The political candidate did her best but could not convince the voters to elect her.
   f. The burglar threatened us with his gun.
3. How, if at all, would you distinguish persuasion from coercion? From the use of force? From pressures toward conformity? From harassment? From teaching? From information giving? From spontaneous expression?
4. Think back to a situation in which you were turned down for a request that you thought should have been granted. In your opinion, what factors of source (i.e., the persuader), message, medium, receiver, and situational context may have influenced the negative outcome?
5. Recalling Aristotle's distinction between issues of judgment and issues of certainty, identify one issue of judgment on which you think reasonable individuals might legitimately differ and another for which you believe the argu-

ments on one side clearly outweigh the arguments on the other. Defend your view.

6. Analyze a course description for one of your courses. Does it communicate interest in persuading? Whether it does so or not, is it persuasive?

7. Are you a part of any consumption communities?

Notes

1. There is, of course, another sense of persuasion as an effect. For example, "The customers were persuaded by the Realtor to buy the house." Or even, "The blizzard persuaded us to go indoors." Occasionally, this book also speaks of persuasion as an effect or cites others who do so (e.g., McGuire on the "communication-persuasion matrix"), but the context of use should make the shift of meaning clear.

2. The figure is actually 6 hours and 57 minutes, according to the National Association of Broadcasters, but oldsters are the chief consumers, averaging close to 8 hours per week, so the "6 or so" figure is used here. See Hickey (1998).

3. As long ago as 1990, companies spent more than $60 billion on product promotion and an additional $150 billion to hire more than 6½ million sales agents. Three hundred companies provided image consulting, and another 500 companies did marketing research (Pratkanis & Aronson, 1992).

4. Horovitz (1999) reports that the figure may have been inflated.

5. Some people view propaganda as evil persuasion; others as one-sided, highly manipulative mass persuasion. This book employs the latter definition and leaves it to you to decide whether all propaganda is unethical persuasion. Note that the term itself is often used in persuasion about persuasion. In wartime, we call what the enemy does to bolster internal morale "propaganda;" they call it "education." Likewise, we export "documentary" films abroad to influence international public opinion; our enemies call them "indoctrination" films.

6. According to Liz Rosenberg, spokeswoman for celebrities such as Madonna, Bette Midler, and Cher, "It's a very fine line. I mean, lying to journalists—you've got to see them the next day. And I guess there's an art to the information that you give out and don't give out" (Gray, 1999, p. 26). Later in the same interview, she says, "I can't stand it when someone doesn't tell me the truth" (p. 28).

7. The approach should not be confused with *behaviorism,* a school of psychology founded in the 1920s by conditioning theorist John Watson. Yet behaviorism's influence on the behavioral study of persuasion has been profound, particularly in the form of theory and research on persuasion as a process of learning (Shavitt & Brock, 1994). Chapter 2 discusses more about persuasion as learning.

8. Drawn from the disciplines of literary studies and the arts, *genre* is a technical term referring to a type or kind of artistic product. The catalog description is a rhetorical genre, however inartistic it may appear on close inspection.

References

Allen, M., & Preiss, R. W. (1998). *Persuasion through meta-analysis.* Cresskill, NJ: Hampton.

Ansolabehere, S., & Iyengar, S. (1995). *Going negative.* New York: Free Press.

Barber, B. R. (1996). *Jihad vs. McWorld: How globalism and tribalism are reshaping the world.* New York: Ballantine.

Burke, K. (1969). *A rhetoric of motives.* Berkeley: University of California Press. (Original work published 1950)

Cohen, J. R. (1998). *Communication criticism: Developing your critical powers.* Thousand Oaks, CA: Sage.

Combs, J. E., & Nimmo, D. (1993). *The new propaganda.* New York: Longman.

Cooper, L. (1932). *The rhetoric of Aristotle: An expanded translation with supplementary examples.* New York: D. Appleton Century.

Farrell, T. B. (1993). *Norms of rhetorical culture.* New Haven, CT: Yale University Press.

Gates, H. L. (1998, June 1). Net worth. *New Yorker, 74,* 48-61.

Gray, G. W. (1946). The precepts of Kagemni and Ptah-Hotep. *Quarterly Journal of Speech, 32,* 446-454.

Gray, K. (1999, February 21). When it's o.k. to lie. *New York Times Magazine,* 26, 28.

Gronbeck, B. E. (1978). Celluloid rhetoric: On genres of documentary. In K. K. Campbell & K. H. Jamieson (Eds.), *Form and genre: Shaping rhetorical action.* Falls Church, VA: Speech Communication Association.

Hall, T. (1998, June 14). You are getting very confused: Psychologists' split decisions. *New York Times,* p. 7.

Hample, D. (1980). Purposes and effects of lying. *Southern Speech Communication Journal, 46,* 33-47.

Hart, R. P. (1997) *Modern rhetorical criticism* (2nd ed.). Needham Heights, MA: Allyn & Bacon.

Hickey, J. G. (1998, June 8). Knowing who watches what. *Insight on the News,* pp. 12-13.

Hopper, R., & Bell, R. (1984). Broadening the deception construct. *Quarterly Journal of Speech, 70,* 288-302.

Horovitz, B. (1999, January 28). Super Bowl ad rates appear inflated. *USA Today,* p. 01B.

Jamieson, K. H. (1992). *Dirty politics: Deception, distraction, and democracy.* Oxford, UK: Oxford University Press.

Klein, J. (2000, Septemb.er 18). Changing places. Gore has fun. Bush has none. *New Yorker,* 90-92.

Leventhal, H. (1970). Findings and theory in the study of fear communications. In L. Berkowitz (Ed.), *Advances in experimental social psychology* (Vol. 5, pp. 119-188). New York: Academic Press.

Malcolm, J. (1999). *The crime of Sheila McGough.* New York: Knopf.

McGuire, W. (1978). Persuasion. In G. A. Miller (Ed.), *Communication, language and meaning.* New York: Harper.

Michie, G. (1998, Winter). Room to learn. *American Educator, 21,* 36-42.

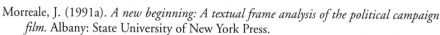

Morreale, J. (1991a). *A new beginning: A textual frame analysis of the political campaign film*. Albany: State University of New York Press.

Morreale, J. (1991b). The political campaign film: Epideictic rhetoric in a documentary frame. In F. Biocca (Ed.), *Television and political advertising* (Vol. 2, pp. 187-202). Hillsdale, NJ: Lawrence Erlbaum.

Page, C. (2000, September 1). You know how to win an election, don'cha? Just pucker up and kiss. *Philadelphia Inquirer*, p. A33.

Plato. (1952). *Gorgias* (W. C. Helmbold, Trans.). New York: Bobbs-Merrill. (Original work n.d.)

Pratkanis, A., & Aronson, E. (1992). *Age of propaganda: The everyday use and abuse of persuasion*. New York: Freeman.

Purdum, T. (2000, September 24). A kiss for the ages. *New York Times, Week in Review*, p. 2.

Shavitt, S., & Brock, T. C. (Eds.). (1994). *Persuasion: Psychological insights and perspectives*. Needham Heights, MA: Allyn & Bacon.

Simons, H. W. (1996). Judging a policy proposal by the company it keeps: The Gore-Perot NAFTA debate. *Quarterly Journal of Speech, 82*, 274-287.

Simons, H. W., Stewart, D., & Harvey, D. (1989). Effects of network treatment of a political campaign film: Can rhetorical criticism make a difference? *Communication Quarterly, 37*, 184-198.

Smith, C. R. (1998). *Rhetoric and human consciousness*. Prospect Heights, IL: Waveland.

Statistical Abstracts of the United States. (1992). Washington, DC: Government Printing Office.

U.S. Bureau of Labor Statistics. (2000). *Occupational outlook handbook 2000-01 edition*. Washington, DC: U.S. Department of Labor. Available: http://stats.bls.gov/oco/ocos053.htm

CHAPTER **2**

The Psychology of Persuasion

Basic Principles

Beliefs and Values as Building Blocks of Attitudes

Persuasion by Degrees: Adapting to Different Audiences

Schemas: Attitudes as Knowledge Structures

From Attitudes to Actions: The Role of Subjective Norms

Elaboration Likelihood Model: Two Routes to Persuasion

Persuasion as a Learning Process

Persuasion as Psychological Unbalancing and Rebalancing

Summary

Questions and Projects for Further Study

References

By the conclusion of the 1999 Senate trial on William Jefferson Clinton's impeachment, *Newsweek* and *Time* had between them run a record 26 covers on the "Monicagate" scandal, and the network news shows had given it more than 2,300 minutes of airtime (Seplow, 1999). During that time, the American people had absorbed a great deal of information about the scandal that formed the core of their *beliefs*. They learned, for example, that Clinton had misled them for several months about his illicit relationship with the White House intern and that he had probably misinformed his close aides as well in an effort to derail the investigation by Independent Counsel Kenneth Starr. Beginning with the revelations contained in

▶   25

surreptitiously taped phone conversations between White House intern Monica Lewinsky and her supposed friend, Linda Tripp, and concluding with DNA evidence on Monica's dress, the fact of Clinton's sexual involvement with Lewinsky had become well nigh incontrovertible.

Yet Americans' *attitudes* toward President Clinton's job performance and toward whether he should be removed from office stemmed not just from their beliefs about sex, lies, and audiotapes but also from their *values*. Were Clinton's transgressions important? Were they *as* important as the good job most people believed Clinton had been doing in managing the economy and conducting foreign policy? Most Americans believed that President Clinton was untrustworthy but placed a higher value on the job he was doing. They saw him as a "low virtue, high competence" president, and most liked what they saw (McGee, 1998, p. 1).

Together, these beliefs and values strongly influenced Americans' attitudes toward President Clinton's performance and continuation in office. Their attitudes, in turn, served as knowledge structures, called *schemas,* for the filtering of new information. They performed, as it were, the work of a mental secretary, determining what new information would be allowed in the door, what importance it would be assigned, and how it would be interpreted. Americans were polarized about the impeachment issue, making it unlikely that either side would be moved very much by new information or new arguments. Their attitudes toward the proposal to impeach ranged from hostile to enthusiastically supportive, with relatively few people on the fence. These attitudes influenced people's perceptions of the Senate trial as well as what they said to friends and coworkers.

But were attitudes *alone* fully predictive of what people would say to their friends and coworkers about the Clinton affair? Probably not. Another important predictor for many Americans (not all) was *subjective norms.* Many persons' public *actions* (as opposed to their privately held attitudes) were influenced by what they believed was most socially acceptable. Should they snub their noses at the Clinton-Lewinsky affair as unworthy of serious attention? A great many Americans publicly dismissed the importance of the scandal even as they tuned in to CNN and MSNBC each night for the latest salacious details. Their public actions may have been attitude related, but subjective norms played an important role as well.

Of course, some Americans thought hard about the Clinton-Lewinsky matter, whereas others were either unwilling or unable to perform the necessary mental labor. The former pursued what Petty and Cacioppo (1981/1996) call the *central route* to judgment making; the latter pursued a *peripheral route,* probably relying for their judgments on *cognitive shorthands.* These are rules of thumb that enable people to get on with their lives without protracted deliberation, for example, "Everybody lies about sex, so what's the big deal?"

Mention of routes to persuasion suggests that *being persuaded* is a *learning process.* Americans learned to like or dislike Clinton on the basis of information, associations, and anticipated rewards and punishments. These constituents of the learning process were also at work as Americans contemplated the policy options of removal or continuation in office. Americans not only learned information but also learned whom to trust. Typically, they tended to be guarded and defensive when exposed to sources they perceived as untrustworthy. To some extent, messages presented in the guise of entertainment (e.g., Jay Leno's jokes about the scandal) or news (e.g., CNN's intensive coverage) had a better chance of influencing their judgments and actions.

Which comes first: attitudes or actions? Actions such as voting for a candidate or signing a petition follow in the wake of attitudes. But the acts of expressing a commitment to a position (such as by voting or signing a petition) have a way of reinforcing privately held attitudes. This helps explain the increasing partisanship in the House and Senate over the issue of impeachment. As members of Congress went public with their views, they became more firmly committed to those views.

Much the same phenomenon occurred among ordinary citizens in response to President Clinton's historic speech on August 17, 1998, in which he admitted to the American people for the first time that he had misled them. It was Clinton's task in the speech to retain the loyalty of his many longtime supporters who had found news of the affair and subsequent cover-up troubling by helping them find ways of understanding and perhaps forgiving his transgressions. For those who had made no secret of their dislike for Clinton and revulsion toward what he had done, the task of winning converts was probably impossible. But perhaps Clinton could *defuse* some of their hostility and even create a sense of cognitive inconsistency between the Clinton they knew and despised and the Clinton they now saw on their television screens.

The Clinton-Lewinsky scandal, then, has much to teach about the psychology of persuasion. The rest of this chapter elaborates on the principles already illustrated.

Beliefs and Values as Building Blocks of Attitudes

Every field has its own jargon, and some fields use familiar terms in special ways, just as the terms *attitude, belief,* and *value* are used in this book in special ways. "Having an attitude" is sometimes used to mean being ornery, stubborn, and hard to get along with, but here the term *attitude* is used differently. Many people speak of their *values* as things they believe in, but in this text, values include judgments of negative worth—for example, negatively valuing adultery. Furthermore, a distinction is made between *believing in* something (e.g., the value of honesty) and *believing that* something (e.g., the belief that Clinton lied). It is in the latter sense that belief is used in this book. The word *opinion* is also used in various ways. Is opinion the same as a belief, a value, or an attitude? Here, it is an all-purpose term for verbalized judgments of every type. Thus, attitudes, beliefs, and values are all types of judgment, and an opinion is any verbalized judgment.

As used here, an *attitude* is a judgment that a given thing is good or bad, desirable or undesirable, or something to be embraced or avoided. The "thing" may be literally anything: a person, an event, an idea, a proposal for action, or an action itself. Attitudes predispose us to act in one way rather than another.

Beliefs are judgments about what is true or probable. I believe you will like this book, for example. I can't say it's true, but I believe it is highly probable.

Values are judgments of relative worth (Devito, 1978). People generally value happiness, self-fulfillment, fair play, and generosity, for example, and are repelled by violence, ugliness, and stinginess. For the most part, their values are relatively stable: They might acquire them in childhood and die still adhering to them at a ripe old age. Some values—such as happiness and self-fulfillment—are ends in themselves. These are called *terminal values* (Rokeach, 1968). Others, such as fair play and generosity, are means to an end. These are called *instrumental values*.

Attitudes, beliefs, and values are connected. Beliefs include judgments that a given object possesses certain attributes. Values include judgments of the worth of these perceived attributes (Ajzen & Fishbein, 1980). A car buyer probably has certain attributes in mind when appraising different makes of car: efficiency, beauty, economy, speed, safety, and comfort. The relative importance attached to each of these attributes probably would not change much from one car to another. Other car purchasers might assign different values to these attributes. Prospective car buyers' attitudes, then, depend on both their beliefs about whether the object possesses particular attributes and the value weightings they assign to those attributes. Buyer A may believe that the new XL7 Zippo sedan is sexy looking and fuel efficient and have a highly favorable attitude toward the Zippo for just these reasons. Buyer B may agree that the Zippo possesses these attributes but view them neutrally or even negatively. Buyer C may value the attributes but not believe that the Zippo possesses them. Buyer D may share the beliefs of Buyer C and the values of Buyer B. For Buyer D, the perception that the Zippo is not sexy looking may even be a decided plus.[1]

These variations in beliefs and values have great importance for persuaders. A sales pitch that succeeds with any one of these customers might backfire with the others. But a presentation specifically tailored to each of the prospective buyers could work wonders.

The *degree* to which beliefs are held and the *degree* to which values are positive or negative also enter into a buying decision. For example, in shopping around for a new sports car, a buyer might be drawn to the XL7 Zippo but have significant doubts about its fuel efficiency and some second thoughts about whether to buy a car primarily because it is sexy looking. Hearing the buyer's doubts, the salesperson would have a number of options:

▶ Play down the value of fuel efficiency or convince the buyer that compared with other cars in its class, the Zippo is highly fuel efficient

▶ Play up the value of buying a sexy-looking car, all the while strengthening the buyer's belief in the Zippo's sexiness

▶ Direct the buyer's attention to other sales features of the XL7, such as its high resale value, relatively low cost, and excellent reputation for reliability

This car-buying scenario is an example of a *theory* of persuasion. *This* theory draws liberally from two well-known theories, Fishbein and Ajzen's (1975) theory of reasoned action and Ajzen's (1991) theory of planned behavior. It is called here *BVA* theory, after its central concepts of belief (B), value (V), and attitude (A).

Theories of every type attempt to summarize and explain a phenomenon while directing the search for additional knowledge. The heart of any scientific theory is a set of assumptions, basic concepts, definitions of those concepts, and explanatory statements or theorems that relate the concepts in a condensed and organized way. BVA is an example of a *psychological* theory of persuasion; it offers assumptions and explanatory statements about what goes on inside the head of the message recipient. A key assumption of BVA theory is that the message recipients are *rational* in the way they form and modify attitudes on the basis of beliefs and values. Compare the rational actor in BVA theory, for example, with a persuadee of Freudian imagining, driven by unconscious urges rather than calculations of perceived costs and benefits. Or compare the persuadee of BVA theory with someone assumed to be a product of conditioning, much like one of Pavlov's salivating dogs. BVA theory comes from the behavioral social-scientific tradition, but it leaves room for thought and decision making. Throughout this book, you will encounter other behavioral theories, some quite general such as BVA, others bearing on more specific phenomena such as the factors contributing to the perceived credibility of communicators.

Persuasion by Degrees:
Adapting to Different Audiences

On any one occasion, a persuader might stop far short of producing wholesale changes in the persuadee from one way of thinking or behaving to another and yet still consider the effort successful (Figure 2.1). Broadly speaking, persuaders may succeed in shaping a response, reinforcing a response, and changing a response (Miller, 1980).

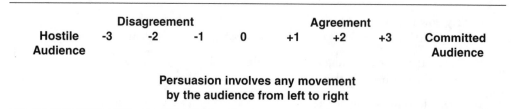

Figure 2.1. Persuasion by Degrees

Response shaping occurs when people acquire new beliefs on controversial matters or when they are socialized to learn new attitudes or acquire new values. Shaping may involve, for example, teaching a child to become a Lutheran, a Democrat, a capitalist, or a patriot. Political campaigns may shape voters' attitudes toward previously unknown candidates. Commercial advertising may shape favorable consumer responses to new products and product brands. The key characteristic of shaping is that it leads to the formation of new beliefs, values, and attitudes.

Response reinforcing consists of strengthening currently held convictions and making them more resistant to change. A campaign on behalf of a charity might begin by transforming lip service commitments into strongly felt commitments (*intensification*), then transforming those commitments into donations of time and money (*activation*), then working to maintain strong behavioral support and discouraging backsliding (*deterrence*). All these are forms of response reinforcing (Figure 2.2). Says Miller (1980),

> The response-reinforcing function underscores the fact that "being persuaded" is seldom, if ever, a one-message proposition; instead, people are constantly in the process of being persuaded. If an individual clings to an attitude (and the behaviors associated with it) more strongly after exposure to a communication, then persuasion has occurred as surely as if the individual has shifted from one set of responses to another. Moreover, those beliefs and behaviors most resistant to change are likely to be grounded in a long history of confirming messages, along with other positive reinforcers. (p. 19)

Response changing involves *converting* others—getting them to switch parties, change cigarette brands, or perhaps quit smoking. In extreme cases, this may require *defusion,* getting a strongly opposed audience to become less hostile. The persuader's goal on any one occasion may be *neutralization,* bringing an audience from the point of disagreement to a point of ambivalence or indecision. Yet a third stage on the way to response changing is *crystallization,* getting those persons who were uncommitted because of mixed feelings about an idea to endorse the persuader's position or proposal. Sometimes—although not usually on ego-involving matters—it is possible to

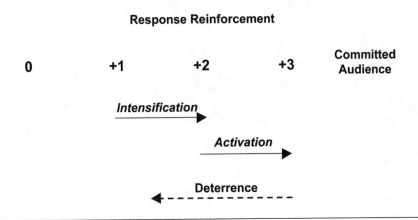

Figure 2.2. Response Reinforcement

achieve conversions in a single message presentation. Usually, it involves multiple presentations.

An extreme case of conversion is attempts to undermine an entire belief system, such as one's commitment to Catholicism or to the American way of life. The 1970s were rife with reports of the alleged brainwashing of newspaper heiress Patty Hearst by an urban guerrilla group known as the Symbionese Liberation Army; of massive conversions to religious cults such as the Unification Church of Sun Myung Moon (the "Moonies"); and, most bizarre of all, of a mass suicide in Jonestown, Guyana, by followers of the charismatic firebrand the Reverend Jim Jones. Recent years have seen the destructive power of cult leaders Luc Jouret in Switzerland and Canada (see Picture 2.1) and David Koresh in Waco, Texas; the nerve gas attack on a Tokyo subway by followers of the Aum Shinrikyo group; a mass suicide by adherents of Heaven's Gate in San Diego, California; and the deaths by fire of hundreds of members of a doomsday sect in Uganda. The indoctrination efforts of cults combine a variety of forms of influence. In extreme cases, they chip away at basic beliefs under highly controlled conditions; sleep, social contact, exercise, and the like are contingent on "progress" at giving up long-held convictions. In less constricted environments where, for example, a college student might come to a meeting of a religious group "just to see what it's all about," the student's guiding belief system is ripe for attack. Zimbardo, Ebbesen, and Maslach (1977) described one such meeting with a group of Moonies. If new recruits made an unacceptable response, they received an immediate, uniformly sad reaction from the other members of the group. The group was saddened, but never angered, by deviant acts or thoughts. As a result, new recruits would feel guilty for upsetting the group by their disagreement (p. 184). By

Picture 2.1. Cult leader Luc Jouret, 1994, described by police as founder of the Order of the Solar Temple. The painting on the left is supposed to show Jouret. Jouret was linked by Swiss radio to two deaths in Canada and more than 40 deaths of possible cult members in Switzerland.
SOURCE: Reuters/Ruben Sprich Archive Photos. Used with permission.

this point (if not before), many of the new recruits in the group had become conflicted and were ripe for crystallization.

Schemas: Attitudes as Knowledge Structures

Audiences often resist persuasive messages or, at the least, process them selectively, that is, message recipients expose themselves to some messages and not to others. When they are exposed, they sometimes are prone to hear what they want to hear and to see what they want to see.[2] Guiding the selection process are *schemas* (Tesser & Leone, 1977).

Attitudes are formed from beliefs and values, and they, in turn, as knowledge structures, influence the receipt of new ideas. The stereotypes associated with groups in society are examples of schemas; they influence people's encounters with persons who are aged, infirm, or affluent and, of course, with persons identified as members of racial and ethnic groups. Groups such as these are defined by an associative network of schema-directed features that presumably apply to members of that category. Not just groups are schematized—so, too, are programs and practices. Kuklinski and Quirk (1997) have illustrated how schemas have affected welfare reform.

In 1996, a Democratic president signed off on a bill sent to him by a largely Republican Congress to end the federal welfare program called Aid to Families With Dependent Children (AFDC). That program, in place since the 1930s, was highly unpopular with large segments of the voting public, and this was undoubtedly one reason that President Clinton agreed to terminate it (Morris, 1997).

It was learned, however, that many people held inaccurate beliefs about welfare. They were not simply uninformed; they were *misinformed* (Kuklinski & Quirk, 1997). Moreover, their erroneous beliefs exhibited high belief strength, that is, people were fairly certain they were true (Ajzen & Fishbein, 1980). Their errors were fairly consistent with an antiwelfare bias. For example, they overestimated the cost of AFDC to the taxpayers while underestimating the percentage of whites on welfare compared with the number of blacks and Hispanics. Kuklinski and Quirk maintained that these erroneous beliefs were inferred from negative attitudes toward welfare. The schema served as a knowledge structure in the sense of linking a number of beliefs together.

> Once the welfare schema is activated, the person can easily fill in whatever is missing. "Welfare" activates "welfare mothers," which in turn activates "wasteful spending on nonessentials." Given the activation of this set of interconnected nodes, it follows that "welfare mothers must receive a lot of money," "the government must spend a good portion of its budget on welfare," and the like. Although admittedly not specific, "factual" derivations such as "a lot of money" and a "good portion of its budget" nevertheless translate into "annual payments of $15,000, not $5,000 a year," and "ten percent of the budget, not one percent," respectively. (Kuklinski & Quirk, 1997, p. 6)

Schemas are resistant to change, but they can be altered. One way to modify attitudes is to give people the correct information. In the Kuklinski and Quirk (1997) study, correcting participants' antiwelfare factual errors resulted in far more favorable attitudes toward keeping welfare and not cutting the federal welfare program than did leaving the errors uncorrected.

Moreover, much depended on *how* an error was corrected. Consistent with the theory of reframing, to be discussed in Chapter 6, the amount of federal spending on welfare seemed relatively small to respondents if AFDC payments were described as about 1% of the annual federal budget. Attitudes toward AFDC were less favorable, however, if the same fact was presented in dollar figures ($10,497,346,981). The $10 billion-plus figure seemed even more alarming if described as equivalent to three stacks of thousand dollar bills as high as the Empire State Building.

Finally, much depended on how a figure was interpreted for the respondents. For example, was $10 billion-plus a lot or a little? Informing the respondents that the average welfare payment for a family with two children was not $15,000 (as many believed) but $5,000 plus Medicaid and food stamps prompted them to regard AFDC more favorably. So did learning that AFDC was 30 times less expensive than the nation's defense.

From Attitudes to Actions:
The Role of Subjective Norms

Fishbein and Ajzen's (1975) theory of reasoned action is a much more elaborate, highly quantified formulation of the problem posed earlier: How do beliefs about an object and evaluations of its attributes influence attitudes toward it? Also, what is the relationship between attitudes and actions, such as purchasing a XL7 Zippo sedan or using birth control pills?

One of the puzzles that Fishbein and Ajzen (1975) wrestled with in constructing their theory was evidence that an attitude toward an action or behavior (they used the terms interchangeably) was not always predictive of what action the holder of that attitude might eventually take. Buyer A might be favorably inclined toward purchasing the XL7 Zippo sedan and still not buy it. By contrast, a woman might have a negative attitude toward using birth control pills but still use them.

Fishbein and Ajzen (1975) concluded that the best predictor of behavior is *intentions,* which are a joint product of *attitudes toward behaviors* (A_B) and *subjective norms* (SN). Just as A_B has belief and value components, so SN is said to depend both on what we believe people whom we value highly would have us do and how desirous we are of complying with those norms. Some people are highly influenced by what other people they value would have them do; others are more self-reliant. In the case of the woman who had a negative attitude toward birth control pills but continued to use them, Fishbein and Ajzen's theory predicts that subjective norms were at work. In any event, attitudes toward a contemplated behavior together with subjective norms indicate rather accurately how an individual will act in a given situation.

Elaboration Likelihood Model:
Two Routes to Persuasion

The elaboration likelihood model (ELM) is an attempt to integrate a vast body of persuasion theory and research about an important insight: Persuasion is a consequence not just of external cues but also of the thoughts that the persuadee generates in response to external communications (Petty & Cacioppo, 1981/1996; 1986). Fundamental to the ELM approach is the distinction between *central* and *peripheral* routes to persuasion.

The central route involves greater elaboration of thoughts than the peripheral route. People who process information centrally ask themselves probing questions, generate additional arguments, and possibly seek new information. Those who become persuaded after mental labor of this sort tend to be resistant to counterarguments and to remain persuaded months afterward. Attitudes formed or changed via the central route are also more easily called to mind and are more predictive of behavior.

But not everyone has the motivation or ability to engage in central processing. Indeed, none of us engage in central processing all the time. We couldn't possibly, even if we wanted to, given the demands on our psyches of the hundreds of messages to which we are exposed every day. Peripheral processing involves the use of cognitive shorthands, sometimes called *heuristics* (Chaicken, 1987). If central processing is mindful, peripheral processing is relatively mindless—but not entirely so. Sales customers traveling the peripheral route may be taken in by a pretty face, the lure of a free gift, the appeal of a celebrity figure, or the number, rather than quality, of reasons presented to them. Such persuasive effects tend to be short-lived, however.

Central and peripheral processing are not mutually exclusive; much of the time, we use them in combination. Degree of involvement is a major determinant of which route we emphasize. When we truly care about a matter—for example, when we genuinely need information and know we need it—the lure of a free gift or of a pretty face isn't as likely to work on us. This has been demonstrated in numerous experiments.

These experiments have revealed that the degree to which a person is involved in an issue determines how much he or she thinks about the issue. For example, if you are told that a proposal to divide your university into undergraduate and graduate campuses has a good chance of being put into effect while you are enrolled there, you are more likely to generate pro- or antidivision arguments than if you believe that university division is a long way off (Petty & Cacioppo, 1981/1996, p. 257).

Whatever your prior predispositions, they are likely to intensify if you are led to anticipate that a message is important or will have significant consequences for you. For example, if you learn that a speaker favors adding a comprehensive exam in all majors as a condition for graduation at your university, and if, like most students, you aren't particularly wild about taking such tests, then chances are that you will rehearse counterarguments to yourself even before you hear the speaker and thus become further entrenched in your opposition. If you're the unusual student who believes that tests of this sort are a good idea, you're likely to think of supporting arguments and thus strengthen your support in advance of hearing the speaker. If you expect that the speaker will be advocating these pregraduation tests for use at some other university, however, it is a good bet that your opinions will moderate, rather than intensifying, in advance of the speaker's presentation (Petty & Cacioppo, 1981/ 1996, p. 233).

High issue involvement also leads to greater attention to quality of arguments. In the study from which the foregoing example was taken, Petty and Cacioppo (1981/1996) exposed half the students to eight powerful and half to eight relatively weak arguments. An example of a strong argument was that "graduate and professional schools show a preference for undergraduates who have passed a comprehensive exam." A weak argument was that "by not administering the exam, a tradition dating back to the ancient Greeks was being violated." As predicted, involved participants paid more attention to the quality of arguments, generating favorable thoughts and persuasion for the strong arguments and counterpersuasion based on internal counterarguing for the weak arguments (p. 233).

If, as a persuader, you believe you have strong arguments, you may wish to stimulate involvement by your audience. One way to do so, of course, is to make your message personally relevant to them, but you can do so as well by such simple expedients as using second person pronouns (e.g., *you*) as opposed to such third person pronouns as *one* or *he* and *she* (Burnkrant & Unnava, 1989).

Some people enjoy thinking about a wide range of topics, whereas others have what Cacioppo and Petty (1982) call a low *need for cognition*. For example, some persons report thinking "only as hard as I have to" and say that they "like tasks that require little thought once I've learned them" (Petty, Cacioppo, Strathman, & Priester, 1994). These people apparently are far less affected by the quality of an argument than are people with a high need for cognition (Cacioppo, Petty, & Morris, 1983).

People cannot always be induced to care about that which should be important to them, nor is there any guarantee that the central route to persuasion will lead to an attitude change. Other things being equal, central processors are likely to generate thoughts consistent with their initial predispositions (Petty & Cacioppo, 1981/ 1996, p. 266). Still, if one side of an issue has demonstrably superior arguments going for it, those arguments are most likely to influence people via the central route— hence the vital importance in our society of facilitating central processing on highly consequential matters.

Persuasion as a Learning Process

Overheard at the deli counter of a large supermarket:

Salesperson (S):   Sir, how would you like to try a sample of our newest imported cheese? It's called Sagamento.

Customer (C):   Well, I'm not sure. I'm not much of a cheese eater.

S: [Noncommittally] Oh? How's that?

C: Well, you see I do like some cheese, but—

S: Mhm! [Enthusiastically]

C: But I don't like the presliced stuff, and I don't enjoy slicing it myself either.

S: [Laughing] Great! This is a spread. Do you like pimentos?

C: Yes, I do.

S: [Nods vigorously] Well, Sagamento combines pimentos and Brie. It's delicious!

C: Sounds good, but—

S: Here, try some on this cracker. It won't cost you a penny.

C: Ummm, good! I'll take a small slice.

S: This package okay?

C: Well, all right.

This customer just underwent a learning process. The three parts of that process—acquiring new information, incentives to act, and favorable associations—are examined in this section.

Persuasion as Information Processing

Persuasion takes place in stages: from conception of the message to reception, from reception to acceptance or yielding, from yielding to overt action (McGuire, 1985). These stages are like a chain, the chain no stronger than its weakest link. Reception alone includes *exposure* to the message (tuning in to Clinton's August 17, 1998, speech, rather than switching the channels), *attention* to the message (actually looking and listening), *comprehension* (understanding what Clinton had to say), and *recall* (remembering it accurately).

Ironically, those people who are best able to comprehend and recall a persuasive message (the reception stage) are least likely to yield to it (to alter their judgments). The customer at the deli counter seems to have been one such hard sell. On the other hand, people most likely to yield to a persuasive message are least likely to process it accurately (McGuire, 1968; 1985). Intelligent, self-confident, well-educated people are competent at receiving persuasive messages but also more likely to be critical of them. Their opposite numbers tend to be more gullible but also are likely to find some persuasive messages difficult to understand and remember. Hence, people of moderate intelligence tend to be most persuasible (McGuire, 1985; Rhodes & Wood, 1992).

Persuasion and Incentives

Persuasion theorists agree that incentives are essential in getting people to act, but they often disagree about why people are motivated to act. Consider once again the purchase of Sagamento cheese at the supermarket deli. One possible explanation for the successfully concluded exchange is that the customer was "trained" to buy the cheese in a manner not unlike a pigeon in a psychological learning laboratory. The process of successively *shaping* appropriate customer responses by use of positive reinforcements is known as *operant conditioning* (Skinner, 1953). But an alternative explanation is that the conversants had simply reasoned together until a rational decision to purchase the Sagamento had formed in the customer's mind.

Operant conditioning works by rewarding desired behavior and withholding rewards—perhaps even using punishments—until the desired behavior is forthcoming. But in a noninteractive situation, the persuader can only help the persuadee *imagine* a rosier future by adoption of the recommended action and perhaps a bleaker future unless the proposal is adopted. In Clinton's televised speech, for example, the incentives had to consist of *projected* rewards and punishments.

Television and film can also be used to dramatize potential rewards and punishments. Using a technique known as *vicarious modeling,* O'Connor (1972) was able to reverse the lifelong patterns of social inactivity of severely withdrawn children simply by having them view a 23-minute movie. Each scene of the movie showed a child such as themselves first watching a social activity, then joining in to everyone's enjoyment (see also Bandura, 1977).

As a general rule, the greater the incentive, the greater the likelihood of successful persuasion. But an exception to this rule is the principle of *insufficient justification* (Wicklund & Brehm, 1976). Here is how it works. Step 1: Encourage half the participants in your experiment to perform an objectionable action—perhaps role-playing a position repugnant to them or writing a counterattitudinal essay. Be sure to provide insufficient justification for performance of the act. That is, don't pay them much, have the request come from an unattractive source, or require that a good deal of effort be spent on the task. Step 2: Compare the attitudes of the participants given insufficient justifications for performance of the act with those given sufficient justification, for example, those paid 10 times as much, those urged to participate by an attractive source, or those required to expend minimal effort. The predicted outcome is counterintuitive but typically confirmed by research (Preiss & Allen, 1998). Counterattitudinal action under conditions of insufficient justification for the action tends to lead people to modify their attitudes, bringing them into line with their actions. This is a reversal of the ordinary process of persuasion in which messages first alter attitudes, with subsequent changes in behavior (Cooper & Scher, 1994). Are they now more favorably inclined toward performance of the objectional action? Might they now even come to argue with positions they initially found repugnant? The result of these studies are fairly consistent. One explanation is that people tend to infer their attitudes from their actions when they have reason to believe that their actions are not the result of external causes. Another is that acting one way and feeling another under conditions of insufficient justification is cognitively dissonant and uncomfortable; attitude change brings relief from the psychological pain of cognitive dissonance. Want to know why volunteers for the unpopular war in Vietnam reported greater satisfaction with it (especially if they had been wounded in the war) than those who had been drafted? Try explaining it by way of the principle of insufficient justification.

Persuasion by Association

In some of the earliest research on animal learning, a previously neutral stimulus was paired with a stimulus known to evoke favorable or unfavorable reactions. Then the original stimulus was removed. In this way, then, the hungry dogs in Pavlov's animal laboratory learned to salivate at the sound of a bell previously linked with food. The phenomenon, known as *classical conditioning,* has widespread applications (Staats & Staats, 1963). Classical conditioning theorists have developed principles governing the acquisition of responses to new stimuli, their transfer to new situations, their extinction, and so on. One immediate application to persuasion is the menu so enticing that we can "almost taste the food." Much as we may scoff at dogs that salivate to the sounds of bells, how different are we who salivate to words?

Indeed, humans form all types of associations to objects, some conscious, others unconscious. Inferences about people are formed in this way. For example, in Tolstoy's *Anna Karenina,* Anna's husband is unimpressed with the attorney who had been recommended to him until the lawyer, without looking up from his desk, suddenly snatches a housefly in midair and crushes it in his hand. Inferences of this type are often spontaneous and automatic, according to Uleman and Bargh (1989), and they are by no means confined to judgments about other people. Try comparing oranges and grapefruit on the basis of the traits of sunny versus cloudy, intimate versus distant, faster versus slower, older versus younger, more intellectual versus less intellectual. Don't think about the task very much: Just let your mind go. Students confronted with this task frequently complain that the task is meaningless. Why should "sunny" attach to orange any more than to grapefruit? Yet overwhelming numbers of respondents report viewing the orange as sunnier, more intimate, and faster; the grapefruit as older and more intellectual (Dichter, 1960). Findings of this sort are not lost on persuaders, as the discussion in Chapter 12 on analyzing product advertising indicates.

Persuasion as Psychological Unbalancing and Rebalancing

Psychological inconsistency disturbs people, enough so that they will often go to great lengths to reduce or remove it. Numerous consistency theories have been put forward by psychologists, some referred to by that name, others labeled as balance theories, dissonance theories, or congruity theories (Petty & Cacioppo, 1981/1996). Already discussed was the likelihood of attitude change under conditions of insufficient justification for performance of a counterattitudinal act, such as role-playing a lifestyle you believe is unethical.

A common denominator in cases of psychological inconsistency is the sense that something is discrepant. In the foregoing case, the obvious discrepancy is between actions and attitudes, but pride hangs in the balance as well; for example, a binge drinker may suffer the sense of wounded pride at knowing that she occasionally drinks to wild excess while realizing that it is irrational and even dangerous.

Another source of psychological inconsistency stems from perceived discrepancies between our attitudes toward other people, our attitudes toward objects, and their attitudes toward the same objects. For most of us, balanced states are preferable to imbalanced states. For example, if Wallace likes (+) pizza and Wallace likes (+) Kate, Wallace would find it psychologically consistent for Kate to like (+) pizza. But a sense of imbalance (psychological inconsistency) is created for Wallace if Kate says she hates (-) pizza or if Kate reports liking (+) pizza but Wallace loses his stomach for the food (-).[3] Even discrepancies in *degree* of liking can be uncomfortable, according to some consistency theorists. For example, if Kate's favorite food was pizza and Wallace liked it only a little, this too could be discomfiting for Wallace, perhaps leading him to think less of Kate, more of pizza, or both.

Imbalances create motivation for attitude change, and persuaders may be quick to exploit them, even foster them. To senators repulsed by Clinton's private behavior and efforts to deny or make light of it, the president's successes in office were psychologically inconsistent and so, too, was the public's willingness to look past the transgressions as long as they approved of his performance in office. By repeatedly calling attention to Clinton's pluses during the impeachment trial, Clinton's attorneys hoped to increase the sense of psychological inconsistency. Acquittal, they suggested, was the only rebalancing alternative.[4]

Balanced Triads

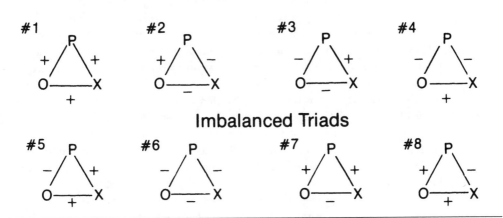

Figure 2.3. Balanced and Imbalanced Triads
SOURCE: From *Attitudes and Persuasion: Classic and Contemporary Approaches* by Petty, R.F. and Cacioppo, J.T. Copyright © 1996 by Westview Press. Reprinted by permission of Westview Press, a member of Perseus Books, L.L.C.

Summary

This chapter has presented basic psychological principles of persuasion and, in the process, has introduced you to psychological theories. From its origins as a field of study, psychology has been divided between theories emphasizing similarities between humans and other animal species and theories emphasizing humans' seemingly distinctive capacity for reason. It should not be surprising, therefore, that psychological theories of persuasion should divide in similar ways. One possible explanation for the successfully concluded exchange at the supermarket deli is that the customer was conditioned to buy a package of Sagamento not unlike a pigeon in a psychological laboratory being trained to hop on one foot, then the other. But an alternative explanation is that the conversants had simply reasoned together until a rational decision to purchase the Sagamento had formed in the customer's mind.

The theorists featured in this chapter were by no means unmindful of such features of human animality as the role of emotion in persuasion, of seemingly unconscious associations, as well as of incentives for action. Petty and Cacioppo (1981/ 1996) describe a *central route* to persuasion in which the quality of an argument is likely to make a great deal of difference to persuadees, but they also recognize that there are times when humans are likely to rely on cognitive shorthands, using what the theorists call a *peripheral route* to persuasion.

BVA theory pictures humans as distinctive by virtue of their capacity to derive attitudes from their beliefs and values but does not exclude the roles of emotions and unreason in the formation of beliefs and values. Likewise, Fishbein and Ajzen (1975) see human action as a weighted combination of attitudes toward the behavior in question and subjective norms—the weight varying depending on how much importance is assigned in the given case to what valued others think. The product of this type of seemingly rational calculation, however, might be the decision to join a religious cult or a right-wing militia. Poorly supported group stereotypes can also influence the formation of beliefs and values, say the proponents of schema theory.

The persuadees in McGuire's (1968) theory vary between those who remain unpersuaded because they are critical of what they understand, those unlikely to be persuaded because of difficulties comprehending and recalling the message, and a middle-range group that is most persuasible because it is neither too critical to resist accepting the persuader's recommendations nor incapable of understanding them.

Again and again, reason is mixed with unreason and downright irrationality—most clearly, perhaps, in theories of psychological consistency. Although the attempt to reconcile conflicting cognitions or attitudes seems rational, it can lead two friends to sever a relationship over something as trivial as the taste of pizza.

So what should the persuader make of all this? Explicit in some theories, implicit in others, are guidelines for selling an XL7 Zippo sedan, coaxing a deli customer into trying a package of Sagamento, and convincing Americans that William Clinton should have been impeached and removed from office or continued as president and celebrated for his accomplishments. For example, if your goal is conversion, encourage people to role-play positions counter to their existing attitudes but offer minimal incentives to try out these roles. If your goal is a fully convinced ally who will remain supportive of your position in the face of counterarguments, appeal to the message recipient by way of the central route to persuasion. But if it's a quick sell that you're after, consider providing cognitive shorthands. (These will be discussed in far more detail in Chapter 7.)

These same guidelines should be warning signals to you as persuadees. Beware, for example, that the innocent "yes" you give to the deli salesperson's question may land you with far more Sagamento than you really wanted. As for that sexy-looking XL7 Zippo sedan, why not? We only live once!

Questions and Projects for Further Study

1. In light of your reading of this chapter, how different are humans from laboratory rats, dogs, pigeons, and so forth?
2. The best way to learn new terms is to try your hand at illustrating them with examples of your own. Try doing that with respect to the following:
   a. The relationship between beliefs, values, and attitudes
   b. The relationship between attitudes, subjective norms, and public actions

   c. The differences between central and peripheral processing
   d. How the learning of an attitude (e.g., liking yogurt) might be influenced by new information, by associations, and by expected benefits
   e. How the act of publicly expressing a commitment to a position may reinforce privately held attitudes
   f. The differences between response reinforcement, response shaping, and response changing
   g. How schemas influence information processing
   h. The principle of insufficient justification
   i. Balancing and unbalancing

3. What is a theory? What is your theory about the relationship between logic and emotion in persuasion? How might research be used to test your theory?

Notes

1. You may find it surprising to find values mentioned in connection with something as mundane as the purchase of a car. But safety is as much a value in thinking about car purchases as fair play is in thinking about modes of conduct and as self-fulfillment is in thinking about goals in life. As used here, then, values are relative to contexts of judgment.

2. Even when audiences are predisposed to decode messages accurately, there are apt to be problems. Numerous examples can be provided of persuasive efforts that failed because of difficulties in translation or other problems in bridging linguistic divides. A notorious example was the campaign to market in South America a style of Chevrolet, the Nova, that had been selling well in North America. Unfortunately, *no va* in Spanish means "it doesn't go."

3. There isn't anything terribly rational about this state of affairs. Why, after all, should the people we like necessarily like the same foods we like? Shouldn't it be possible for us to like them just as much despite minor differences in food tastes? Still, the preference for balanced states seems to be powerful (Heider, 1958).

4. Consistency theories vary considerably in the options they identify for reducing psychological imbalances. For some, an asymmetry between attitudes toward a person (e.g., Kate) and attitudes toward an object (e.g., pizza) could be resolved only by a complete rebalancing. But as other theorists have observed, humans are capable of lesser remedies. Said Festinger (1957) in his original *Theory of Cognitive Dissonance,* they can decide that some discrepancies are not important. They can also *compartmentalize,* keeping separate in their heads, for example, Clinton's moral transgressions and his apparent competence as president. Similarly, said Abelson and Rosenberg (1958), they can *differentiate:* deciding, for example, that there is a difference between lying about matters of state (very bad) and lying about personal matters (not as bad). From distinctions such as these, many a politician has crafted successful defenses against charges of wrongdoing in

office. This is yet another *genre* of rhetoric, the *political apologia*—one that requires sure knowledge of the psychology of persuasion.

References

Abelson, R. P., & Rosenberg, M. J. (1958). Symbolic psycho-logic: A model of attitudinal cognition. *Behavioral Science, 3,* 1-13.

Ajzen, I. (1991). The theory of planned behavior. *Organizational Behavior and Human Decision Processes, 50,* 179-211.

Ajzen, I., & Fishbein, M. (1980). *Understanding attitudes and predicting social behavior.* Englewood Cliffs, NJ: Prentice Hall.

Bandura, A. (1977). *Social learning theory.* Englewood Cliffs, NJ: Prentice Hall.

Burnkrant, R. E., & Unnava, H. R. (1989). Self-referencing: A strategy for increasing processing of message content. *Personality and Social Psychology Bulletin, 15,* 628-638.

Cacioppo, J. T., & Petty, R. E. (1982). The need for cognition. *Journal of Personality and Social Psychology, 42,* 116-133.

Cacioppo, J. T., Petty, R. E., & Morris, K. J. (1983). Effects of need for cognition on message evaluation, recall and persuasion. *Journal of Personality and Social Psychology, 45,* 805-818.

Chaicken, S. (1987). The heuristic model of persuasion. In M. P. Zanna, M. Olson, & C. P. Herman (Eds.), *Social influence: The Ontario Symposium* (Vol. 5, pp. 3-39). Hillsdale, NJ: Lawrence Erlbaum.

Cooper, J., & Scher, S. J. (1994). When do our actions affect our attitudes? In S. Shavitt & T. C. Brock (Eds.), *Persuasion: Psychological insights and perspectives.* Needham Heights, MA: Allyn & Bacon.

Devito, J. A. (1978). *Communicology: An introduction to the study of communication.* New York: Harper & Row.

Dichter, E. (1960). *The strategy of desire.* Garden City, NY: Doubleday.

Festinger, L. (1957). *A theory of cognitive dissonance.* Palo Alto, CA: Stanford University Press.

Fishbein, M., & Ajzen, I. (1975). *Belief, attitude, intention, and behavior.* Reading, MA: Addison-Wesley.

Heider, F. (1958). *The psychology of interpersonal relations.* New York: John Wiley.

Kuklinski, J. H., & Quirk, P. J. (1997, February 26-28). *Political facts and public opinion.* Paper presented at conference on "The Future of Fact," University of Pennsylvania, Philadelphia.

McGee, M. (1998, August 31). Judging presidential character. *CRTNET* (listserv of National Communication Association).

McGuire, W. (1968). Personality and susceptibility to social influence. In E. F. Borgatta & W. W. Lambert (Eds.), *Handbook of personality theory and research.* Chicago: Rand McNally.

McGuire, W. (1985) Attitudes and attitude change. In G. Lindzey & E. Aronson (Eds.), *Handbook of social psychology* (3rd ed., Vol. 2, pp. 233-346). New York: Random House.

Miller, G. R. (1980). On being persuaded: Some basic distinctions. In M. E. Roloff & G. R. Miller (Eds.), *Persuasion: New directions in theory and research.* Beverly Hills, CA: Sage.

Morris, D. (1997). *Behind the Oval Office.* New York: Random House.

O'Connor, R. D. (1972). Relative efficacy of modeling, shaping, and the combined procedures for the modification of social withdrawal. *Journal of Abnormal Psychology, 79,* 327-334.

Petty, R. E., & Cacioppo, J. T. (1986). *Communication and persuasion: Central and peripheral routes to attitude change.* New York: Springer-Verlag.

Petty, R. E., & Cacioppo, J. T. (1996). *Attitudes and persuasion: Classic and contemporary approaches.* Boulder, CO: Westview. (Original work published 1981)

Petty, R. E., Cacioppo, J. T., Strathman, A. J., & Priester, J. R. (1994). To think or not to think: Exploring two routes to persuasion. In S. Shavitt & T. C. Brock (Eds.), *Persuasion: Psychological insights and perspectives.* Needham, MA: Allyn & Bacon.

Preiss, R. W., & Allen, M. (1998). Performing counterattitudinal advocacy: The persuasive impact of incentives. In M. Allen & R. W. Preiss, *Persuasion: Advances through meta-analysis.* Cresskill, NJ: Hampton.

Rhodes, N., & Wood, W. (1992). Self-esteem and intelligence affect influenceability: The mediating role of message reception. *Psychological Bulletin, 111,* 156-171.

Rokeach, M. (1968). *Beliefs, attitudes, and values.* San Francisco: Jossey-Bass.

Seplow, S. (1999, February 14). Magnitude of Monica Lewinsky boosted by media. *Philadelphia Inquirer,* p. E5.

Skinner, B. F. (1953). *Science and human behavior.* New York: Free Press.

Staats, A. W., & Staats, C. K. (1963). *Complex human behavior.* New York: Holt.

Tesser, A., & Leone, C. (1977). Cognitive schemas and thought as determinants of attitude change. *Journal of Experimental Social Psychology, 13,* 340-356.

Uleman, J. S., & Bargh, J. A. (Eds.). (1989). *Unintended thought.* New York: New York University Press.

Wicklund, R. A., & Brehm, J. (1976). *Perspectives on cognitive dissonance.* Hillsdale, NJ: Lawrence Erlbaum.

Zimbardo, P., Ebbesen, E. B., & Maslach, C. (1977). *Influencing attitudes and changing behavior* (Rev. ed). Reading, MA: Addison-Wesley.

Persuasion Broadly Considered

O n the first day of the freshman seminar, Professor Steven Jones approaches student Linda Smithers and says, "Ah, you must be Linda." She says, "And you must be Steven." "No," says the professor, "I'm Dr. Jones" (Lakoff, 1990, p. 154). Is this guy putting me down? Linda asks herself. Is he on some kind of ego trip? Or is he merely letting me know how he prefers to be addressed? She looks to his nonverbals for the answer.

Beyond the paradigm cases of persuasion are the gray areas of persuasion where persuasive intent is mixed with other motives or hidden from the audience (and perhaps even from the persuader) or persuasion is combined with other forms of influence. These more complex forms of persuasion are actually quite commonplace in society, and often we are taken in by them because they appear as something entirely trustworthy: as spontaneous expression, for example, or as mere entertainment, or as objective news reporting. But to fully grasp their power and significance, you will need a far more sophisticated view of the communication process than that presented in Chapters 1 and 2.

The view of communication presented here begins with the theory that the individual communicative act is the bearer of multiple meanings. Linda and Steven (or should we call him Professor Jones?) don't just communicate information about who they are; their exchange is also about such relational matters as how they see themselves, how they see the other, how they see the other seeing them, and how they would like to be seen. This, moreover, is just the beginning of the story. Human communication is often multimotivated. It takes place through multiple channels. It is seldom fully explicit. Even then, intended meanings and received meanings may be different. There is seldom an arbiter available to say who is "right." Thus, in a sense, persuader and persuadee cocreate meaning. Sometimes, as in a long-term relationship, meanings may be fought over and ultimately negotiated.

From a concern with individual messages, Chapter 3 moves to consideration of the cumulative effects of multiple messages. Think, for example, of the differences between individual advertise*ments* and advertis*ing* as a recurring institutional practice. What happens to a society when its consumers are repeatedly bombarded with the message that their happiness depends on what they own? What happens to that society when the heroes and heroines of its television dramas are predominantly white middle class? Of special interest here is how multiple meanings and their cumulative effects shape ideologies.

An *ideology* is the glue that joins attitudes together, helping to explain, for example, why someone who is pro-life is also likely to favor prayer in schools, capital punishment, and a reduction in food stamp programs for the poor. Because they are widely shared systems of beliefs and values, ideologies bind people together in such groups as the religious right, the cultural left, libertarians, liberals, fiscal conservatives, and radical feminists. More fundamentally, ideologies join people of an entire society together; these systems of thought are called *cultural ideologies.* Rich or poor, conservative or liberal, Americans tend to be far more committed to materialism and individualism than, say, a village in rural India today or a New England village 300 years ago. Some theorists believe that ideologies are at their most powerful when people are least aware of their hold on them. According to this view, the ideas most basic to the functioning of capitalist societies, such as the "right" to own private property, are also the most taken for granted. (Imagine, said Karl Marx, if we were to view private property as "theft.") In modern society, *hegemonic* (all-controlling) ideas such as ownership of private property are shaped and reinforced from childhood on in a thousand ways, some deliberate, some unintentional, with the news and entertainment media playing a major role. This chapter will highlight the role of the "infotainment" media in the shaping of cultural ideologies, both in the United States and abroad.

Two Levels of Communication:
Content and Relational

People do not just talk about substantive matters (content level of communication); they also, at the very same time, tell us something about themselves in relationship to their audiences (relational level of communication). The "substance" of their communication may be Lou's report to Sue on yesterday's stock market plunge. The relational level is the underlying feeling/tone of the message—as intended by Lou and as received by Sue. Wrapped together in Lou's stock market report may be all manner of *image projections:* "I think I'm smart. I think you're cute. I perceive you as someone who's interested in me and in what I have to say" (Watzlawick, Beavin, & Jackson, 1967).

All of this is likely to be communicated indirectly, by manner and tone—if it is communicated at all. Despite Lou's good intentions, Sue may be hearing Lou as once again seeing her as the little woman and himself as smugly superior. In conflict situations (discussed in Ch. 13), the dispute is often over the relational component of a prior message, even one so matter-of-fact as a stock market report.

Not always are message senders and message receivers out of sync at the relational level. Lou's tone might have heightened Sue's interest in the stock market report (as Lou intended), and it might also have increased her interest in him; but always the relational component is "present" in a message, and it frequently is a continuing source of conflict between people, even when they are trying to straighten out their differences.

Think, for example, about a conversation designed to clear up a misunderstanding between an adviser and her student. The advisor had said simply, "There's a meeting at 8 tonight," but the student had heard something more ominous; hence the need for further conversation. "When I said that there was a meeting at 8:00 p.m. tonight, Winston, I didn't mean that I thought you had to go." "Oh?," says Winston, glaring at his adviser, "I thought it was an order." "Well, maybe it was a suggestion," says the adviser.

Would this "problem-solving" conversation reduce the hard feelings between adviser and advisee? Not necessarily. In the initial encounter the relational component of the message (sometimes called simply the "relational message")—whether the adviser is providing an announcement, giving an order, or offering a suggestion—is what was in dispute. Now, in the airing out of their differences, the relational component of the initial encounter becomes the content component of the second encounter, but much depends on how advisor and advisee express themselves stylistically, nonverbally—at the relational level—in this second exchange. It could be a source of intensified conflict.

Every utterance about substantive matters (about content), Watzlawick et al. argue, is also an interpersonal encounter that invariably projects an image of the communicator. These image

projections, in turn, "comment" on the substantive component of the message. Thus, Watzlawick et al. speak of "levels" of communication. Messages at the relationship level *metacommunicate:* they communicate about communication.

Take the substantive message "Two eggs over light." A simple "please" at the end of that sentence may transform an order to a waiter into a request. Also, at the relationship level, it tells the waiter something about the customer: "See, I'm not the type of person who orders other people about." This is not only what gets metacommunicated, because the customer also transmits relationally by way of gestures, inflections, facial expressions, timing, distance, dress, and grooming. Thus, a smile may reinforce the "please," but the customer's hurried manner may suggest that both the smile and the "please" were perfunctory. (Note in this example how communication may take place at multiple levels. Humans are forever communicating about communication, then communicating—verbally and nonverbally—about them.)

People cannot *not* project relational images of themselves as they communicate about substantive matters (Watzlawick et al., 1967). Those who try to *not* present an image to others—when they try to be natural, to avoid artifice, to express their thoughts or feelings directly—often wind up communicating the image of not appearing to project an image. This is one of the many paradoxes of communication we will have to confront.

The distinction between substantive messages and image projections is important for the study of persuasion. Whether or not we are functioning as persuaders at the content level, we may still be persuading at the relationship level. At the content level, the sportscaster who brings you the latest scores may be doing little more than reciting a series of facts. At the relationship level, however, she may, by the manner of her presentation, help to reinforce or undermine your identification with the station as one that shares your enthusiasm for the local basketball team. Indeed, a large part of the job evaluation of the sportscaster may consist of an assessment of how convincingly she promotes the impression that her own happiness depends on the fate of the home team. In long-term relationships between friends or relatives, relational image projections are often more important than what gets said at the content level. Rarely, for example, is a dispute between husband and wife about who should pick up whose socks from the floor and place them in the laundry basket only about dirty socks (Haley, 1976). Images about self and other invariably get communicated, including images of power, trust, and affection.

Although substantive messages are carried largely by verbal means, messages at the relationship level are transmitted mostly by nonverbal means. These are discussed at some length in Chapter 5. Nonverbal stimuli range from clearly intentional winks to innocent-appearing blinks. But even the blinks, as we shall see, can be contrived.

Impression Management

Just how much of our lives is occupied with concerns about the images we project is a matter of some debate. The issue is a sensitive one, particularly for those who pride themselves on their individuality or who regard manipulation of any type as intrinsically immoral (Johannesen, 1996). Nevertheless, it appears that sensitivity to how others perceive us develops early in life and leads to rhetorical sophistication at impression management. From the recognition that we communicate images of ourselves whether or not we want to come attempts at doing something about how we are perceived—at *promoting* an image and not just projecting one.

Yet this does not mean that most people care *only* about how others see them. Rather, their efforts at impression management may be paired with or balanced against other concerns, including some that they ordinarily view as exclusively nonrhetorical. Some of their acts may be *multimotivated.* They may wear blue jeans, for example, because jeans are comfortable and relatively inexpensive, they like the way they look, *and* wearing the jeans may please or impress valued others. Similarly, they may attempt to inform or entertain or please others aesthetically *and* seek to impress them.

Sometimes, our motivations are so complex that we ourselves have great difficulty deciding which ones are primary. A former student commented in a paper that she had "banished" makeup from her face because she did not like having to be careful of the finished product, unable to laugh, cry, or touch for fear of marring the surface. She added that she had grown ashamed of her need to fix and angered by the feeling that something always needed repair. But on further reflection, it occurred to her that another motive might have been operative. By not wearing makeup, she could protect her ego with the belief that if she really wanted to, she could be a raving beauty. Not wearing makeup allowed her the security of not trying, much like the second grader who dares not risk failure by attempting to read.

Impression management is sometimes goal-specific, for example, a means of gaining the trust we need to win over audience support for a controversial proposal. Yet much of the "imaging" we do is not designed for any particular or immediate purpose. It is more like putting money in the bank and trading on it when we need it. We literally bank on our images.

Deception About Persuasive Intent

From the recognition that we cannot *not* communicate, it is but a short step to the realization that it is impossible in some contexts not to function as persuaders. Consider, for example, a "no-frills" box of tissues. Ordinarily, boxes of tissues, like most supermarket packages, announce themselves as instances of attempted persuasion.

They are attractively adorned and delicately scented. They display a brand name made famous by expensive advertising.

Not so this generic box. It presents a surface image of "the real" as opposed to the rhetorical. Indeed, there is something so starkly "unrhetorical" about the package that one gets the impression of extra effort expended to distance the product from its brand name competitors by making it seem "antirhetorical." No name (not just the absence of a brand name) appears on the box. The lettering announcing its contents is plain black on white. We are told with rather unnecessary exactitude that its 200 2-ply tissues are 8.25 inches by 9.71 inches in size. Perhaps the packagers, while providing a reduction in price, are also trying to persuade us that the box is in some sense "virtuous" for being nonrhetorical. They would be hard-pressed, in any case, not to present a persuasive message of any type within a supermarket context.

No-frills packages are by no means the only things made to seem nonrhetorical. Persuaders often go to great lengths to persuade us that they are not persuaders, and they often succeed as persuaders by disarming us in precisely this way. "I'm not trying to advise you," says the clever parent of a rebellious teenager, "I just want to ask you a question." Of course, the advice is couched as a question.

Planting a thought in a message recipient's mind can be accomplished even by declaring a rumor about an electoral candidate to be untrue, for example, a headline stating mayoral candidate "Andrew Winters *Not* Connected to Bank Embezzlement." The effects of *innuendo* in newspaper headlines have been well illustrated in studies by Wegner, Wenzalaff, Kerker, and Beattie (1981). They compared the success of headlines aimed at fictitious candidates such as Andrew Winters that took the form of questions ("Is Karen Downing Associated With a Fraudulent Charity?") with directly incriminating statements about a candidate ("Bob Talbert Linked With Mafia"). All these headlines resulted in negative perceptions of the candidate; the form that they took made little difference.

Deceptive Deception

The reason that masked persuasive intent works is well known to communication researchers. Persons forewarned that a communicator intends to persuade them probably will mount a psychological defense, perhaps tuning out, perhaps reciting counterarguments to themselves even in advance of exposure to the communicator's message (e.g., Petty & Cacioppo, 1981/1996). This defensive reaction is especially likely if the issue is of some importance to the persuadees or if they suspect that the communicator is up to no good—that he or she is manipulative, exploitative, and perhaps deliberately deceptive (Benoit, 1998; Fukada, 1986; Papageorgis, 1968; Petty & Cacioppo, 1977). Knowing this, persuaders often present themselves as innocent of any persuasive designs on the recipients of their messages. Rather, they are just out to inform, to entertain, to ask a few questions, or perhaps to express their innermost feelings.

This happens even in television ads when, for example, a professional actor completes a commercial pitch and, with the cameras still on him, turns in obvious relief from his task to take real pleasure in consuming the product he has been advertising (Goffman, 1974, p. 475). This is just one way in which the appearance of naturalness is used by advertisers in an attempt to dispel audience suspicions. Radio and TV ads have used children's voices, presumably because these seem unschooled. Street noises and other effects give the impression of interviews with unpaid respondents. False starts, filled pauses, and overlapping speech simulate actual conversation.

As a general rule, whatever yardsticks may be used by one person to distinguish persuasion from nonpersuasion will be exploited by others to deceive their listeners or viewers about their persuasive intent or at least to make their messages appear more authentic or more objective. Is seeming unrehearsed a sign of the nonpersuader? In 1980, the makers of campaign commercials for Ronald Reagan deliberately staged scenes to look unstaged, and they encouraged Reagan himself to seem as little like an actor (or former actor) as possible. Is looking away from the job interviewer a sign of the nonpersuader (or at least the not very skilled persuader)? By a type of perverse logic, some persuaders deliberately shift their gaze away from the job interviewer from time to time to create the appearance of being sincere, honest, not too slick. Similarly, "yes-men" learn to disagree with their bosses enough to negate the impression of being panderers while still playing up to them. Is one-sided argument evidence of promotional intent? Skilled persuaders learn to appear impartial by presenting both sides of an issue while subtly minimizing the merits of the opposing view.

In the category of deception about persuasive intent is deception about deception. This takes us beyond the relational level of communication to meta-meta levels (communications about relational communication and beyond). Most deceptive messages carry with them the implicit metacommunication: "This is not a deceptive message." To carry conviction, these deceptive metacommunications may require deceptive meta-metacommunications in their support. Note here that all deception is persuasion, although not all persuasion is deception. (See Box 3.1.)

In situations in which people are suspected of concealing or distorting information, observers heed their expressions rather than their apparently deliberate messages. For example, if Lucy thinks her friend Tom is lying to her, she is more likely to study his face, body, or vocal cues than to listen to what he is saying. Here, the semantic content of a verbal message counts for less than its style. If she detects a furtive glance, an embarrassed hesitation, or a trembling lip, Lucy may not be able to determine what Tom may be concealing, but she will assume that he is concealing something.

BOX 3.1 Embrace and Pose

Deep into the Paula Jones scandal, with reporters chasing down leads about possible past affairs, Bill and Hillary Clinton "just happened" to be caught embracing on a Virgin Islands beach. Was this an assault on their privacy by an unscrupulous, paparazzi-like photographer? Or was this a shrewd attempt to offset bad publicity under cover of pretended outrage at the press? Most newspapers bought the official White House line on the event, despite reports that the Secret Service had blocked access to the beach area from which the photo was taken but left it unprotected on the day of the kiss.

One person who voiced suspicion was Bill Kovach, then curator of the Nieman Foundation, who "wondered about whether the Clintons, as they were dancing, really believed they were alone. 'I'm skeptical how candid it was. I have difficulty believing that we have, in that photograph, been witness to something deep and meaningful in the relationship between the president and the first lady'" (Shogren, 1998, p. A10).

Expression Games

Expression games are contests over the control, and detection of control, of expressive behaviors (Goffman, 1967). For example, Tom may deliberately show signs of guilt or embarrassment over a relatively minor concealment in the hope that Lucy will not investigate a more serious evasion. Apparently, much behavior that is regularly assumed to be uncontrollable is, in fact, controllable. Psychiatric and physical symptoms ranging from headaches to paralysis of limbs may be consciously or unconsciously faked or used rhetorically as "loss of control" tactics in conflict situations (Haley, 1963).

Expression games can get extremely complicated, particularly in military conflicts. Rival nations may go to great lengths to stage deceptions or to conceal their detection from those who staged them. During World War II, for example, the British arranged for the Germans to discover false secrets on the corpse of a high-ranking but fictitious military officer. They constructed dummy airfields to camouflage real air war preparations and to entice the Germans to expend effort and ammunition on false targets. Vials of chemicals were dropped behind enemy lines with instructions to German troops on how to foil their medical officers by creating the impression that they had succumbed to major diseases. When German spies were detected, they were allowed to remain in the field and generally fed innocuous or false information. Sometimes, however, they were fed true and important information as a way of persuading them and their superiors that they had not been detected.

To deceive the enemy about manipulative intent, it was often necessary to mislead the communicator of the deceptive message as well. Rather than instructing

French resistance workers not to warn the Germans about Allied invasion plans, the British gave them false information, instructed them to keep it secret, and assumed that as a matter of course, some would be captured by the Germans and would reveal the false information very credibly under torture.

More commonly, however, people deceive themselves about their manipulative designs on others. They can then appear sincere while avoiding conscious feelings of guilt or shame. Any person who is consistently sincere is probably suffering from a good dose of self-deception. Indeed, people deceive themselves far more than they deceive others (Berger, 1963). Such deceptions range from relatively harmless rationalizations for manipulative stratagems (e.g., the parent who denies any selfish motives in persuading a child to go to bed) to the development of psychosomatic illnesses (e.g., an excessive need for sleep as a way of warding off anxiety).

Persuasion in the Guise of Objectivity

Another gray area of persuasion is persuasion in the guise of objectivity. Accounting statements and cost-benefit analyses, news reports, scientific articles, history textbooks, and reported discoveries of social problems, among other things, fall into this gray area. But aren't these really forms of "nonpersuasion?" Not really. Messages classified as objective make serious claims on the human psyche, often for good reason. Each purports to provide "truth" or "knowledge" of some sort, arrived at disinterestedly. Yet because the appearance of objectivity can be a powerful form of persuasion, it is wise to view claims to pure objectivity with suspicion.

Accounting Statements and Cost-Benefit Analyses

In the early days of capitalism, the introduction of double-entry bookkeeping did more than provide the basis of rational business calculations (Mayhew, 1997). These records "displayed character, a basis for trust" (p. 39). Yet companies often employed them as a way of covering over their own sloppiness. Indeed, companies today continue to covet the legitimizing functions of accounting statements.

Although Leon Mayhew (1997) concedes the rational basis for modern accounting methods, Theodore M. Porter (1994) maintains that the "rhetoric of impersonality" in cost-benefit analysis is intended to deceive. As with double-entry bookkeeping, its public message is one of objectivity. But the task of cost-benefit analysis—to assess the economic consequences of adopting a given policy—is fraught with perils that tend to be covered over. One such difficulty is quantifying values, such as that of a schoolchild's life against that of an adult. What matters in these estimates, says Porter, is not accuracy—which is impossible to achieve—but the appearance of precision, giving policymakers something to go on.

News Reporting

News reporting, unlike commentating and editorializing, is supposed to be objective, and sometimes it approaches that ideal. But journalists are aware that their choice of what news to cover and what not to cover, as well as their decisions about how to cover it, can have enormous consequences (e.g., Iyengar, 1991). Indeed, some theorists have argued that objectivity in news reporting is virtually impossible (Cappella & Jamieson, 1997; Hackett, 1984; Malcolm, 1999). Storytelling of every kind requires selection. Not everything can be said about an object, and not everything can be given equal emphasis. Thus, selections deflect even as they reflect; in calling attention to some things, they prompt inattention to others (Burke, 1966).

The process of selection-deflection is by no means random. Institutional pressures force editors and reporters to play up the dramatic, the sensational, and to play down news that doesn't sell newspapers or ad time. For example, a report on an important but complicated new insurance regulation may be shoved aside on the evening news and replaced by an arresting human interest story of little consequence. Increasingly, to remain competitive, news outlets must entertain. These same outlets may be under pressure to bow to one or another constituency. Former *Newsweek* reporter Robert Parry (1992) tells the story of a photo of George Bush and accompanying caption that appeared on the cover of *Newsweek* magazine just as the then vice president was preparing to announce his intention to run for the presidency in 1988. On first impression, said Parry, nothing on the cover should have concerned even a hypersensitive person such as Bush. The cover picture showed Bush driving his powerboat and staring steely-eyed out to sea. He was wearing a yellow slicker and a slight scowl. But it was not the picture but the caption that drove Bush to distraction. "George Bush: Fighting the 'Wimp Factor,'" the cover language read. The much feared "w word" had come into prominent national view (p. 45).

But Bush's public relations problem could have been worse, reported Parry (1992). *Newsweek* had been refused authorization to photograph Bush playing tennis, a request that the Bush people believed was cruelly designed to play up the vice president's preppie roots. Within days of the "wimp" cover, said Parry, Bush denied the *Newsweek* reporters preparing a book on the 1988 presidential election access to his campaign. *Newsweek* was granted a reprieve only after a "summit meeting" between the two sides. Although *Newsweek* editors claimed that the meeting on the "wimp" cover had no influence on subsequent news decisions, they were not about to make the same mistake twice.

> So as Bush headed for the Republican National Convention in New Orleans in August, *Newsweek* featured the vice-president in a pressed white shirt, dark blue tie with thin red stripes. The backdrop was blue sky, fluffy white clouds and an American flag fluttering in the distance. In the August GOP convention issue, the respectful cover language read: "Bush. High Stakes in New Orleans. A Revealing Interview. Nixon on the Race." Nothing that could possibly offend this time. (p. 49)

Parry added that several critical stories on Bush that had been originally slated for convention week were also whisked away.

Scientific Reporting

Scientific reporting, like news journalism, purports to give information rather than persuade, but the trappings of science can be used as tools of advertising and public relations (Jackall, 1995). Not uncommonly, for example, industries set up seemingly disinterested scientific institutes whose professed purpose is to serve the public good but whose real aim is to discredit opponents' charges that the industry's product, whether it be cosmetics, explosives, paints, leathers, furs, or medicines, is a threat to the public good. For example, the stated purpose of the Formaldehyde Institute was "for the sound science of formaldehyde and formaldehyde-based products and to ensure that the data are used and interpreted properly" (p. 372). To this end, the institute sought to appear objective in its compilations of research evidence and collaborations with other investigative agencies, but this association of formaldehyde producers and industrial users just happened to play down the potential dangers posed by the chemical (e.g., evidence of nasal cancer in rats) and to play up the benefits (e.g., its indispensability).

Of course, science at its most objective is a far cry from such paradigm cases of persuasion as product advertising and political campaigning. But to speak of the scientific report as fully objective is to ignore too much evidence to the contrary. For example, in a series of articles, John A. Campbell (1970, 1997) revealed evolutionist Charles Darwin to be something of a persuader in disguise: purporting to be purely objective in his fact gathering and theorizing, whereas acknowledging in his private writings that the appearance of objectivity was for him a persuasive strategy. Darwin claimed publicly, for example, that his theorizing had been guided entirely by what the raw facts disclosed, yet in private he acknowledged the reverse: that his theorizing guided the search for facts. This, at the time, was a highly unorthodox approach to science, one that he was reluctant to disclose publicly. Darwin was also not above attempting to mollify religious believers or to court England's agrarian aristocracy by his likening of evolution to animal breeding.

Even if we were to assume that scientific inquiry is simply a matter of fact gathering and logical inference, it would be hard to deny persuasion's role in scientific reporting. To cite a contemporary example, the AIDS researcher who prepares a scientific report for an AIDS research conference must decide how to title the report, how to frame the issues, how to write the report stylistically, how to make interpretations of the research data appear convincing, and how to deliver the report orally and visually with maximum clarity and believability. Even so seemingly straightforward a process as citing past work on the AIDS researcher's topic becomes an opportunity to impress research foundations with the importance of the work, to forge alliances with respected colleagues, and to attack rivals (Latour, 1987). Bruno Latour likens the citational stratagems of the clever researcher to the moves and countermoves of an expert billiard player.

The report of a major clinical trial of a cholesterol-lowering drug named cholestyramine provides vivid evidence of an attempt at making research findings appear impressive (Lipid Research Clinics Program, 1984). For example, the researchers boasted that use of the drug resulted in eight fewer deaths than in a control group not given the drug (30 versus 38), but they neglected to say that this difference was rather minuscule given the more than 1,800 participants in the study, roughly 900 in each group. Similarly, the potential for rather severe gastrointestinal side effects from use of cholestyramine was nowhere mentioned in the abstract of the study, which is what most physicians tend to read. The first mention of these side effects speaks of "*the ability of* certain lipid-lowering drugs . . ." Suppose the report had said instead, "*the danger that* . . ." (Simons, 1993)?

History Textbooks

History textbooks also fall in the gray area of persuasion in the guise of objectivity. According to Alexander Stille (1998), the need to cater to the two largest markets in the United States, Texas and California, has prompted publishers of American history texts to promote multicultural diversity while avoiding anything that might offend the conservative religious right. Says Stille, "The words 'tribe' and 'Indian' are out, in favor of 'group' and 'Native American,' even though many Native Americans use and prefer the former terms" (p. 15). On the other hand, according to Stille, the religious right vigorously opposes any critical references to America's cultural heroes, opposes harsh accounts of slavery, and brings pressure on publishers to avoid positive descriptions of the New Deal or the charter of the United Nations.

Reported Discoveries of Social Problems

Do societies discover social problems objectively, or do they construct them rhetorically? This question continues to perplex social theorists (Hacking, 1991). Fifty years ago, for example, the terms *child abuse, date rape,* and *sexual harassment* did not exist. But did that mean that the problems designated by the terms also did not exist? There are at least three schools of thought on the matter: (a) *Mundane realists* argue that problems such as child abuse are every bit as real as skin cancer or infant mortality; putting a name to them only assists in talking about conditions that have long existed. (b) *Strict constructionists* argue that language is constitutive of reality, rather than merely reflective of it. Who we are as individuals and as groups, how we understand ourselves to be joined together in time and space, and what we consider to be problems or nonproblems all depend on the language we select to "create," as it were, the worlds we inhabit. For example, in cultures past, even infant mortality was not labeled as a problem; it was seen rather as a routine occurrence. (c) *Contextual constructionists* argue that social problems are neither entirely discovered nor entirely fabricated. They point to widely varying statistics on alleged problems such as child abuse to show that these problems do not simply exist "out there." For example, estimates of the magnitude of child abuse in the United States have ranged from the minuscule to the all-inclusive, depending on how the term was defined. At the same time, contextual constructionists reject the "antirealism" of their strict constructionist colleagues. Child abuse may be a social construction, they concede, but the problem would not have been categorized, named, quantified, and the like, had there not been a basis in fact for multiple injuries to children, documented by pediatric radiologists and shown by investigators to be the work of parents or parent substitutes. Like strict constructionists, contextual constructionists assign persuasion a significant role in explaining what estimates of the nature and magnitude of a social problem any given society takes to be real. Still, they believe that some estimates are better than others (Best, 1989; Hacking, 1991; Miller & Holstein, 1993).

How Multiple Messages Shape Ideologies

One communicative act may stem from many motivations, operate on many levels, and have many effects via multiple forms of influence, some of them unintended. (See, for example, Picture 3.1.) For example, the producer of a television sitcom might very well want to entertain viewers *and* build an audience for potential big-money sponsors. In the process, it might persuade viewers that the nuclear family is a good thing. The producers of television sitcoms in the late 1950s and early 1960s did precisely that with such shows as *Leave It to Beaver, Ozzie and Harriet,* and *Father Knows Best.* Other types of shows combine multiple forms of influence. Today's

Picture 3.1. Politics as Entertainment, Entertainment as Politics
SOURCE: Used with permission of the artist, Ward Sutton.

BOX 3.2 Political Persuasion in the Guise of Late-Night Television Comedy

"Have you seen George W. Bush trying to pronounce the word 'subliminal'? He pronounces the word 'subliminable'—not 'subliminal,' 'subliminable.' And it makes me wonder, do you think this guy is 'electimable'?" (David Letterman, quoted in "Campaign Laugh Track," 2000, p. wk5)

"Al Gore has been accused of polling voters and using the result of that poll to write his policy statements. This made him mad, he shot back. Today Gore said, 'I pay no attention to the polls and neither do 73.3% of the American people.'" (Jay Leno, quoted in "Campaign Laugh Track," 2000, p. wk5)

Political experts have belatedly come to appreciate the power of the David Lettermans and Jay Lenos to influence voting decisions. In a survey conducted by the Pew Research Center for the People and the Press, nearly half of Americans aged 18 to 29 and 25% of their elders reported that they often gleaned information about the 2000 presidential campaign from late-night comedy shows (cited in Sella, 2000, p. 74).

Comedy's most powerful contribution is to cast campaign rivals as cardboard characters. In 2000, the presidential contest was reduced by the comics to Bush the Fool and Gore the Stiff. Variations on these archetypes were repeated daily, making it virtually impossible for the candidates to undo them (Sella, 2000). In 2000, the *New York Times* signaled its acknowledgment of the importance of late-night comedy by providing a weekly tally of late-night jokes about the candidates. For the week of September 8 through September 14, said the *Times,* the numbers of jokes per candidate were nearly even: 24 about Bush, 23 about Gore. As Sella maintains, however, these numbers can be deceptive. For one thing, "stiff" isn't as worrisome to most voters as "dumb" or "stupid." For another, the comedians and their writers seemed to take special delight in pillorying Governor Bush.

Says Sella (2000), the late-night comics tend in general to be more liberal than conservative, and they reflect their political leanings in their work even as they claim to be apolitical and powerless to shape electoral outcomes:

Mainstream comedy—especially the sly, rounded-scissor-blade gibes of Letterman and Leno—is presented as a last bastion of impartiality. Yet it is a form of propaganda. From the ideology of those who write the shows, straight down to the arcane structure of TV humor itself, political bias is comedy's secret sharer. (p. 74)

By way of response, the comics insist that their barbs would not resonate with viewers were they not accurate. In short, Bush is a fool; Gore is stiff. Yet as Sella observes, Bush and Gore are many things. Why pick on these two attributes? Why especially did the comedians not fasten on a more damning cardboard cutout for the Democratic candidate: Gore the Fraud? The evidence was readily available of Gore having bent repeatedly to the political winds—exploiting, for example, the lung cancer death of his own sister, although he had personally accepted large campaign gifts from Big Tobacco. Sella provides an impressive list.

Yet as Sella himself acknowledges, lampooning Gore as a fraud would have been more difficult for the comics. It would have required more setup time for each joke and depended on typical viewers knowing more than they did.

Thus has presidential politics been shaped by the rhetorical requirements of late-night comedy.

infomercial is designed to sell a product or service, but it does so in the guise of a lecture, interview, or scientific demonstration. The docudrama combines fact and fiction in an informative, entertaining, and persuasive manner. The news magazine specializes in entertaining news, all the while pulling in potential customers for the program's sponsors.

Any given episode of a sitcom may have unintended effects, including ideological effects. Dress styles might be imitated, for example, or a viewer might find inspiration from a Sunday with the Cleavers for a renewal of religious vows. The same is true of more recent television programming such as *ER* or *The West Wing*.

If any given television or advertising segment may affect a viewer's ideology, what are the effects of a daily dose of television? The difference that multiple messages can make is well illustrated by product advertising.

An ad may be both *informational* and *transformational*—that is, it tells you about a product and, if effective, makes a customer out of you (Leiss, Kline, & Jhally, 1986, p. 46). But the combined effect of multiple advertisements is truly transformational. As consumers, we generally assume that the arguments and slogans and pretty pictures used to argue for a product are merely means to an end. We fail to recognize that these means are being reinforced even as the product is being promoted.

Consider television ads for medicinals such as pain relievers and nutritional supplements. An underlying and oft-repeated premise of these advertisements is this: Got a problem? Take a pill! No advertiser deliberately strives to turn America into a nation of pill poppers, and no single advertisement has that effect. Still, the combined effect of these multiple messages is pronounced. These messages combine with yet others—for one-stop shopping, for easy listening, for dinner in a box or even education in a box—that mold and reinforce the values not just of material acquisition but of a certain type of acquisition: of purchased passivity, of being served, of life made unthinkingly, unblinkingly easy.

These values come with a belief—or perhaps a quasi-religious faith—in technology. Got any problem? Technology can solve it. These beliefs and values combine with others to form the bedrock of contemporary Western culture's dominant ideology. Advertising not only proposes solutions to problems but also helps construct them. It does so, moreover, without being particularly noticeable. For example, a thousand or more ads for "a sexier you" (or some such slogan) sell not just the hair rinse or beauty cream or breath freshener but also the assumption—learned from childhood on—that sexuality needs to be purchased; what we bring to relationships on our own is not good enough.

As Michael Schudson (1986) put it, advertising "surrounds and enters us" (p. 210). American advertising, he observes, "simplifies and typifies" (p. 215).

It does not present life as it is but reality as it should be—life and lives worth emulating. It always assumes that there is progress. It is thoroughly optimistic, providing for any troubles that it identifies a solution in a particular product or style of life. (p. 215)

Its underlying message is a serious one even when it is self-mocking. Of course, many of the values it celebrates are already in the common culture. But advertising "picks up some of the things that people hold dear and re-presents them to people as *all* of what they value, assuring them that the sponsor is the patron of common ideals" (p. 233).

This is not to say that product advertising's version of the good life is monolithic and unchanging. Together with news and entertainment programming, advertising reflects currents in the culture—some of them conflicting—even as it molds and re-inforces them. Some components of the culture's dominant ideology have remained in place through the years—for example, its celebration of "family values." But just as today's high school history books promote multiculturalism, so television advertising reflects America's increased diversity, including a greater diversity of family lifestyles.

That diversity also extends to television programming. Compare, for example, the television entertainment of today with the family-oriented television sitcoms of the 1950s and early 1960s. These shows had a great deal in common. Each presented what appeared to be a realistic portrayal of the newly suburbanized, largely white, middle-class American family. These families consisted of a working father, home-maker mother, and children experiencing the everyday crises of growing up. Each show ended with a moral lesson that taught appropriate roles and behavior in the new postwar consumer culture. A weekly diet of these shows sent an ideological message far more powerful than any one of them alone. Their central message was the need for conformity to white, male, mainstream, middle-class values.

To illustrate the ideological effects of multiple messages, this chapter has focused, not by accident, on television. Television is at once the great reflector of cultural values and the great shaper of those same values. Television exerts ideological influence by portraying "appropriate" and "inappropriate" social relations, defining norms and conventions, providing "common sense" understandings, and articulating our central preoccupations and concerns. In so doing, it confirms, reinforces, and often helps create our sense of ourselves and our place in the world (Fiske, 1987). Together with other mass media of communication, it is remaking the world itself.

The Making of McWorld

According to numerous experts, the world has undergone an ideological revolution of immense proportions (e.g., Barber, 1996; Combs & Nimmo, 1993; Lakoff,

1997). In the United States and in much of the rest of the world, traditional values such as those epitomized in the television sitcoms of the 1950s have been called into question, making thinkable and even doable shows in which two lesbians are locked in a passionate embrace, a television anchor has a baby out of wedlock, and an inter-racial couple beds down for a night without so much as a murmur afterward from mainstream TV commentators. Meanwhile, capitalism has triumphed indisputably, and with it has come a celebration of consumerism, of materialism, and of what some critics lament as unbridled narcissism. This revolution in lifestyles and values has a distinctively American flavor, creating imitations and adaptations of American popular culture in Tokyo and London, Shanghai and Buenos Aires, Moscow and Tel Aviv (Picture 3.2). Benjamin Barber (1996) has an apt name for this ideological globalization: He calls it "McWorld." Says Barber, McWorld turns the old Marxist war cry, "Workers of the World Unite; you have nothing to lose but your chains," into the new cry, "Consumers of the world unite! We have everything you need in our chains" (p. 78).

What has been said thus far about multiple messages having unintended (or only partially intended) ideological effects goes a long way toward explaining the Americanization of the world's cultures. Mattel's Barbie doll is but one of a number of internationally marketed and merchandised symbols of America that participate in the making of McWorld. A recent special issue of the *New York Times Magazine* showed Pepsi drinkers in New Delhi; the Nike insignia over a store in Beijing; the Lucky Strikes logo in Yangon, Myanmar (Burma); the familiar symbols of Burger King in Germany and of IBM in Ho Chi Minh City, Vietnam; and signs for Marlboro in Tripoli, Libya, and for Texas Fried Chicken in Cairo. McWorld is a little girl clutching her very own Barbie doll in that Burger King in Germany or Texas Fried Chicken in Cairo consuming not just the products to be had but also their functions as symbols of things and lifestyles American.

Thus Barbie and her friends need to be seen not just as instruments of domestic propaganda but as a vital part of America's unrivaled power in the world. Josef Joffe (1997), one of the contributors to the *Times* special issue, remarked that "unlike cen-turies past, when war was the great arbiter, today the most interesting types of power do not grow out of the barrel of a gun" (p. 41). He added that although the classic way was to force other nations to act against their wills, today there is a much bigger payoff in "getting others to want what you want" (p. 42).

What the world thinks it wants, what it fantasizes it wants, says Barber (1996), is increasingly influenced by Hollywood versions of the good life. A 1991 survey of top-grossing films revealed that of the top three in 22 countries, 58 of a possible 66 were American (p. 93). McWorld is MTV, CNN, the NBA play-offs, the NFL Super Bowl, and *Dynasty, Dallas,* and *Baywatch* in syndication—just to mention some of

Picture 3.2. Huge Lines Outside Moscow's First McDonald's Restaurant, 1990
SOURCE: Reuters/Archive Photos. Used with permission.

the TV fare that reaches across the globe. McWorld is the names and logos and trade-marks of Nike, Marlboro, Levi, IBM, Microsoft, Coca-Cola, KFC, and a hundred other familiar brands—together constituting a new international language. McWorld is theme parks such as Euro-Disney, located just kilometers away from what used to be the cultural capital of Europe. McWorld is American-style malls fea-turing American products: These, says Barber, have become theme parks in their own right.

Above all, McWorld is the combined effects of these component parts on the hearts and minds of the world's citizens, particularly its young people. These effects, suggest Barber (1996), are synergistic. *Synergy* in persuasion is most clearly illustrated by mammoth "infotainment" corporations such as Disney seeing to it that all their component parts—Disney Studios, Disney theme parks, Disney stores, ABC television—are coordinated to produce maximum profits for such blockbuster hits as *Lion King,* the movie; *Lion King,* the video; and *Lion King,* the Broadway play.

But synergy is also at work at a broader, ideological level in the combined effects of American films, food chains, sitcoms, and the rest inviting the world to buy American, think American, and fantasize American. Most obviously, that ideology is one of consumerism, with its attendant cry of "gimme, gimme, gimme" (Barber, 1996). Along with consumerism, says Barber, has come a devaluation of class consciousness; there are no workers in McWorld, only consumers. But this is not all. Hollywood and Madison Avenue also shape values of secularism, passivity, vicariousness, and an accelerated pace of life (p. 97). Meanwhile, MTV, with a half billion viewers in 71 countries as early as 1993, celebrates youth, disdains authority, flirts with violence, and makes a sport of sex (p. 109). It is little wonder that traditional cultures such as Iran's find McWorld threatening.

Barber himself (1996) asks whether the world has become a better place as a result of its Americanization. Have we lost patience with such traditional forms of persuasion as political oratory, the newspaper editorial, and the Sunday sermon? Can the market for European art films survive the competition from American blockbusters? Will radio stations playing classical music give way to Top 40 rock? Will the centuries-old Japanese tea ceremony be displaced by Coca-Cola?

One thing seems certain: The clearly intentional, single-track, effects-limited messages that come to mind when speaking of paradigm cases of persuasion are not the only influences, nor necessarily the most significant influences, on the world's judgments and actions.

Summary

The conventional view of persuasion confines it to such paradigm cases as political oratory, religious sermons, product advertisements, and newspaper editorials. But there are other instances of communication in which intent to persuade is not so clear-cut or in which persuasive intent is commingled with other motives for communicating. Cases such as these fall outside the core of persuasion, but they are important nevertheless. Appreciating their influence on society requires a perspective on any given communicative act as multileveled. Then, too, communication can have persuasive effects beyond those that were clearly intended; the cumulative effects of advertising provide an example. Moreover, in some contexts, persuasion is unavoidable.

TABLE 3.1 Gray Areas of Persuasion

Type of Cases	*Examples*
Unclear or masked intent	• Persuasion in the guise of news reporting • Innuendo
Unavoidable persuasion	• The generic box of tissues on a supermarket shelf
Unintended effects of intentionally persuasive messages	• Ideological effects of advertising and entertainment programming
Mixed intent	• Blue jeans worn for comfort and to impress • A sportscast designed to sell the station as it gives the news

Table 3.1 charts these gray areas around the core, identifying four areas that were the focus of this chapter. In the gray areas are persuasion masked as—or mixed with—information giving, scientific demonstration, entertainment, and seemingly authentic, spontaneous expression.

Still, not all guises are deliberate disguises, intended to deceive and manipulate. The professions of science, journalism, and accounting make legitimate claims on our attention, however much we may find evidence of persuasion rather than "pure" logic or "pure" description. Entertainment does not cease to amuse us or interest us just because it also persuades us. The generic box of tissues that attracts us by its "realness" still contains objects that we can really use. The blue jeans that promote an image of unadorned authenticity also cover the lower half of the body—comfortably, durably, and relatively inexpensively.

Although Part 2 of this book focuses on paradigm cases of persuasion, the perspective on communication introduced in this chapter to help you identify nonobvious instances of persuasion applies to persuasion's core as well. Moreover, the principles presented here fit well with those articulated in Chapter 2. Consider the following as you are introduced in Chapter 4 to the coactive approach to persuasion.

1. Human beings project images of themselves as they communicate about substantive matters.

2. Communicators are not entirely in control of the effects they produce.

3. Messages make connections between things—between, say, the car being advertised and the life of luxury with which it is linked. As the ad sells the car, it also reinforces desire for a life of luxury.

4. Message recipients are cocreators of meaning. In so doing, they often self-persuade in ways unintended by communicators.

5. The message is mostly thought of as what is said by the communicator, whether verbally or nonverbally. But broadly speaking, the message is anything to which the message recipient attends and assigns meaning. It may include the context of the message, not just the text; it will probably include the source of the message, not just what is said.

Taken together, these principles should help us better understand a number of things: how, for example, product advertising promotes ideologies, not just products; how what we take to be reality is in part rhetorically constructed; and how news of Michael Jordan's latest contract with Nike helps sell both Air Jordans and Michael Jordan.

Questions and Projects for Further Study

1. Do you actively seek to promote an image of yourself to others, or do you merely project one?
2. How do you address your professors? How do they address you? What's being metacommunicated about power, respect, and liking by these interactions?
3. Is there a dominant, widely shared ideology in this country, or are there many competing ideologies with no single dominant ideology? How would you describe your own ideology?
4. What is objectivity? As a communicator, is it possible to be fully objective? Discuss in relation to news, textbooks, tax statements, scientific reports, and so forth.
5. Review the discussion of consumption communities in Chapter 1. Are there consumption communities in the United States? Do you "belong" to one? How would you describe it?
6. Is the Americanization of cultures around the world a good or bad thing?

References

Barber, B. (1996). *Jihad vs. McWorld: How globalism and tribalism are reshaping the world.* New York: Ballantine.

Benoit, W. L. (1998). Forewarning and persuasion. In M. Allen & R. A. Preiss (Eds.), *Persuasion through meta-analysis.* Cresskill, NJ: Hampton.

Berger, P. (1963). *Invitation to sociology.* Garden City, NY: Anchor.

Best, J. (1989). *Images of issues.* New York: Aldine de Gruyter.

Burke, K. (1966). *Language as symbolic action.* Berkeley: University of California Press.

Campbell, J. A. (1970). Darwin and *The origin of species:* The rhetorical ancestry of an idea. *Speech Monographs, 37,* 1-14.

Campbell, J. A. (1997). Strategic reading: Rhetoric, intention, and interpretation. In A. G. Gross & W. M. Keith (Eds.), *Rhetorical hermeneutics: Invention and interpretation in the age of science.* Albany: State University of New York Press.

Campaign laugh track. (2000, September 17). *New York Times,* Week in Review, p. 5.

Cappella, J. N., & Jamieson, K. H. (1997). *The spiral of cynicism.* New York: Oxford University Press.

Combs, J. E., & Nimmo, D. (1993). *The new propaganda.* New York: Longman.

Fiske, J. (1987). *Television culture.* New York: Methuen.

Fukada, H. (1986). Psychological processes mediating the persuasion inhibiting effects of forewarning in fear arousing communications. *Psychological Reports, 58,* 87-90.

Goffman, E. (1967). *Interaction ritual.* Garden City, NY: Anchor.

Goffman, E. (1974). *Frame analysis.* New York: Harper & Row.

Hackett, R. A. (1984). Decline of a paradigm: Bias and selectivity in news media studies. *Critical Studies in Mass Communication, 1,* 1-14.

Hacking, I. (1991). The making and molding of child abuse. *Critical Inquiry, 17,* 275-288.

Haley, J. (1963). *Strategies of psychotherapy.* New York: Grune & Stratton.

Haley, J. (1976). *Problem-solving therapy.* San Francisco: Jossey-Bass.

Iyengar, S. (1991). *Is anyone responsible? How television frames political issues.* Chicago: University of Chicago Press.

Jackall, R. (1995). The magic lantern: The world of public relations. In R. Jackall (Ed.), *Propaganda* (pp. 351-399). New York: New York University Press.

Joffe, J. (1997, June 8). America the inescapable [Special issue: How the world sees us]. *New York Times Magazine, 38,* 41-42.

Johannesen, R. L. (1996). *Ethics in human communication* (4th ed.). Prospect Heights, IL: Waveland.

Lakoff, G. (1997). *Moral politics: What conservatives know that liberals don't.* Chicago: University of Chicago Press.

Lakoff, R. (1990). *Talking power: The politics of language in our lives.* New York: Basic Books.

Latour, B. (1987). *Science in action.* Cambridge, MA: Harvard University Press.

Leiss, W., Kline, S., & Jhally, S. (1986). *Social communication in advertising: Persons, products, and images of well-being.* New York: Methuen.

Lipid Research Clinics Program. (1984). The Lipid Research Clinics coronary trial results. *Journal of the American Medical Association, 251,* 351-364.

Mayhew, L. H. (1997). *The new public: Professional communication and the means of social influence.* New York: Cambridge University Press.

Miller, G., & Holstein, J. A. (Eds.). (1993). *Constructionist controversies: Issues in social problems theory.* New York: Aldine de Gruyter.

Papageorgis, D. (1968). Warning and persuasion. *Psychological Bulletin, 70,* 271-282.

Parry, R. (1992). *Fooling America: How Washington insiders twist the truth and manufacture the conventional wisdom.* New York: William Morrow.

Petty, R. E., & Cacioppo, J. T. (1977). Forewarning, cognitive responding, and resistance to persuasion. *Journal of Personality and Social Psychology, 35,* 645-655.

Petty, R. E., & Cacioppo, J. T. (1996). *Attitudes and persuasion: Classic and contemporary approaches.* Boulder, CO: Westview. (Original work published 1981)

Porter, T. M. (1994). Objectivity as standardization: The rhetoric of impersonality in measurement, statistics, and cost-benefit analysis. In A. Megill (Ed.), *Rethinking objectivity.* Durham, NC: Duke University Press.

Schudson, M. (1986). *Advertising: The uneasy persuasion.* New York: Basic Books.

Sella, M. (2000, September 24). The stiff guy vs. the dumb guy. *New York Times Magazine,* 72-80, 102.

Shogren, E. (1998, January 6). Candid Clinton photos hit, hailed. *Los Angeles Times,* p. A10.

Simons, H. W. (1993). The rhetoric of the scientific research report: "Drug-pushing" in a medical journal article. In R. H. Roberts & J. M. M. Good (Eds.), *The recovery of rhetoric: Persuasive discourse and disciplinarity in the human sciences* (pp. 148-163). Charlottesville: University Press of Virginia.

Stille, A. (1998, June 11). The betrayal of history. *New York Review of Books, 45,* 15-16.

Watzlawick, P., Beavin, J. H., & Jackson, D. D. (1967). *Pragmatics of human communication.* New York: Norton.

Wegner, D. M., Wenzalaff, R., Kerker, R. M., & Beattie, A. E. (1981). Can media questions become public answers? *Journal of Personality and Social Psychology, 40,* 822-832.

PART 2

THE COACTIVE
APPROACH

CHAPTER 4

Coactive Persuasion

Using Receiver-Oriented Approaches

Being Situation Sensitive

Combining Similarity and Credibility

Building on Acceptable Premises

Appearing Reasonable and Providing Psychological Income

Using Communication Resources

Summary

Questions and Projects for Further Study

References

When the U.S. Congress refused to provide funding for an expensive but highly promising vehicle for research in physics known as the supercollider, their refusal was termed "the revenge of the 'C' students." Yet, says communication scholar John Angus Campbell (1996), one might ask who really deserved the middling grade. "Were the 'C' students the legislators who failed to grasp the national interest in physics, or were they the physicists who failed to adapt their arguments to a popular forum?" (p. 212).

Persuasion is a process of bridging differences—reducing psychological distances—to secure preferred outcomes. The physicists' job was to close the gap between their belief in the merits of building a supercollider and what Congress saw as the public interest. Even attempts to reinforce existing beliefs may involve perceived differences of a sort. For example, a political campaign manager, perceiving a gap between the current level of activity by campaign volunteers and the amount needed to win at the polls, may attempt to reinforce their commitments to the cause. How persuaders can best bridge the psychological divide is the subject of this chapter and the focus of Part 2 of the book. It has direct implications for persuadees as well. The principles and techniques of coactive persuasion introduced here are also employed by persuasion professionals via the mass media—where ordinary citizens are far more likely to function as persuadees.

Coactive persuasion is an umbrella term for the ways that persuaders might *move toward* persuadees psychologically so that they will be moved, in turn, to accept the persuaders' position or proposal for action. This book's conception of it derives primarily from Aristotle's *Rhetoric* (Cooper, 1932), from Kenneth Burke's *A Rhetoric of Motives* (1950/1969b), from social-psychological theory and research (e.g., Allen & Preiss, 1998; Shavitt & Brock, 1994), and from reports by practitioners in fields as diverse as politics and psychotherapy.

Just what form coactive persuasion takes depends on the situation, for example, whether it uses the mass media or involves interpersonal communication: if interpersonal, on whether persons A and B are locked in a conflict of interests or merely have a difference of opinion; if the mass media, whether the object of their talk is to convince each other or to persuade some third party such as the voters in a political contest. In a staged confrontation, as when two presidential candidates are facing each other in a television debate, coactive persuasion may be highly combative toward the adversary even as it appeals coactively to the target audience. Thus, although coactive persuasion is essentially "friendly" persuasion, it is not without its weaponry.

Taken together, the components of the coactive approach (listed in Box 4.1) constitute a logic of "rhetorical proof," as opposed to the logics expected from scientists or mathematicians. Above all, it is a logic of adaptation, finding in audiences and situations the grounds on which appeals are presented and arguments addressed.

Using Receiver-Oriented Approaches

Coactive persuasion recognizes that receivers of messages are by no means cut from the same cloth. As an extension of this principle, it underscores the need to provide "different strokes for different folks." For example, the department of communication at a large university sought to have its course in public speaking made mandatory for all undergraduates. To the college of business, it appealed for the practical benefits. To colleagues in education, it characterized public speaking as especially relevant for teachers and their students. The department recognized, however, that these appeals would cut little ice in its own college of liberal arts, which prided itself

> **BOX 4.1** Components of Coactive Persuasion
>
> ▷ Is receiver oriented, taking place largely, although not entirely, on the message recipients' terms
> ▷ Is situation sensitive, recognizing that receivers (e.g., audiences, persuadees) respond differently to persuasive messages in different situations
> ▷ Combines images of similarity between persuader and persuadee while promoting images of the persuader's unique expertise and trustworthiness
> ▷ Addresses controversial matters by appeals to premises the audience can accept
> ▷ Moves audiences from premises to desired actions or conclusions by both appearing reasonable and providing psychological income
> ▷ Makes full use of the resources of human communication

on maintaining traditional academic values in the face of pressures for practicality and relevance. Accordingly, the chairman of the department circulated to his colleagues in liberal arts a long and scholarly memo on the humanistic rhetorical tradition that characterized public speaking training as a venerable practice that began with the preparation of citizen-orators in ancient Greece and Rome. They were duly impressed.

This important principle can be illustrated with another example, this one from psychotherapy. One of the hardest things for patients to do, report Watzlawick, Weakland, and Fisch (1974), is to display to the therapist the symptoms they are so eager to control. Here is how Watzlawick et al. use the principle of "different strokes for different folks" in working to overcome their patients' resistance:

> To the engineer or computer man we may explain the reason for this behavior prescription in terms of a change from negative to positive feedback mechanisms. To a client associating his problem with low self-esteem, we may concede that he is evidently in need of self-punishment and that this is an excellent way of fulfilling this need. To somebody involved in Eastern thought we may recall the seeming absurdity of Zen koans. With the patient who comes and signals, "Here I am—now you take care of me," we shall probably take an authoritarian stand and give him no explanation whatsoever ("Doctor's orders!"). With somebody who seems a poor prospect for any form of cooperation, we shall have to preface the prescription itself with the remark that there exists a simple but somewhat odd way out of his problem, but that we are almost certain that he's not the kind of person who can utilize this solution. (p. 126)

Coactive persuasion, then, is *receiver oriented* rather than *source oriented*. This distinction may become clearer by contrasting these receiver-oriented examples with one that is source oriented. When computers were first coming on the market, the sales manager of the computer division of a large electronics firm lamented,

> I can't understand why my company isn't selling computers as effectively as IBM. We have the best computers in the world. What's more, I've written out a sales spiel for my people that's dynamite. All they have to do is memorize it and say it smoothly. Our products should do the rest.

When the sales manager was asked how IBM achieved its success, he explained,

> Oh well, you see they use a different type of salesperson than we do. Our sales staff are all former engineers; what we care about is our products, and our people know them inside and out. IBM hires these "personality types" who sit down with the customers and get real chatty with them. The fact is, they spend more time listening to the customers yak about their problems than on selling their products. It's a waste of time to me, but I have to admit that it works.

What the sales manager failed to realize, of course, is that by "wasting time" listening to the customers' problems, IBM's salespeople were accomplishing a great deal. Besides showing interest in the customer as a human being—a factor of no small consequence in itself—they were learning firsthand how to tailor their messages to achieve their intended effects. IBM's approach might be characterized as receiver oriented. The approach contrasts quite favorably with the source-oriented approach of IBM's competitor. The differences in the two approaches are summarized in Table 4.1.

Being Situation Sensitive

Situations vary. What persuades in the boardroom may fail miserably in the bedroom. What works at an outdoor rally before a partisan crowd will surely seem out of place in a televised interview. The clowning that might be appropriate at a fraternity party would be highly inappropriate at a funeral.

Earlier, this chapter distinguished between differences of opinion and conflicts of interest. It is one thing for strangers on a train to disagree about whether abortion is murder; it is quite another for a husband and his pregnant wife to have the same disagreement. Not much is at stake in the first instance, whereas in the second example, the controversy might well end up in a divorce court.

Another situational variable is time. Compare the difference, for example, between a 50-minute college lecture and a 30-second television sound bite. Professors

TABLE 4.1 Comparison Between Source-Oriented and Receiver-Oriented Approaches

Source-Oriented Approach	Receiver-Oriented Approach
Assumes that all receivers are alike	Assumes that all receivers are unique, or, at the least, that some differences make a difference
Decides for receivers what they need, want, know, value, etc.	Learns from receivers if possible what they need, want, know, value, etc.
Selects specific persuasive goals for any one occasion on the basis of persuader's own timetable	Selects specific persuasive goals for any occasion on the basis of the receivers' readiness to be persuaded
Communicates at receivers by means of a "canned" presentation	Communicates with receivers by adapting the message on the basis of a mutual interchange if at all possible
Promotes solutions on the basis of their supposed intrinsic merits	Promotes solutions on the basis of their capacity to resolve or reduce the receivers' special problems

like me who are in the habit of delivering long-winded lectures often discover the pitfalls of condensing what we have to say for television news. Time to think likewise makes an enormous difference in the quality of the receiver's message-processing ability (Petty & Cacioppo, 1981/1996). Faced with message overload and pressing deadlines for decision making, even the most discriminating message recipient is likely to rely on cognitive shorthands.

A major factor to consider in analyzing situations is audience expectations. Situations often impel and constrain communicators in predictable ways, thus giving rise to such rhetorical genres as the eulogy and the commencement address.

Coactive persuaders need to learn what is expected and perhaps even required of them in situations of a given type. Then, having drawn on guidelines for dealing with that type of situation, they must develop a sense of what makes the situation they confront unique. Some situations are easy to deal with, for example, bestowing praise at a retirement dinner for an executive who served the company well. Other situations challenge the rhetorical skills of even the most talented improvisers.

Consider once again, President Clinton's rhetorical situation when he admitted to the American people in his political apologia of August 17, 1998, that he had, since January of that year, misled them about the Lewinsky affair (Simons, 2000). *In theory*, political apologists have numerous options at their disposal:

1. Deny if you can, that is, if the case against you is unproved and is unlikely to be proved.

2. Differentiate if you can between acts committed on your watch and acts for which you are personally to blame. Do so if your personal culpability is unproved and is unlikely to be proved. Combine denials of personal blame with corrective action or pledges of corrective action.

3. Brag if you have bragging rights, that is, if you can point to notable achievements in the past and the potential for more in the future.

4. Attack your attackers, particularly if the case against you is weak and/or the credibility of your attackers is suspect.

5. Minimize, if you can, the significance of the wrongdoing, but do so only if its significance is open to question.

6. Minimize, if you can, the relevance of the wrongdoing to your public position, but do so only if its relevance is open to question.

7. Admit only what you have to admit, that is, wrongdoing, personal culpability, significance, or relevance.

8. Justify, if you can, questionable means for the worthy ends they accomplished or were designed to accomplish. Do so only if the argument is likely to appear credible.

9. Differentiate, if you can, between the impulsive you or momentarily distracted you or otherwise forgivable you who committed the wrongdoing and the normally trustworthy, competent "real" you. Do so only if the excuses you offer are credible and if they won't unduly tarnish your reputation and ability to do your job.

10. Express contrition in proportion to the perceived significance and relevance of your personal wrongdoing, and combine expressions of remorse with corrective action or pledges of corrective action.

11. Appeal, if you can, for closure/termination of the case in the interests of getting on with more important affairs of state. Do so only if the argument is likely to appear credible.

The foregoing seems straightforward enough, but plots have a way of thickening and rhetorical problems, of deepening. Bill Clinton hoped or assumed that his affair with Monica Lewinsky would remain unproved. Then, subsequent to his denials, came incontrovertible evidence, such as DNA traces linking Bill to Monica on Monica's dress.

What should Clinton have said when the cover-up he staged and attempted to keep hidden was exposed to public view? Did the exposure effectively undermine his earlier claims that the alleged wrongdoing was strictly a private matter, and thus irrelevant, to the conduct of his office? If so, should he have held fast to his insistence on a right of privacy or shifted to another rhetorical tack? Moreover, Clinton's denials and attempted cover-up were linked by the media to previous patterns of evasion and were thus seen by some as indelibly ingrained in his character. Should he then have pleaded for mercy?

But Clinton's apparent defects of character—including, perhaps, an addiction to illicit sex and to risk more generally—are not readily forgiven in American society. If offered as excuses, might they have further tarnished his reputation and ability to govern? What then? What if the legal appeals and objections devised by his attorneys to spare him from further embarrassment were repeatedly turned down by the courts? This happened.

What could Clinton possibly have said when, having finally admitted to some degree of wrongdoing after prolonged denials and delays, his expressions of contrition in leaked grand jury testimony were not believed? Should Clinton have exploited the vulnerability of his attackers to attack, at the risk of undermining the apparent sincerity of his expressed remorse?

What if complete candor at the point of exposure could have placed him in severe legal jeopardy, while a legalistic defense risked alienating him from the citizenry? This question is not merely hypothetical; the dilemma was quite real. What happens if, in light of the circumstances, Clinton's pleas for closure, for getting on with the nation's business, are seen by many as transparently self-serving? What happens if those who are on his side or who are at least reluctant to remove him from office are themselves divided as to what sort of apologia would satisfy them? What should be done then?

From such hypothetical problems—quite real in Clinton's case—dilemmas are created, and it becomes the persuader's central task to grapple with them successfully. Chapter 10 will present a critical assessment of Clinton's handling of this difficult rhetorical situation in his apologia of August 17, 1998.

Combining Similarity and Credibility

The coactive persuader moves toward the audience psychologically by establishing relational bonds. Verbally but also nonverbally, the coactive persuader expresses caring and concern for the audience as people, respect for their feelings and ideas, and perhaps affection as well. Coactive lecturers, for example, may deliberately breach the rules for a platform speech by stepping out from behind the podium to address the audience directly, perhaps interrupting the formal presentation to address members of the audience in conversation. Even in a formal presentation, the coactive persuader will give the impression of communicating *with* the audience rather than communicating *at* them.

Especially important to audiences are evidences of membership group similarities. The persuader may move toward the persuadees psychologically by emphasizing similarities in background, experience, and group affiliation and also by displaying evidences of commonality through dialect, dress, and mannerisms.

These signs of commonality not only enhance the persuader's attractiveness to the audience but also serve indirectly to express shared beliefs, values, and attitudes. It is little wonder, therefore, that advertisers often feature testimonials by "plain folks." In 30-second spots, the advocate of a brand-name detergent is often the neighbor next door. In longer infomercials, the advertiser may feature a variety of role models, each representative of a different demographic group or culture type. Former governor of Louisiana Huey Long is supposed to have launched his fabulous political career during the Depression of the 1930s by use of the plain folks device. In the film *All the King's Men* (1950/1986), Huey Long (given the name Willie Stark in the movie) stands before a group of downtrodden farmers at a local carnival and says,

> You're all a bunch of hicks! That's right.
> Hicks! You're hicks and I'm a hick
> and us hicks are gonna run the state legislature.

Evidences of interpersonal similarity are clearly essential, but so, too, is it important on most occasions for persuaders to appear *different* in ways that make them appear more expert, better informed, and more reliable than most members of their audience. The general point is that although interpersonal similarity almost always results in *attraction* toward the persuader as a person, it doesn't always yield *credibility.* Attraction is generally important on issues of value and taste; dissimilar but more expert sources tend to be more effective on questions of belief (McGuire, 1985). If, for example, you were looking around for a new brand of coffee, chances are that you would be more influenced by the judgments of friends than by experts. But you would ordinarily trust experts on medical matters, or on the question of where to invest your money. The "ideal" communicator is often one who seems both similar enough and different enough to appear overall as a *superrepresentative* of the audience. This is equally true of ordinary friends and acquaintances whom we count as *opinion leaders* as it is of celebrity figures such as leading politicians (see Picture 4.1). An interesting exercise is to think about the persons whose opinions you value most. How are they similar to you? How are they different?

Picture 4.1. Superman in a Wheelchair: Christopher Reeve (who played Superman in film) at the 1996 Democratic National Convention lends his celebrity status to the party's cause while making a pitch for the disabled.

The major determinants of source credibility are perceived expertise and trustworthiness. This includes such qualities as perceived intelligence, honesty and dependability, and maturity and good judgment. Other important credibility factors are power and dynamism. Power is the extent to which the speaker is perceived by the audience as willing and able to use rewards and punishments. Dynamism includes verve, passion, enthusiasm, and the like.

Hart (1997) argues that persuasion is always, to some extent, credibility driven. "Persuasion," he says, "comes to us embodied. Most people cannot separate the substance of a message from its author. This is especially true in spoken persuasion where the speaker's attitudes, voice, and personal appearance interact constantly with what the speaker says" (p. 84).

Building on Acceptable Premises

The distinctive character of coactive persuasion is nowhere more manifest than in conflict situations or where there are sharp differences of opinion between people.

Picture a persuader, A, and a persuadee, B, who differ about issue X. In the face of their disagreement, a number of options are available for settling their differences. One approach is that of the *objectivist*. Operating from what he or she perceives as greater knowledge or wisdom on the matter, A may elect to tell B what is best for him or her. Parents, and sometimes teachers as well, do that—not always with great success. Or A may attempt to "demonstrate" the cold logic why his or her way of thinking is the only way. This is the "sage on the stage" method. For the thoroughgoing objectivist, hard fact and cold logic are, and ought to be, the sole arbiters of disputes, and everyone ought to reason as the objectivist does. A second way is that of the *privatist,* who merely asserts his or her feelings on the matter at hand, offering no reasons, no appeals, and no support for the views of any type. If B remains unconvinced of the merits of A's views, that's okay. If B shifts position, so much the better, but A does nothing to bring that shift about. Privatism stems from a deep-seated antipathy toward persuasion. To the privatist, all persuasion is immoral manipulation.

Should B remain unmoved by declarations of truth, cold logic, or personal feelings, A may be tempted to move against B combatively by vilifying, ridiculing, or threatening B. These *combative* modes of influence often prompt message recipients to become increasingly antagonistic or perhaps to withdraw from further discussion.

The coactive persuader tends to prefer the carrot (inducements) to the stick (coercion) in conflict situations but prefers, where possible, to rely exclusively on talk to ameliorate or resolve differences. It is not, however, talk of a merely uncalculated, expressive nature. Coactive persuaders reason with their audiences. They offer arguments in support of their more controversial claims and evidence in support of their arguments. In these respects, the methods of the coactive persuader are not unlike those of the objectivist. The coactive persuader, however, is less concerned with showing that he or she is right—with winning arguments—than with *winning belief.* This requires arguments that begin from general premises that the audience can accept.

Reasoning is discussed in more detail in Chapter 8. A *premise* is a hook on which to hang an argument. Depending on the context of the discussion, it may be a definition, a value assumption, or a general observation. Get people to grant the premise, and they are halfway to granting the conclusion as well. Sometimes, it may be enough to appeal to an accepted or acceptable premise. For example, an organization specializing in securing adoptions of difficult placements manages to get the cooperation of a pro-choice advocate and a pro-life advocate who had once been friends but who had long since stopped speaking to one another. It accomplishes this seemingly remarkable feat by identifying a premise common to both: Neither views abortion as the preferred option for poor, unmarried pregnant women, if indeed there can be a viable alternative to bringing up children the women don't want and can't afford. Both the pro-choice and pro-life activists agree that increasing the opportunities for adoption is consistent with their otherwise opposed philosophies.

In other situations, it may be necessary to make the case for the reasonableness of a premise. Thus, for example, you may oppose awarding formal recognition to the new Slobovian regime on the grounds that it is ruthlessly tyrannical. But someone may be able to convince you that our government and most other governments typically extend formal recognition to regimes that violate the rights of their citizens. Once you grant the premise that recognition does not necessarily mean moral approval, the persuader is then in a much better position to convince you that our government should recognize the Slobovian regime:

> (Major premise) To recognize a government isn't necessarily to signal approval of it but rather to acknowledge that it exercises control over its people.

> (Minor premise) The new Slobovian regime surely is in control of its people.

> (Conclusion) Therefore, the United States should recognize the new Slobovian regime.

In building from acceptable premises, persuaders generally start from premises that they themselves accept, and they make a point of emphasizing their points of agreement. In addition to providing hooks on which to hang arguments, these *common ground* appeals make the persuader appear more trustworthy and more attractive. Typically, the coactive persuader moves from agreement to disagreement on highly sensitive controversial issues, or at least delays direct confrontation until agreed-on issues have been identified. Two variants of this bridge-building process are the *yes-yes* technique and the *yes-but* technique. In both cases, little or no hint of any disagreement with the audience is expressed until after a whole string of assertions is communicated about which agreement is sure. The object is to establish a habit of assent, to get receivers nodding "Yes," "That's right," and "You said it" either aloud or to themselves. Once this is done, the audience will presumably be receptive to more controversial assertions.

Using the yes-yes approach, the persuader lays the groundwork for the case by identifying a number of acceptable principles or criteria by which the case will later be supported. Thus, the vacuum cleaner sales rep might say,

If you're like most of the people I meet, you also want a vacuum cleaner that really cleans, one that picks up the ashes and the threads and the crumbs that hide in the corners. I'd guess too that in these tough times you don't feel like getting stuck with big bills. . . . Well, okay, I know just what you mean. . . . Here's our new kind of vacuum cleaner, and it fits your specifications exactly.

Using the yes-but approach, persuaders begin by noting those arguments of the message recipient with which they can agree, and then, having shown how fair-minded they are, they offer a series of "buts" that constitute the heart of their case. Here are the beginnings of an argument on the perennial question of how much a government should tell its citizens about its more sensitive operations:

Look, I'm not one of these people who'll tell you that our government has got to tell all, that it's got to conduct diplomacy in a fish bowl, that it's got to give away secrets that are vital to national security, that it's got to make its wildest contingency plans public. These are valid reasons for keeping things under covers, *but* . . .

Although coactive persuasion generally builds on areas of agreement between persuader and persuadee, it need not do so to be successful. What counts from a purely practical standpoint is that the persuadee find the arguments attractive, not that the persuader be enamored of them. Suppose that Rachel is an agnostic, and her friend Rashid is fervently religious. Although it might enhance Rachel's credibility if she were able to share Rashid's religious convictions, Rachel need not be a believer herself to convince Rashid of the disadvantages to believers of mandating prayer in schools. Rachel can make the case from the believer's perspective, pointing out, for example, the many occasions in history when religious groups have benefited from separation of church and state.

Similarly, a college professor may not care whether students get As or Cs in her courses; she may even decry their obsession with grades and be concerned only with whether they learn what she has to teach them. But knowing that grades are a major concern of most students, the professor may nevertheless appeal to their desire for good grades as a way of inducing them to keep up with the readings in the course. In these, as in other examples, coactive persuaders may move toward the message recipient to the point of offering reasons for belief or action that are not their own and that they even find personally distasteful but that they expect the receiver will find compelling.

The approaches of the college professor, and of Rachel in the previous example, are known as *reasoning from the perspective of the other*. How ethical is the approach? Is it dishonest to advance reasons for belief or action that one does not personally find appealing? Reason giving of this sort is surely one reason that mere mention of the word persuasion often elicits negative feelings. The persuader may take a coldly calculating approach to the task, much like the ancient Roman poet Ovid in his playful advice to would-be Casanovas:

> On deceiving in the name of friendship; feigning just enough drunkenness to be winsome; on astute use of praise and promises; inducement value of belief in the gods; deceiving deceivers; the utility of tears; the need to guard against the risk that entreaties may merely feed the woman's vanity; inducement value of pallor, which is the proper color of love; advisability of shift in methods, as she who resisted the well-bred may yield to the crude, ways to subdue by yielding; the controlled use of compliments; become a habit with her; enjoy others too, but in stealth, and deny if you are found out; give each of her faults the name of the good quality most like it. (quoted in Burke, 1950/1969b, p. 160)

Appearing Reasonable and Providing Psychological Income

American culture tends to separate fact from value, reason from emotion, and to decide that only questions of fact and logic can be addressed rationally. Correspondingly, there is a tendency to denigrate all appeals to emotion and all expressions of emotion as in some sense irrational. This may be one reason that persons who are scientifically minded often object to the use of dramatic narratives; they tug at the heartstrings, sometimes eliciting emotional responses in place of coolheaded analysis. Although persuaders ought not to allow emotion to stand in place of reason or to overwhelm reason, they are entitled to provide their audiences with a feeling for problems and not just a dry accounting of them.

As suggested in Chapter 2, audiences also need incentives to act. In Rank's (1982) colloquial terms, they need to be convinced that proposals for action will help them either "get a good" (acquisition), "keep a good" (protection), "get rid of a bad" (relief), or "avoid a bad" (prevention) (Rank, 1982, p. 1). In providing incentives, persuaders might well tap into audience emotions. For example, a public service announcement warning viewers not to drink and drive is likely to play on the emotion of fear. But surely there is nothing irrational about fearing the consequences of drinking and driving.

In the 1950s and 1960s, the field of psychology spawned what is now regarded as "classical" theories of persuasion (Petty & Cacioppo, 1981/1996). These provided the springboard for much of the theorizing reviewed in Chapter 2 on how to appeal to audience needs and desires while at the same time not appearing unreasonable. From those theories emerge some guidelines for the coactive persuader.

> Attempt where possible to link your position or proposal with beliefs and values already held by the audience. Remind your audience of beliefs and values consistent with your position; challenge undesired beliefs and schemas with new information. Likewise, attempt to elevate the importance of congruent values while challenging or minimizing the importance of undesired values.

> In urging action on your proposal, convince your audience not just that the proposal is a good one but also that it has the support of people they most admire. But if the audience's subjective norms are likely to work against adoption of your proposal, urge self-reliance, rather than dependence on what others think.

> Facilitate information processing by simplifying the message for those who would otherwise have difficulty understanding it. At the same time, anticipate and respond to possible objections from those who are more informed, more confident, better educated, or more intelligent. Similarly, encourage issue involvement and provide strong arguments for persons whose opinions will matter in the long run, and help them resist counterarguments. Help those unable or unwilling to engage in central processing to find the cognitive shorthands necessary to make short-term commitments.

> Exploit the potential benefits of interactive situations by positively reinforcing desired responses to your questions while withholding reinforcements for undesired responses.

> Exploit the tendency of persuadees to form conscious as well as unconscious associations to people and ideas. Dress and act such that audiences will form favorable inferences about your competence, trustworthiness, and attractiveness. Likewise, dress up your ideas in a language that audiences will find attractive.

> With persuadees opposed to your position, encourage role-playing of the desired behavior but under conditions of minimal justification for performance of the act. Similarly, encourage those sympathetic to your views to act on them, even in modest ways, because this will provide reinforcement.

Using Communication Resources

Coactive persuasion at its best makes artful use of the various ways in which messages may be framed (see Chapter 6) and delivered (see Chapter 5). The persuader's message includes not just what is said but how it is said, both verbally and nonverbally. Every utterance is the end product of a set of conscious or unconscious decisions, from among a huge array of possible choices, that constitute what Burke (1945/1969a) has called the *"resources of ambiguity"* in language (p. xix). Burke's phrase is a way of suggesting that there are multiple ways to label something; categorize it; define it; illustrate it; or compare, contrast, or contextualize it. For example, at the annual company holiday party, a coworker whispers to you in anger that the boss "has been hitting on half the people in the office." Want to *intensify* your coworker's rage? Agree that yes, the boss is a pig or a roach or a worm or simply an animal. Want to *downplay* the matter? Assure your coworker that your boss is just an old goat.

Language choices may involve far more than mere labeling. Responding to another animal label—the charge that he and some of his colleagues in the House of Representatives had been behaving like "ostriches" in refusing to see the wisdom of President Ronald Reagan's policy toward Nicaragua—Representative Barney Frank responded with an ancient rhetorical technique known as *peritrope* (a table-turning). According to Representative Frank, the member of Congress who had heaped insult on the ostrich, not to mention on his colleagues, was sadly deficient in his ornithological knowledge. The ostrich, Frank said, was a great survivor, capable when riled of delivering a lethal kick. With its large eyes and keen vision the ostrich was ever alert. And, contrary to myth, the ostrich does not stick its head in the sand. "So there you have it," concluded Frank. "The ostrich is a rugged, wily, and frugal bird. Indeed, in a scrap between an ostrich and a Member of Congress, I would bet on the ostrich" (Jamieson, 1998, p. 18).

Communication is not confined to words alone. The surroundings in which the message is delivered make a difference, and persuaders are sometimes able to select and arrange them. In keeping with the notion of moving toward the persuadee psychologically, the coactive persuader tends to prefer close physical settings over more distant ones. Better to lecture in a room with too few chairs than too many. Better to air disagreements over a drink or a meal than in an atmosphere that announces itself as "strictly business." Better to be seated next to the other than in a position directly opposite the other.

The persuader's choice of *medium* can make a difference as well. A medium is a carrier of messages, a means through which messages may be expressed. Broadly speaking, the medium may be oral or written, verbal or nonverbal, direct or indirect, but within these general categories, communicators may select from among a wide variety of message forms. An advertiser may choose among newspapers, magazines, word of mouth, and television. An executive may elect to convey the same message by telephone, memo, e-mail, bulletin board, platform speech, conference, loudspeaker, informal conversation, or company newspaper. The modern protester may be credited with having invented any number of message forms: be-ins, sit-ins, lie-ins, swim-ins, rock festivals, festivals of life, performance art, and guerilla theater.

Strictly speaking, a medium is nothing but a message carrier. The various media differ, however, not just in their technical capabilities but also in the feelings generated toward them. For example, face-to-face communication is generally perceived as warmer and more personal than indirect forms of communication. As anyone knows who tries summarizing the experience of an engaging film to a friend, a medium is also a source of information in its own right. Each medium has its own range of expressive potential. Each has a *grammar* based on the medium's unique production capacities. Grammar variables in photography, for example, include camera angle, selection of focus, depth of focus, shot framing from close-up to long-shot, and focal length of the lens. Television and film add to photography such variables as dissolves, fades, cutting speed, zooms, tilts, pans, and changes in focus, as well as objective or subjective perspective (Meyrowitz, 1991). It makes a difference, for example, whether we see the action of a film from an outsider's perspective or from the subjective perspective of one of the actors. In these respects, the visual can get us to take sides in a controversy every bit as powerfully as a well-crafted verbal argument.

Summary

Coactive persuasion is a method of bridging differences, of moving toward persuadees psychologically in the hope that they will be moved in turn to accept the persuader's position or proposal. It consists, essentially, of six components:

1. Being receiver oriented rather than source oriented—communicating on the message recipient's terms

2. Being situationally sensitive

3. Combining expressions of interpersonal similarity with manifestations of expertise, knowledge of subject, trustworthiness, and the like—responding to the persuadee's desire to be addressed by a credible, not just a likable, source

4. Building from shared premises but also, if necessary, reasoning from the perspective of the other

5. Moving audiences to the desired conclusion or action by both appearing reasonable and providing psychological income

6. Using fully the resources of human communication

Coactive persuasion functions somewhat differently in conflict and nonconflict situations. More will be said about persuasion in conflict situations in Part 3, where it will be suggested that the object is not always to persuade the antagonist. Sometimes, the coactive persuader behaves competitively or even combatively with his or her antagonist to win support from third parties. This is typically the case in political campaigns and in struggles in behalf of a cause by social movements.

Questions and Projects for Further Study

1. Illustrate how the idea of *bridging differences* can be brought to bear on receivers who already agree with you.
2. Is it possible to "move toward" someone psychologically if your initial positions on a controversial issue are miles apart?
3. How might the principle of "different strokes for different folks" be applied to a situation in your own life?
4. Illustrate the differences between winning an argument and winning belief.
5. Have you ever had to defend yourself against charges of wrongdoing? Describe the situation, including the problems of persuasion you confronted. How did you handle the situation?
6. Think about recent candidates for high office. Which one of them best combined similarity and credibility? Which one was least successful at this?
7. What did Hart mean when he said that persuasion is always to some extent credibility driven?
8. Illustrate the differences between the yes-yes approach and the yes-but approach with examples of your own choosing.
9. Illustrate reasoning from the perspective of the other with examples of your own.
10. Vast sums have been spent recently in efforts to convince teenagers not to smoke but with little success. Rather than reminding teenagers of smoking's harmful effects, a Florida-based organization sought to arouse their anger at the tobacco companies for having covered up tobacco's harmful effects. How do you think the arousal of anger would work in getting teenagers not to smoke, compared with the use of fear appeals?
11. When is it appropriate to use emotional appeals? When is it not?
12. Try applying the principles derived from classical theories of persuasion to an example of your own choosing, perhaps something as familiar as a disagreement among friends or at work. Use the exercise to refresh your memory of the theories, including such technical terms as schema and central processing.
13. As a way of appreciating further what coactive persuasion entails, try composing two versions of a letter to someone with whom you disagree on a matter of concern to both of you.

Version 1 should exhibit the style of the objectivist. In this form of the letter, you should state your position, provide the best reasons you can find to support that position, and undermine your opponent's arguments. Prove that you are "right."

Version 2 should exhibit a coactive style. Rather than lecturing at your reader, reason with him or her. Try organizing your letter as follows:

a. State the issue under consideration.
b. State the reader's position as clearly and as fairly as you can. Show that you understand the opposing position.
c. Indicate areas of agreement, including contexts in which the reader could be "right."
d. Identify areas of doubt or disagreement, while at the same time affirming your respect for the other. Don't at any point antagonize the other.
e. Suggest consideration of your ideas. Promote them with premises the reader is likely to find attractive. Perhaps point out ways in which your respective ideas are complementary, each supplying what the other lacks.

References

All the king's men [Video] (R. Rossen, Director and Writer). (1986). New York: RCA/ Columbia Pictures Home Video. (Original film 1950, Columbia Pictures Corporation, based on the novel by R. P. Warren)

Allen, M., & Preiss, R. W. (1998). *Persuasion: Advances through meta-analysis.* Cresskill, NJ: Hampton.

Burke, K. (1969a). *Grammar of motives.* Berkeley: University of California Press. (Original work published 1945)

Burke, K. (1969b). *A rhetoric of motives.* Berkeley: University of California Press. (Original work published 1950)

Campbell, J. A. (1996). Oratory, democracy, and the classroom. In R. Soder (Ed.), *Democracy, education, and the school* (pp. 211-243). San Francisco: Jossey-Bass.

Cooper, L. (1932). *The rhetoric of Aristotle: An expanded translation with supplementary examples.* New York: D. Appleton Century.

Hart, R. (1997). *Modern rhetorical criticism* (2nd ed.). Boston: Allyn & Bacon.

Jamieson, K. H. (1998, June 22). *Civility in the House of Representatives: The 105th Congress* (Report #24). Available: www.appcpenn.org

McGuire, W. J. (1985). Attitudes and attitude change. In G. Lindzey & E. Aronson (Eds.), *Handbook of social psychology* (3rd ed., Vol. 2, pp. 233-346). New York: Random House.

Meyrowitz, J. (1991). The questionable reality of media. In J. Brockman (Ed.), *Ways of knowing: The reality club.* New York: Prentice Hall.

Petty, R. E., & Cacioppo, J. T. (1996). *Attitudes and persuasion: Classic and contemporary approaches.* Boulder, CO: Westview. (Original work published 1981)

Rank, H. (1982). *Questions you can ask about advertising.* Park Forest, IL: Counter-Propaganda Press.

Shavitt, S., & Brock, T. C. (1994). *Persuasion: Psychological insights and perspectives.* Boston: Allyn & Bacon.

Simons, H. W. (2000). A dilemma-centered analysis of William Clinton's August 17th apologia: Implications for theory and method. *Quarterly Journal of Speech, 86*, 438-453.

Watzlawick, P., Weakland, J., & Fisch, R. (1974). *Change: Principles of problem formation and problem resolution.* New York: Norton.

CHAPTER 5

Resources of Communication

Resources of Language

Nonverbal Resources

Visual and Audiovisual Resources

Resources of the New Media

Summary

Questions and Projects for Further Study

References

The last two decades of the first millennium A.D. were not particularly kind to the tobacco industry. With newscasts announcing new evidence of the dangers of secondhand smoke, pressures mounted to ban the smoking of tobacco in public places. The tobacco industry responded with a campaign of its own. Prohibited from advertising on radio and television, it turned to the print media. One such ad, by the R. J. Reynolds Tobacco Company (now RJR Nabisco), was apparently designed to defuse or neutralize the attitudes of nonsmokers hostile to the cigarette industry while providing emotional support to smokers for what was already becoming a socially undesirable habit (Picture 5.1).

Reynold's key language strategy was *typification*. Reynolds typified smokers and nonsmokers by, in effect, putting words in their mouths and excluding other, more damning, words. In playing down the negatives while playing up the positives, Reynolds was doing with language what persuaders since time immemorial have done. Suppose the nonsmokers had been represented as saying, "We're hopping mad. To us, the smoke from your cigarettes can be anything from a minor irritant to

A message from those who don't to those who do.

We're uncomfortable.

To us, the smoke from your cigarettes can be anything from a minor nuisance to a real annoyance.

We're frustrated.

Even though we've chosen not to smoke, we're exposed to second-hand smoke anyway.

We feel a little powerless.

Because you can invade our privacy without even trying. Often without noticing.

And sometimes when we speak up and let you know how we feel, you react as though *we* were the bad guys.

We're not fanatics. We're not out to deprive you of something you enjoy. We don't want to be your enemies.

We just wish you'd be more considerate and responsible about how, when, and where you smoke.

We know you've got rights and feelings. We just want you to respect our rights and feelings, as well.

A message from those who do to those who don't.

We're on the spot.

Smoking is something we consider to be a very personal choice, yet it's become a very public issue.

We're confused.

Smoking is something that gives us enjoyment, but it gives you offense.

We feel singled out.

We're doing something perfectly legal, yet we're often segregated, discriminated against, even legislated against.

Total strangers feel free to abuse us verbally in public without warning.

We're not criminals. We don't mean to bother or offend you. And we don't like confrontations with you.

We're just doing something we enjoy, and trying to understand your concerns.

We know you've got rights and feelings. We just want you to respect our rights and feelings, as well.

Brought to you in the interest of common courtesy by

R.J. Reynolds Tobacco Company

Picture 5.1. R. J. Reynolds Messages for Those Who Do and Those Who Don't a real threat. . . ." Suppose that their message had gone on to mention the health dangers they attributed to secondhand smoke, not just their exposure to it.

By the same token, why are the smokers "on the spot"? Why is smoking for them a "choice" (not to mention a "very personal choice"), rather than an addiction? Surely a comparable ad by the American Cancer Society would have put things in different ways.

As in this example, then, language offers *resources* that can be exploited by persuaders to suit their own ends (Burke, 1950/1969). This chapter identifies intensifying and downplaying stratagems as well as tactics persuaders can employ for purposes of compliance gaining. It also catalogs the persuaders' nonverbal resources and briefly surveys media resources, including the rhetorical potential of so-called new media. Chapter 6 is reserved for the powerful devices of framing and reframing. Chapter 7 focuses on influence mechanisms for peripheral processing by persuadees, Chapter 8 on types of argument and evidence used in central processing (Petty & Cacioppo, 1981/1996). All told, then, Part 2 of *Persuasion in Society* is designed to do for today's reader what Aristotle long ago characterized as rhetorical theory's most essential function: that of identifying the "available means of persuasion." But persuaders need always to keep in mind that these means of persuasion will fall short of their mark and may even backfire unless they are well adapted to ends, audiences, and situations.

Resources of Language

Anyone using language to communicate faces many choices. A word, a phrase, or an entire speech might accent some features of an object while deemphasizing others. Similarly, matters might be stated in ways that conceal or reveal, magnify or minimize, elevate or degrade, sharpen or blur, link or divide, simplify or complexify, or make good, bad, or indifferent.

Chapter 1 provided the example of the catalog description for COM 390R as evidence of how the *style* of a persuasive message can prompt suspicion, even incredulity. The absence of verbs and adjectives, the failure to define terms, and the seemingly bureaucratic character of the language created the impression that the authors of this description were not particularly interested in encouraging enrollments in the course.

Intensify/Downplay

As in the Reynolds ad, language is most often used to play up the positives and play down the negatives. One need look no further than the 2000 presidential campaign for examples of intensifying and downplaying. In contesting for the Republican Party nomination, George W. Bush played up his experience as governor of a large state; Senator John McCain played up his heroism in the Vietnam War. Bush played down rumors of drug use in his younger days; McCain played down his past involvement in a corruption scandal.

Correspondingly, persuaders play down their opponents' positives and play up their opponents' negatives. As former Senator Bill Bradley told it, Vice President Al Gore's many years of service in Washington had made Gore rather timid—reluctant to push ahead with bold initiatives. As Gore told it, Bill Bradley's ambitious health care plan was fiscally irresponsible. Intensifying and downplaying of this type by the Democratic and Republican nominees continued into the general election.

Flattery is another form of intensify/downplay, in this case used to extol the other's virtues. Recall Ovid's advice to the suitor: "Give each of her faults the name of the good quality most like it" (quoted in Burke, 1950/1969, p. 160).

Hugh Rank's Six Components of Intensify/Downplay

The National Council of Teachers of English has long been involved in efforts to help students analyze persuasive discourse. Hugh Rank (1976), a member of the council's Committee on Public Doublespeak, identified repetition, association, and composition as key components of intensifying and omission, diversion, and confusion as key components of downplaying (Figure 5.1). His analytic scheme is further illustrated below.

Tactics for Intensifying

Repetition. One way to intensify good or bad points about a person, a product, or an idea is to repeat them again and again. People are comfortable with what is familiar, which is one reason why all cultures have chants and rituals based on the principle of repetition. The most common example of repetition in persuasion is the use of slogans and jingles in advertising. Some advertisers keep the same slogans for years. For example, we are all familiar with "M&M's melt in your mouth, not in your hand." Notice the alliteration of the letter *m*. Another example is "Midas. The Right Muffler. The Right Price."

Association. Another tactic that persuaders favor is to intensify by linking a person, idea, or product to something already either loved/desired by or hated/feared by the intended audience. Advertisements often play on our most basic desires, such as security, love and belonging, esteem, relaxation, and self-improvement. Many of the words that persuaders associate themselves with are *glittering generalities:* words that

Questions about Advertising
You can ask

based on Hugh Rank's **Intensify/Downplay** pattern, a simple framework to analyze complex communications.

 INTENSIFY

☐ Expect people to **intensify their own "good"** by means of repetition, association, and composition.

Repetition

How often have you seen the ad? On TV? In print? Do you recognize the **brand name? trademark? logo? company? package?** What key words or images repeated within ad? Any repetition patterns *(alliteration, anaphora, rhyme)* used? Any **slogan?** Can you hum or sing the **musical theme** or **jingle?** How long has this ad been running? How old were you when you first heard it? (For information on frequency, duration, and costs of ad campaigns, see *Advertising Age.)*

Association

What **"good things"** - already loved or desired by the intended audience - are associated with the product? Any links with basic needs *(food, activity, sex, security)?* With an appeal to save or gain money? With desire for certitude or outside approval (from *religion, science,* or the *"best," "most,"* or *"average" people)?* With desire for a sense of space *(neighborhood, nation, nature)?* With desire for love and belonging *(intimacy, family, groups)?* With other human desires *(esteem, play, generosity, curiosity, creativity, completion)?* Are **"bad things"** - things already hated or feared - stressed, as in a **"scare-and-sell"** ad? Are *problems* presented, with products as *solutions?* Are the speakers (models, endorsers) **authority figures:** people you respect, admire? Or **friend figures:** people you'd like as friends, identify with, or would like to be?

Composition

Look for the basic strategy of "the pitch": Hi . . . TRUST ME . . . YOU NEED . . . HURRY . . . BUY. What are the **attention-getting (HI)** words, images, devices? What are the **confidence-building (TRUST ME)** techniques: words, images, smiles, endorsers, brand names? Is the main **desire-stimulation (YOU NEED)** appeal focused on our benefit-seeking *to get* or *to keep* a "good," or *to avoid* or *to get rid of* a "bad"? Are you the **"target audience"?** If not, who is? Are you part of an unintended audience"? When and where did the ads appear? Are **product claims** made for: superiority, quantity, beauty, efficiency, scarcity, novelty, stability, reliability, simplicity, utility, rapidity, or safety? Are any **"added values"** suggested or implied by using any of the association techniques (see above)? Is there any **urgency-stressing (HURRY)** by words, movement, pace? Or is a "soft sell" conditioning for *later* purchase? Are there specific **response-triggering** words **(BUY):** to buy, to do, to call? Or is it conditioning (image building or public relations) to make us *"feel good"* about the company, to get favorable public opinion on *its* side *(against government regulations, laws, taxes)?* **Persuaders seek some kind of response!**

 DOWNPLAY

☐ Expect people to **downplay their own "bad"** by means of omission, diversion, and confusion.

Omission

What "bad" aspects, disadvantages, drawbacks, hazards, have been **omitted** from the ad? Are there some unspoken assumptions? An unsaid story? Are some things implied or suggested, but not explicitly stated? Are there concealed problems concerning the **maker,** the **materials,** the **design,** the **use,** or the **purpose of the product? Are there any unwanted or harmful side effects:** *unsafe, unhealthy, uneconomical, inefficient, unneeded?* Does any **"disclosure law"** exist (or is needed) requiring public warning about a concealed hazard? In the ad, what gets less time, less attention, smaller print? *(Most ads are true, but incomplete.)*

Diversion

What benefits (low cost, high speed, etc.) get high priority in the ad's claim and promises? Are these **your** priorities? Significant, important to you? Is there any **"bait-and-switch"?** *(Ad stresses low cost, but the actual seller switches buyer's priority to high quality.)* Does ad divert focus from **key issues,** important things *(e.g., nutrition, health, safety)?* Does ad focus on **side-issues,** unmeaningful trivia *(common in parity products)?* Does ad divert attention from your other choices, other options: buy something else, use less, use less often, rent, borrow, share, do without? *(Ads need not show other choices, but you should know them.)*

Confusion

Are the words clear or ambiguous? Specific or vague? Are claims and promises absolute, or are there qualifying words *("may help," "some")?* Is the claim measurable? Or is it **"puffery"?** *(Laws permit most "sellers's talk" of such general praise and subjective opinions.)* Are the words common, understandable, familiar? Uncommon? Jargon? Any parts difficult to "translate" or explain to others? Are analogies clear? Are comparisons within the same kind? Are examples related? Typical? Adequate? Enough examples? Any contradictions? Inconsistencies? Errors? Are there frequent changes, variations, revisions *(in size, price, options, extras, contents, packaging)?* Is it too complex: too much, too many? Disorganized? Incoherent? Unsorted? Any confusing statistics? Numbers? Do you know exact costs? Benefits? Risks? Are **your own goals,** priorities, and desires clear or vague? Fixed or shifting? Simple or complex? *(Confusion can also exist within us as well as within an ad. If any confusion exists: slow down, take care.)* © 1982, Hugh Rank. Permission granted to photocopy for classroom use.
Counter-Propaganda Press, Box 365, Park Forest, Illinois 60466

Figure 5.1a. Questions You Can Ask About Advertising: Rank's Intensify/Downplay Pattern
SOURCE: From "Questions You Can Ask About Advertising," copyright © 1982 by Hugh Rank. Counter-Propaganda Press, Box 385, Park Forest, Illinois 60466. Based on Hugh Rank's Intensify/Downplay pattern, copyright © 1976 by Hugh Rank, endorsed by the Committee on Public Doublespeak, National Council of Teachers of English. Reprinted with permission. For more information, go to www.govst.edu/users/ghrank

INTENSIFY

Repetition

Intensifying by repetition is an easy, simple, and effective way to persuade. People are comfortable with the *known*, the *familiar*. As children, we love to hear the same stories repeated; later, we have "favorite" songs, TV programs, etc. All cultures have chants, prayers, rituals, dances based on repetition. Advertising slogans, brand names, logos, and signs are common. Much education, training, indoctrination is based on repetition to imprint on *memory* of the receiver to identify, recognize, and respond.

Association

Intensifying by linking (1) the idea or product with (2) something *already loved/desired by-* or *hated/feared by* (3) the intended audience. Thus, the need for **audience analysis**: surveys, polls, "market research," "consumer behavior," psychological and sociological studies. Associate by *direct* assertions or *indirect* ways; (metaphoric language, allusions, backgrounds, contexts, etc.) Some "good things" often linked with products are those common human needs/wants/desires for "basics," "certitude," "intimacy," "space," and "growth."

Composition

Intensifying by pattern and arrangement uses *design, variations in sequence* and *in proportion* to add to the force of words, images, movements, etc. How we put together, or compose, is important: e.g. in **verbal** communication: the choice of words, their level of abstraction; their patterns within sentences, the strategy of longer messages. Logic, inductive and deductive, puts ideas together systematically. **Non-verbal** compositions involve *visuals* (color, shape, size); *aural* (music); *mathematics* (quantities, relationships); *time* and *space* patterns.

The INTENSIFY/DOWNPLAY schema is a pattern useful to analyze communication, persuasion and propaganda. All people intensify (commonly by *repetition, association, composition*) and downplay (commonly by *omission, diversion, confusion*) as they communicate in words, gestures, numbers, etc. But, "professional persuaders" have more training, technology, money and media access than the average citizen. Individuals can better cope with organized persuasion by recognizing the common ways how communication is intensified or downplayed, and by considering who is saying what to whom, when and where, with what intent and what result.

DOWNPLAY

Omission

Downplaying by omission is common since the basic selection/omission process *necessarily omits* more than can be presented. All communication is limited, is edited, is slanted or biased to include and exclude items. But omission can also be used as a *deliberate* way of concealing, hiding. Half-truths, quotes out of context, etc. are very hard to detect or find. Political examples include *cover-ups, censorship, book-burning, managed news, secret police activities.* Receivers, too, can omit: can "filter out" or be closed minded, prejudiced.

Diversion

Downplaying by distracting focus, diverting attention away from key issues or important things: usually by intensifying the side-issues, the non-related, the trivial. Common variations include:"hairsplitting," "nit-picking", "attacking a straw man," "red herring"; also, those emotional attacks and appeals *(ad hominem, ad populum)*, plus things which drain the energy of others: *"busy work," "legal harassment,"* etc. Humor and entertainment *("bread and circuses")* are used as pleasant ways to divert attention from major issues.

Confusion

Downplaying issues by making things so complex, so chaotic, that people "give up," get weary, "overloaded." This is dangerous when people are unable to understand, comprehend, or make reasonable decisions. Chaos can be the accidental result of a disorganized mind, or the deliberate flim-flam of a *con man* or the political *demagogue* (who then offers a "simple solution" to the confused). Confusion can result from *faulty logic, equivocation, circumlocution, contradictions, multiple diversions, inconsistencies, jargon* or anything which blurs clarity or understanding.

Figure 5.1b. Questions You Can Ask About Advertising: Rank's Intensify/Downplay Pattern

SOURCE: From "Questions You Can Ask About Advertising," copyright © 1982 by Hugh Rank. Counter-Propaganda Press, Box 385, Park Forest, Illinois 60466. Based on Hugh Rank's Intensify/Downplay pattern, copyright © 1976 by Hugh Rank, endorsed by the Committee on Public Doublespeak, National Council of Teachers of English. Reprinted with permission. For more information, go to www.govst.edu/users/ghrank

seek to make us approve or accept without examining the evidence. Most often, the associations are indirect, but they can also be direct, as when a political candidate declares that he or she is for "faith, freedom, and family." Candidates for public office have a list of "positive, governing words" that they use when speaking about themselves and their policies. Just some of the words beginning with the letter *c* are *candid, caring, challenging, change, children, citizen, commitment, common sense, compete, confident, control, courage,* and *crusade.* George W. Bush opened his crusade for the Republican presidential nomination in the year 2000 with "compassionate conservatism."

In addition to the use of association to intensify the persuader's good points, association can also be used to play on the audience's fears or hatreds (intensifying the other's bad). An ad for home insurance, for example, may show a picture of a house ravaged by a fire, followed by directions for how to obtain insurance. A public service announcement may show an image of eggs frying in a pan, followed by the warning, "This is your brain on drugs." In politics, association is often accomplished by *name-calling*—linking a person or idea to a negative symbol. The persuader hopes that the receiver will reject the person or idea on the basis of the negative symbol, rather than by examining the evidence. For example, those who oppose budget cuts may refer to fiscally conservative politicians as "stingy," thus creating a negative association, although the same person could equally be referred to as "thrifty" by supporters. Similarly, candidates have a list of negative words and phrases that they use when speaking about their opponents. Some of these are *betray, coercion, collapse, corruption, crisis, decay, destroy, endanger, failure, greed, hypocrisy, incompetent, insecure, liberal, permissive attitude, shallow, sick, traitors,* and *unionized.*

Composition. The arrangement of words in a print advertisement and the organization of ideas in a speech are examples of composition. Reynolds positioned itself as somehow "above the battle" between smokers and nonsmokers by its symmetrical counterbalancing of the two messages and by the ad's simple black-and-white design. It reinforced the image of neutrality by its tag line: "Brought to you in the interest of common courtesy." Some print advertisers combine repetition with association in compositions that link brand names with little more than verbal reminders, such as Pepsi's "the pause that refreshes." Other print ads are thick with technical details, not because the average reader is ever going to read them but because they suggest know-how and instill customer confidence.

Tactics for Downplaying

Omission. One downplaying tactic involves omitting information about the bad points about a person, product, or idea. This is sometimes called *cardstacking*— selecting only information that supports the persuader's point of view. All communication involves some omission because not everything can be said about an object. But omission can also be used to deliberately hide or conceal information. Some other common cases of omission involve telling a half-truth and quoting someone out of context. Unfortunately, these tactics have become part of the thrust and parry of political commercials. For example, a George W. Bush ad in the heat of the heavily contested South Carolina primary in 2000 boasted that "while Washington politicians deadlocked, I delivered a patients' bill of rights" (cited in Jamieson, 2000, p. 216). But according to Jamieson, Bush was far from enthusiastic about the patients' bill of rights in Texas.

Meanwhile, Bush's principal campaign opponent in the primaries, Senator John McCain, declared in South Carolina that he had forsworn the use of attack advertising and would hence forward run a purely positive campaign. He challenged his opponent to do the same. But in a subsequent televised debate, Bush pulled from his pocket an attack flyer from McCain's campaign (Jamieson, 2000).

Advertisers often omit drawbacks, hazards, or disadvantages, such as the high cost of a product. They may omit mention of concealed problems. For example, "fat-free" cookies or ice cream often have more calories than some regular brands. Ads for alcohol, coffee, or laxatives never say, "This is an addictive drug." Until required by law, cigarette companies never told consumers that cigarettes were linked to lung cancer. Finally, one well-known baby food manufacturer (naturally) omits to mention in its ads that apricots and pears from concentrate have little nutritional value.

Diversion. Diversion consists of downplaying by shifting attention away from another's good points or one's own bad points or away from key issues by intensifying side issues. During election campaigns, candidates are often accused of diversion by concentrating on abstract concepts such as "family values," rather than concrete issues such as changing Medicare benefits. Another type of diversion used frequently in political arenas is the ad hominem argument, whereby the person, rather than the idea, is attacked. This was used repeatedly in a 1996 debate between Al Gore and Ross Perot on the North American Free Trade Agreement (NAFTA) that aired on *Larry King Live.* Vice President Al Gore repeatedly questioned Ross Perot's motives in opposing NAFTA, whereas Perot intimated that Gore was a liar. Both men diverted attention from the real issues.

Confusion. Yet another tactic for downplaying one's own weaknesses or the other's strengths is to make things so chaotic and complex that people give up trying to understand. This can be done by use of intentionally faulty logic, euphemisms, jargon, or anything that blurs clarity or understanding. A general name for this is *doublespeak:* language intentionally used to mislead. According to William Lutz (1989), four types of doublespeak are prevalent in contemporary culture.

Euphemism is a device used to make an unpleasant reality more acceptable. In ordinary social discourse, for example, we might say that someone "passed away" or "went to the other side," rather than died. A bathroom may be referred to as a "rest room." Used in this way, euphemisms are not problems. They become problematic, however, when they are used to deceive. For example, comedian George Carlin notes that traumatized veterans returning home from World War I were referred to as "shell-shocked," a term that accurately conveyed the horrors of war. After the World War II, people began to refer to the same phenomenon as "battle fatigue," a term that was a bit more euphemistic but still conveyed the notion of combat as a source of discomfort. After the Vietnam War, people referred to "post-traumatic stress disorder," a phrase that is almost completely disconnected from the realities of war.

Jargon is the specialized language of a trade or profession. Within a specialized group, it is often a type of verbal shorthand that allows people to communicate quickly and efficiently. When used as a downplay tactic, however, jargon often obscures meaning and makes simple things seem complex. A good example of jargon is referring to smelling as "organoleptic analysis," glass as "fused silicate," and a thermometer as a "fever computer." Legal language is full of such jargon: If you lose your property through theft, it is called "involuntary conversion." In advertising, we often see jargon in ads for drugs, automobiles, and equipment such as cameras and computers. Academia is also a good source of jargon. A controversy erupted recently when a physicist (Sokal, 1996) wrote a nonsensical article, "Transgressing the Boundaries: Toward a Transformative Hermeneutics of Quantum Gravity." The author pretended to use quantum theory to "prove" that reality is socially constructed, and his article was accepted by a leading journal in the field of literary criticism. His intention was to point out the prevalence of jargon in academia, and he succeeded all too well.

Gobbledygook or *bureaucratese* is similar to jargon, except that gobbledygook occurs when a persuader attempts to overload the audience with long, complex sentences that sound impressive but actually don't make any sense. The quantum theory article demonstrates the use of gobbledygook:

In quantum gravity, as we shall see, the space-time manifold ceases to exist as an objective physical reality; geometry becomes relational and contextual; and the foundational conceptual categories of prior science—among them, existence itself—become problematized and relativized. (Sokal, 1996, p. 218)

Inflated language is designed to make the ordinary and mundane seem important or things that are simple seem quite complicated. Sometimes, this is merely funny, as when a manicurist is called a "nail technician" or an elevator operator is called a "vertical transport captain." It becomes controversial, however, when used in military "technospeak," where death is "collateral damage," destroying cities is a

---

BOX 5.1 A Sampling of Compliance-Gaining Methods

1. *Altercasting (negative):* Try to get others to comply by pointing out that *only a bad person would not* do what is wanted. That is, try to gain their compliance by noting that only a person with negative qualities would not comply.

2. *Altercasting (positive):* Try to get others to comply by pointing out that a *good person would do* what is wanted. That is, try to gain their compliance by noting that any person with positive qualities would comply.

3. *Altruism:* Try to get others to comply by asking them to *give you a hand* out of the goodness of their heart. That is, try to gain their compliance by asking them to be altruistic and just do it for you.

4. *Audience-Use:* Try to get others to comply by having a group of other people present when you make your request. That is, try to gain their compliance by *asking them in front of other people* as a way to back up your request.

5. *Self-Feeling (negative):* Try to get others to comply by stating that not doing so will result in an automatic decrease in self-worth. That is, try to gain their compliance by pointing out that *they will feel better about themselves* if they do what you want.

6. *Self-Feeling (positive):* Try to get others to comply by stating that doing so will result in an automatic increase in their self-worth. That is, try to gain their compliance by pointing out that *they will feel better about themselves* if they do what you want.

"countervalue attack," the MX missile is a "damage limitation weapon," and a nighttime invasion is a "predawn vertical insertion." The effect of such language is not only to create confusion but to mask the reality behind the words.

Compliance-Gaining Tactics

Compliance-gaining tactics are those used to effect changes in overt behavior, not just in beliefs, values, or attitudes. Compliance gaining is most often associated with interpersonal encounters: a sales negotiator clinching a deal after protracted talks with a client, a physician convincing a sick patient to take the prescribed medication, a son or daughter getting parental permission to use the family car for the evening.

Compliance gaining isn't always a matter of persuasion. Force or the threat of force can coerce compliance. Large sums of money or promises of same can in-

7. *Suggest:* Try to get others to comply by *offering suggestions* about what it is you want them to do. That is, try to gain their compliance by subtly proposing an idea that indirectly points out and describes what it is you want them to do.

8. *Surveillance:* Try to get others to comply by indicating your awareness and observation of what they do. That is, try to gain their compliance by *referring to your general vigilance, surveillance, scrutiny, and/or monitoring of their behavior.*

9. *Third Party:* Try to get others to comply by *having someone else ask them for you.* That is, try to gain their compliance by getting someone else to intervene and do it for you.

10. *This Is the Way Things Are:* Try to get others to comply by telling them they have to because *that is just the way things are.* That is, try to gain their compliance by referring to rules, procedures, policies, or customs that require them to comply.

11. *Value Appeal:* Try to get others to comply because of *important values* that compel action in this instance. That is, try to gain their compliance by pointing to *central and joint beliefs* that should guide what they do.

12. *Why Not?* Try to get others to comply by making them justify why they should not. That is, try to gain their compliance by pointing out there are *no real grounds for not doing so.*

SOURCE: From "Classifying Compliance Gaining Messages: Taxonomic Disorder and Strategic Confusion," by K. Kellermann and C. Cole, 1994, in *Communication Theory, 4,* pp. 3-60. Copyright © by Oxford University Press. Used with permission.

duce people to work long hours, endure unpleasant working conditions, and even risk their lives. But these "power" strategies need persuasion to make them palatable; without it, coercion and material inducements produce only grudging compliance.

What, then, are the resources for compliance gaining available to the persuader? Researchers have found that the relative success of alternative tactics depends on situational factors. What works with intimates may not work with strangers. What works for physicians may not work for their patients (e.g., Boster, 1990). Ensuing chapters compare the use of compliance-gaining stratagems in a number of settings, for example, in health education campaigns (Chapter 10), in sales negotiations (Chapter 13), and in gaining privileged access to a photocopy machine (Chapter 15). For now, this chapter merely identifies verbal resources for persuasion-based compliance gaining. Box 5.1 provides a partial list, along with examples. It is taken from an article that has done much to advance our understanding of compliance-gaining possibilities (Kellermann & Cole, 1994).

Picture 5.2. Bill Clinton is seemingly in command as he provides grand jury testimony, August 17, 1998.

Nonverbal Resources

In his 4 hours of testimony before a grand jury looking into the "Monicagate" scandal, Bill Clinton alternately lectured his inquisitors, complained about trick questions, tossed off veiled insults and condescending put-downs, quibbled and quarreled, and occasionally allowed that he had made mistakes (Purdum, 1998). But Clinton's cameo performance would have failed to impress had not his verbal dexterity been matched by nonverbal acumen (Picture 5.2).

Shaky at first, he warmed to his task, sometimes displaying wounded dignity, at other times exhibiting controlled anger or intense concentration on the matters before him. Like a good novelist, reporter Todd Purdum (1998) has found the verbal resources for capturing the nonverbal twists and turns. When Clinton is forced to concede wrongdoing, he appears as a "sheepish cookie-thief caught red-handed" (p. A1). As he reads from a statement admitting inappropriate intimate contact, he looks "ashen, crumpled, flat." But when he takes the measure of his interrogators, his muted anger takes the form of "a flexed jaw, a jabbed finger, a spit-out 'sir'" (p. A1).

Contrast Clinton's dexterous use of body language in testimony to the grand jury on August 17, 1998, with his nonverbals that evening. Perhaps it was a matter of simple exhaustion. In any event, said Gronbeck (1999):

> The "up close and personal" Bill Clinton—the man able to shift into a reedy voice, capable of adjusting the smallest facial muscles to convey his hurt, his love for the people, his indignation, his joy for future possibilities—spoke contra this usual practice. The vocal characteristics of personal relationship were gone; his face was a rigid mask; his jaw was set through much of the speech; and his gestures were minimal. (p. 2)

Experts on nonverbal communication have identified a number of channels of expression, each capable of influencing receivers in myriad ways.

Vocalics, the auditory channel, includes rate, volume, pitch, voice quality, and articulation. As Chapter 3 suggested, vocal cues play a significant role in projecting images of self and in metacommunicating relational messages about how speakers intend their substantive messages to be understood. But communicating the right inflections isn't always easy. Much of what persuaders say nonverbally is outside their conscious control.

Kinesics, the visual channel, includes posture, gestures, fidgeting, and other body movements, as well as eye behavior and facial expressions. Birdwhistell (1970) has estimated that the face is capable of producing 25,000 different expressions. Ekman and Friesen (1975) claim to have discovered eight positions for the eyes alone. Smiling and direct eye contact are generally found to increase attractiveness and perceptions of trustworthiness, but as suggested in Chapter 3, message recipients are often wary of contrived expressions. Still, this has not stopped some persuaders from using a technique known as *mirroring.* As its name implies, mirroring involves matching the looks or behavior of the person you are trying to influence. Lexis, a former student, discovered at a sales training seminar that it could be taken to wild extremes:

> Fresh out of college, a lump of educated clay, I entered the world-famous Techno executive sales training program. The first words out of the instructor's mouth were: "The key to your success at Techno is the principle that people buy from people they like." I sat in my chair very nonplussed by this comment as we spent virtually the remainder of the day talking about how to make your customer like you.
>
> One component of "similarity" Techno called the "chameleon technique," meaning, do exactly what your customer does. Imitate body posture, speech volume, visual cues, etc. In training, we put this theory into practice by role-

playing: leaning forward when the customer leaned forward, lowering or raising our voices in accordance with the customer's volume, etc. I can vividly
remember my first sales call, hearing my mother's faint, gentle commands to sit
up straight and cross my legs while my customer, a toy manufacturer, lounged
and swiveled in his chair. I glanced nervously at my manager, normally a very
erect dude, but he too was slouched in his seat giving me the visual cue to do
the same. Within a few months this "mirror and matching" became second
nature, customer in relaxed posture, me in relaxed posture.

The whole "similarity" principle, we like people who are similar to us, was
delivered at Techno via the "15-second rule." Within the first 15 seconds in the
customer's office, it was critical to uncover one or two key things about the person: weekend sailor, a kid the same age as your pre-schooler, animal lover, etc.
Once this information was gathered, it was then used to begin the rapport
building or "similarity" creating process. Typical customer meetings began with
a 10- to 15-minute discussion of last night's game, next month's fishing trip, or
where your kid was applying to college.

One particular example was instructive. Robert, the same upright sales
manager in my "chameleon" example, had 20/20 vision. One day, while on a
sales call with a spectacled customer, Robert reached into his pocket and pulled
out a pair of glasses. When the meeting was over, on the way to the car, I asked
Robert when he found out he needed glasses. He said, "I don't, but lots of my
clients wear them so I bought a pair." I looked at him, perplexed. "But Robert,
if you don't need them, doesn't wearing them make you feel dizzy?" He replied,
"They aren't real. They're just frames with glass; they're fakes."[1]

Proxemics is the study of how space and spatial relationships communicate. Hall
(1969) distinguished among zones or territories of communication ranging from
about 18 inches (*intimate* distance) to 25 feet or more (*public* distance). Between
these extremes are *personal* distance (18 inches to 2 feet) and *social* distance (4 to 12
feet). Cultures vary in zones of comfort. For example, Latin Americans tend to be
comfortable at closer distances than do persons reared in Northern European cultures, according to Hall. Still, all cultures seem to place taboos on excessive closeness
by strangers and excessive distance by intimates. Persuaders violate them at their
peril when they communicate interpersonally, but our culture permits all manner of
visual displays of intimate distance, as in magazine advertising.

Proxemics also covers spatial positioning, as in who sits where around a table.
Diplomatic negotiations between rival nations have been known to stall intermina-
bly over the size and shape and seating arrangements of the negotiating table.
Pellegrini (1971) discovered that people seated at the head of the table tended to
be regarded as more persuasive, more talkative, more dominant, and more self-
confident.

Haptics refers to the tactile channel of communication, the arena of touch. Hornick (1992) has demonstrated the rhetorical benefits of touch. Bookstore customers touched on the arm tended to shop longer and buy more; supermarket customers who had been touched were more likely to taste and purchase food samples; restaurant customers tipped servers better if they had been touched by them.

But touch can be discomfiting, both for the touchee and the toucher. A former student, Carol Mickey, tested the effects of touch and closeness in her role as head waitress at a busy downtown restaurant that catered to men. For several weeks, Mickey and the waitresses who worked under her supervision alternated between their normal, businesslike way of approaching male customers and a more intimate style that included increased eye contact (the servers looked at the customers as they ordered, then wrote the orders down on their pads), greater physical proximity (the servers rubbed shoulders with customers as they pointed out specials), and greater individuation (the servers wore name tags). When the more intimate style of service was adopted, tipping increased as much as 20% to 30%. But, although Mickey and her team enjoyed the money, they could not sustain the requisite level of closeness. Some felt guilty, others embarrassed at intruding themselves in these ways.

As with space and touch, cultures assign meanings to being fast or slow, early, late, or on time. These are among the variables of *chronemics,* the study of how time communicates. Clinton's reluctant admission of wrongdoing came late by most persons' reckoning, but his sense of timing in testimony before the grand jury was adept, as Purdum (1998) observed. One moment he would forcefully interrupt his interrogator, the next he would pause for longer than is customary as though to assert his control over the situation.

Americans as a whole tend to value speed. The success of fast-food and fast-lube establishments testifies to that, but there are those who prefer leisurely dining to McDonald's or Burger King. This latter group tends to regard the gulping down of greasy hamburgers as an unhappy marriage of fast food and fast lube.

As for time of arrival for prescheduled appearances, this too has its pluses and minuses. The old joke of the psychoanalyst was actually not so funny: If you arrived early for therapy, you were anxious; if you arrived late, you were angry; if you arrived precisely on time, you were clearly compulsive. You couldn't win.

Deciphering nonverbal communications is seldom reducible to formula, despite what the psychoanalyst would have patients believe. Often, it is not clear what a wink or a blink (or other nonverbal behavior) means in a given context; also, contexts themselves may be no less complex than the nonverbal "texts" we are trying to interpret. Moreover, because even when we think we've discerned "the meaning" (recall the discussion of multiple meanings in Chapter 3), we often have difficulty finding the words to describe it. Gergen (1982) provides the example of a couple coming down to breakfast with their friends at a vacation house. Ross reaches over to stroke

Laura's hair. Is this a sign of real love, or is Ross merely trying to convey the impression of love but without the real feelings? What could we possibly learn about the context to decipher this text with confidence? Mightn't the answer we finally arrive at admit of both possibilities, but in a way that is difficult, if not impossible, to verbalize?

Minimally speaking, nonverbal communications seem to be capable of having six effects, according to Hickson and Stacks (1985):

▶ Repetition: Nodding while saying "yes"

▶ Contradiction: Coldly, perhaps sarcastically, saying to an intimate, "Je t'adore"

▶ Accentuation: "*No way!*" as opposed to "no way." Try stressing a different word each time as you repeat this question: When was the last time you saw Paris?

▶ Complement: Laughing while saying "That's funny"

▶ Substitution: Nodding agreement instead of verbalizing it

▶ Regulation: Fidgeting, putting books away, and so forth as your professor drones on after class was supposed to end

But this list of effects is indeed minimal and does not capture the range of meanings in something as apparently simple as the stroking of Laura's hair. After all, messages (nonverbals included) may be multimotivated and multileveled, much communication is implicit rather than explicit, and receivers coparticipate in the making of meaning. Lists such as this also do not capture the "both-ands" of experience. Does a bikini reveal or conceal, for example, or does it do both?

Visual and Audiovisual Resources

On his way to a charity ball, Senator Jones is photographed walking down a hotel corridor with a priest on one arm and a gorgeous model on the other. This presents the photo editor of a newspaper with an interesting question. Should the photograph be used as is to accompany the newspaper's story on the charity ball? Why not? The senator, after all, is Catholic *and,* at the time of the photograph, had something of a reputation as a philanderer. Photographing the senator between the priest and the model is therefore appropriate. On the other hand, the newspaper could dramatically *reframe* the senator's visit to the charity ball by cropping the photograph. Depending on its politics, it could cut out the priest and leave the model, or cut out the model and leave the priest, or perhaps downplay the senator's presence altogether by selecting instead a photograph of the charity host and hostess dancing together.

As this example makes clear, language is not alone in being able to link or divide, elevate or downgrade, and play up or play down. Indeed, the six linguistic components of Intensify/Downplay identified by Rank (1976) have their visual and audiovisual counterparts. The newspaper, for example, could have played up the senator's promenade to the charity ball by placing its photo of him on the front page. Alternatively, it could have buried the photo on the society page.

Another aspect of visual persuasion is the scene that creates a backdrop for persuasive messages. For example, in ads for diapers, a neat and tidy home is in the background. Ads for cognac usually take place against a background of sophistication and elegance. Ever since Ronald Reagan mastered the art of visual presentation in 1984, political candidates have been careful to be photographed against visually compelling backdrops to air on the evening news. It is far more compelling to see a candidate surrounded by American flags, speaking to a full house of cheering admirers, than it is to see a candidate speaking inside a warehouse to an audience that is half asleep.

Other aspects of visual and audiovisual persuasion appear in film, television, and video presentations and call for consideration of the use of camera angle, editing, lighting, sound, and music. Generally speaking, high-angle shots give the impression of a character's vulnerability, whereas low-angle shots make a character look powerful. Wide-angle shots of a crowd cheering on its leader can arouse intense emotion from a film or television audience. Fast cuts convey dynamism and action, whereas slow dissolves indicate softness (these operate much like the use of straight lines versus curves in pictorial design). Lighting, too, can be soft or harsh, meant to convey dreamlike sentimentality or documentary realism. Advertising exploits the grammar of the visual and audiovisual every bit as effectively as feature-length films do. A 30-second spot for Diehard batteries rehearses for viewers the memory of a winter snowstorm. The familiar sounds are heard of an engine that wants to turn over but cannot. The camera zooms to a high-angle close-up of the driver whose look of utter frustration says it all. Time for a Diehard battery.

Media guru Tony Schwartz (1974) argues that scenes such as these correspond to *scripts* in our heads. The appeal of the Diehard commercial resides in our having been there before. But our brains also lock away fantasy scripts in memory that clever advertisers can evoke. We know that Jeep Cherokees can't climb rugged cliffs, just as we know that Budweiser's bullfrogs can't talk—not English, anyway—but we also know how to suspend disbelief for the sake of a vicarious adventure or a good laugh. What we generally aren't aware of at the moment is how the conventions of the visual and audiovisual are working their magic on us.

Resources of the New Media

In its efforts to "hear from" as many people as possible, the board of an affluent, fast-growing suburban school district decided to post its controversial proposal for student school transfers on the Internet and invite responses. It succeeded beyond expectations, garnering 2,000 hits on its Web site and about 500 comments. It also avoided the usual raucous meetings on school transfers, where, in the past, angry parents had registered long-winded objections in person. This time, the process was orderly, and many people expressed satisfaction with the amended plan. Yet even its supporters expressed regret that the board had essentially made up its mind on the basis of e-mail commentary in advance of any face-to-face engagement. Moreover, at the one meeting it did hold, speakers were limited to 2 minutes each. Summaries of e-mail responses were provided by the board, but what was the *feeling-tone* of the objections? If surveying by way of the Internet became routinized, what would happen to the old sense of community?

The new millennium has been abuzz with talk not just of "new" media such as the Internet but also of a *convergence* of the resources of telecommunication, made possible by greatly expanded bandwidths. Some experts forecast that the Internet alone will revolutionize political campaigning, usher in direct democracy in place of representative government, and redistribute power across the globe. Others, such as Richard Davis (1999), maintain that the politics of tomorrow will be little changed by the Internet.

> Rather than acting as a revolutionary tool rearranging political power and instigating direct democracy, the Internet is destined to become dominated by the same actors in American politics who currently utilize other mediums. Undoubtedly, public expression will become more common and policy makers will be expected to respond hastily. But the mobilization of public expression will still largely be the creation of groups and individuals who currently dominate the political landscape. (p. 5)

Similar disputes can be heard about the private sector. One cartoonist pictured it as a gravity-less outer space with lots of paper money floating about, seemingly at random. Some forecasters predict a sales revolution: Online advertising will be a $24 billion industry by the year 2003, 20 million households will trade stocks online in 2003, and $6 billion will be spent online in the last 2 months of that year. But as *Money* magazine's Jim Frederick (1999) has argued, much of this forecasting is unscientific and much of the hoopla behind it is smoke and mirrors. The forecasters, he observes, "do nothing to contradict the idea they are virtual oracles" (p. 70), but they retreat when their methods of forecasting are subjected to critical scrutiny.

To be sure, the Internet opens up possibilities for persuaders that did not exist a decade or two ago. By its nature, the technology increases the speed with which persuadees can be reached and enables persuaders both to learn more about their target audiences and to target each market segment with greater precision. Increasingly, then, political campaigners, advertisers, and movement leaders can custom-tailor their messages, a process known in the trade as *narrowcasting* (Shapiro, 1999).

Persuadees, for their part, can order up messages, including persuasive messages, by way of the Internet. The Internet enables users to order up the portions of newspapers they wish to read online, plus in-depth follow-ups, and to make similar selections from television news. Specialized news and opinion services are created to service specialized readerships. Search engines such as Yahoo! exist to scan the various universes of information available on any given topic. The much vaunted freedom afforded by the Internet, however, usually requires exposure to advertisements that Internet browsers don't want to see. From the advertiser's perspective, of course, this is a decided plus: the chance to reach a nearly captive audience (Shapiro, 1999).

The Internet also permits considerable interactivity. On listservs and in online chat groups, participants can function as persuaders one moment, persuadees the next. This indeed could have occurred in advance of the suburban school district's decision on a student transfer policy. A discussion hotline could have been created, and angry parents could even have made their feelings known.

It is difficult to imagine cyberspace in the imminent world of complete technological convergence. Convergence could greatly increase the choices available to consumers, while at the same time rendering choice making relatively simple. In a broadband world, says columnist Andrew Sullivan (2000),

> Even the distinctions among telephone wires, cables, and satellites will be erased. There will be one cultural-economic tube, and you'll be at the end of it—eagerly clutching your credit card that can make telephone calls, get cash out of A.T.M.s, and earn you frequent-flier miles. (p. 31)

Summary

One way of thinking about persuasion is as an art of the sayable. Many things can be said pro or con about a person, an idea, or a proposal for action; moreover, the things to be said can be said in many ways. By their choice of labels, descriptions, comparisons, definitions, and so forth, persuaders can make a difference in the way things are perceived and evaluated. They can, for example, minimize or maximize, reveal or conceal, sharpen or blur, link or divide, and make something seem good, bad, or somewhere in between.

The persuader, then, has many choices, and this chapter's exploration of language resources focused on tactics for intensifying and downplaying while also providing illustrations of persuasive compliance-gaining techniques. Getting people to comply—that is, to act as you wish they would act—is not always a matter of persuasion. The power of monetary incentives and of coercive pressures are sometimes an adequate substitute for persuasion, but unless accompanied by persuasive arguments and appeals, they generally produce only grudging compliance.

Besides being an art of the sayable, persuasion is an art of the nonverbal: of gestures and inflections, settings and physical arrangements, timing and touch. The nonverbal can reinforce the verbal or nullify what's been said, in effect contradicting it. As with language, this chapter explored the resources of the nonverbal.

Brief consideration was given as well to the resources of the visual and audiovisual. The example of the senator photographed between the model and the priest reminds us that the visual, too, can intensify or downplay, especially in these days of digital imaging whereby, with no difficulty at all, reality is created in the editing room.

What, then, of the new media and of the emerging convergence of telecommunications transmission systems? There seems little question but that persuaders will be able to custom-tailor messages to ever narrower audience segments and with incredible speed. Message recipients will have greater freedom to select messages, except those they are forced to see and hear as a condition for signing on with transmission providers. There will also be greater opportunity for interactivity. Just what effects these changes will have on the private sector, or on the way the nation's business is conducted, remains a matter of considerable dispute at this point. The question is not whether product advertising, political campaigning, and other such paradigmatic forms of persuasion will be transformed but the extent of that transformation.

Questions and Projects for Further Study

1. Think of the ways you use the resources of the verbal and the nonverbal in the course of a day. What do you routinely play up and play down?
2. Think of an incident when you had to choose your words carefully. How did you use language to conceal or reveal, magnify or minimize, elevate or degrade, sharpen or blur, link or divide, simplify or complexify, or make good, bad or indifferent? What functions were performed by labels, definitions, and descriptions; by contrasts and comparisons; and by the way things were contextualized or decontextualized? How would you say things differently if you had a chance to choose your words again?

3. Repeat the same exercise, but this time focus on the nonverbal elements in a difficult rhetorical situation. How many did you deliberately choose?
4. Is it possible to know whether someone is genuinely in love or merely acting the part? How can you know? How can you know that you know? Are nonverbals as easily decipherable as verbal expressions? Can they be seen through more readily? What features of the context need attention to decipher the nonverbal text?
5. Provide your own examples of nonverbal communication's six meaningful effects.
6. Illustrate how the six verbal components of intensify/downplay, identified by Rank, have their visual and audiovisual counterparts.
7. What changes has the Internet produced in the choices available to persuaders and persuadees? What will persuasion be like with increased telecommunications convergence?

Note

1. Used with permission of the student.

References

Birdwhistell, R. L. (1970). *Kinesics and context.* Philadelphia: University of Pennsylvania Press.

Boster, F. J. (1990). An examination of the state of compliance-gaining message research. In J. Dillard (Ed.), *Seeking compliance: The production of interpersonal influence messages* (pp. 7-17). Scottsdale, AZ: Gorsuch Scarisbrick.

Burke, K. (1969). *A rhetoric of motives.* Berkeley: University of California Press. (Original work published 1950)

Davis, R. (1999). *The web of politics: The Internet's impact on the American political system.* New York: Oxford University Press.

Ekman, P., & Friesen, W. V. (1975). *Unmasking the face.* Englewood Cliffs, NJ: Prentice Hall.

Frederick, J. (1999, Dec. 19). The virtual science of high-tech forecasting. *New York Times Magazine,* 70-73.

Gergen, K. J. (1982). *Toward transformation in social knowledge.* New York: Springer-Verlag.

Gronbeck, B. (1999). Underestimating generic expectations: Clinton's apologies of August 17, 1998. *American Communication Journal, 2,* 1-4. Available: www.americancomm.org

Hall, E. T. (1969). *The hidden dimension.* New York: Doubleday.

Hickson, M. L., & Stacks, D. W. (1985). *NVC: Nonverbal communication.* Dubuque, IA: William C. Brown.

Hornick, J. (1992). Tactile stimulation and consumer response. *Journal of Consumer Research, 19,* 449-458.

Jamieson, K. H. (2000). *Everything you think you know about politics—and why you're wrong.* New York: Basic Books.

Kellermann, K., & Cole, C. (1994). Classifying compliance gaining messages: Taxonomic disorder and strategic confusion. *Communication Theory, 4,* 3-60.

Lutz, W. (Ed.). (1989). *Beyond 1984: Doublespeak in a post-Orwellian age.* Urbana, IL: National Council of Teachers of English.

Pellegrini, R. J. (1971). Some effects of seating position on social perception. *Psychological Reports, 28,* 887-893.

Petty, R. E., & Cacioppo, J. T. (1996). *Attitudes and persuasion: Classic and contemporary approaches.* Boulder, CO: Westview. (Original work published 1981)

Purdum, T. S. (1998, September 22). On camera, president shows his many sides. *New York Times,* pp. A1, A14.

Rank, H. (1976). *Intensify/downplay.* Urbana, IL: National Council of Teachers of English.

Rank, H. (1982). *Questions you can ask about advertising.* Park Forest, IL: Counter-Propaganda Press.

Schwartz, T. (1974). *The responsive chord.* New York: Anchor.

Shapiro, A. (1999). *The control revolution.* New York: Public Affairs.

Sokal, A. D. (1996). Transgressing the boundaries: Toward a transformative hermeneutics of quantum gravity. *Social Text, 4,* 217-252.

Sullivan, A. (2000, June 11). Dot.communist manifesto. *New York Times Magazine,* 30-32.

Framing and Reframing

Jamie wants to connect the nine dots shown in Figure 6.1 by four straight lines without lifting his pen or pencil from the paper. (The solution to the problem appears in Figure 6.2, but do not peek until you too have worked on the problem for at least 2 minutes.)

At first, like nearly everyone who comes across this problem for the first time, Jamie assumes that the nine dots comprise a rectangle and that he can't go outside the box formed by the dots. But this self-imposed rule dooms all attempts to solve the problem. Only by questioning the assumption, recognizing that the ambiguity of the task allows greater freedom than initially assumed, can those trying to solve the puz-

The Nine-Dot Problem

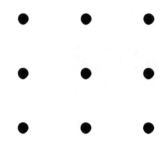

Connect the nine dots using four continuous straight lines

Figure 6.1. The Nine-Dot Problem
SOURCE: From Watzlawick, P., Weakland, J. & Fisch, R. (1974).*Change: Principles of Problem Formation and Problem Resolution.* Copyright ©1974 by W. W. Norton & Company, Inc. Used by permission of W. W. Norton & Company, Inc.

zle step outside the frame of their own making and deal with the problem effectively (Figure 6.2).

This lesson has enormous implications for persuasion. Persuaders can encourage their audiences to think in new ways. Message recipients can refuse the frames proposed by communicators or at least challenge their assumptions. In working together, people can learn to *dissolve* problems that seemed impossible to resolve or *resolve* them in ways that had previously been unimaginable.

But reframing isn't always easy. As Watzlawick, Weakland, and Fisch (1974) point out, it is not simply the perspective people have on particular issues that impedes solutions to problems but their more general tendency to regard any and all categories as fixed and proper:

> Once an object is categorized as the member of a given class, it is extremely difficult to see it as belonging also to another class. This class membership of an object is called its "reality;" thus anybody who sees it as the member of another class must be mad or bad. Moreover, from this simplistic assumption there follows another, equally simplistic one, namely that to stick to this view of reality is not only sane, but also "honest," "authentic," and what not. "I cannot play games" is the usual retort of people who are playing the game of not playing a

game, when confronted with the possibility of seeing an alternative class membership. (p. 99)

Frames, then, can become a reality for people. The categories that persuaders construct can be every bit as constraining as a prison and every bit as emancipating as a liberating army. People experience this most vividly, perhaps, when they are in the grip of a powerful metaphor.

Metaphors as Frames

Like its close cousin the simile, a metaphor is a comparison of sorts, a way of seeing one thing in comparison with another. Metaphors are nonliteral comparisons, however, and for that reason they tend to be more powerful than simile expressions. In the metaphorist's hands, for example, "love" is not "*like* a red, red rose;" it *becomes* a red, red rose.

Some metaphors serve only to add force or drama or life to a description (screaming headlines, yellow journalism), but others serve also as framing devices by which to direct or redirect thought on a matter. Consider, for example, the many uses that former presidents have made of the "This means war" metaphor. President Lyndon Johnson declared a War on Poverty. Ford pledged an all-out War on Inflation. Carter insisted that the energy problem presented us with "the moral equivalent of war." As Lakoff and Johnson (1980) observe, the war metaphor was not simply an emotionally loaded term: It structured thought and directed action. For example, when Carter used the war metaphor, it generated a network of entailments. There was an "enemy," a "threat to national security," which required "setting targets," "reorganizing priorities," "establishing a new chain of command," "plotting a new strategy," "gathering intelligence," "marshaling forces," "imposing sanctions," "calling for sacrifices," and on and on (pp. 156-157). The war metaphor highlighted certain realities and hid others. The metaphor was not merely a way of viewing reality; it constituted a license for policy change and political and economic action. The very acceptance of the metaphor provided grounds for certain inferences: There was an external, foreign, hostile enemy (pictured by cartoonists in Arab headdress); energy needed to be given top priority; the populace would have to make sacrifices; if we didn't meet the threat, we would not survive. It is important to realize that this was not the only metaphor available.

Anyone choosing a framing metaphor must decide what will be intensified and what will be downplayed. Consider the following slogan for the ad agency Spiro and Associates, "the low cholesterol ad agency." In small print, the ad agency boasts, "no fat," "low cholesterol," "no gimmicks," no "drawn-out, formal presentations." The

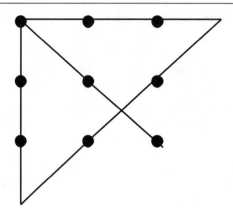

Solution to the Nine-Dot Problem

Figure 6.2. Solution to the Nine-Dot Problem
SOURCE: From Watzlawick, P., Weakland, J. & Fisch, R. (1974).*Change: Principles of Problem Formation and Problem Resolution.* Copyright ©1974 by W. W. Norton & Company, Inc. Used by permission of W. W. Norton & Company, Inc.

style of the ad reinforces this boast. It is spare, unadorned, and black and white. It "speaks" to its readers in a clipped, informal, decidedly conversational tone.

To better appreciate the low-cholesterol frame, consider a couple of framing alternatives. Might Spiro and Associates do better as the "no frills" agency? But that suggests a reduction in quality as well as in price. What if its competitors who prefer dining to dieting find a different gustatory image more appealing: "the filet mignon of ad agencies" that "sells the steak, not just the sizzle"? But in these days of widespread health concerns, the low-cholesterol appeal is likely to have more takers. Besides, the "filet mignon" frame would *downplay* what the Spiro and Associates agency wants to *highlight*—that is, because of its "no fat" approach, it is able to undercut its competitors in price.

The artful use of a metaphor is an important mark of the polished speech or essay, but finding the right metaphor isn't always easy. Sometimes, however, just the right one comes along. Wayne Booth (1978) has provided this particularly good example of reframing by metaphor:

A lawyer friend of mine was hired to defend a large Southern utility against a suit by a small one, and he thought he was doing fine. All of the law seemed to be on his side, and he felt that he had presented his case well. Then the lawyer for the small utility said, speaking to the jury, almost as if incidentally to his legal case: So now see what it is. They got us where they want us. They holding us up with one hand, their good sharp fishing knife in the other hand, and they sayin' "You sit still, little catfish, we're just going to gut ya'." (p. 178)

In this example, a contest between relative equals is transformed into a saga of David versus Goliath. Moreover, the speaker not only manages to link himself with his audience in opposition to the lawyer for the larger utility but also redirects attention from the substantive issues toward the personalities involved. Every last detail of this seemingly casual remark, from its Southernisms and "down home" grammatical style to the choice of a catfish (as opposed, say, to a carp), supports the frame the lawyer is trying to create. Imagine, says Booth (1978), that the speaker had tried to frame the picture of victimization using a different metaphor:

> The big utilities just expect us to stand around helplessly while they sap our vital forces.
>   or
> And so the big utility is trying to disembowel the company I represent, right before our very eyes.
> Clearly, the catfish motif is superior. (p. 178)

Creative Reframing Through Generative Metaphors

Problem solvers, including those approaching the nine-dot problem, often fix on the task of problem solving before they have given sufficient thought to how they have framed the problem. Schön and his colleagues devised an especially provocative application of the concept of reframing problems (Schön, 1979; Schön & Argyris, 1978). Their *generative metaphor* refers to verbal frames that lead us to see one thing as another in novel ways. Generative metaphors structure perceptions, and new generative metaphors may stimulate thought and discovery.

In providing an example of reframing by generative metaphor, Schön (1979) describes how a group of product development engineers some years ago deliberated on how to improve the performance of a new paintbrush made with synthetic bristles. Compared with the old natural bristle brush, the new one delivered paint to a surface in an uneven "gloppy" way. The researchers had tried a variety of alternatives. They had observed, for example, that natural bristles had split ends, whereas the synthetic bristles did not, and they tried (without significant gain) to split the ends of the synthetic bristles. They experimented with bristles of different diameters. Nothing seemed to work very well.

Then someone observed, "You know, a paintbrush is a kind of pump!" He pointed out that when a paintbrush is pressed against a surface, paint is forced through the spaces between bristles onto the surface. The paint is made to flow through the "channels" formed by the bristles when the channels are deformed by the bending of the brush. He noted that painters will sometimes vibrate a brush when applying it to a surface, so as to facilitate the flow of paint.

The researchers tried out the natural and synthetic bristle brushes, thinking of them as pumps. They noticed that the natural brush formed a gradual curve when it was pressed against a surface whereas the synthetic brush formed a shape more nearly an angle. They speculated that this difference might account for the "gloppy" performance of the bristle brush. How then might they make the bending shape of the synthetic brush into a gentle curve?

This line of thought led them to a variety of inventions. Perhaps fibers could be varied so as to create greater density in that zone. Perhaps fibers could be bonded together in that zone. Some of these inventions were reduced to practice and did, indeed, produce a smoother flow of paint. (p. 257)

"Paintbrush-as-pump," said Schön, "is an example of what I mean by a generative metaphor" (p. 257).

"Frame" as Metaphor

Paradoxically, just as metaphors are frames, so the term *frame* as applied to language is itself metaphorical. The metaphor of a linguistic frame is at least partially visual,[1] conjuring up images of photographic frames (the senator photographed with or without his escorts), frames in a motion picture (e.g., a battle between cowboys and Indians, first seen from the perspective of the cowboys, then from the perspective of the Indians), and picture frames (e.g., gilt-edged versus unadorned). *A frame, then, is one among a number of possible ways of seeing something, and a reframing is a way of seeing it differently; in effect changing its meaning.* Just as there are frames around pictures, so may there be talk about frames as *frames of frames;* recall the discussion of *levels* of communication in Chapter 3.

There is clearly a good deal of ambiguity surrounding the notions of framing and reframing, and some writers have therefore attempted to rein the terms in. To frame, suggests Entman (1993),

is to *select some aspects of a perceived reality and make them more salient in a communicative text, in such a way as to promote a particular problem definition, causal interpretation, moral evaluation, and/or treatment recommendation* for the item described. (p. 52)

Note how this definition fits the examples provided thus far. Indeed, the war metaphor diagnoses, evaluates, *and* prescribes (Entman, 1993; Gamson, 1992). The catfish metaphor shifts attention from the *substantive* frame and presents instead a *metacommunicational* frame, one that makes salient the *relationship* between the two utility companies, suggesting a negative moral evaluation of the larger one. The paintbrush-as-pump metaphor offers no moral evaluation, but it clearly diagnoses and prescribes.

Entman (1993) adds that frames reside in four locations in a communicative process, which may or may not coincide. These are the communicator, the text, the receiver, and the culture.

> *Communicators* make conscious or unconscious framing judgments in deciding what to say, guided by frames (often called schemata) that organize their belief systems. The *text* contains frames, which are manifested by the presence or absence of certain key-words, stock phrases, stereotyped images, sources of information, and sentences that provide thematically reinforcing clusters of facts or judgments. The frames that guide the *receiver's* thinking and conclusion may or may not reflect the frames in the text and the framing intention of the communicator. The *culture* is the stock of commonly invoked frames. In fact, culture might be defined as the empirically demonstrable set of common frames exhibited in the discourse and thinking of most people in a social grouping. (pp. 52-53)

Cultural Frames and Verbal Repertoires

This last notion—of cultural frames—is particularly interesting. On many a social or political issue, the culture seems to supply competing aphorisms. Should the heroine of a favorite soap opera risk an affair with that handsome doctor who's just come into town? Perhaps yes. After all, "nothing ventured, nothing gained," "love must have its way," and "the early bird catches the worm." On the other hand, "safety first," "look before you leap," "the grass is greener on the other side," and "thou shalt not commit adultery."

These are just a sampling of the seemingly opposed framing expressions that pass for the common sense of Western culture. They are seemingly opposed because as Billig (1987) has observed, the aphorisms don't directly contradict one another when taken literally. Moreover, they are typically invoked selectively, as needed, to make a point or craft an image. In this respect, they are like the lines of argument that the ancient Greek and Roman rhetoricians taught would-be orators and that law schools still teach prospective lawyers today. For example, a lawyer wishing to prove that O. J. Simpson could have murdered his wife and her friend in the time he had available could turn to Aristotle's *Rhetoric* (Cooper, 1932) for lines of argument—called *topoi*—that can be used in establishing possibility. Aristotle's *Rhetoric* could also provide ways to establish impossibility—for example, that Simpson's alibi was ironclad.

People hold in their heads not just seemingly opposed aphorisms and lines of argument but entire *repertoires* of verbal response that they invoke, depending on what they take to be the relevant frame in a given situation. Americans are willing to support "preventing Medicare from going bankrupt by reducing the annual rate of increase in Medicare funding." But they are strongly opposed to "cutting back on Medicare spending."

Americans are able to shift repertoires, especially when competing cultural myths about the meaning of being an American are called into play. As reflected in decades-long controversies about welfare, affirmative action, and universal health care, they tend to shift between the two dominant cultural frames of "self-reliance" and "equality." Let a politician emphasize either frame, and people tend to nod their support for it, at least until they hear another politician evoking the competing frame. The frames are not easily reconciled; thus, public opinion tends to be divided on such issues as welfare and affirmative action, with many persons registering ambivalence and with pronounced shifts in expressed attitudes depending on how questions are worded or to whom they are talking or listening (Edelman, 1971; Gamson & Modigliani, 1989). When efforts are made to reconcile the two frames, confusion frequently results. For example, most Americans favor being race conscious in providing opportunities to blacks to compensate them for past mistreatment (here emphasizing the frame of equality). They want their governing institutions to be color-blind, however, in allocating rewards (here emphasizing the frame of self-reliance). But admission to college or graduate school is both an opportunity and a reward (Gamson & Modigliani, 1989). What do they do then?

Faced with challenges to their positions, proponents and opponents of affirmative action (or welfare, or government-subsidized health insurance) engage in *spin control*. Correspondingly, they reframe incoming information or opposing arguments in an effort to make them fit with their positions. Supporters of affirmative action insist that they are not opposed to self-reliance; they simply want to "help minorities help themselves." Opponents of affirmative action declare that they are not opposed to equality, but the equality that is most truly "American," they insist, is "equality of opportunity." Similarly, although opponents of affirmative action castigate it as "preferential treatment," supporters call it "compensatory treatment." Each group, meanwhile, invokes rival sayings, mottoes, slogans, and catchphrases that have been woven throughout centuries into the fabric of the culture (Billig, 1987). "God helps those who help themselves," says the champion of self-reliance. "Love thy neighbor as thyself," says the egalitarian. And so the battle of competing frames goes on.

Research on Frames and Reframes

The difference that a frame (or reframe) can make has been amply demonstrated by social psychologists (e.g., Kahneman & Tversky, 1984). A few examples of research findings are reviewed below.

Example 1:

   A. This beef is 75% lean.

   B. This beef is 25% fat.

In this study, focusing on positive product attributes produced more favorable ratings (Levin & Gaeth, 1988). But consider the following:

Example 2:

   A. Women who do breast self-examinations (BSE) have an increased chance of finding a tumor in the early, more treatable stage of the disease.

   B. Women who do not do BSE have a decreased chance of finding a tumor in the early, more treatable stage of the disease.

Here, the negatively worded message produced greater compliance with recommendations for BSEs (Meyerowitz & Chaiken, 1987). Negatively framed messages appear to be more persuasive when detailed processing is called for.

Example 3: In studying how leading questions can influence eyewitness testimony in the courtroom, Loftus and Palmer (1974) showed participants a film depicting a multicar accident. After the film, participants were asked one of two leading questions:

   A. About how fast were the cars going when they *smashed* into each other?

   B. About how fast were the cars going when they *hit* each other?

Participants presented with wording A not only estimated that the cars were going faster but also were more likely to report having seen broken glass at the accident scene, although none was shown.

Metacommunicative Frames

As Chapter 3 discussed, a metacommunication is a communication *about* a communication. Two types of metacommunications are *reflexive* and *responsive.*

Reflexive Metacommunications

Reflexive messages interpret, classify, or in other ways comment on one's own messages. Much of this is done nonverbally (see Chapter 3). But consider the following response by then President Richard Nixon when a reporter asked why he held press conferences irregularly: "It's not that I'm afraid to do it. I have to determine the best way of communicating, and also, *and this will sound self-serving, and is intended to be,* I have to use the press conference" [italics added] (Cohen, 1988, p. 7). The reporter supplies the substantive frame: Why do you hold press conferences irregularly? Nixon merely stays in frame when he answers that question directly. But he "goes meta" to himself when he says "and this will sound self-serving," and he goes "meta-meta" when he says, "and is intended to be."

Reflexive metacommunications are especially important at the beginning of a speech or essay. Here speakers or writers generally classify the message, indicate their purpose or purposes in communicating, preview the upcoming substantive message, and metacommunicate explicitly as well as implicitly about themselves in relation to the audience. The strategic character of these framing opportunities is revealed by comparing what is said with what could have been said.

For example, Congressman Fudge has returned to his home district to address an audience of business leaders and to consult privately with a few of them regarding what they want from him and what they're prepared to give in return. His subject is a national sales tax, which many in his audience oppose but which he is inclined to support. Fudge decides against open confrontation with the sales tax opponents in his audience. Instead, he elects to present his speech as a "discussion of options for raising federal revenues to support needed programs." Rather than stating overtly that he wants the audience's support for House Bill 237, he says that he intends to "inform" them of recent research by his staff on "revenue enhancement." Rather than organizing his speech around the benefits of Bill 237 and the costs of not passing it, he declares that he first wants to "explore" other alternatives with them. All these are framing maneuvers that Fudge uses in talking about his own subsequent talk.

Responsive Metacommunications

Responsive metacommunications reply to what others have said in interactive situations. Note the following responses to the question "Have you got the time?"

A1. If you've got the money, honey, I've got the time.

or

A2. Your English is improving.

or

A3. What is time, anyway?

The central point of these examples is that responsive metacommunications are frame altering (and sometimes frame breaking). If the expectation is that we should directly reply to questions in a given situation, then we will have "gone meta" (and broken the frame of direct address) if we choose to step back from a question to question the questioner's motives, tone, premises, right to ask certain questions, or right to ask any questions at all. Going meta also occurs when we comment favorably on a question or on the questioner's mode of delivery.

Moreover, communicators may comment not just on immediately preceding utterances but also on segments of an interaction ("This conversation is getting out of hand"), on the interaction as a whole ("I didn't know this was to be a cross-examination"), or, for that matter, on multiple interactions involving different groups of interactants ("Why do you European Americans always seem to privilege your own cultural premises?"). All these are instances of metamoves.

Reframing in Political Confrontations: "Going Meta"

During the intensely watched Senate Judiciary Committee hearings in 1991 on allegations of sexual harassment by Supreme Court nominee Clarence Thomas, Professor Anita Hill engaged consistently in communicational activities that might be characterized as direct exchange—that is, she concentrated on doing what was expected of her at the hearings, according to all the explicit rules of communication and implicit "taken-for-granteds" (Hopper, 1981) for that situation. Asked a question, she answered it directly. Challenged by a follow-up to her response, she

Picture 6.1. Anita Hill gives testimony at the Senate Judiciary Committee hearing.

attempted to meet the challenge directly. What she did not do was "go meta" (Picture 6.1).

By contrast, in his opening statement, Thomas sought to place the hearings themselves in question: "This is not American. This is Kafkaesque. It has got to stop." Then he let his questioners know which questions he would answer and which questions he considered out of bounds. "I am here specifically to respond to allegations of sex harassment in the workplace. . . . I will not allow this committee or anyone else to probe into my private life." In his second statement, Thomas found new ways to castigate the hearings: a "circus," a "national disgrace," a "high-tech lynching." Then he proceeded to inform the committee that he had chosen not to listen to Anita Hill's testimony: "No I didn't: I've heard enough lies." Admonished by Democratic Senator Howell Heflin for not listening to the testimony and thus denying himself a chance to refute it, Thomas challenged Heflin's premise: "Senator, I am incapable of proving the negative." Only after Thomas had engineered a reframing of the committee hearings did he deign to respond directly to questions, and even then he maintained nonverbally the persona of the beleaguered victim ("Excerpts," 1991, p. A30; Thomas, 1991, p. A10).

When Judge Thomas cast himself as the victim of a "high-tech lynching," he reframed the hearings in two important respects. First, by the act of "stepping outside the circle" of question and reply, he broke from the frame of business as usual. Second, by his lynching metaphor, he placed a particular stamp on that business, a particular way of seeing it. The effect of Thomas's metamoves was to displace attention from his own guilt or innocence to that of the Judiciary Committee. Now it was the Democratic majority's turn to shift in their seats as Senator Heflin sought in vain to regain control of the situation. Arguably, the Democrats could have so bolstered Anita Hill's case against Clarence Thomas during the hearings that Thomas's later repudiation of the process would have seemed shrill, unfair, self-serving, and hypocritical. Perhaps someone among the members of the Democratic majority could have "gone meta" to Thomas's metamoves, effectively calling them into question. Surely, Thomas and his Republican handlers had to know that "going meta" in such a confrontational way was a risky undertaking.

But the Thomas forces also knew that the Democratic majority's legitimacy had been significantly eroded in the regular hearings on Judge Thomas's nomination, during the negotiations leading up to the Hill-Thomas hearings, and at the Hill-Thomas hearings themselves. Having observed, for example, the Democrats' failure to come to Anita Hill's aid in the face of withering questioning by Republican Senator Arlen Specter, they concluded that they could attack with impunity (Nelson, 1991).

This is not to say that Thomas's success was foreordained. On the face of it, after all, the metaphor of a high-tech lynching hardly suited a congressional hearing peopled by supporters and not just opponents, at which the principal accuser of a conservative appellate judge was another African American. But Thomas managed rhetorically to deflect attention from the questionable logic of the metaphor, providing what television critic Walter Goodman (1991) saw as having all the earmarks of a theatrical performance. Said Goodman, "He was innocent and hurt, indignant and outraged. His frequent references to family and his language—'a living hell'— seemed to have been influenced by television melodrama" (p. 30).

Judge Thomas's undoing of the Democratic majority at the hearing by way of biting commentaries on his situation provides vivid illustration of the power of metamoves. In keeping with the notion of levels of communication, these are a way of going "one up" in the situation by arrogating to oneself the role of interpreter, hence, the frequent references here to going meta. But going meta requires a rhetorical balancing act, pivoting on the high wire of perceived legitimacy. There were reasons, after all, that Anita Hill did not go meta. Her almost exclusive reliance on direct exchange promoted an image of demure self-confidence, of politeness and a sense of propriety, of consideration for her interlocutors' interests and not just her own, and of someone who had nothing to hide. Thus, meta-goers must skillfully balance the potential gains of enhancing their reputations, shaping agendas, and influencing judgments against the dangers of appearing unjustifiably intrusive, disruptive, contentious, or evasive. Meta-goers in confrontational situations must also weigh into the balance their relative legitimacy against that of their opponents.

"Having" legitimacy is rhetorically akin to holding the chips necessary to call or raise in a poker game. In each case, it is a matter of rights or entitlements. But calculations of legitimacy are by no means as easy as chip counting. Ultimately, legitimacy is performative, a matter not simply of what one has but of what one can do to shape audience perceptions of what one has. Legitimacy, then, is also subject to frame altering.

Legitimacy is also contextual. Were Judge Thomas sitting on his own bench, there would be little question of his right to deflect questions by commenting on them. Were he a teacher responding to a student or a therapist responding to a patient, he might be granted the right to provide not just any interpretation but the "authoritative" interpretation in that situation. But what are the rights of a Supreme Court nominee at a Judiciary Committee hearing on charges of sexual harassment? The waters were uncharted. Surely, a complex mix of counteracting factors entered into the public's determination of Thomas's rights, as they typically do in all political confrontations.

Reframing in Psychotherapy

When people come into psychotherapy, it is often because the meanings and interpretations they have given to the events in their lives haven't worked to remedy their problems and may indeed have contributed to them. Much of what falls under the rubric of reframing in psychotherapy involves helping people create new meanings and new ways of making sense of their experiences that might lead to new possibilities for adaptive action. Clinical psychologist Paul Wachtel (1993) provides the example of Bret, whose wife experienced considerable anxiety at parties with people she didn't know. When Bret's wife reluctantly agreed to attend these parties, she stayed so close to him that Bret would inevitably berate her for her excessive "clinginess." Bret was troubled by his attitude toward his wife, however, whom he loved and enjoyed being with when they were together by themselves. Wachtel chose to reframe Bret's report by responding, "Your wife seems to feel most relaxed when she's alone with you" (p. 196). Said Wachtel,

It is interesting to note that the comment simply restated what Bret had been describing, but from the opposite vantage point. One could equally describe Bret's wife as *less* comfortable with strangers, or as *more* comfortable alone with him. But although the two ways of framing the facts were logical equivalents, they were not at all equivalent psychologically. The second vantage point highlighted a different meaning to the behavior and had different implications for their relationship. Moreover, by interrupting the pattern of bickering that had developed between them about this issue, the reframing created space for a different equilibrium to develop and for them to renegotiate how they would deal with their differing experiences of social occasions. (p. 196)

Just as it is impossible to *not* metacommunicate when an individual is joined in time and space with others, so it is impossible to *not* supply a frame. A central issue for psychotherapists is whether to provide an objectivist or coactive frame in registering interpretations of the patient's reported problems.

Consider the familiar case of two persons locked in a vicious cycle of reproach and recrimination. Husband withdraws from the relationship because he feels trapped by wife's possessiveness. But wife says she clutches because she senses him slipping out of the marital bond. Conceivably, the therapist could declare objectively that each is contributing to the problem and suggest steps that they could take to rectify it. But matters are seldom that simple. Husband and wife may be invested in their own "objective" analyses of the source of the problem and in their anger toward the other. Neither may be consciously aware of their own role in contributing to the problem. One or both may become defensive on being questioned about it, fearing, perhaps, that they will be judged mad or bad. They may resist change in the relationship because, bad as it is, it has its satisfying moments and may be preferable to some untried alternative.

The objectivist approach to psychotherapy assumes that there is one best description of the patient's problems and one best explanation for their causes. The job of the therapist is to help the patient overcome defenses to face up to the deep, dark, disturbing truths denied to consciousness by the patient's self-deceiving nature. By this account, knowledge of the repressed "real" self is an essential step toward cure. Insofar as patients resist self-discovery, they must also be confronted with their resistance. Never mind that this frequently sets up an adversarial relationship between therapist and patient.

An extreme example of the objectivist approach is found in a case report by classic psychoanalyst Otto Kernberg (Wile, 1984). It involved a conflict between Kernberg and a female patient who had gotten increasingly angry at Kernberg for telling her that she was masochistic, defensive, and infantile and that she wanted to have intercourse with her father as well as with him. According to Wile, "Although this may be everyday common sense talk to psychoanalysts, such statements may seem strange and accusatory to many others" (p. 354).

The coactive approach to psychotherapy rejects objectivism in favor of a view of the therapist as one who helps the patient construct a *version* of the truth, one that will be more productive for the patient than the perspective that helps perpetuate and perhaps aggravate the patient's problems. This pragmatic orientation assumes that there is no single truth about problems and their causes but rather multiple truths or perspectives. This perspective on truth itself licenses the therapist to use language flexibly, strategically, and coactively, whether in questioning the patient or in offering interpretations of what the patient presents. Here, as in ordinary persuasive discourse, attention must be paid not just to the substantive message but to the attitudes toward the patient expressed in the therapist's metacommunications. Of crucial importance are verbal framings (and nonverbal accompaniments) that elicit cooperation, enhance self-esteem, and lead to conflict-resolving, fear-reducing, or skill-enhancing action.

Wachtel (1993) has done an admirable job of illustrating the differences in objectivist versus coactive approaches. Instead of phrasing interpretations in forms such as "You are trying to hide . . . ," "You are denying . . . ," and "You're really very . . . ," Wachtel urges "framing comments whose meta-message conveys permission for the patient to reappropriate previously warded-off feelings" (p. 73). Here are some examples:

> *You seem rather harsh with yourself when you sense any hint of sexual feeling.* [instead of "You avoid acknowledging sexual feelings."]
>
> *You seem to expect something terrible to happen to you if you have any wish to be taken care of.* [instead of "You're defending against feelings of dependency."]
>
> *I have the sense that you're angry at your mother but think it's awful of you to feel that.* [instead of "You're a lot angrier at your mother than you realize."] (p. 73)

In these examples, the therapist moves toward the patient psychologically by opening a permissive space for mutual exploration of the patient's problems. A coactive persuader, rather than an objectivist, is at work here.

Summary

The terms *framing* and *reframing* are ambiguous yet useful nonetheless. Cultures supply frames (e.g., the power of positive thinking and the need to avoid wishful thinking), people select them (being in an optimistic or pessimistic frame of mind), and texts contain them ("Think positive." "Be realistic."). In all these cases, the organizing of a perceived reality is taking place. The persuader who urges positive thinking is connecting life's dots in a particular way. The dots may include ideas about causation ("When there's a will, there's a way"), about problems ("You're too picky"), and solutions ("Always look on the bright side of life"). As Entman (1993) maintains, frames may also suggest moral evaluations ("It's unfair of you to put down my hopes and aspirations"). As addressed to a person who is routinely pessimistic, the recommendation to "chill out" is a reframe, a proposal to restructure life's dots, or, to use a different metaphor, to think outside the boxes of pessimism and despair. As in these examples, not only are "framing" and "reframing" metaphors, but also reframing is often accomplished by the use of metaphor (e.g., Schön's [1979] "paintbrush as pump").

Cultures typically offer competing frames on a controversial topic—justice versus mercy as applied to capital punishment, for example. This is a source of ambivalence or indecision for many people. Persuaders, then, have an opportunity to tilt audience opinion in one direction or the other—toward the rough justice of capital punishment or toward the tender mercy of limited incarceration.

So what difference does a frame make? It has been well documented in framing research that respondents will often prefer one framing alternative to another by wide margins, although only the language has been altered, not the actual meanings or consequences. Most impressive, perhaps, is research showing that eyewitnesses to an accident can be persuaded to conjure up memories of broken glass in a video of an accident simply by being asked, via a leading question, about the cars "smashing" into each other, rather than "hitting" each other.

Frames (and reframes) may be *substantive* or *metacommunicative*. In the latter category are two subtypes: reflexive metacommunications and responsive metacommunications. Reflexive metacommunications figure importantly in the introductions to speeches or essays where, in effect, persuaders strategically frame the substantive messages they will later be presenting.

Responsive metacommunications are of particular significance in interactive situations. Here, a communicator may "go meta" to a prior communication or to the message context, rather than staying within its frame. The notion of going meta suggests communicating not just *about* but also *above* (at a higher level), and, indeed, metamoves in political confrontations are typically a form of one-upmanship.

In psychotherapy, therapists can often defuse unnecessary anxiety in patients by offering coactive reframes rather than objectivist reframes. Instead of phrasing interpretations in forms such as "You are trying to hide . . . ," "You are denying . . . ," and "You're really very . . . ," Wachtel (1993) urges framing comments whose metamessage conveys permission for the patient to face up to previously warded-off feelings; for example, "You seem to expect something terrible to happen to you if you have any wish to be taken care of" (instead of "You're defending against feelings of dependency").

Questions and Projects for Further Study

1. Most people are unable to solve the nine-dot problem. Then, after it is explained to them, they say, "Of course! Why didn't I think of it?" How would you account for their difficulty?
2. Think about the differences between playing by the rules and playing with the rules. What examples do you come up with? Is one of these alternatives always better than the other? If not, what should be the metarule about rule-playing?
3. Provide examples of your own of metaphors and similes. Can you think of any generative metaphors?
4. Try reframing what initially seemed like a hopelessly difficult problem.
5. Provide examples of the difference between reflexive and responsive metacommunications.
6. What is "going meta"? Provide examples of your own choosing of successful metamoves.

Note

1. Cappella and Jamieson (1997) also call attention to its structural features, for example, the frame of a building.

References

Billig, M. (1987). *Arguing and thinking: A rhetorical approach to social psychology.* Cambridge, UK: Cambridge University Press.

Booth, W. (1978). Afterthoughts on metaphor: Ten literal "theses." *Critical Inquiry, 5,* 175-188.

Cappella, J., & Jamieson, K. H. (1997). *Spirals of cynicism.* New York: Oxford University Press.

Cohen, N. (1988, September 8). Meta-musings. *New Republic,* 7-8.

Cooper, L. (1932). *The rhetoric of Aristotle: An expanded translation with supplementary examples.* New York: D. Appleton Century.

Edelman, M. (1971). *Politics as symbolic action.* Chicago: Markham.

Entman, R. M. (1993). Framing: Toward clarification of a fractured paradigm. *Journal of Communication, 43,* 51-58.

Excerpts from Senate hearings on the Thomas nomination. (1991, October 13). *New York Times,* p. A30.

Gamson, W. (1992). *Talking politics.* New York: Cambridge University Press.

Gamson, W., & Modigliani, A. (1989). Media discourse and public opinion on nuclear power: A constructionist approach. *American Journal of Sociology, 95,* 1-37.

Goodman, W. (1991, October 13). Thomas' testimony: Not the usual Saturday morning fare. *New York Times,* p. A30.

Hopper, R. (1981). The taken-for-granted. *Human Communication Research, 7,* 195-211.

Kahneman, D., & Tversky, A. (1984). Choices, values, and frames. *American Psychologist, 39,* 341-350.

Lakoff, G., & Johnson, M. (1980). *Metaphors we live by.* Chicago: University of Chicago Press.

Levin, I. P., & Gaeth, G. J. (1988). How consumers are affected by the frame of attribute information before and after consuming the product. *Journal of Consumer Research, 15,* 374-378.

Loftus, E. E., & Palmer, J. C. (1974). Reconstruction of automobile destruction: An example of the interaction between language and memory. *Journal of Verbal Learning and Verbal Behavior, 13,* 585-589.

Meyerowitz, B. E., & Chaiken, S. (1987). The effects of message framing on breast self-examination attitudes, intentions, and behavior. *Journal of Personality and Social Psychology, 52,* 500-510.

Nelson, J. (1991, October 15). Democrats give little aid to Hill. *Philadelphia Inquirer,* p. A6.

Schön, D. A. (1979). Generative metaphor: A perspective on problem-setting in social policy. In A. Ortony (Ed.), *Metaphor and thought.* New York: Cambridge University Press.

Schön, D. A., & Argyris, C. (1978). *Organizational learning: A theory of action perspective.* Reading, MA: Addison-Wesley.

Thomas, C. (1991, October 12). My name has been harmed. *New York Times,* p. A10.

Wachtel, P. L. (1993). *Therapeutic communication.* New York: Guilford.

Watzlawick, P., Weakland, J., & Fisch, R. (1974). *Change: Principles of problem formation and problem resolution.* New York: Norton.

Wile, D. B. (1984). Kohut, Kernberg and accusatory interpretations: Do we have to harm clients to help them? *Psychotherapy, 21,* 353-364.

CHAPTER 7

Cognitive Shorthands

Cialdini's Seven Principles

    1. Contrast

    2. Reciprocity

    3. Consistency

    4. Social Proof

    5. Authority

    6. Liking

    7. Scarcity

Mother Turkeys or Faulty Automatic Pilots?

Summary

Questions and Projects for Further Study

References

I can admit it freely now. All my life I've been a patsy. For as long as I can recall, I've been an easy mark for the pitches of peddlers, fund raisers, and operators of one sort or another. True, only some of these people have had dishonorable motives. The others—representatives of certain charitable agencies, for instance—have had the best of intentions. No matter. With personally disquieting frequency, I have always found myself in possession of unwanted magazine subscriptions or tickets to the sanitation workers' ball.

So confides Robert B. Cialdini (1993, p. xiii), a leading social psychologist, in the introduction to his highly popular book on social influence. Readers of Cialdini's book discover that Cialdini is not alone; many suspect that they, too, are among the gullible. Cialdini compiled some powerful techniques of persuasion. But he offers two contrasting explanations for the power of these techniques, and he never reconciles them. One is that people are like mother turkeys—programmed to respond automatically to specific triggering stimuli. "Click" goes the triggering stimulus, "whirr" goes the fixed-action response. This explanation assumes that there isn't much they can do about their gullibilities.

The other explanation is that people are like fliers who have put their planes on automatic pilot at precisely those times when they need to be in direct control. Maybe the problem is with the automatic pilot device. Maybe the problem is with the information it is getting. But the important thing is that people can do something about their gullibilities. They can disengage their automatic pilots and engage in thoughtful, rather than mindless, message processing. This chapter will critically examine these rival frames. It is designed in part to illustrate how critical methods can be brought to bear on textbook persuasion, including the rhetoric of textbooks such as this one that are *about* persuasion. In the process, it will pave the way for Chapter 8 on reasoning and evidence. First, however, this chapter will survey Cialdini's compilation of influence techniques. The techniques he identifies are immensely important, especially in a message-dense society. These are among society's *cognitive shorthands;* none of us can do without them.

Cialdini's Seven Principles

Cialdini (1993) organizes his collection of influence techniques around seven principles: (1) contrast, (2) reciprocity, (3) consistency, (4) social proof, (5) authority, (6) liking, and (7) scarcity. These cognitive shorthands are especially needed when individuals haven't the inclination or wherewithal to engage in more mindful message processing.

For example, a visitor from a foreign shore decides to stop in her hotel's bar for a beer. She knows nothing about American beers, and the question of which beer to choose isn't terribly important to her. The bartender seems like a competent, friendly sort of person, so she asks him for a recommendation. Rather than indicating his personal preference, he tells her that Budweiser is the most popular beer in America. On the basis of the cognitive shorthand that "popular = good," she decides to order a Budweiser. Besides, she assumes, an authoritative, likable source wouldn't lead her astray. Let us examine Cialdini's principles more carefully.

Contrast

Contrast has to do with the sequencing of message stimuli. Just as a moderately heavy object may seem heavy after you have lifted a light one or relatively light after you have lifted a heavy one, so the order of occurrence of social stimuli can make a difference in how you perceive them. Our own mates may seem less attractive after we view exceptionally attractive models in magazine ads (Cialdini, 1993, p. 25). So, too, may photos of a possible blind date seem relatively unattractive after we see good-looking actors or actresses on a TV sitcom.

On the basis of this same "psycho-logic," clothing sales personnel are instructed to attempt to sell an expensive suit first and then offer a comparatively inexpensive item, rather than the other way around. Even a moderately priced sweater may seem affordable by comparison. Were the salesperson to sell the sweater first, the cost of the suit might well seem exorbitant (Cialdini, 1993, pp. 25-26). Similarly, real estate brokers sometimes take customers through undesirable setup properties before showing them the ones they truly intend to promote. Car dealers try to sell optional extras to the customer after the price of the car itself has been agreed to. They know that the cost of each option will seem minuscule relative to the cost of the car the customer has already agreed to buy.

Reciprocity

Persuaders can exploit our inclination to repay in kind what others have done for us. Presented by a charitable organization with an envelope containing unrequested address labels, we are more likely to send back envelopes with a donation to their cause. Want to sell a lot of raffle tickets? Cialdini (1993) reports on a suggestive experiment by Regan (1971) in which a confederate—that is, an accomplice of the experimenter—increased raffle sales to those research participants for whom he had earlier provided the unsolicited gift of a soft drink. Department stores exploit this principle by providing free samples of selected items. The Amway Corporation likewise gave potential customers an entire kit of trial items in a hand-delivered package called the "bug." The salesperson emphasized that the customers might try the trial items "for 24, 48, or 72 hours, at no cost or obligation," but the salesperson knew that precisely this pitch was likely to incur a felt obligation by the customers to buy at least some of what they had been tempted to try.

A variant of the reciprocity principle is the *rejection-then-retreat approach,* sometimes known as the *door-in-the-face* (DITF) technique. Make an extreme request of a potential donor, favor giver, or authority figure. Then, having placed the persuadee in a position where she or he is likely to turn you down, come through with a comparatively more reasonable request. This approach clearly has echoes of the contrast principle as well.

For example, a Boy Scout approaches a stranger with a request to buy some $5 tickets to a Boy Scout-sponsored circus. The customer refuses but feels guilty for turning the youngster down. The Boy Scout suggests an alternative: "If you don't want to buy any tickets, how about buying some of our big chocolate bars? They're only a dollar each."

Consistency

A key principle, consistency is the impulse to bring our beliefs, values, and attitudes into line with what we have already done or decided. For example, gamblers at a racetrack express greater confidence in their decisions after they have actually laid down their bets (Cialdini, 1993, p. 66). Contestants who bother to write "in 25 words or less" why they like Bozo Corn Chips are apt to increase their regard for the chips as a result. The impulse to consistency increases with voluntary, overt commitments—with publicly expressed decisions and with actions already taken.

Like the contrast and reciprocity principles, consistency is a useful cognitive shorthand much of the time. Certainly there is value in *appearing* consistent; we are called fickle if we change our minds too often but are thought strong-minded if we hold the line. Even unthinking consistency has its rewards, says Cialdini (1993), in that it substitutes for difficult, sometimes painful thought. "Sealed within the fortress walls of rigid consistency," he says, "we can be impervious to the sieges of reason" (p. 69).

Cialdini (1993) offers numerous examples of rigid consistency. Recruits to Transcendental Meditation, a self-help organization, began to have doubts about the organization after another visitor effectively demolished the leader's presentation at the first meeting of the group. But rather than allowing these doubts to overcome their earlier decision to join, many of the recruits decided to pay up at their first opportunity (pp. 69-71). One of the recruits explained that he hadn't intended to put down any money that evening. But when he heard the one visitor's powerful critique, he knew he had better give the organization money immediately or he would never join up (p. 71).

Consistency can build on small commitments. For instance, during the Korean War, the Chinese effectively indoctrinated some American prisoners at their "training sessions" by first having them admit publicly that "the United States is not perfect." Then the prisoner might be asked to prepare a list of problems in the United States. Later, he might be asked to read his list to other prisoners. Each step in the indoctrination process seems harmless enough on its own, but, together, these voluntary, public commitments can be powerful sources of self-persuasion (Cialdini, 1993, pp. 76-77, 82-85; Schein, 1961).

A counterpart to the door-in-the-face technique is the *foot-in-the-door* (FITD) technique. Here the persuader secures a modest commitment as a prelude to a far bigger one. Freedman and Fraser (1966) are credited with one of the most impressive demonstrations of this phenomenon. A researcher, posing as a volunteer campaigner, went door-to-door in a residential California neighborhood pleading with homeowners to accept placement on their front lawns of a rather large, public service billboard with the words "Drive Carefully" scrawled clumsily on it. Nearly all in one experimental group refused. But another group had been visited 2 weeks earlier by a different volunteer worker and had been asked to display a little 3-inch square sign saying "Be a Safe Driver." This group complied with the subsequent request by a margin of three to one.

Social Proof

Canned laughter on TV sitcoms, salted tip jars in bars, salted collection boxes in church, "everybody's doing it" appeals in ads, and product testimonials by satisfied customers—these are among the many examples Cialdini (1993) provides of *social proof,* that is, evidence that what other people think is correct. Why are people such imitators? Social proof is generally a serviceable cognitive shorthand, as the Budweiser example revealed.

But social proof also can be misleading, such as when drivers fail to go to the aid of an accident victim on the highway because no one else seems to be stopping and when, as actually happened, 38 residents of a Queens, New York, neighborhood watched a killer stalk and stab Catherine Genovese to death without so much as calling the police. Again, one possible explanation for the inaction: Nobody else seemed to be going to the woman's aid. In one experiment, a college student appearing to have an epileptic seizure received help nearly all the time when a single bystander was present but only 31% of the time when five bystanders were present (Cialdini, 1993, p. 133; Latané & Darley, 1968). The assumption that individuals make that "because nobody is concerned, nothing is wrong" is appropriately called *pluralistic ignorance.*

Imitation can also work for the social good, such as when children in a nursery school learned to overcome their fears of dogs after seeing one youngster playing happily with a dog for just 20 minutes a day (Bandura, 1973). In another experiment, film clips showing children successfully interacting with their dogs had a similar fear-reducing effect. Bandura calls this *behavioral modeling.* Consistent with the principle of social proof, it seems to be most effective when there is more than one model to imitate.

A striking example of social proof was the mass suicide at Jonestown, Guyana, at which nearly all of the 910 people who died did so in a seemingly orderly, voluntary way. No doubt one reason for their conformity was the charismatic power of the group's spiritual leader, the Reverend Jim Jones, who had urged his followers to drink a strawberry-flavored poison. But as Cialdini (1993) underscores, this incredible event could not have occurred had the group been subjected to normal social influences. A year earlier, however, the group had moved from San Francisco to the hostile environs of a jungle clearing in Guyana, far removed from any social influences but their own. In these circumstances, they could be led to choose social proof over survival.

Liking

Cialdini's (1993) first example of the principle of liking is the Tupperware party, featuring not only the Tupperware salesperson as persuader but also, and perhaps more important, as the hostess who has invited all her good friends to attend (pp. 163-166). A source of influence, then, is the party goers' *liking* for their hostess. The Tupperware party also builds on several of Cialdini's preceding principles. Everyone receives a gift from the Tupperware lady, not just those who compete successfully at party games. Thus the impulse of reciprocity is at work. All party goers are also urged to speak publicly about the virtues of the Tupperware items they already own. This creates pressures toward new purchases for the sake of consistency. Each new purchase at the party is a kind of social proof to the others present.

Authority

Expressed liking and authority can be powerful motivators. Cialdini (1993) offers the example of the physician who orders ear drops for the right ear of a patient. But rather than writing out the words "right ear," the doctor writes "place in R ear." Obediently, the duty nurse places the prescribed number of drops in the patient's anus (pp. 212-213).

Like coercion and material inducements, authority in and of itself is not persuasion. But just as there is a rhetoric of coercion and a rhetoric of inducements at a relational or image management level (see Chapter 3), so individuals are taken in by the mere trappings of authority. This indeed *is* persuasion, and Cialdini (1993) provides some outstanding examples.

Actors who *play* authorities on TV shows aren't the same authorities in real life. Yet there is carryover. For example, Robert Young, who played the role of Marcus Welby, M.D., in a TV sitcom, was perceived as a highly authoritative figure in commercials counseling against caffeine and for decaffeinated Sanka coffee (Cialdini, 1993, p. 180).

In another example, a researcher posing as a doctor was able to get 95% of regular duty nurses to comply with a phoned request to administer 20 milligrams of Astrogen to a specific ward patient. But phoned-in prescriptions were contrary to hospital policy, and Astrogen was not an authorized drug on the ward stock list. Moreover, the dosage prescribed was dangerously excessive and obviously so. Fortunately, the nurses were stopped from actually administering the drug by an observer who explained to them the nature of the experiment (Cialdini, 1993, p. 219).

Picture 7.1. "Authority" is a cognitive shorthand in a cigarette advertisement. Note how this Camels ad trades on associations between real doctors and a fictional doctor and between a fictional character and the real actor who plays him. Pavlov would be salivating if he saw this ad.

Finally, clothes, as well as titles, can make the nonauthority into an apparent authority. In one simple experiment, the same 31-year-old man jaywalked half the time in a freshly pressed business suit and half the time in a work shirt and trousers. He was followed by pedestrians against the traffic light three and a half times as often when wearing the suit (Cialdini, 1993, pp. 220-221).

The praise for Camels in the ad shown in Picture 7.1 comes not from a licensed physician but from a television actor who played the role of physician in a long-running series. He succeeded as a salesman by having taken on the trappings of authority. Lesson to be learned: Why bother with medical school?

Scarcity

"On sale for a limited time only." "Hurry, only two left in stock." In another example from Cialdini (1993), two customers are observed by a salesperson to be interested in a certain appliance item.

> I see you're interested in this model here, and I can understand why; it's a great machine at a great price. But, unfortunately, I sold it to another couple not more than twenty minutes ago. And, if I'm not mistaken, it was the last one we had. (p. 197)

The customers register dismay. Couldn't the salesperson check to be sure? one of them asks. "Well, that is possible, and I'd be willing to check," says the salesperson. "But do I understand that this is the model you want, and if I can get it for you at this price, you'll take it?" Once the scarce item has been magically "found," the principle of consistency takes over. Having committed themselves to the purchase, many customers actually buy it (Cialdini, 1993, p. 197).

Seemingly scarce items appear even more valuable if consumers believe there is competition for them. Thus, there may be a mad scramble when the department store announces a close-out sale of sports shoes. A prospective buyer may show renewed interest in a house when told by the Realtor that "a physician and his wife moving into town" are likely bidders on the house (Cialdini, 1993, p. 252). Teens may find a dance club more attractive when customers are kept waiting in line outside although there may be space inside.

Like authority, it is perceived scarcity, not real scarcity, that counts. Perceived scarcity is relative to what we have known or expect to know. Not surprisingly, the chocolate chip cookie in a jar with but two cookies is rated more attractive as a consumer item than the same cookie in a jar with nine other cookies. More interesting, when one group of research participants discovered that the number of cookies in a jar had been reduced from 10 to 2, the cookies just made "scarce" were rated more positively than when there were only two cookies in the jar all along (Cialdini, 1993, pp. 247-248). Cialdini likens this perception to the anxiety and unrest that occur during an economic downturn (pp. 248-251).

Mother Turkeys or Faulty Automatic Pilots?

The devices Cialdini (1993) identifies are powerful. They work because people rely on cognitive shorthands, which are fallible. The question, however, is whether gullible persuadees are incapable of resistance or are capable of doing something about their naïveté. An answer to that question will require further exploration of the *rhetoric* of Cialdini and some *central* message processing.

The Mother Turkey Hypothesis

Cialdini is not only an expert *on* persuasion but also an expert *at* persuasion. We should have gathered that from his opening confessional. Rather than speaking of others (his readers?) as the gullible ones, he names himself. Recall the lines: "I can admit it freely now. All my life I've been a patsy." The rhetorical technique of including himself among the foolish is called *humble irony* (Burke, 1937/1961). Its effect is to disarm the readers, creating the impression of a warm and fuzzy guy who shares the readers' vulnerabilities. The first line is an implicit invitation to his readers to let down their defenses, perhaps to look back unashamedly on those moments when they were too trusting—when they were "patsies." It's as if Cialdini were testifying at something akin to an Alcoholics Anonymous meeting. Call it "Patsies Anonymous." Appropriately disarmed, we are ready to assume the role of mother turkeys.

"Mother Turkey" may be the wrong metaphor—others could easily be substituted—but it is a metaphor for human beings as essentially and irremediably reflexive animals, responsive as persuadees to specific triggering cues in precisely the same way that the turkey responds to specific triggering cues.

> Consider the case of the mother turkey. Turkey mothers are good mothers— loving, watchful, and protective. They spend much of their time tending, warming, cleaning, and huddling the young beneath them. But there is something odd about their method. Virtually all of this mothering is triggered by one thing: the "cheep-cheep" sound of young turkey chicks. Other identifying features of the chicks, such as their smell, touch, or appearance, seem to play minor roles in the mothering process. If a chick makes the "cheep-cheep" noise, its mother will care for it; if not, the mother will ignore or sometimes kill it. (Cialdini, 1993, p. 2)

Cialdini's (1993) mother turkey may be a bit too rigid for some tastes, but the worst is yet to come. Cialdini cites a study by an animal behaviorist, appropriately named M. W. Fox, of a mother turkey's reactions to a stuffed polecat:

> For a mother turkey, a polecat is a natural enemy whose approach is to be greeted with squawking, pecking, clawing rage. Indeed, the experimenters found that even a stuffed model of a polecat, when drawn by a string toward a mother turkey, received an immediate and furious attack. When, however, the same stuffed replica carried inside it a small recorder that played the "cheep-cheep" sound of baby turkeys, the mother not only accepted the oncoming polecat but gathered it underneath her. When the machine was turned off, the polecat model again drew a vicious attack. (p. 2)

Now, the turkey seems not only rigid but downright stupid. Indeed, Cialdini (1993) likens the female turkey to an automaton whose maternal instincts are under the automatic control of that single sound (pp. 2-3). This sort of thing is not unique to the turkey, he adds. Mechanical patterns of action such as these can involve intricate sequences of behavior, such as entire courtship or mating rituals. A fundamental characteristic of these patterns is that the behaviors that compose them occur in virtually the same fashion and in the same order every time. It is almost as if the patterns were recorded on tapes within the animals. When the situation calls for courtship, the courtship tape gets played; when the situation calls for mothering, the maternal behavior tape gets played. *Click* and the appropriate tape is activated; *whirr* and out rolls the standard sequence of behaviors.

Thus far, Cialdini (1993) has been talking only about lower-order animals. Now comes the crucial linking argument to humans:

> Before we enjoy too smugly the ease with which lower animals can be tricked by trigger features into reacting in ways wholly inappropriate to the situation, we might realize . . . that we too have our preprogrammed tapes; and, although they usually work to our advantage, the trigger features that activate them can be used to dupe *us* into playing them at the wrong times. (p. 3)

A Critique of the Mother Turkey Hypothesis

Cialdini (1993) mounts some impressive evidence of human vulnerabilities. Moreover, he points out the cues that trigger our "click-whirr" responses. For example, a Canadian study found that good-looking politicians got more than two and one half times as many votes in a federal election as less attractive candidates. Yet few voters admitted to having been influenced by physical attractiveness (p. 140; Efran & Patterson, 1976, as discussed in Cialdini, 1993).

Still, Cialdini's Mother Turkey hypothesis is not completely convincing. In the final analysis, Cialdini does not seem convinced as well. His rhetorical purpose may have been to shock his readers into attention, rather than to win their literal assent. If that was his aim, it certainly was achieved.

What, then, can be said about Cialdini's Mother Turkey hypothesis? Four aspects are open to criticism. First, some of the principles Cialdini identifies are stated vaguely; in so doing, he obscures important differences in the phenomena he groups together.

Second, tensions or inconsistencies exist between principles, suggesting that the task of the persuader is far more complex than Cialdini would have his readers believe.

Third, although Cialdini likens the triggers that activate humans to the concrete stimuli that produce click-whirr responses in lower-order animals, the human activators he identifies are stated fairly generally. If there are equivalent activators of human influence, Cialdini doesn't name them.

Finally, as Cialdini himself emphasizes in subsequent chapters, persuadees can learn to say "no" to persuaders. No lower-order animal can make that statement. This, then, is the key point, for it provides the basis for an alternative to the Mother Turkey metaphor.

Concealed Differences

The principle causing the biggest problem on this account is consistency. Cialdini treats it as an impulse to bring beliefs, values, or attitudes into line with one's commitments, especially one's expressed, public commitments. Fishbein and Ajzen (1975) group this type of reasoning under the heading of *evaluational consistency.* The key ingredient here is alignment of desires. If we've bet on a horse to win, we want to believe that it will win. If we value our lives, we want to believe that we will be immortal. Cialdini provides a perfect example of evaluational consistency in the case of the recruits to Transcendental Meditation who preferred to put up their money rather than be overcome by doubts. Examples such as this one make us seem silly indeed.

Another broad class of consistencies that is the essence of good reasoning and the enemy of blind, evaluational consistency is called *belief consistency* (Fishbein & Ajzen, 1975). It is manifested, for example, when we reason correctly from premises to conclusions, from facts to empirical generalizations, and from beliefs and values to attitudes (see Chapter 2).

Tensions Between Principles

Each of Cialdini's principles seems to stand nicely on its own, and sometimes they combine powerfully, as in the Tupperware example—but not always. Recall the research on behavioral modeling in which young children's inappropriate fears were overcome by what Cialdini calls social proof. Conceivably, that "proof" could have come from an authority figure, such as a teacher, or from someone who was better liked but less respected, such as another child. In the two research studies cited, successful persuasion resulted from using child models, but sometimes authority figures are more persuasive, for example, when questions of fact are in dispute.

Rarely is one approach to persuasion superior to a comparable alternative in all circumstances. Instead, multiple research studies are needed to derive *contingent generalizations.* A contingent generalization is one that states the conditions under which one approach is likely to be superior to its alternatives. All other things being equal, for example, a similar and presumably more likeable source should be more persuasive than a dissimilar and presumably more expert source *when the facts are not at issue.* But the reverse should be the case, for example, when someone is uncertain of the best way to treat a newly acquired medical problem (Norman, 1976).

Consider in this context two persuasive devices discussed by Cialdini: the door-in-the-face (DITF) technique (discussed under the heading of reciprocity) and the foot-in-the-door (FITD) technique (discussed under the heading of consistency). As O'Keefe (1990) points out, "The door-in-the-face strategy turns the foot-in-the-door strategy on its head" (p. 171). At no point, however, does Cialdini compare the two to tell us under what conditions one is likely to be more effective than another. But others have, and the research findings are complex. For example, a delay between initial and subsequent request seems to markedly lessen the effects of DITF but not FITD. Persuasion researchers still aren't sure why (O'Keefe, 1990, pp. 171-174).

Unidentified triggers

Are humans really like mother turkeys? Cialdini seems to say so but identifies nothing quite comparable to the "cheep-cheep" sound of the turkey chick or the rage-inspiring shape of the approaching polecat in his descriptions of human influence processes. The closest he comes to it is in an anecdotal report of a jewelry sale somewhere in Arizona.

It seems that the proprietor of an Indian jewelry store was having immense difficulty selling a certain allotment of turquoise jewelry to her tourist clients. Exasperated, she scribbled a note to her head saleswoman before leaving town, "Everything in the display case, price × ½." When she returned, she discovered that everything had been sold—and at twice the price, rather than half the price. The head saleswoman had misread her scribbled note, marking *up* all the items by a factor of two.

Why had the customers purchased the marked-up jewelry? Cialdini (1993) explains as follows:

> The customers, mostly well-to-do vacationers with little knowledge of turquoise, were using a standard principle—a stereotype—to guide their buying: "expensive = good." Thus, the vacationers, who wanted "good" jewelry, saw the turquoise pieces as decidedly more valuable and desirable when nothing about them was enhanced but the price. Price alone had become a trigger feature for quality; and a dramatic increase in price alone had led to a dramatic increase in sales among the quality-hungry buyers. *Click, whirr!* (p. 19)

The first thing to notice about this example is the identified *contingencies* of persuasion. These weren't *any* message recipients; they were well-to-do vacationers. This wasn't *any* product; it was difficult-to-assess Indian turquoise. Presumably, the trigger "expensive = good" would not have worked on other customers buying other items. Presumably, too, there was no Indian jewelry store nearby at which to do comparison shopping.

But more to the point, is "expensive = good" really comparable with the "cheep-cheep" of a turkey chick? Probably not. Consider whether even these well-to-do vacationers would have applied the same click-whirr principle had the items been marked up by a factor of 20, rather than 2. Even among consumers brought up to believe that "you get what you pay for," is there not a countervailing impulse to avoid getting ripped off?

The key observation here is made by Michael Billig (1987), who maintains that consumers tend to position their decisions between opposed or nearly opposed frames such as "you get what you pay for" and "value for the money." These "triggers," moreover, are more like general guidelines than concrete "cheep-cheeps;" they are invoked as the situation demands.

Saying "No"

Cialdini (1993) emphasizes at various points how we can choose to say "no" to compliance seekers who would subvert our cognitive shorthands. His advice is instructive, although blatantly inconsistent with his Mother Turkey hypothesis. For example, if we have determined that a compliance professional's gift or concession was a tactic rather than a genuine favor, "we need only react to it accordingly to be free of its influence" (p. 63). If we realize "in the pit of our stomachs" that we have been trapped into complying with a request that we have no wish to perform, we can turn tables on the influence-seekers, explaining to them exactly how we think they've been manipulating us (pp. 108-111). If we "feel in our hearts" that we've been foolishly consistent, then we can learn to trust those feelings and stop being foolish (pp. 112-114). If we have reason to suspect that social evidence has been purposely falsified, as in the case of canned laughter tracks on a TV comedy, we can make conscious decisions not to be influenced by it.

Sounds simple, doesn't it? Indeed, if our stomachs, our hearts, and our reason have all been working for us, how turkeylike could our responses have been in the first place?

An Alternative Hypothesis: The Faulty Automatic Pilot

Midway through his book, Cialdini (1993) provides a perfect example of reframing. Without, unfortunately, abandoning his Mother Turkey metaphor, he interposes another metaphor, that of the flier running on faulty automatic pilot. This device, he says, does some wonderful work. "With it we can cruise confidently through a myriad of decisions without personally having to investigate the detailed pros and cons of each" (p. 155).

But there are occasional problems with automatic pilots:

> These problems appear whenever the flight information locked into the control mechanism is wrong. In these instances, we will be taken off course. Depending upon the size of the error, the consequences can be severe. But, because the automatic pilot . . . is more often an ally than an enemy, we can't be expected to want simply to disconnect it. Thus we are faced with a classic problem: how to make use of a piece of equipment that simultaneously benefits and imperils our welfare.
>
> Fortunately, there is a way out of the dilemma. Because the disadvantages of automatic pilots arise principally when incorrect data have been put into the control system, our best defense against these disadvantages is to recognize when the data are in error. If we can become sensitive to situations where the automatic pilot is working with inaccurate information, we can disengage the mechanism and grasp the controls when we need to. (pp. 155-156)

Now Cialdini has found an appropriate metaphor. Never mind that he doesn't say how to recognize *when* the data are in error or what to do should we suspect that the machine itself is defective.

But notice the differences between the mother turkey and the automatic pilot. Both operate automatically, but the automatic pilot operates only insofar as we choose, and the mother turkey has no choice in the matter. We control the automatic pilot even as we allow the automatic pilot to control the movement of our airplane. Moreover, automatic pilots have sophisticated sensing and error-correcting devices;

they are not likely to confuse an airstrip with a shiny roof. Just in case, we can check our automatic pilots against our manual controls. We can look out the windows of our mental cockpits to see if we're taking an intellectual nosedive. Unlike the mother turkey, we can generally bring multiple sensing and error-correcting devices to bear on a given situation. We can read and interpret these multiple cues, rather than merely reacting to them reflexively. We can, for example, let belief consistency serve as a corrective to evaluative consistency and can have tests of the expertise and trustworthiness of authority figures serve as a corrective to the mere trappings of authority.

The Highly Persuasible Persuadee

Nothing that has been said by way of criticism of the Mother Turkey metaphor negates Cialdini's (1993) central point about the widespread use of cognitive shorthands. To paraphrase Abraham Lincoln, you can persuade nearly all the people some of the time, and you can persuade some of them nearly all the time. Cialdini's numerous examples of persuadees flying dangerously on faulty automatic pilots fit nicely with Petty and Cacioppo's (1981/1996) elaboration of likelihood model with its distinction between central and peripheral processing. Some people apparently have great difficulty defending against the seductive appeals of professional persuaders.

Children, persons who are old, recent immigrants, and persons with little education or low intelligence are especially vulnerable to advertising messages (Schudson, 1984). People with low self-esteem and low to moderate intelligence tend to be relatively easy marks for these messages, particularly if they are kept simple enough for them to understand (McGuire, 1985; Stiff, 1994). Insecurities about social status make some persuadees highly receptive to snob appeals for upscale brand names, particularly if these appeals are coupled with reminders of social shame (Messaris, 1997). An inability to process complex messages thoughtfully leads many people to engage in peripheral processing, as discussed in Chapter 2. Stereotypical thinking is yet another way of flying on automatic pilot. Rather than judging a complex case on its merits, jurors unable to follow its technical details are apt to let oversimplified schemas do their thinking for them. This defendant has an innocent face; that one looks like the type of person who should be behind bars.

Yet peripheral processing, including reliance on cognitive shorthands, is impossible to avoid in today's fast-paced, message-dense society. All of us do it when the stakes are low, and many of us rely on cognitive shorthands even when the stakes are high. Following are examples of sales techniques that engaged customers' automatic pilots.

Get-Rich Scheme

Literally hundreds of venture capitalists, officers and directors of charitable institutions, and prominent civic leaders entrusted large sums of money—in some cases millions of dollars—to the Foundation for New Era Philanthropy, falling prey to "a phony, primitive get-rich scheme" by its founder, John G. Bennett, Jr., that promised a 6 months' return of two dollars for every dollar they entrusted to the foundation (Arensen, 1995, p. E4). The story vividly illustrates how even the rhetorically sophisticated can be prompted to fly dangerously on automatic pilot. Seven explanations for their gullibility repeatedly came up in interviews with those taken in by Bennett (Arensen, 1995; Dobrin, Sataline, & Ferrick, 1995).

> *Wanting to Believe.* Many of the charitable institutions and civic organizations that succumbed to the appeal of the now bankrupt and defunct foundation were desperate for money. They were facing declines in government and corporate giving and increased competition for fewer dollars. "Not having government funding, there's more pressure on the boards to create more dollars, bigger investments," said the president of the Philadelphia Chamber of Commerce (Dobrin et al., 1995, p. A18).

> *Leader's Credibility.* There was Bennett himself, a supreme salesman—a man, his friends say, of great decency, a born-again Christian who has spent his adult life helping others: first as a drug-abuse counselor and administrator; later as a man who trained nonprofits to obtain money from foundations; finally, as head of his own foundation (Dobrin et al., 1995, p. A18).

> *Endorsements.* Respondents testified to the importance of endorsements from intermediaries who had the trust of the financial, religious, and civic communities that invested with Bennett's foundation. The *New York Times* account echoed Cialdini; the donors were busy people; as such, they looked for shortcuts. What better way than to turn to their friends for advice? (Arensen, 1995)

> *Document's Attractiveness.* The 30-page document explaining the "get-richer" scheme had the look of believability. It was enclosed in a white binder bearing the foundation's logo—a woodcut of a farmer sowing seeds under a glorious sun. "Sowing the seed God gives us today cultivates excellence tomorrow" was its motto.

> *Glow of Backers' Anonymity.* Basically, the document promised that investments would be matched in 6 months by a network of esteemed, extremely wealthy givers who insisted on remaining anonymous. For

some message recipients, the cloak of anonymity raised problems, but for those who succumbed, it was often a major selling point, suggesting that the foundation's chief backers were especially worthy because they were not in it for self-interest and publicity. Some givers assumed that they knew who these behind-the-scenes backers were. It turned out that they did not exist.

➤ *Scarcity.* Not every nonprofit was eligible to invest with New Era, the document said. It had to meet rigorous criteria. It had to be willing to invest at least $50,000. It had to be screened and sponsored. It had to be one of the select few.

➤ *Commitment.* Giving was dissonant with continued doubt; hence, one way of relieving the dissonance was to suppress the doubt. As one investor put it, "By the time you get your hook in your mouth, you're saying, Hey, another $100,000? Sure!" (Dobrin et al., 1995, p. A18)

Telephone System Anyone?

Yet another example of smart people succumbing to appeals that activated cognitive shorthands is provided by Lexis, whose lessons in persuasion as a Techno, Inc. sales trainee were briefly described in Chapter 5. Lexis's account team sold expensive, highly sophisticated telephone systems, ranging in price from $250,000 to $25,000,000 and consisting primarily of a large computer that ran the system (housed off-site) and telephones. Said Lexis, "These phones were cool, with lots of buttons, a display screen to tell you who was calling, and customized features. The customer's generic black dial paled in comparison."

Techno, Inc. managed these sales by first securing modest commitments from customers, then encouraging them to take the big plunge. It was a textbook case of the foot-in-the-door technique.

Very early in the sales cycle, we would ask the customers if they would like to have one of these slick, executive-looking phones on their desks in nonoperational form, just to see how they looked and felt. A few weeks passed, and with their curiosity piqued as to how these phones actually worked, we explained that for a nominal fee, we could temporarily activate these phones so they could receive incoming calls, see who was calling them, and get to "play" with the other neat features. We even offered to customize the phone by putting their name and number on the display screen. By asking the customer to spend small amounts of money from the beginning, we laid the groundwork for getting the customer to spend greater and greater sums of money.

Once we had the customer in the groove of spending money with us, a letter of intent was the only thing left on the path to a signed contract. The letter of intent, which did no more than state the customer's intention to purchase, was rarely legally binding, and most customers knew this, yet it was very effective, ultimately resulting in signed contracts. Techno had such success and confidence with the technique that in many cases computers, telephone systems, etc. were ordered and books balanced based solely on the customer's signed letter of intent.[1]

Summary

The alternative to mindful processing, according to Cialdini, involves reliance on a variety of external cues and automatic, information-processing mechanisms, including the none-too-reliable filter of evaluational consistency. Cialdini organizes these mental shorthands under seven principles: contrast, reciprocity, consistency, social proof, liking, authority, and scarcity.

These frequently operate in tandem, as in the example of the Tupperware party. To take another example, suppose that your neighbors takes exception to your habitually parking your car in front of their house. You could, of course, try reasoning with them: You prefer to park in front of your house, but your housemates always seem to get there first. This argument metacommunicates caring, which should at least make you appear more likable to your neighbors, even if it isn't entirely convincing. Perhaps, too, you could elicit from your neighbors an expression of sympathy for your plight, and you could then exploit their self-professed caring by appealing to the principle of consistency. Also, you could, without being asked, shovel the snow off their sidewalk; that would incur a reciprocal obligation. You could inform them that there's nothing illegal about what you've been doing; you have it on the highest authority. You could point out that the practice of parking in front of other people's houses is common on your street—thus invoking the principle of social proof. You could, if worst came to worst, try the rejection-then-retreat approach. You are thinking about buying a motorcycle and keeping it in front of their house along with the car. Would they object? Yes? Well, all right then, you'll stick with the car. By contrast, this smaller violation may actually appear reasonable.

Cialdini's seven principles are by no means original with him. But this chapter has focused on his compilation of them for several reasons. First, because of his rich and varied examples from the field, Cialdini shows that these mental shorthands are used by real people in everyday situations, and not just in contrived experiments. Second, Cialdini is an uncommonly adept persuader in addition to being expert on persuasion; his writings are examined as an example of textbook rhetoric.

But most important, Cialdini provides dramatic illustration of the difference a frame makes. Humans as mother turkeys? We might as well resign ourselves to our gullibilities. Human beings as "turner-oners" and "turner-offers" of our automatic pilots? This gives us real reason to hope. Cialdini gives us both metaphors but never reconciles them.

There is more hope for persuadees than Cialdini's book suggests. Although we cannot and should not abandon our mental shorthands, we can learn to process messages critically when it is truly important for us to do so, and we can make it a habit to check out our automatic pilots on a regular basis. By the same token, persuaders cannot always count on winning over audiences by appeal to cognitive shorthands. In some circumstances, they must truly reason with audiences, and when they do, the quality of their arguments often makes a difference.

Questions and Projects for Further Study

1. This chapter has argued that Cialdini uses techniques of persuasion in the very process of writing about persuasion. Can the same be said of the writing in this book?
2. What did you think of the critique of Cialdini's Mother Turkey hypothesis? What might you say in Cialdini's defense?
3. Interview people who make a living as persuasion professionals. Ask them to reveal to you some of their tricks of the trade. Mention principles identified by Cialdini. See if they ring true to the people you interview. Summarize the results of your interview survey in a 3- to 4-page report.
4. How have you used or been influenced by the seven principles Cialdini discusses? Think about jobs you've had, relationships you've been in, or shopping you've done. Summarize your reflections in a 3- to 4-page report.

Note

1. Used with permission of the student.

References

Arensen, K. W. (1995, May 21). Embarrassing the rich. *New York Times,* p. E4.
Bandura, A. (1973). *Aggression: A social learning analysis.* Englewood Cliffs, NJ: Prentice Hall.

Billig, M. (1987). *Arguing and thinking.* Cambridge, UK: Cambridge University Press.

Burke, K. (1961). *Attitudes toward history.* Boston: Beacon. (Original work published 1937)

Cialdini, R. B. (1993). *Influence: Science and practice* (3rd ed.). New York: Harper-Collins.

Dobrin, P., Sataline, S., & Ferrick, T., Jr. (1995, May 21). New Era played on dire need for cash, and nonprofits swallowed their doubts. *Philadelphia Inquirer,* pp. A1, A18.

Efran, M. G., & Patterson, L. R. (1976). *The politics of appearance.* Unpublished study, cited in Cialdini (1993).

Fishbein, M., & Ajzen, I. (1975). *Belief, attitude, intention, and behavior.* Reading, MA: Addison-Wesley.

Freedman, J. L., & Fraser, S. C. (1966). Compliance without pressure: The foot-in-the-door technique. *Journal of Personality and Social Psychology, 4,* 195-203.

Latané, B., & Darley, J. M. (1968). *The unresponsive bystander: Why doesn't he help?* New York: Appleton-Century-Crofts.

McGuire, W. J. (1985). Attitudes and attitude change. In G. Lindzey & E. Aronson (Eds.), *Handbook of social psychology* (3rd ed., Vol. 2, pp. 233-346). New York: Random House.

Messaris, P. (1997). *Visual persuasion.* Thousand Oaks, CA: Sage.

Norman, R. (1976). When what is said is important: A comparison of expert and attractive sources. *Journal of Experimental Social Psychology, 12,* 294-300.

O'Keefe, D. J. (1990). *Persuasion: Theory and research.* Newbury Park, CA: Sage.

Petty, R. E., & Cacioppo, J. T. (1996). *Attitudes and persuasion: Classic and contemporary approaches.* Boulder, CO: Westview. (Original work published 1981)

Regan, R. T. (1971). Effects of a favor and liking on compliance. *Journal of Experimental Social Psychology, 7,* 627-639.

Schein, E. (1961). *Coercive persuasion.* New York: Norton.

Schudson, M. (1984). *Advertising: The dubious persuasion.* New York: Basic Books.

Stiff, J. B. (1994). *Persuasive communication.* New York: Guilford.

Reasoning and Evidence

In 1993, Congress signed into law the Brady bill, named in honor of James Brady, former press secretary to President Ronald Reagan, who was shot and seriously wounded by John Hinckley, Reagan's would-be assassin. Passage of the Brady bill took a dozen years (see Picture 8.1), during which time advocates of stricter gun regulation had to overcome strong resistance from the National Rifle Association (NRA). Jim Brady's wife, Sarah, served as a spokesperson for the gun control movement. In 1986, she wrote an article for *Glamour* describing their ordeal.[1]

> On the morning of January 2, 1981, my husband Jim Brady received a call from President-elect Reagan, asking him to be his press secretary. It was a dream come true for Jim—the culmination of many years of hard work in politics.

Picture 8.1. Jim and Sarah Brady at 1996 Democratic National Convention
SOURCE: C-SPAN archives. Used with permission.

The next two and one-half months whizzed by. There was the excitement of the inaugural, Jim's nightly appearances on network news, the flurry of parties following his long hours at the White House. We never expected it to end so abruptly.

On the morning of March 30, 1981, as Jim was about to leave for work, he decided to go upstairs and wake our two-year old son, Scott. It was to be the last time he would climb those stairs to Scott's bedroom. At 2:30 that afternoon, Jim was shot through the head by John Hinckley. Jim nearly died. The President and two of his security men also were seriously wounded.

Five years later, I still wonder how the John Hinckleys of the world can go into a store, buy a handgun—no questions asked—and shoot people because they hear voices or have strange visions. (pp. 96-97)

Sarah Brady's story contains the rudiments of an argument—about the insanity of allowing the John Hinckleys of the world to purchase handguns—backed up by a piece of evidence, the Hinckley case itself. By strict standards of logic, however, this story is insignificant, because it is about an isolated case, an "*n* of 1," as they say in statistics texts. Clearly, Sarah Brady will need a lot more evidence before she is through making her case.

This chapter connects the principles of reasoning and evidence to the larger tasks of preparing a persuasive case (in the role of a persuader) and of evaluating a persuasive case (in the role of a message recipient). These tasks require balancing the standards of sound reasoning and credible evidence against the realization that persuasion typically takes place under conditions that are less than ideal for reflective argumentative exchange (van Eemeren, Grootendorst, Jackson, & Jacobs, 1993). These conditions include those in which committed, sometimes passionate communicators, operating under time constraints, must adapt their arguments to audiences with limited information on topics that are likely to arouse audience passions and prejudices as well. Accordingly, like Sarah Brady, persuaders cannot always be expected to win belief by logic alone.

Sarah Brady's (1986) story does pack a wallop. Its narrative details—of the parties, of the network news appearances, of Jim Brady's impulsive farewell to his son on the morning before he was shot—are not logically essential to her case for gun regulation, but they give the reader a *feeling* for what the shooting of her husband meant in lived experience. The opening to Sarah Brady's article also contributes greatly to her *ethos;* it literally *authorizes* her to speak as someone who has experienced the tragic consequences of unregulated handgun ownership firsthand. Brady couples this story with another, about a visit to Centralia, Illinois, Jim's hometown.

> A friend invited Scott, then six years old, and me for a ride in his pickup truck. We got in. Scott picked up what looked like a toy pistol and pointed it toward himself. I said, "Scott, don't ever point a gun at anyone, even if it's only a toy." Then, to my horror, I realized it was no toy. It was a fully-loaded handgun that our friend kept on the seat of his truck for "safety" reasons. I wondered how many other careless adults left handguns lying around for children to pick up. My mind went back to the day Jim was shot, then to the day one of my best friends was murdered—with a handgun—by her enraged boyfriend. I decided I had to do more than think about handgun violence—I had to do something to try to stop it. (pp. 96-97)

The tales about the loaded gun and about the killing of one of Sarah Brady's best friends are almost as powerful as the story about Jim Brady. If anything, they establish Sarah Brady as more similar to her readers and less remote from them than does the Jim Brady story. Together, the vignettes about her life give Sarah the image of being a *superrepresentative* of her audience. Lest there be any doubt about her credibility, she adds that she is a Republican and a conservative—not some wild-eyed liberal who wants to ban or confiscate guns and further restrict use of hunting rifles. Sarah Brady takes pains to emphasize that she is not in that camp:

> What I am for is finding a way to keep handguns out of the wrong hands—the hands of the mentally incompetent; small children; drunks, drug users and criminals; and the person who, on the spur of the moment, decides that he wants to purchase a handgun to "settle" an argument. (pp. 96-97)

She also employs *enthymematic* arguments in her article. An *enthymeme* invites the reader to supply and endorse premises that are missing from the argument but left implicit. It is a *truncated* argument that rests on a premise or premises it assumes its audience will accept. Virtually all persuasive discourse is enthymematic, as Aristotle observed long ago.

Most conspicuous in the opening story is the premise that the near killing of the president's press secretary (let alone, of the president) is a bad thing. But numerous other enthymematic premises are embedded in the narrative that derive from our culture. Indeed, Brady is giving back to us our own traditional image of the American dream: of Jim Brady's deserved rise to the top on the basis of hard work; of the call from Mr. Big; of glamorous parties mixed with more hard work; of little Scott fast asleep in an upstairs bedroom; of Mrs. Brady standing up for her beliefs.

Despite the combined power of Sarah Kemp Brady's stories, they still tell us about only three cases, and they offer little insight about what gun regulation would actually accomplish. General claims, such as those made by Brady for gun regulation, are most likely to be believed when they are bolstered by a variety of arguments.

Propositions of Policy, Fact, and Value

Brady's proposal for gun regulation is an example of what argumentation theorists call a *proposition of policy*—a controversial recommendation for action of some sort, to be taken in the future. As with any proposition of policy, certain recurring questions, called *stock issues,* are logically relevant to the decision on gun regulation:

1. Is there a *need* for a change—that is, is there a problem or deficiency of some type in the present way of thinking or of doing things? Persuaders often identify several problems with the current system, rather than focusing on any one of them. Thus, Brady could have dealt separately with the problems of gun availability to drunks, drug users, and criminals, in addition to children and the mentally incompetent.

2. Is the proposed policy *workable?* In theory, at least, should it remedy the problem or deficiency? Does the plan meet the need?

3. Is the proposed policy *practical?* Are the means (money, enforcement machinery, etc.) available for bringing about the change?

4. Is the proposed policy reasonably *free from greater evils,* or is the cure worse than the disease?

5. Is the proposed solution the *best available* solution?

In the limited space that she has available, Brady chooses to focus on the need for a change, on workability, and especially on the issue of greater evils. This last issue is crucial because as she points out in her article, the gun lobby, led by the NRA, had been arguing that "there is no middle ground on handguns in America." Note how Brady turns the gun lobby's arguments against them:

The gun lobby uses scare tactics to play on the fears of women, attempting to make them believe that any gun control laws will make them defenseless. The NRA, for example, produced a brochure to "educate" women on the effectiveness of handguns for self-defense. Black with spatters of red blood, the brochure's cover read: "Tell them what rape is. Be graphic. Be disgusting. Be obscene. Make them sick. If they throw up, then they have the tiniest idea of what it is!"

Women, understandably, feel vulnerable to acts of violence, and the gun lobby takes advantage of these fears in an attempt to increase sales and expand the handgun market. (pp. 96-97)

In addition to putting forth a variety of arguments, the persuader should—if time and space permit—use a variety of evidence. For example, statistics are a nice complement to extended narratives. Brady attempts to show that a handgun kept for self-defense is more likely to hurt or kill a family member than an intruder.

Data collected by Handgun Control, Inc., a pro-control lobbying group, shows that twelve hundred people are killed in handgun accidents each year—as compared to two hundred intruders who are killed by handguns kept for self-defense. And my son's experience with a loaded "toy gun" is repeated hundreds of times each year. On the average, one child a day is killed in a handgun accident—most because they found a loaded handgun carelessly left lying around the house. In addition, according to the Centers for Disease Control, approximately 52 percent of the fifteen-to-twenty-four year old females committing suicide in 1980 used handguns. That represents a sizeable increase from the approximately 32 percent who shot themselves to death in 1970. (pp. 96-97)

Although these data on the dangers of handgun-related accidental deaths and suicides are impressive, they are by no means the last word on the subject. Nor is Brady's take on the NRA pamphlet the only take. Nor, for that matter, is her handling of the other stock issues for a policy proposition irrefutable. The NRA can make a good case that Brady goes too far and that legal restrictions affect only the law-abiding, while others think that the Brady Bill didn't go far enough. At last report, there were more than 60 million gun owners in the United States, with about 35 million owning handguns, according to the NRA-Institute for Legislative Action (www.nraila.org/). The Brady bill is expected to lead to a modest reduction in gun-related deaths. Thus, on a great many issues, including gun control, there may be no demonstrable best solution.

This is another way of saying what was said earlier: Persuasion deals in matters of judgment, rather than certainty. Under the circumstances, it makes little sense to speak of the persuader as proving a case beyond the shadow of a doubt. What constitutes "proof" varies from situation to situation and from audience to audience. Similarly, it makes little sense to think of persuasive arguments as definitive or compelling, or as weapons with which to demolish an adversary.

This, however, is not an invitation to impulsive or random decision making or to perpetual indecision. Indeed, for the persuader, careful inquiry should precede impassioned advocacy. Before you promote ideas to others, you should ask yourself whether the position you are about to endorse is one you truly believe. Check your basic assumptions. Ask yourself whether you have been treating assumptions as facts, ignoring counterarguments, or perhaps trusting too much in the opinions of others without thinking things through yourself. The process of inquiry may lead you to abandon your initially held convictions, or it may strengthen them. It should lead in either case to a more sophisticated sense of the issues at hand and to a position reflecting the topic's complexities. Once persuadees become satisfied that your position, although not without flaws, is "least worst" among the alternatives available, they should become its impassioned advocate.

As a message recipient, you should practice what might be called an art of mistrust. Question the persuader's premises, either verbally or to yourself. Question the links the persuader makes between premises and conclusions and between evidence and generalization, the choice and treatment of language, and claims to authority or expertise. But having practiced the art of mistrust, don't be afraid to commit to the persuader's position, for he or she will have earned your assent.

The Brady proposal, as noted, was a proposition of policy. It suggests that a message recipient should (or should not) engage in some action or be in favor of (or opposed to) some action. Policy propositions may be quite general ("The government should do more to stop ozone pollution") or quite specific ("City Council should pass Bill 239765 to further regulate industrial waste disposal"); positive ("Buy American") or negative ("Let's not let patriotism determine purchases"); important

("Please marry me") or relatively unimportant ("Let's serve duck, not chicken"); and explicit ("Don't go to school at Old Ivy U.") or implicit ("Do you really want to go to a snob-ridden school?").

A proposition is debatable in the sense that there is room for argument about it. *Argument* involves staking out and supporting a claim that is not already known or agreed on. On the one hand, as Brockriede (1990) suggests, argument involves the region of uncertainty: "If certainty existed, people need not engage in what I am defining as argument" (p. 7). On the other hand, suggests Brockriede, "An arguer must perceive some rationale that establishes that the claim leaped to is worthy of at least being entertained" (p. 6). A claim, then, is not truly debatable unless some rationale exists for its support.

Changing, Repairing, or Retaining a Policy: The Stock Issues Revisited

Stock issues (recurring questions), discussed briefly in connection with the Brady example, are systematized common sense. Generally speaking, people assume the desirability of existing policies, practices, systems, and the like *unless the need for a change has been conceded or demonstrated.* This is the first of the stock issues relevant to policy changes. Car owners do not change their cars unless they perceive something wrong with the old car. Physicians do not operate unless they perceive something defective about one of the systems (e.g., respiratory, circulatory) that keep the patient going. In the same way, most people would not endorse basic changes in welfare laws unless they believed there was something seriously wrong with those laws. Existing policies are presumed "innocent" until proved "guilty."

The second commonsense assumption is that the *solution would fit the need or problem.* This is the stock issue of *workability.* Rather than buying a new car when the old one gets a flat tire, a car owner is more likely to repair or replace the flat tire. Rather than operating, physicians prescribe medication to heal a minor respiratory problem. Rather than getting rid of welfare policies on grounds that they are inefficiently administered, lawmakers are likely to prefer keeping the policies but getting rid of the inefficiencies. In the jargon of argumentation theory, persons may opt for *repair* of a policy or system or thing rather than outright *change.*

This being said, a proposed policy or solution should not, if possible, fall short of the need. If an old car is wrecked beyond repair, its owner will feel compelled to get a new one. If medication will not suffice, the physician may decide to operate. If inefficient administration is *inherent* in the present welfare policy—that is, if, whenever and wherever it is administered, problems of inefficiency seem to recur—lawmakers may feel obliged to support a new policy.

The third commonsense assumption is that *compared with other possible policies, the proposed policy must offer the most advantages and the fewest disadvantages.* A brand-new Lexus might handily satisfy a driver's needs, but its costs may render it impractical. An operation might be successful but create new problems for the patient. A new welfare policy might be desirable, but it may not be as workable or as practical as other possible plans being considered. Often, when the need for a change is conceded or when persuaders are reasonably assured that their audiences share their goals, an entire speech or essay may be structured around *comparative advantages.* The persuader's obligations are met by showing that the proposed plan (a) is an improvement on the present system and (b) can be favorably compared with other alternatives. This conversation between two college roommates, Lucas and George, focuses on the first task (Warnick & Inch, 1994).

> Lucas: I think it is time to move off-campus. I hate living in the dorms and I hate eating cafeteria food. In general, I hate living on campus. So many freshmen, so much noise.
>
> George: Yes, but living on campus has many benefits. If we move into an apartment, who will cook our meals? Who will clean the bathroom? Who will we socialize with? It seems to me that what we are doing now is the best alternative.
>
> Lucas: You're wrong. Look at it this way—if we move off campus, we will save a lot of money. In fact, I figure that our housing cost will drop by about a third. Besides, the freedom to come and go without worrying about dorm rules and regulations far outweigh any reason to stay in the dorms. Besides, I like the idea of just having time to stay away from campus and relax.
>
> George: Well, I hadn't thought of it like that. I especially hadn't thought about the cost savings, and I expect that between you and me, we can cook better than the cafeteria. Let's move! (p. 250)

If, as a persuader, you believe that an existing policy or system should be *retained* more or less as is, your first obligation is to refute objections to the present way of doing things. George does this (but then falls for Lucas's argument). Proponents of change, such as prosecutors in a law court, have the burden of demonstrating that something is seriously wrong with the system or policy. This is called the *burden of proof.* You, as a defender of the status quo, have a lesser obligation, called the *burden of refutation.* You may choose to go on the offensive, however, showing how the system being attacked by others actually does its job quite well. You also may argue that the changes being proposed by others would not solve existing problems nearly as well, or that proposals for change would introduce new and greater evils. Insofar as you make positive assertions ("The existing welfare system is doing just fine") rather than merely challenging the claims made by proponents for change or major repair

("Where's their evidence that the current welfare system is inherently inefficient?"), you, too, take on a burden of proof.

Although there is a commonsense logic to the assumptions behind stock issues for a proposition of policy, the way people apply these assumptions often reveals their irrationality. In the first place, the conditions labeled as problems or nonproblems are often branded as such on highly questionable grounds. As a result of the auto manufacturers' careful indoctrination programs, a current automobile can constitute "a problem" simply by being 2 years old. In the absence of substantive information for choosing among headache pills, mouthwashes, or premium beers, the advertiser may promote a product, and consumers may buy it, on the basis of snob appeal, color preference, or because it's "lighter."

Not uncommonly, the solutions we concoct for remedying a problem turn out to have been inappropriate or worse. One common difficulty is balancing workability and practicality. What is most workable in theory may be least doable in practice. Often, we are faced with the choice of seeking to eliminate the causes of a problem or trying to contain its ill effects. That choice is difficult enough, but it is often compounded by the rhetoric of such debates. Effects-oriented advocates label cause-oriented reformers as dreamers or utopians and label themselves as pragmatists; cause-oriented reformers respond that trying to control symptoms or effects of a problem is a bit like putting a Band-aid on a gushing wound or using a pain reliever to get rid of an infection.

Actions aimed at the effects of a problem may be not only more practical but also more workable in the long run. Often (although not always), it is fruitless to try to eliminate causes. They are obscure, they are hopelessly entwined, or there are simply too many of them. Moreover, getting at a bad effect need not be a mere Band-aid. Hunger, unemployment, lack of education, and so on are parts of a system. Change one part of the system, and you may change other parts as well. With enough food in their bellies, poor people may be more prone to look for jobs and be better prepared to succeed once they are hired. These are among the systemwide changes that can occur by getting at particular effects.

Proposals for change not only may be ineffective but also may make a problem worse. Psychotherapists Watzlawick, Weakland, and Fisch (1974) have even suggested that it is not the initial difficulties people experience that get them into real trouble; rather, it is the solutions they devise to remove these difficulties. For example, fearing that you might be at a loss for words if you dare to present a classroom speech from notes, you commit the entire speech to memory but then go blank at the time of the presentation and thus are truly at a loss for words. Concerned that your spouse has been behaving flirtatiously at parties, you react with jealous rage, thus increasing the probability that your spouse will seek solace in the arms of another. Here, once again, effects are looping back on their causes, but this time in negative ways.

Although the focus here has been on what the policy advocate should do, the message recipient has much to think about as well. Stock issues take different forms, depending on whether a persuader advocates change, repair, or retention of a policy. As the message recipient, you should be alert to some of the pitfalls in reasoning and evidence when policy advocates address problems or move from considerations of need to their proposed solutions. Did the policy advocates cover all the stock issues or perhaps treat one or more of them superficially? Did the communicators meet their burden of proof or, in the case of advocates of retention of a policy, their burden of refutation? Consider as well the relation between the alleged need for a change and the claims made for the workability of the proposed policy: They should mesh. Has the appropriate balance been struck between the dream of workability and the realities of practicality? Has a convincing case been made that on balance, the advantages of this plan outweigh its disadvantages? Of the various plans currently under consideration, does the plan advocated have the most advantages? Having directed your critical antennae to the speech or essay, also remember that there is only so much that the communicator can do given the constraints of time or space.

Recall that propositions of any type are debatable; there must be room for argument. Accordingly, propositions of fact are not in themselves established facts. Rather, they are *belief* claims for which factual evidence is needed.

Beliefs are the building blocks of attitudes. At bedrock are claims of the "How do I know?" variety:

My intuition tells me it's so.

My senses tell me true.

My tipster rarely fails me.

The authority quoted in the article I read is very knowledgeable.

The majority is usually right.

Because I said it, it must be so.

Propositions of fact are topics of consideration in their own right. Warnick and Inch (1994) divide them into three types:

Causal claims
  Capital punishment deters crime.
  Smoking marijuana harms your health.
  Violence on television affects children's behavior.

Predictive claims
  A staffed space mission will reach Mars by 2010.
  Our economy is headed for a massive depression.

TABLE 8.1 Structure of the Brady Case

A. Handguns need to be kept out of the wrong hands (subproposition).
1. This includes persons who are mentally incompetent (sub-subproposition).
2. This includes the criminal element (sub-subproposition).
3. Not doing so would be unjust (sub-subproposition).
4. Not doing so would continue to incur great costs to society (sub-subproposition).

B. The Brady bill will help keep handguns out of the wrong hands (subproposition).
1. Its provision of a national safety check will help identify persons known to be mentally incompetent (sub-subproposition).
2. Its provisions of a waiting period and a national safety check will deter criminals from purchasing guns (sub-subproposition).

C. The Brady bill will not interfere with the legitimate interests of ordinary citizens (subproposition).
1. It will not further curtail hunters (sub-subproposition).
2. It will not prevent ordinary citizens from owning handguns (sub-subproposition).

A severe shortage of teachers will occur by the year 2005.

Historical claims
> The Shroud of Turin was worn by Jesus in the tomb.
> The author of *On the Sublime* was not Longinus.
> Lee Harvey Oswald was the sole assassin of John F. Kennedy. (pp. 64-65)

More often then not, however, factual claims serve in subordinate roles to propositions of policy. For example, when discussing the policy proposition that capital punishment should be made legal (or illegal, depending on the state), people generally debate whether capital punishment deters crime. The same is true of value claims such as the assertion that capital punishment is immoral. These are *subpropositions* or *sub-subpropositions* of the broader policy claim. Table 8.1 should help make this last point clearer by illustrating the structure of the Sarah Brady case.

Most, but not all, of the supporting claims in Table 8.1 are factual. But consider such value terms as "unjust," "the wrong hands," and "legitimate interests." Terms such as these signal the possibility that disputants may become embroiled in a battle over definitions. What do "unjust," "the wrong hands," and "legitimate interests" mean? Controversies over propositions of fact can be just as intense, but there is greater likelihood of agreement on the meaning of key terms. Here are some contrasting examples of propositions of fact and value.

Propositions of fact:

1. Cutbacks in the welfare program have helped widen the gap between the rich and the poor.

2. Mandatory seat belts have reduced traffic fatalities by 20%.

3. The People's Republic of China is not really a communist state any longer.

4. Censorship of literature only increases its sales.

5. On the average, the top hitters in baseball get paid more than the top pitchers.

Propositions of value:

1. Widening the gap between the rich and the poor is immoral.

2. Mandating seat belt use is more ethical than merely advising people to wear them.

3. It's better to try and then fail than never to make the attempt.

4. It's not the government's job to regulate morals.

5. Basketball is more fun to watch than baseball.

Although values tend to be resistant to change, they are not impossible to change. Through the years, for example, Americans have become more open to ethnic and racial diversity, more accepting of gay and lesbian rights, and more tolerant of religious differences. At the same time, they have become more insistent on marketplace freedoms and less accepting of government regulations. But these changes have taken a good deal of time.

More realistically, on any one occasion, it may be possible to place value controversies in a new light, perhaps reframing the issues, perhaps downplaying objectionable values while highlighting values consistent with a proposed policy. For most of us, the basic values that we hold dear exist in a precarious state of balance. We want freedom but also order, spontaneity but also control, property rights but also human rights, stability but also change, what is equitable but also what is profitable. Thus, for example, opponents of gun control may believe that the right to bear arms is inviolable while at the same time valuing the safety and sanctity of human lives. These conflicts within ourselves can provide an opening for persuaders. For example, supporters of the Brady bill could (and did) argue that they opposed gun-related violence but not gun ownership. More recently, in Philadelphia, proponents and opponents of gun control came together in behalf of an experimental program to reduce gun-related violence.

Types of Evidence as Resources of Argumentation

The believability of factual claims rests on evidence and on inferences drawn from that evidence. Evidence can also be brought to bear on value issues. Josina, for example, favors locking up cocaine users for possession of even small quantities of the drug. She argues that drug use is immoral, and when pressed on the matter, she explains that no person has a right to inflict harm to self or others. Kristina counters with questions about the consequences of Josina's position. How is cocaine dangerous, she asks, and for whom? For the user, perhaps, but what evidence is there that others are directly affected? If we lock up cocaine users for harming only themselves, does this set a dangerous precedent? If, on the other hand, we were to decriminalize use of the drug, would this bring its users out into the open, making them more likely to go for treatment? Are there studies, she asks, that might address this question, or at least experts who can render informed opinions?

Picture 8.2 sends a powerful message by way of statistical comparison. Ironically, in this case, freedom leads to self-control, whereas government controls increase drug dependency. The big question that remains in any such contrast, however, concerns comparability. Do the significant similarities between the United States and the Netherlands outweigh the significant differences?

Evidence can take the form of stories (narratives), statistics, or testimony. The Sarah Brady (1986) article provides ample illustration of the power of extended narratives. The stories she tells wrap evidence and reasoning together in a way that both paints a vivid picture and drives home the intended conclusion. But stories of this sort take a lot of time (or space), and they cover a limited number of cases. Hence, persuaders sometimes combine extended narratives with a series of specific examples as well as statistical generalizations.

Specific examples contain the bare bones of a story: the who, what, when, where, how, and possibly the why, but without the detail: "In 1981, my husband was shot by a crazed gunman who'd been allowed by the government to have a gun—no questions asked." "When my son was six years old, he nearly killed himself playing with a loaded handgun that had been left on the seat of a pickup truck in which we'd been riding." Abbreviated stories of this sort give the persuader ample opportunity to

General McCaffrey says the Dutch approach to drugs "hasn't worked."

The Facts say: It has!

ISSUE	United States	The Netherlands
Use of marijuana by older teens (1994)	38%	30%
Use of marijuana by 15-year-olds (in 1995)	34%	29%
Heroin addicts (in 1995)	430 per 100,000	160 per 100,000
Murder rate (in 1996)	8.22 per 100,000	1.8 per 100,000
Crime-related deaths	8.2 per 100,000 (1995)	1.8 per 100,000 (1994)
Incarceration rate (1997)	645 per 100,000	73 per 100,000
Per capita spending on drug-related law enforcement	$81	$27

Are we so committed to past mistakes that we cannot shift to more effective strategies?

Visit Drug War Facts at: www.drugsense.org

Paid for by Common Sense for Drug Policy Foundation
Kevin B. Zeese, President, 703-354-5694, 703-354-5695 (fax), csdp@drugsense.org

These facts are based on official statistics from Holland and the United States.
Citations are available from the Web site of the Netherlands http:www.netherlands-embassy.org/drug-inf.htm or from Common Sense

Picture 8.2. A case for drug legalization based on statistical comparison: Assuming the factual claims are accurate, should marijuana and other street drugs be legalized in the United States?

exhibit the range and variety of cases covered by the factual claim. Even then, critical audiences might ask: Are the alleged facts true? Are they relevant and representative, and are there enough of them to warrant the generalization?

These same questions may be asked about statistics. The great virtue of statistics is that they quickly cover the territory marked out by the claim. But statistics may also lead to faulty inferences, as when the sampling is unrepresentative, when the statistical unit is inappropriate, or when a comparison is made between noncomparable data.

Suppose, for example, that the data gathered by Handgun Control, Inc., on the number of people in the United States killed in handgun accidents each year had been drawn from a few atypical states and then extrapolated to the others. Or consider the possibility that the organization's category of "intruders killed by handguns kept for self-defense" had excluded anyone previously known to the handgun user, including would-be rapists or other assailants who just happened to be acquaintances or family members. Should only strangers be counted in the statistical unit known as "intruders"?

Evidence also can include first-person accounts, testimony by witnesses, secondhand reports, such as those provided by journalists or historians, and finally testimony by authorities. These, too, can help substantiate a factual claim but can also be misleading. First-person accounts are often self-serving, whereas witnesses, as to an auto accident, are often inaccurate. Secondhand reports are only as trustworthy as the firsthand reports on which they're based.

War coverage provides an outstanding example of problems in secondhand reporting. In the early years of the war in Vietnam, seasoned reporters returned from visits to that troubled nation with glowing accounts of the progress of the South Vietnamese regime at beating back the communist, Vietcong guerrillas. Usually, however, they relied for their information on what government officials told them. These officials, in turn, relied on reports from the front. Thus, for example, the journalists might be told that the "kill ratio" in a recent battle was 10 Vietcong for every government soldier. Little did they realize at the time that combat officers were grossly misrepresenting the facts and that government officials were distorting them further. Clearly, an accurate picture of progress in the war could not be gained from press briefings in Saigon.

Despite the potential unreliability of first-person accounts, testimony by witnesses, and secondhand accounts, these can also be invaluable in substantiating a factual claim, and the claim can be bolstered as well by appeal to authority. For example, Sarah Brady's case would be much more impressive if she had cited an expert on handgun use, preferably a lifelong member of the NRA, who conceded, on the basis of his or her own studies, that passage of the Brady bill was likely to reduce gun crime by a substantial amount each year.

As with all other forms of evidence, message recipients have reason to be suspicious of authority; some arguments from authority are fallacious. Still, few have the resources to check matters out firsthand. Indeed, most of what people call "fact" is accepted on the authority of someone (e.g., teachers) or something (e.g., newspapers). (Science is in itself a major source of authority these days.) Even if most of our factual knowledge were based on direct observation, we could still benefit from the judgments of authorities on how to interpret those facts.

The characteristics we tend to value in authorities cited by persuaders are much like the characteristics we value in the persuaders themselves. Are they competent? Are they trustworthy? Do they exercise good judgment? Are they in a position to render informed judgments in the matter at hand? These virtues are all the more important when we have reason to be suspicious of the persuader's own credibility. A case in point was the Nixon "Checkers" speech.

Former President Richard Nixon is best known for being the only president to have resigned from office under threat of impeachment. But Nixon had been embroiled in another scandal many years earlier involving allegations that he had acquired an illegal slush fund, amounting to $18,000 (a substantial sum 50 years ago), while he was running for vice president. Under pressure from his running mate, Dwight Eisenhower, Nixon went on national television in 1952 to plead his case. The speech is memorable for many things, not least Nixon's passionate defense of his decision to keep a cocker spaniel given to him by a campaign contributor for his daughter Julie—a dog by the name of "Checkers." But the most credible evidence for Nixon's innocence of any wrongdoing in the slush fund case came in the way of an authoritative report. Nixon (1952/1986) said about the report,

And I am proud of the fact that the taxpayers by subterfuge or otherwise have never paid one dime for expenses which I thought were political and shouldn't be charged to the taxpayers.

Let me say, incidentally, that some of you may say, "Well, that's all right, Senator; that's your explanation, but have you got any proof?"

And I'd like to tell you this evening that just about an hour ago we received an independent audit of this entire fund.

I suggested to Gov. Sherman Adams, who is the chief of staff of the Dwight Eisenhower campaign, that an independent audit and legal report be obtained. And I have that audit here in my hand.

It's an audit made by the Price, Waterhouse & Co. firm, and the legal opinion by Gibson, Dunn & Crutcher, lawyers in Los Angeles, the biggest law firm and incidentally one of the best ones in Los Angeles.

I'm proud to be able to report to you tonight that this audit and this legal opinion is being forwarded to General Eisenhower. And I'd like to read to you the opinion that was prepared by Gibson, Dunn & Crutcher and based on all the pertinent laws and statutes, together with the audit report prepared by the certified public accountants.

"It is our conclusion that Senator Nixon did not obtain any financial gain from the collection and disbursement of the fund by Dana Smith; that Senator Nixon did not violate any Federal or state law by reason of the operation of the fund, and that neither the portion of the fund paid by Dana Smith directly to third persons nor the portion paid to Senator Nixon to reimburse him for designated office expenses constituted income to the Senator which was either reportable or taxable as income under applicable tax laws. (signed) Gibson, Dunn & Crutcher by Alma H. Conway."

Now that, my friends, is not Nixon speaking, but that's an independent audit which was requested because I want the American people to know all the facts and I'm not afraid of having independent people go in and check the facts, and that is exactly what they did. (pp. 199-208)

Whatever view one holds of Richard Nixon, it must be admitted that he knew how to select and cite credible authorities.

Fallacies Reconsidered

A fallacious argument is one that fails to stand up to careful scrutiny. At first blush, it appears convincing, perhaps even compelling, but then cracks begin to appear. For example, Tom appears to have undermined John's position on capital punishment, but John responds that Tom has misrepresented his arguments, presenting them in weakened form so that they could more easily be knocked down. This type of misrepresentation is called the *straw man* fallacy. The straw man, says John, is one of Tom's imagining. John's real case has gone unrefuted.

Tom responds, perhaps, with charges of his own. John is claiming to have been misrepresented only because his case is truly weak. John is guilty of having illogically reduced complex matters to an either-or, known as a *false dichotomy.* Or John resorts to name-calling rather than addressing Tom's arguments—the *ad hominem* fallacy. Or Tom compares two unlikes as if they were sufficiently alike to treat them as analogous—the *false analogy.* Or John draws faulty inferences about causation. A *common causal* fallacy involves treating one among many causal factors as the sole cause. Another causal fallacy, known as *post hoc,* involves assuming that because something preceded an event, it must be its cause. Defective arguments of this type are called *false cause* fallacies.

Textbooks on logic and on argumentation list many categories of fallacies (e.g., Walton, 1992)—too many all to be identified and discussed in this book. The important thing is to get a sense of when to accept an argument and when to reject it;

labels are less important. Yet it isn't always easy to decide whether an argument is sound or fallacious. Often, fallacy claims are *arguable,* that is, subject to legitimate dispute. Each side in the dispute may argue about what features of the context are most relevant, about what the communicator intended, or about how the message was received. These factors can be important, as illustrated in the following examples.

▶ False dichotomy? Some complex issues are usefully clarified by reducing them to two sides or to two alternatives. Mayoral candidate Chris says, "I know there are five candidates running for mayor, and of course you don't have to vote at all. But let's face it: This race is going to be won by the Democrat or the Republican, and your vote could make a difference.

▶ Post hoc? "When Clinton became president," says his Democratic supporter, "the economy was in the dumps. Now it's riding high. Clearly, Clinton was good for the economy." "Post hoc fallacy!" cries the critic of Clinton. "Clinton may have just been lucky to be in the right position at the right time." But the Clinton supporter has a comeback: "Luck, nothing. You've forgotten that the tax package he pushed through Congress in 1993 was what got the economy on track."

▶ Inappropriate ad hominem? When council member White's character is attacked, she cries foul, insisting that her critics stick to the issues. "You are the issue," one of them replies. "After all, the question is whether you should be reelected."

▶ False analogy? "This is no time to remove Governor Green from office," says his supporter. "After all, you don't switch quarterbacks when the quarterback you've got is taking the team down the field." "Politics isn't football," says the critic. "Besides, you do change quarterbacks if the team's been heading down the field the wrong way. That's what's wrong with our state. Governor Green has moved it backward rather than forward."

As these examples illustrate, arguments should rarely be rejected at the first suspicion of a fallacy. They are best played out in the give-and-take of argumentative exchange. Sometimes, the real culprit turns out to be the one making the initial charge of fallacy. The fallacy accusation can be like the proverbial hammer, a new tool in danger of being overused and misapplied. Those of us who write about argument are not immune. For example, in a textbook on argumentation, author Don Trent Jacobs (1994) accused Rush Limbaugh of being unfair to astrophysicist Carl Sagan. Sagan, Limbaugh claimed, commented on matters about which he had little expertise, such as global warming and nuclear winter. But Jacobs's criticism of

Limbaugh's critique was also suspect. He argued that because astrophysics covers "everything that lies beyond the dominant influence of the earth," Sagan could be considered an authority on subjects relating to global climate (p. 129). But this is akin to saying that a urologist is an expert on the big toe. After all, a urologist is a medical doctor, and the field of medicine deals with every part of the human body. For all we know, the late Carl Sagan may have been an expert on global warming and nuclear winter, but the reasoning behind Jacobs's fallacy accusation is itself fallacious.

The point thus far has been that fallacy charges are often arguable, best played out through argumentative exchange, and sometimes fallacious in their own right. Yet the concept of fallacy would have no meaning if all arguments were fallacious. This is seen most clearly in the case of well-argued disputes. Just because two people disagree does not mean that at least one of them must be committing a fallacy. Here is an example of a well-argued disagreement.

In ancient Judea, so the story goes, the Jewish elders were challenged in their opposition to idolatry by some unnamed, but presumably Roman, idol worshippers. A Roman asks the first question: "Why, if God so opposes idolatry, doesn't he destroy all the idols?" The elders ponder this tough question but then reply, "God would certainly do just that, if the idolators only worshipped useless objects. But the idolators also worship necessary objects like the sun, moon, stars, and planets. Destroying these would put an end to God's whole creation. Shall He then make an end of His world because of fools?" The Romans are not satisfied. They counter the argument with one of their own: "If God does not want to destroy the world, then let Him destroy only the useless idols." But this clever retort does not satisfy the Jewish elders. They answer with one of their own: "If God destroyed your useless idols, but kept the moon, sun, stars, and planets, you would say these are the true deities because they had been untouched by the destruction of the idols" (Billig, 1987, pp. 100-101).[2]

Are there ever times when an argument can be shown to be clearly fallacious? Our answer to that is an emphatic *yes*. Sometimes, a communicator commits an obvious error in reasoning. "You say that he's not in Reno? And of course we both know that Reno is in Nevada. Well, I guess that proves he's definitely not in Nevada." Or take another type of error: "If he's in Reno, he must be in Nevada. He's in Nevada. Therefore, he must be in Reno."

These errors are fairly straightforward. But sometimes, a fallacious argument goes undetected for years, even centuries. Masses of people coalesce in support of the idea. As it gains supporters, it becomes more difficult to undermine. The argument itself may have more than a surface plausibility. Religious cults are often accused of errors of this type, but none of us are immune to them. Consider this story about a false cause fallacy, one that nearly everyone in the media was ready to believe at one point. It is the story of Gulf War Syndrome.

The Case of Gulf War Syndrome

Some of the most moving evidence heard in recent times concerned the real possibility that American soldiers serving in the Persian Gulf War against Saddam Hussein had been exposed to a toxic chemical that had caused thousands of them to experience a baffling set of war-related symptoms. A health survey found a majority of vets reporting that they had delayed having children, fearing that the babies would be born deformed. Vets also feared passing on their illness to loved ones. But the principal victims appeared to be the veterans themselves. As recounted on PBS's *Frontline* ("The Last Battle of the Gulf War," 1998), veterans who had been healthy going into the war independently reported having problems with concentration, fatigue, nausea, and an inability to focus. These seemingly independent accounts were made all the more believable by visual evidence of the sorry state of those testifying, and the testimony was confirmed by eyewitnesses. So credible were the accounts that Congress was persuaded to hold a hearing on the complaints. Said Representative Bernard Sanders, (I), of Vermont, on *Frontline:* "There is no question in my mind— none, zero—that tens and tens of thousands of our soldiers are suffering from a wide range of illnesses, which I believe are attributable to their service in the Gulf."

In addition to Congress, the news media—including such highly respected programs as *Nightline, 20/20,* and *60 Minutes*—lavished considerable attention on Gulf War Syndrome. There was no shortage of plausible explanations for the alleged problem, some of them coming from respected news sources. *Dateline* speculated that radioactive debris from the uranium shell casings used to pierce Iraqi tanks might be the cause of Gulf War Syndrome. *60 Minutes* wondered if side effects from PB, a drug given to protect against the nerve gas soman, might be the cause of Gulf War Syndrome. It had, after all, been given to large numbers of troops. Several news sources speculated that chemical weapons might be to blame. Said the *Frontline* narrator, "Since the war, the DoD had repeatedly denied that U.S. troops had been exposed to chemical agents. But many vets were skeptical of these denials because during the war hundreds of chemical alarms had gone off."

Was there, then, a Gulf War Syndrome? One reason a viewer practicing an art of mistrust might have remained suspicious was that the facts and proffered explanations did not add up to create a single coherent narrative. In the case of Gulf War Syndrome, there were apparently too many disparate, unrelated symptoms and too many plausible explanations. Moreover, according to *Frontline,* once the claims and explanations were subjected to careful scientific investigation, the case for Gulf War Syndrome fell apart like a house of cards. Not always is science in a position to resolve controversies; after all, many of them are outside the purview of scientific investigation. Nor, as argued in Chapter 3, is scientific reporting purely objective. Still, science proved to be immensely helpful in the controversy about Gulf War Syndrome.

To lead its medical investigation of Gulf War Syndrome, the Pentagon appointed Dr. Stephen Joseph, a seasoned public health physician who had worked in New York at the height of the AIDS epidemic. Working with the Veterans Administration, Joseph invited Gulf War veterans who reported feeling ill to register and undertake a full exam. Panels of scientists were asked to review everything known about any toxin that vets might have been exposed to in the Gulf. Millions were spent on a series of epidemiological studies to see whether reports of veterans' hospitalizations and deaths occurred at a higher rate than normal. Several blue-ribbon panels were set up, including the Defense Science Board, the Institute of Medicine, and a special panel created by the president, the Presidential Advisory Committee.

On the basis of all these investigations, Dr. Joseph concluded that there was no unique Gulf War Syndrome. Said Joseph on *Frontline,* "There was no magic bullet. There was no mystery illness." Rather, there were lots of common illnesses, illnesses that people would have had whether they went to the Gulf or not. Then, too, there were injuries resulting from being in the Gulf but not an extraordinary number of them. There were those with symptoms that couldn't be easily understood or accounted for—symptoms such as headaches, fatigue, depression, muscle soreness, and joint pains. But considered as a proportion of the estimated 700,000 servicemen and servicewomen who went to the Gulf, these numbers were also not unusual.

Particularly impressive was the scientists' systematic examination and subsequent refutation of each of the theories offered to explain Gulf War Syndrome. The matter is not fully resolved. There remains the possibility that multiple vaccines injected in soldiers already deployed to the Gulf may have added to their trauma and to chronic fatigue in many returning vets (Hilts, 2000). Research continues, as it should, but the initial claims were clearly overblown. Even previously suppressed news that the United States had blown up an Iraqi ammunition dump containing a lethal nerve gas proved less than convincing as evidence for Gulf War Syndrome. Subsequent studies showed that a large proportion of vets reporting symptoms were nowhere near the dump site at the time it was exploded. The story of Gulf War Syndrome ultimately stands not just as testimony to the potential pitfalls in causal reasoning but also to the persuasive power of statistics, eyewitness accounts, personal experience, and authoritative opinion—all of them forms of evidence that can assist audiences in making sound judgments but that in this case may have led them astray.

Summary

Persuasion typically takes place under conditions that are less than ideal for reflective argumentative exchange. Under the circumstances, persuaders cannot be expected to win belief by logic alone. Arresting narratives, for example, go beyond logic in providing a feeling for a problem, but this doesn't mean they are illogical. Nor is it antithetical to logic for persuaders to provide evidences of their own credibility on a topic. As Aristotle emphasized in his treatise on rhetoric, *logos, pathos,* and *ethos* can go hand in hand.

When persuaders reason, they typically do so by use of truncated arguments called *enthymemes* that call on their audiences to supply and endorse implicit premises. In support of a position on a complex issue, they are well-advised to offer a variety of supporting arguments and evidence.

No amount of argument and evidence is likely to provide the last word on complex issues. But this does not mean that the persuaders ought to be haphazard in investigating a topic and coming to a conclusion about it or that they are unwarranted in defending what—after investigation—they consider the best, most sensible position on the matter. To put it more positively: Persuaders should practice thoroughgoing inquiry *and* advocacy. When in the role of message consumer, persuadees should listen (or read) critically but also be willing to commit to the persuader's position after questioning it.

Much of this chapter has been given over to a discussion of types of propositions and the arguments and evidence necessary to support them. Propositions are debatable assertions, of which three types are generally recognized: policy, fact, and value.

Propositions of policy urge support for or opposition to a proposed action or decision. As the discussion in connection with the Sarah Brady article indicated, policy advocates are logically obligated to advance arguments on five stock issues: need, workability, practicality, freedom from greater evils, and superiority relative to other possible solutions. Sometimes, one or more of these issues will be bypassed under the impress of time or of limited space; sometimes the persuader will treat a stock issue enthymematically, assuming audiences will agree there is not much reason to discuss it. Not uncommonly, the focus shifts from issue of need to questions of comparative advantage or to the question of which proposed solution best meets some delimited set of goals or criteria.

Advocates of change from the status quo generally are assumed to have a burden of proof, whereas those advocating retention of the present system have only a burden of refutation—unless they choose to make positive claims for the system or against proposals for change, in which case they, too, take on burdens of proof. Between the alternatives of advocating full-scale change or retention of a policy, policy proponents may urge that the current system be repaired to one degree or another—each increment of repair incurring an increased burden of proof.

Propositions of fact urge acceptance (or rejection) of a belief claim that something is true or probable. The belief claim may be causal, predictive, or historical. Often, belief claims are themselves supports for propositions of policy or value. They can be thought of as subpropositions (or sub-subpropositions, etc.).

Value propositions arise in controversies about morality, taste, propriety, and the like, or, as so often happens, when two persons share the same values but prioritize them differently. The difference between propositions of fact and value often hinges on whether persuader and audience agree on the meaning of key terms in the proposition. The guilt or innocence of O. J. Simpson was generally considered to be an issue of fact, for example, but the propriety of Simpson's attorneys in their handling of the case was generally seen as a question of value. Three methods of dealing with value controversies were identified: (1) examining consequences, (2) attaching a disputed value to higher-order values, and (3) appealing to shared assumptions. These often go hand in hand.

A fallacious argument is one that fails to stand up to careful scrutiny. Some arguments are clearly fallacious. But arguments should rarely be rejected at the first whiff of trouble. Often, the charge of fallacy can be successfully defended against and turned back on the accuser. Among the most common of fallacies is the fallacy of having falsely labeled an opponent's argument fallacious.

Questions and Projects for Further Study

1. Do you believe that it's reasonable that existing ways of doing things should be assumed to be preferable to proposals for change? What might be said for reversing the burden of proof in the case of policy propositions?
2. Why is it sometimes better to get at the effects of a problem, rather than its causes? Can you provide examples of when the reverse is true?
3. Why as part of an analysis of a problem is it often a good idea to investigate what was done in the past to remedy the problem?
4. Can you think of value conflicts between people when efforts at persuasion are bound to be fruitless? Can you think of any that could prove fruitful?
5. Generate five examples each of a proposition of policy, fact, and value.
6. Provide five examples of your own of clear-cut fallacies and five examples that you think could be reasonably argued either way.

Notes

1. Article excerpts reprinted by permission of Sarah Brady.
2. This exchange is so good that you might be tempted to continue the conversation. In Billig's (1987, p. 107) imagining, one of the Jews at the time did just that. Seeing that the Romans were stuck for the moment by the Jews' last rejoinder, he proposed to

the Romans an argument that could give the Jews further difficulty: If your God does not wish to destroy the useful or the useless idols, why does He not destroy us useless idolators? Assisting one's opponent in a debate is a characteristic of what is called the *persuasion dialogue* in Chapter 13. Says Billig, the Jews themselves entertained this fascinating question in the Talmudic commentaries of the Gemara, a recorded exchange among rabbinic sages throughout many years. Confronted with this clever argument, they asked themselves, what would be the best reply?

References

Billig, M. (1987). *Arguing and thinking: A rhetorical approach to social psychology.* Cambridge, UK: Cambridge University Press.

Brady, S. K. (1986, May). Handguns must be kept away from the John Hinckleys of the world. *Glamour, 84,* 96-97.

Brockriede, W. (1990). Where is argument? In R. Trapp & J. Schuetz (Eds.), *Perspectives on argumentation: Essays in honor of Wayne Brockriede.* Prospect Heights, IL: Waveland.

Hilts, P. J. (2000, September 8). Study fails to reveal the causes of Gulf War syndrome. *New York Times,* p. A21.

Jacobs, D. T. (1994). *The bum's rush.* Boise, ID: Legendary Publishing.

The last battle of the Gulf War. (1998, January 20). In *Frontline.* New York and Washington, DC: Public Broadcasting Service. Available: www.pbs.org/wgbh/pages/frontline

Nixon, R. M. (1986). My side of the story. In H. W. Simons, *Persuasion: Understanding, practice, and analysis* (2nd ed.). New York: McGraw-Hill. (Original speech September 23, 1952)

van Eemeren, F. H., Grootendorst, R., Jackson, S., & Jacobs, S. (1993). *Reconstructing argumentative discourse.* Tuscaloosa: University of Alabama Press.

Walton, D. (1992). *Plausible argument in everyday conversation.* Albany: State University of New York Press.

Warnick, B., & Inch, E. S. (1994). *Critical thinking and communication* (2nd ed.). New York: Macmillan.

Watzlawick, P., Weakland, J., & Fisch, R. (1974). *Change: Principles of problem formation and problem resolution.* New York: Norton.

CONTEXTS FOR PERSUASION

Going Public

Frederick Douglass, born in 1818 to a slave and her master, escaped from a Southern prison-house of bondage to become one of the great orators and essayists for racial equality of the 19th century. His early life is testimony to the potential of humankind to triumph over adversity. His adult life is testimony to the power of public persuasion. Douglass committed the crime, punishable by death at the time, of secretly teaching himself to read and write while a slave. The fugitive-orator came to the attention of abolitionist leader Henry Lloyd Garrison, who reported in the preface to Douglass's (1845/1968) autobiography that he was spell-bound by Douglass's oratory on first hearing him at an antislavery convention in Nantucket, Massachusetts, in 1841.

> I shall never forget his first speech at the convention—the extraordinary emotion it excited in my own mind—the powerful impression it created upon a crowded auditory, completely taken by surprise—the applause which followed from the beginning to the end of his felicitous remarks.

He came forward to the platform with a hesitancy and embarrassment, necessarily the attendants of a sensitive mind in such a novel position. After apologizing for his ignorance, and reminding the audience that slavery was a poor school for the human intellect and heart, he proceeded to narrate some of the facts in his own history as a slave, and in the course of his speech gave utterance to many noble thoughts and thrilling reflections. As soon as he had taken his seat, filled with hope and admiration, I rose, and declared that *Patrick Henry*, of revolutionary fame, never made a speech more eloquent in the cause of liberty, than the one we had just listened to from the lips of that hunted fugitive. So I believed at the time—so I believe now. (Garrison, 1845/1968, pp. vi-vii)

"Going public" is that moment when the private self goes public in support of a position or proposal. For audiences, it is often the moment of decision. For speakers such as Douglass, it is generally the moment *after* decision, and after a commitment to exercise leadership has been made.

The focus of this chapter is on the one-shot presentation or message, as opposed to persuasive campaigns, which are organized, sustained attempts to influence groups or masses of people through a series of messages. Campaigns—political, product advertising, and issue-oriented—are covered in the rest of Part 3 on the contexts of persuasion. This chapter looks primarily at what the communicator must do to win over audiences.

The Genuinely Committed Persuader

Going public is scary for most people. Communications scholar John Angus Campbell (1996) provides the all-too-painful picture of a first round of presentations in a public speaking classroom.

> Here is a speech with no point; here is another with twelve! Here is a speech crammed with technical evidence incomprehensible to the audience. Here is a light speech backed with little thought and no research. Here is an adequate speech, if one could listen to it, but that is all but impossible because of the speaker's odd dexterity in jingling, chewing gum, and talking all at once. Here is a speech that is being read. Here is a speech so obviously memorized that the speaker looks out at the class as though his body had been snatched by space aliens. (p. 222)

Anyone who has ever taken public speaking probably recognizes that Campbell is exaggerating only slightly. Yet these problems can be overcome, especially if students are willing to do the necessary work of gathering research materials, coming to an informed judgment on the topic at hand, preparing the message, rehearsing if it is an oral presentation, then risking themselves in genuine expressions of commitment.

As Campbell observes, authentic, knowledgeable expression makes for the most moving, most memorable moments in the life of a public speaking class. It also helps overcome the debilitating fears of public address.

Campbell's immediate context is the classroom speech, but as he points out, the same combination of commitment and craft skills is needed in the writing classroom as in the public speaking classroom, and it is surely required in most situations outside the classroom. The chief exceptions are those in which the communicator is a hired gun, paid to persuade on behalf of a client or employer. Even then, it helps to believe in what is being promoted.

Yet as Campbell (1996) also observes, many students prefer to go through the motions of speech making without the risks of genuine commitment. Playing it safe, he laments, is often a habit, rewarded in classrooms from childhood on. Campbell tells the story of a former student who when asked why she had chosen to speak on drug abuse in high school, replied matter-of-factly that her best friend had died of a drug overdose during their junior year. Until that moment, the student's speech had been competently mechanical. But now, as her revelation registered on the faces of her classmates, the speaker, too, came alive. Out came details about the reactions of fellow high schoolers to news of the event, about its devastating impact on her, and about the urgency of the problem for those with sisters and brothers still in high school. This "second speech," as Campbell termed it, offered evidence that was at once personal yet public. What before had been merely adequate content and delivery "was now transformed into brilliance as the student spoke with feeling, emphasis, tone, movement, and commanding presence" (p. 223). Sadly, however, the student also gave unwitting testimony to the stifling effects of learning to speak mechanistically as if one were painting by the numbers. Asked why she didn't include the fact of her best friend's drug overdose in the speech, she said, "I didn't think it was relevant."

Strategic Planning: A Three-Step Process

Persuasion tends to work best when the communicator is genuinely committed, but it also requires strategic planning and skillful presentation. The following scheme for strategic planning pulls together much of what has been said thus far in this book about how to persuade. Two fictitious case studies, one of a speech planning effort, the other of planning for delivery of a radio editorial, are used to illustrate the three steps of strategy formulation.

Step 1: Goals, Audience, Situation

1. What do I want, know, believe, value, and so forth? What do they want, know, believe, value, and so forth?

2. What's expected, and perhaps required, of me in this situation? What's the rhetorical exigency, if any, and what are the chief constraints?

These are the primary questions that persuaders need to address at this step, but depending on the situation, there may be others. For example, if your speech is part of a larger effort at persuasion, say a communitywide campaign, you will need to think about how your speech can best serve that larger cause. Are there, for example, key opinion leaders in your audience who can be recruited to energize others in the community? If, as often happens, your audience is divided on the issues being addressed, you may need to develop different strategies for different audience segments or perhaps target some of them for primary attention while striving not to antagonize others.

Questions 1 and 2 address goals in relationship to the audience and situation. Ideally, speakers want to energize their audiences to take action in behalf of their cause, but the audience may not be ready to make public commitments or the situation may not permit that type of active recruiting. Thus, perhaps a better goal in some situations is to give the audience a better appreciation of the problem and convince audience members that the proposed solution is worthy of further consideration.

These are substantive goals. Relational goals are important as well. When you've finished speaking, what impression do you want to leave with the audience of who you are as a person and how you feel about them? It's possible, after all, that you may want to come back. It's even possible that you'll be able to capitalize on their initial favorable impression in your subsequent efforts at persuasion. This has happened repeatedly in classroom presentations.

But how can a speaker determine what the audience is like? What can be learned about the situation? The answers to these questions vary with the extent of the persuader's ambitions. Running a national or even a communitywide campaign typically involves scientific polling. Campaign planners also attempt to learn more about audience attitudes and situational expectations by gathering together selected individuals for intense questioning. For occasions such as a classroom speech assignment, two other approaches are recommended. First, draw inferences about the audience from *demographic* information, such as sex, age, and socioeconomic status. For example, older, well-educated audiences are probably more open to complex verbal arguments, whereas younger audiences exposed to daily diets of television and little else will probably be more drawn to visual displays (Hamlin, 1998).

Second, *talk* informally with audience members or persons similar to them. Learn from them what their attitudes are to the position or action you'll be defending (hostile? mild disagreement? indecision? strong agreement?) and what beliefs and values support those attitudes, including their perceptions of you as a person. Determine as well what they know (or think they know) about the topic and whether and why they care about it. Also ask them about other audience members and about the audience and situation as a whole. If you've been invited to give a speech, for example, how large will the audience be, and what will the physical setting be like? Who will introduce you? How much time will you have? Will there be questions afterward? What form will they take? Will they be hostile or friendly? Who is likely to ask them? What will you be expected to know or admit you don't know in the question and answer period?

Above all, find out from these conversations what it will take to convince audience members and perhaps turn them on. On what common ground can you build? What arguments and evidence are they likely to find believable? What appeals (to reason *and* emotion) can you offer that will make them feel that they have a personal stake in the outcome of this controversy?

Example 1: Richmond, Virginia, Tobacco Marketing Speech

Emily's class in persuasion at the University of Richmond has decided to launch a communitywide campaign to get corporate executives of tobacco companies in the Richmond area to agree to voluntary restraints on marketing to young people around the globe. As part of that campaign, she has wrangled an invitation to address members of the Richmond Teachers Association (RTA) at their annual conference. She has 10 minutes to speak plus 10 minutes for questions and answers.

She learns from the president of the RTA that its members are generally undecided about the proposal for voluntary restraints. Many people in Richmond depend on the tobacco companies for employment, and although these public and private schoolteachers care deeply about young people, they tend not to think much about the effects of tobacco on young people outside the United States. Still, virtually everyone in Richmond is aware that the marketing of tobacco products has become highly controversial and that antitobacco groups are pressuring the federal government to cut back on its assistance to U.S. tobacco companies in their international marketing efforts. This is the rhetorical situation that has given rise to the class's campaign and to the audience's willingness to hear Emily out, although she is a total stranger to them and can claim few credentials other than her status as a junior majoring in communication at the University of Richmond. She decides on the basis of this analysis that she had better tread lightly with this audience, perhaps urging support for the campaign but not enjoining the audience to commit to active participation in its behalf.

Example 2: Teenage Pregnancy Radio Editorial

The campus radio station at Big City University airs 1-minute guest editorials at 5:59 each weekday evening by just about anyone connected with the university who's willing to propose a topic, stay within decency guidelines, and come to the studio to tape it. Few people listen to WBCU; its broadcast range doesn't extend much beyond the campus. Still, Maggie is eager to speak in behalf of her favorite cause: free condom distribution to high school students. As a 19-year-old single mother of a 2-year-old boy, she can speak from experience about teenage pregnancy. But what will this mostly college-age audience think of her proposal to provide free condoms to Big City students beginning in the ninth grade? Maggie decides to survey her classmates and discovers little overt opposition, although perhaps those opposed are reluctant to admit their reservations given their awareness of how strongly she feels about the topic. From her conversations with students, it appears that they are divided between those sympathetic to her cause and those who are indifferent and ill informed. Both groups of students seem to perk up when she tells them about her own personal experience. She decides to combine response reinforcing for the former group with response shaping for the latter.

Step 2: Initial Strategizing

1. What are the chief obstacles that I will have to confront? How can I overcome them?

2. What resources can I bring to this situation? How can I best deploy them? What opportunities for persuasion are available? How can I best exploit them?

3. How should I actually prepare my presentation?

The first two questions in this list, focusing on potential problems and on assets and opportunities, should lead you to some sound decisions on overall strategy. Decisions on the particulars of self-presentation are covered in question 3.

In doing your initial strategizing, think once again about goals, audience, and situation, but this time in relation to principles of coactive persuasion, presented in Chapter 4. Think, for example, about ways to overcome skepticism or outright disagreement by building on shared premises and shared experiences. Think about how you can exploit your personal attractiveness and credibility or perhaps how you might work to overcome audience doubts about your competence and trustworthiness. Think about what you know or can learn about your topic that might help to overcome audience apathy and perhaps move audience members to action. Think about how you might best arrange these materials so that your speech (or guest editorial, public service announcement, etc.) is enthusiastically received and easily remembered. Think about what you can do nonverbally to augment your verbal message. Think about the physical and social setting for your presentation and what you can do to overcome such problems as noisy air conditioning or to exploit such opportunities as are provided by friendly questioning from the floor.

Start with your *prior ethos*—what audience members know about you directly and know of you by reputation. If it's a classroom speech you're giving, you already have a major asset: You're one of them—fellow sufferers, all in the same boat. Chances are that at least some class members have come to know you and like you and respect you. Think especially of them as you stand before the class. Well before you present the speech, think about how your day-to-day behavior in class will become part of your prior ethos. Cultivate a favorable reputation.

A second major resource is the message you've prepared. If you've done the necessary research, it will show. If you've exercised good judgment, it will show. If you've organized well (to be discussed), it will show. See Appendix I for a reminder of resources for the persuader.

Think also about the nonverbal resources at your command. You have a voice and a body that can work for you or against you. You can also use time and space to advantage. A poised beginning—not too fast, not too slow—can communicate confidence. A step away from behind the podium can reinforce that perception. Gestures and facial expressions can complement the verbal message, perhaps adding emphasis or metacommunicating feelings that are impossible to express verbally. A speaker's voice can be like a musical instrument, able in a nuanced way to express irony, amusement, interest, detachment, conviction, ambivalence—perhaps sequentially or even simultaneously. The actor inside you can assume the role of teacher, sermonizer, editorialist, or advertiser. You can enjoin the audience to think with you as you puzzle out a problem with them. "Let's do this together," your voice and body can be saying (Picture 9.1). Or of course you can metacommunicate panic, disinterest, condescension, self-loathing, or any of a number of feelings and attitudes that will speak so loudly that your audience won't be able to hear what you are saying. Whatever else you do, you want to create the impression of communicating with your audience, rather than at them.

Example 1: Richmond, Virginia,
Tobacco Marketing Speech

Having determined that she will be permitted 10 minutes of speaking time plus 10 minutes for questions and answers to convince members of the RTA to support her group's campaign, Emily takes stock of the resources she has available to win them over. Her first thought is that this speech will fail. After all, many in the audience will be hostile to any curtailment of international marketing by the tobacco companies; others will be in mild to moderate disagreement; and even those who are on the fence will be listening critically to what she, a total stranger, has to say.

Picture 9.1. Elizabeth Dole at the 1996 Republican Convention Communicating With Her Audience Rather Than at Them

But then the outlines of a strategy begin to form in her mind. This speech will need evidence—plenty of it—of harm from tobacco marketing geared to young people. But before she presents that evidence, she will need to build rapport with the audience, establishing herself as a friend, rather than an enemy. She will also need to build common ground on her central premise that although the good of the tobacco companies and of the Richmond economy are important, serious and widespread harm to children anywhere in the world is an overriding concern.

This is not an easy premise to sell, she realizes. Perhaps she can begin with evidence of harm to American children and then document the worldwide aspects of the problem. Having searched the Web and logged many hours at the library, she is now in possession of a good deal of information:

> ▶ More than 1 million American kids will start smoking this year. One third will die from their addiction.

▶ About 90% of all new smokers in the United States are 18 or younger. The tobacco industry has marketed accordingly; it knows that relatively few adults will take up the habit.

▶ Once kids or teenagers start smoking, it's likely they'll become addicts without realizing it, and then it's too late to stop.

▶ Cigarettes kill more Americans than AIDS, alcohol, car accidents, murders, suicide, drugs, and fires combined.

▶ Forty-six million adults in this country smoke, and most of them want to quit. Nearly all began smoking as children. The average smoker begins at age 13 and becomes a daily smoker by age 14½.

▶ Of Americans in a recent poll, 86% said they wanted their member of Congress to support the proposal of the U.S. Food and Drug Administration (FDA) to decrease smoking in children.

▶ Although agencies such as the FDA have worked to curtail smoking in children, other federal agencies have poured billions through the years in support of marketing of American tobacco products to children overseas. But these practices are increasingly unpopular at home and abroad.

▶ Children everywhere have the same potential for addiction, the same potential for lung cancer and heart disease. Increasingly, they're buying American tobacco products at ages 14, 13, and 12.

And so on. Emily decides to present these points with a computer-generated slide presentation. That way, the teachers will be more likely to remember them.

As to the matter of building rapport, she remembers that she has resources aplenty to accomplish that task as well. Her family, after all, has lived in Richmond through four generations. Her mother is a retired schoolteacher; that's how she got to meet the RTA's distinguished president, Mrs. Foxworth. As for Richmond's bread-and-butter industry, why, Emily was raised like everyone else in this town on the conviction that tobacco could do no wrong. Her uncle, may he rest in peace, used to conclude every dinner table debate—no matter what the topic—with the question, "But is it good for Philip Morris?"

Having established her bona fides, Emily figures she can get down to business. She decides to use the "yes-but" approach. Yes, Philip Morris's welfare is important. Many of us have friends and family who've worked for the company. Others have counted on the price of the stock to go up and up and up; it's been among the best-performing blue chips these last 40 years.

But we can't ignore the effects of tobacco marketing on children. (With this, she will launch the slide presentation.)

Emily concludes with a brief pitch for voluntary restraints on tobacco marketing overseas. Why only a brief pitch? Because she has planted a question about it in the audience. She has also already arranged with the chair of the session to call on this questioner first—so much for leaving things to chance!

In response to the question about voluntary restraints, she intends to argue from the perspective of many in the audience. The technique Emily will use is called the *method of residues.* The tobacco companies, she will say, have three choices. They can hope the government does nothing. That's unlikely.

They can wait for the government to impose restraints. If it does, the restraints are likely to be harsh.

They can curtail their overseas marketing to children voluntarily. This is the third and remaining option (the "residue"). Voluntary curtailment can give a much needed public relations boost to the industry while weakening the movement for government-imposed restraints.

As for the rest of the question and answer period, Emily anticipates the questions and rehearses her answers as best she can. At no point does she write out or memorize those answers; she wants to stay fresh and alive during this. Much as she is tempted to memorize all but the slide presentation, she resists committing any part of her introduction or conclusion to manuscript form. She doesn't want this speech to appear as an "essay on its hind legs."

Example 2: Teenage Pregnancy Guest Editorial

Maggie thought initially that her guest editorial was going to be easy. How much can you say, after all, in just 60 seconds?

But that turns out to be the major problem. On reflection and after some library research, she realizes that she has much too much to say. Moreover, she has concluded that trying to squeeze everything in by talking quickly is precisely the wrong way to go.

She decides on a sixfold strategy:

1. Use a loud and prolonged sound—something similar to the beep of the emergency radio control system—to get attention. Then follow with a startling statistic. "Hi, I'm Maggie Friendly. During the time of the sound that you just heard, X number of children were born to single teenage mothers." (Maggie plans to compute the exact number on average from yearly statistics.)

2. Paint a vivid picture of the problems of teenage pregnancy for child and parent. (Time limit: 20 seconds)

3. Make an example of herself. "I know because I've been there, done that, paid the price. My son, Reginald, and I are lucky we've got my mom to help support us."

4. State her position. "Let's face it, teens are having sex. They're not going to stop just because some teacher lectures them not to."

5. Accent the positive. (This is a framing decision. Maggie could have stayed negative.) "But you know, the teenage birthrate is going down. One big reason is that high schools around the country are giving out condoms to their students as early as the ninth grade."

6. Design a conclusion especially for listeners already on her side: "Help support Big City Planned Parenthood in their efforts to get free condoms distributed in our high schools. Call 555-5111 for further information."

Maggie writes out her editorial word for word, tries it out on her little tape recorder, sees that its timing is about right, brings the tape to the radio station, gets an okay, then heads for the studio to cut the tape that will be aired.

Step 3: Test-Marketing and Revision

1. Now that I've prepared my speech, written my guest editorial, and so forth, what do the sorts of people I want to persuade think of it? Is it the "right" message after all?

2. Assuming that there are problems (or missed opportunities) in my initial strategizing, how can I best revise my plans?

Does this step seem unnecessary? Lots of people, including many professional persuaders, think it is. But they ignore it at their peril.

Dick Morris (1997), the man who engineered Bill Clinton's second-term presidential victory, described a conversation with Clinton in which the then attorney general of Arkansas expressed surprise at Morris's habit of composing all the ads and all the arguments for a political campaign, then showing them to typical voters and finding out how they were affected. Back then, it was new to politics; now it is common practice. Of course, once the composition of an ad or argument for a speech is found wanting, it is revised or discarded.

BOX 9.1 Putting It All Together: A Formula for the Extemporaneous Speaker

You want to be skilled at the crafts of self-presentation. You also want to use available knowledge on the psychology of persuasion. How do you prepare and practice while at the same time expressing genuine commitments? Some speakers manage to combine craft eloquence with the appearance of utter genuineness. For most of us, a display of the necessary craft skills with genuine commitments doesn't come easy. But for that 10-minute speech before the class (and for most other public speaking situations), there is a formula that seems to work for most students.

1. Detailed speech outline: Don't write out your speech word for word, but assemble and organize the materials you plan to use. Do this well before the due date for your speech. Begin the process of test-marketing by showing it to a friend.

2. Revision: The first speech outline will almost always reveal problems needing attention. This point needs development. This point has none. This controversial claim lacks evidence, or the evidence is weak. (Lesson: Back to the library or to the Internet.) This speech would be great if I had 47 minutes to deliver it. This introduction doesn't say enough. This conclusion says too much. This framing metaphor is great, but not for this speech. Continue the process of test-marketing by talking through the revision process with a few fellow students. Volunteer to do the same for them.

3. Key word outline: On a few note cards or a sheet of paper, *clearly type out* the key words you'll need to remind you of whole chunks of material. If necessary, type out quotes or difficult-to-remember statistics. Consider outlining your speech using PowerPoint or one of the other software tools for projecting main ideas on to a screen. Then use that visual aid in your classroom speech.

Example 1: Richmond, Virginia,
Tobacco Marketing Speech

In preparation for her speech to the RTA, Emily has lost nearly every friend she's ever had in the process of anticipating questions from the audience and testing out possible responses. She has also met with Mrs. Foxworth and a couple of her friends. They think that her slide presentation will be effective, but they recommend including more information on the nature and effects of marketing by U.S. tobacco companies overseas. They also suggest that she bring along some reading materials for the folks, and maybe even a campaign sign-up sheet, "just in case they get turned on by what you have to say." Emily takes their advice. (See Box 9.1 for tips on delivering speeches.)

4. Informal rehearsal: When you have completed the key word outline, use it to talk through the speech with a friend or two, developing in the process a conversational style for communicating its key ideas. Have the key word outline in front of you, but use it as little as possible. If you discover additional reminders that need to be inserted into the outline, include only the most essential of them.

5. Stand-up rehearsal: Before friends or just a mirror, stand up and deliver from your key word outline, *deliberately altering your wording to avoid unintentional memorizing.* Having produced the speech on a detailed outline, transformed it to a key word outline, heard yourself say it a few times in different ways, and placed its contents in the different parts of your brain corresponding to sight and sound, you are ready to sleep comfortably, for the next day you will be ready to "knock 'em dead."

6. Presentation: Stand up and deliver, knowing in advance that the speech you present will be different in small and perhaps big ways from the speech you planned. Treat these departures as a potential opportunity, rather than an obstacle. Perhaps the moment-by-moment reactions of your audience have been telling you something. Perhaps the point you planned to emphasize but barely remembered can be safely forgotten. Or perhaps you can improvise a bit: "Oh yes, and back to my first point, I want to add . . ." Be alive to audience feedback as you speak. Show by your attention to their reactions that for you, communication is a two-way street. When you have finished, if time permits, don't say, "Any questions?" Ask, "What questions do you have?" This small difference in framing devices will metacommunicate your interest in continuing the conversation.

Example 2: Teenage Pregnancy
Radio Editorial

On arriving at the studio, Maggie had given no thought to test-marketing her audiotape, but the station manager, who happens to be a friend of hers, says he likes everything except her own testimonial. There's nothing wrong with the words, he says; it's how you're saying them. Sure enough, on rehearing, it sounds to Maggie as if she's not too sorry she got pregnant; after all, her mom is helping her and Reginald out.

In the studio, Maggie tries out another reading of the script, and then another, and another. Each time, the nonverbal message—the metacommunication—about her own pregnancy changes. Sometimes, it sounds like too much of a confession of wrongdoing, sometimes as if she's a victim, sometimes as if she just happened to get pregnant. Just when she's about ready to give up on this whole idea of making a radio editorial, the station manager suggests that they take some time out, have a Coke, talk about the weather. The two of them sit down together, and Maggie begins to cry. Memories come back to her of the pain of rejection by her lover, of the embarrassment at telling her mom that she was pregnant, of the loneliness she felt on having to stay home every day with her newborn, of the joy she felt at seeing Reginald smile for the first time. All this and much more comes flooding back to Maggie.

When she has finished crying, she goes back into the studio. She is now ready to tell the world what she really means by those two lines about herself.

Organizing Messages

Because message recipients process information in stages, audience members for Emily's presentation are unlikely to act on her proposal unless they evaluate it favorably. But they will not evaluate it favorably unless they understand it. To understand it, they must attend to it. But they may not expose themselves to her message if they suspect they won't benefit from it.

This Attention-Comprehension-Evaluation-Action model is simple, but it has its drawbacks. For one thing, evaluation begins from the moment of attention and includes assessments of the speaker as well as what the speaker has to say. Attention doesn't stop with comprehension. A vague or ambiguous message may, under some circumstances, yield a more favorable evaluation than a clear one. Much depends on the audience and the situation.

All this has implications for organizing messages. For example, as the next section describes, the tasks of getting attention and orienting receivers belong primarily to the introduction of a speech. Yet these tasks must be carried out throughout the speech (or other public message). As the chapter later notes, sometimes it is advantageous not to reveal all about purpose or position in the introduction, although *as a rule* you should. Consider what follows, then, provisionally. The same might be said, incidentally, about other rules of thumb offered in this chapter. Campbell (1996), for example, asserts that speakers and others ultimately need to rely on their own judgment:

> Rules accepted on faith produce wooden speeches—and worse, a wooden and gimmicky understanding of the art. The fun happens when mind happens, when students use rules as initial guidelines to the right way and then, through the arduous discipline of judging the particulars of their own cases, transcend them. (p. 221)

Introduction

The introduction to a speech is the place to get the attention of receivers and then orient them to the message. It is the place to create a favorable first impression. Indeed, building rapport with the audience and projecting just the right image to the audience must accompany everything else a speaker does. (See Table 9.1 for factors to consider in establishing your credibility.)

Although the introduction is presented first, the final draft of the introduction should not be prepared until the body and conclusion of the message are firmly established. Persuaders tend to make conclusions too long and introductions too short. They are anxious to delve into the meat of their presentations, and once into it, they have difficulty wrapping it up succinctly.

Getting Attention

Audiences heed selectively the messages they see and hear. Countering these tendencies often requires careful planning and great ingenuity, especially at an event such as an outdoor rally. Even with a captive audience, and even when the situation is conducive to careful listening, speakers may have to fight their way past apathy and competing stimuli. Consider the job of a visiting speaker at a campus convocation. At first, the listeners make physical adjustments. Books are placed under the seat. Sweaters are pulled off. Students shift in their seats. Next comes the social adjustment, which may go on for several minutes. "Hi Josh, Hi Luisa. Guess who I saw at the cafeteria this morning." In the midst of all this is the guest lecturer, all but forgotten on the stage.

Among the attention-getters often used as openers in a public speech are the humorous anecdote, the brief quotation, the startling statistic, the thought-provoking question, the pithy reference to the audience or the occasion, and the factual illustration. Sometimes, it is enough to go directly into the topic or to open conversationally with a greeting and a smile.

Orienting the Audience

"First I tell 'em what I'm gonna tell 'em. Then I tell 'em. Then I tell 'em what I told 'em."

Why follow the example of the minister quoted above? Why not simply "tell 'em"? Although persuaders may sometimes wish to postpone revealing purpose and position or to mask illogic behind a veil of ambiguity, at least some understanding of a message is almost always a prerequisite to acceptance of a proposition.

TABLE 9.1 Factors Affecting Communicator Credibility (A Specific Example of a Student Attempting to Persuade Others Not to Use Drugs)

Conceptual Factors	Examples of Assets	Examples of Liabilities	How to Do It
Power	Not much. I might be able to show them that my speech could save their lives.	They see me as just another person in class, with no special power to reward and punish.	Dramatize the horrors of drug addition; back it up with plenty of painful examples.
Competence	They know from Bob's comment in class that I made the dean's list last semester.	I've never told them about my interest in drug addiction. Could be starting from scratch with most of them.	Mention early in speech about my work with the Crisis Center. Get that *Time* article.
Trustworthiness	Some of them know I really followed through on the group assignment. They shouldn't feel that I'd trick them.	This will be a new topic for me. Most unlike my last speech on the campus election scandal.	Don't have much to worry about here. Might remind them that I stuck with them when the professor tried to spring a quiz on us!
Good will	My strong suit. By now the group knows that I'm majoring in social work—who could hate a social worker?	No problem as long as I stay with hard drugs. Can't come down hard on pot.	Many of them smoke, so I'd better steer clear of the marijuana issue or they'll see me as caring more about preaching than about them.

Speakers begin to orient their audiences by stating in the introduction the thesis—the central idea that sums up what the entire speech is about. The thesis determines what the main points will be, what types of material the speaker will select to support the main points, and how the speaker will introduce and conclude the message. Listeners should generally have a clear notion of what will be discussed and why. Rather than saying, "I think something should be done to change divorce laws," Lionel might say, "I'm here to ask your support for a proposal to abolish no-fault divorce in the Commonwealth of Pennsylvania."

But it is not enough to simply state the thesis; whatever the structure of the body of a speech or essay, it is generally useful to *preview* it in the introduction. Thus, Lionel might indicate that he will first discuss flaws in the present divorce system, then their causes, and then their solutions. Or he might preview only the first section of the body of the message, identifying the three or four inherent problems with the

TABLE 9.1 Continued

Conceptual Factors	Examples of Assets	Examples of Liabilities	How to Do It
Idealism	They know that I'm always up in the clouds and generally aspire to the same things they do.	Got to be careful not to get too carried away with the moral stuff. Stick to the "fully functioning human being" idea.	Should probably stress our common goals early in the speech before I mention drugs.
Similarity	I've been in class with them all semester. They know I dress and talk like most of them.	Could be a problem if I come on like Ms. Know-It-All. Have to steer clear of my religious views on the subject with these heathens!	Better tie this in with Claire's speech on legalizing pot. This should build more common ground between me and them.
Dynamism	My biggie! They know that they can't shut me up when I get committed to a topic.	No problem! (As long as I remember not to talk too fast!)	Pace yourself, baby, pace yourself.

SOURCE: Reprinted from Zimbardo, Ebbeson, & Maslach (1977), pp. 60-61. Originally adapted from Hart, Friedrich, & Brooks (1975). Used with permission.

present divorce laws and the order in which they will be discussed. Previews key receivers in to main ideas and their logical relationships.

In a longer and more complex treatment of a subject, the speaker should prepare the audience thoroughly for what is to come. Still, he will need to be strategic in deciding how to prepare them. He may have to indicate what he will *not* be talking about. In a speech advocating no-fault divorce, for example, Lionel could say, "Now I'm not here to promote divorce. What I'll be asking you to support is the plan proposed by former divorce lawyer Herbert Sherbert of the Commonwealth of Pennsylvania."

Lionel might also want to define key terms. What exactly is no-fault divorce? On almost any controversial issue, there are bound to be key terms that need defining. The most familiar form of definition is the dictionary definition. It names something, puts it into a category, and then separates it from members of that category. No-fault divorce might be defined as "a system of divorce that allows dissolution of a marriage, without findings of wrongdoing by either party." In and of themselves, however, dictionary definitions tend to be too abstract. Often, it is helpful to supplement them with examples and perhaps with further explanation. Definitions should ordinarily be acceptable to the audience, but the speaker may need to take time to defend his definition. Perhaps Lionel could cite an authority in its support or ask his audience to accept the definition for purposes of discussion (like a ground rule in baseball or football) without necessarily endorsing it fully.

In a 10-minute speech, a persuader might well want to introduce historical or other background material before beginning the body of the message. How many states have no-fault divorce at present? How did the idea originate? What other states are considering it? These are just some of the factual questions that might be discussed briefly in the introduction.

Chances are that the body of a speech or essay favoring passage of no-fault divorce legislation will begin with an indictment of the present system: its manifest evils and the reasons that it must be replaced, rather than simply repaired. Such an indictment assumes that there is something wrong with the system in principle, that the alleged evils stem from the nature of the system, rather than from particular practices associated with it. But what is "the system"? What are its underlying principles? Often, the basic principles of the system are not at all obvious. An indictment of the present divorce laws might well be preceded by analyses and explanations of their underlying principles—their inherent assumption, for example, that every marital breakup is caused by a "guilty" party.

Body

After stating the thesis, the next step is to come up with *main points,* or reasons that justify the thesis. These may be organized around the stock issues discussed in Chapter 8. Or Lionel could simply say, "I support no-fault divorce for the following five reasons." In the body of the speech, the persuader may also raise and refute counterarguments (more on this later in the chapter).

Main points should usually be simple, declarative sentences that contain one memorably stated idea. Lionel won't say, "No-fault divorce, by eliminating the requirement of blame on either party and the possible sense of embarrassment one of them might have at having wronged the other, is preferable to the existing system. That, in any event, is my first reason for advocating it." Instead, Lionel might say, "Why am I for no-fault divorce? Reason One: No government-required blame or shame."

A useful mnemonic device for remembering how to organize discussion of a main point is NESC: Name it. Explain it. Support it. Conclude it. Having stated the main point (naming), you may well need to clarify it (explaining) and to provide evidence and arguments in its defense (supporting). As you do so, remember the importance of holding the audience's attention. Supporting materials may be made more interesting by rounding out statistics, paraphrasing long or dull quotations, interspersing seriousness with humor, and using vivid analogies or other comparisons. Once having nailed down your main point, it often helps to restate it (concluding).

A coactive, conversational style, one that communicates with the audience, rather than at them, is important. Part and parcel of that style is the transformation of dry, abstract statistics into terms that audiences can understand on a personal level. Rather than saying that "51.5% of married people in the Commonwealth of Pennsylvania terminate their marriages by way of divorce," Lionel might say, "More than half of all marriages in Pennsylvania end in divorce." Better still, "You probably know at least two couples planning to tie the knot in the next year. Well, if past is prophet, Becky and Sam may hang in there, but don't count on Tanya and Tim. More than half of all Pennsylvania marriages end in divorce."

As you plan your speech, think of ways to make its language robust. Even the language of normally dull orienting materials can be livened up. For example, longish speeches with four or five points typically need *transitional statements* that remind audiences of where the speech has been and alert them to where it is heading. But instead of saying, "Now that my time-savings point has been established, I want at this juncture to discuss how no-fault divorce can save money as well," Lionel might say, "We've seen that no-fault divorce saves time. But does it save money?" Connectives such as these invite curiosity. Should Lionel then say, "It is my second contention that no-fault divorce does in fact provide significant cost savings"? Probably not. Instead he might say, "I think it does. Lots of money. And that's my next point."

Conclusion

The rule of thumb for speeches is to wrap things up quickly—perhaps in one third the time required for the introduction. But that depends on whether the persuader's goal is to convince the audience and stop at that or attempt to activate them. A 10-minute speech to convince might close with a vivid restatement of the thesis and a summary of the main points. Says Lionel, "And so in conclusion, I repeat: The people of Pennsylvania need no-fault divorce for these reasons: . . ." Should he wish to activate his audience, he will probably need to tell them how to act (who, what, when, where, and how?), and he may need to pound home the need for urgency.

You can make a difference by calling or e-mailing State Senator Getwirthy, chair of the Senate committee that's considering this legislation. But you'd better act now because the Getwirthy committee is about to make its recommendation to the full Senate. Here's how you can contact Getwirthy. . . . Let him know that you give a damn.

If time permits, the persuader should probably try to solicit overt pledges of support, preferably from respected audience members. He might ask the audience to consider ways of making a difference on this issue. Suggestions on how to act will probably have more influence coming from them.

Issues in Message Design

Behavioral research has weighed in on a number of knotty issues in message construction. In addition, as indicated in Chapter 1, researchers now have the benefits of *meta-analysis* (Allen & Preiss, 1998). This is a methodological device by which to pool the findings from multiple studies of the same or similar phenomena. This section takes up several issues, offering judgments about what conclusions to draw from the research and from meta-analyses of the research findings.

Explicit Versus Implicit Conclusion Drawing

When, if at all, should you hold back on stating your thesis, perhaps building up to it in stages by use of the yes-yes or yes-but approaches? You run a risk if you leave your position unstated and merely implied; the audience may not draw the same conclusion that you intended. The same holds true for concealing your conclusion until the end; what if the audience fails to follow your logic? What if the act of concealment damages your credibility? Shouldn't you be frank and forthright with your audience?

Considerations such as these have made explicit, up-front conclusion drawing the equivalent of the default options on your computer drive. It is the recommendation of choice for most situations. But leaving your position unstated has the theoretical advantage of preventing defenses from being raised. This could be particularly important when facing a hostile or highly critical audience. Moreover, audiences that do follow your logic and generate supportive thoughts of their own in the process of attending to your arguments are likely to be your most enduring supporters (Petty & Cacioppo, 1981/1996). So the matter is not clear-cut.

An analysis of the findings from seven studies of explicit versus implicit conclusion drawing gives a slight edge to explicitness but reveals considerable variation from study to study (Cruz, 1998). This is not unusual. For example, Kardes (1988) and Sawyer and Howard (1991) found a significant advantage for implicit conclusion drawing under conditions of high audience involvement. But unlike the other researchers, they used brief advertisements as opposed to longer messages; hence problems of audience comprehension were probably not as great.

Up-front, explicit conclusion drawing (stating the thesis in the introduction) is the best way to go, *other things being equal.* But there is no need to settle this thorny issue in an either-or fashion. As Cruz (1998) points out, it is possible to reason with audiences, drawing partial conclusions along the way, then treat these conclusions as premises in subsequent chains of reasoning. This is advisable with hostile or even intelligent, discriminating audiences that have the motivation and ability to engage in central processing.

Campbell (1996) tells the story of a student named Mike from conservative northern Idaho who addressed his public speaking class at the liberal-leaning University of Washington in Seattle on the question of whether vengeance was ever a legitimate motive for capital punishment. Having raised this incendiary question, should Mike have immediately answered it in the affirmative, thus further inflaming the audience? He chose not to, but neither did he wait until the end of the speech to state his conclusion.

Instead, Mike followed his incendiary question with another question, one designed to get the yes-yes process going. "How many of you have ever heard of Simon Wiesenthal?" he asked. Several hands went up. "What does he do?" was the next question. A student answered the question with a question. "Isn't he the fellow who hunts Nazis?" "That's right," said Mike. "Why do you suppose he does it? Do you think he is trying to rehabilitate them?" He paused to let the import of the question sink in. Then he looked directly at the class and said, "He does it for vengeance." Mike then dispensed with the usual arguments for capital punishment, announcing instead that his case for capital punishment would be based exclusively on the social value of vengeance. Said Campbell, the speech was successful even if it won no converts to Mike's position. "He had convinced his audience that his position was not grounded in values foreign to their own." (p. 253). On the basis of previous speeches, Mike had been perceived by many in the class as a right-wing alien. Not after this speech—he had become one of them.[1]

"One-Sided" Versus "Both-Sided" Presentations

A one-sided message presents only the arguments favoring a given proposition. "Vote for Mervin for these reasons: . . ." Or "Vote against Mervin's opponent for these reasons: . . ." A both-sided message considers pros and cons. But how should the pros and cons be considered—by treating the two sides equally and without partisan bias? "Here are five reasons to vote for Mervin; here are five to vote for his opponent." Or, as used here, considering opposing arguments but refuting them where possible? "It's sometimes said that Mervin doesn't know how to compromise. Well, I say that's baloney. Perhaps what his opponents don't like is that Mervin is a person of principle."

The conventional wisdom has been that treating the two sides equally doesn't persuade very well, and this is clearly confirmed by research (Allen, 1991; Allen et al., 1990). The conventional wisdom *had* been that a both-sided approach with refutation of the opposing arguments worked best on reasonably well-educated audiences, on persons who were undecided or in disagreement with the communicator's position, and on audiences that would later be exposed to counterarguments. A one-sided approach, it was assumed, worked best with less-educated, already sympathetic audiences who would not be exposed to counterarguments.

Allen's (1991) meta-analysis calls this received wisdom into question. Almost always, it suggests, the refutational both-sides approach works best. Yet this approach generally takes more time than a one-sided approach, and time may be in short supply. Moreover, although consideration of an opposing position can enhance the persuader's credibility, it can backfire if strong con arguments are raised that the audience previously hadn't thought of or if the persuader's refutations appear weak. Allen's meta-analysis notwithstanding, it is probably a good idea to concede what you can't deny. "Yes, Mervin was in detox for a drug problem, but that was 20 years ago, and he's been drug-free ever since." (See section below on adapting to different types of audiences for more measured advice.)

Magnitude of Discrepancy Controversy

Explicitly or implicitly, the persuader always communicates a position that is more or less discrepant from the position initially endorsed by the audience. Perhaps an advocate of a 6% sales tax is addressing those who believe only a 3% tax is needed. A fund-raiser for a charity may address an audience that is sympathetic to the cause but not as committed to it. In any case, the persuader must discern when the discrepancy between the proposition and the attitude of the audience will be too great to gain acceptance.

A review of the early research literature by Aronson, Turner, and Carlsmith (1963) suggested that communicator credibility plays an important role in the magnitude of discrepancy controversy. Their conclusion was the product not of a meta-analysis but of some careful detective work. In study after study, they discovered that extremely discrepant positions tended to be accepted if the source of the message was described as highly credible—for example, a highly regarded sleep researcher (as opposed to an ordinary college student) claiming that most people slept far longer than they needed to and could really get by on just 2 hours per night. Less credible communicators, they found, had to make less extreme claims than the highly credible sources or risk being disbelieved altogether. The clear implication of their literature review is that if speakers intend to secure audience acceptance of extreme claims, they had best be highly credible themselves or provide testimonial support from persons who are. Testimonial evidence can be highly effective (Reinard, 1998). It tends to be especially persuasive when the sources are identified and their qualifications briefly explained. Another factor that bears on the relationship between extremity of position and opinion change is an audience's ego involvement. On controversial issues such as gun control, some people on each side feel a direct personal stake in the matter; others are relatively indifferent. For example, the citizens of Littleton, Colorado, became far more ego involved in the gun control issue after the tragic killings at Littleton's Columbine High School in 1999.

Ego involvement strengthens beliefs and attitude commitments, making them much harder to dislodge and much easier to reinforce. For example, after the Columbine shootings, a gun control advocate would probably have become less receptive to persuasive messages from leaders of the National Rifle Association and even more receptive than before to arguments from Handgun Control, Inc.

The way ego involvement relates to magnitude of discrepancy was elegantly formulated by Sherif, Sherif, and Nebergall (1965) in their *social judgment-involvement* theory. They began with the truism that attitudes toward any issue can be arranged along a continuum from very unfavorable to very favorable. On this continuum, there will be some positions the receiver can agree with, some positions the receiver will reject, and a middle range of positions on which the receiver has no strong feelings. For example, an advocate of banning guns entirely would probably be receptive to proposals calling for prohibitions on assault weapons, the registration of all guns, and the introduction of safety locks on guns. These proposals fall within what Sherif et al. label as the *latitude of acceptance.* According to Sherif et al., proposals falling within this zone are assimilated. That is, they are seen as more similar to one's favorite position than they really are. Other proposals would fall within this person's *latitude of rejection,* for example, a call for legislation permitting ordinary citizens to carry weapons on their persons at all times. This proposal would be contrasted. That is, it would be seen as more different from the gun control advocate's favorite position than it really is. Finally, the gun control advocate might be indifferent to proposals inviting hunters to take voluntary safety education courses and other proposals calling for training in marksmanship. These would fall within the gun control advocate's *latitude of neutrality.*

Sherif et al. maintain that ego involvement shrinks the latitudes of acceptance and neutrality and widens the latitude of rejection. After the shootings at Columbine High School, for example, an advocate of total bans on gun ownership might now regard proposals for marksmanship training and even for safety locks on guns as palliatives that should be rejected. When before, a proposal to require safety locks on guns would have been assimilated, now a speech advocating this position might boomerang, prompting greater hostility toward safety locks than before the speech had been given. The ego-involved listener can be energized by increased involvement and perhaps made more receptive to calls for action in support of the gun control cause

An Attitudes Continuum on Gun Control

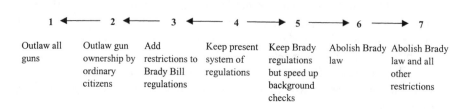

1	2	3	4	5	6	7
Outlaw all guns	Outlaw gun ownership by ordinary citizens	Add restrictions to Brady Bill regulations	Keep present system of regulations	Keep Brady regulations but speed up background checks	Abolish Brady law	Abolish Brady law and all other restrictions

Figure 9.1. An Attitudes Continuum on Gun Control

but will be highly resistant to conversion or even neutralization. In general, the greatest degree of attitude change occurs with well-crafted messages that fall within the message recipient's latitude of neutrality.

The best thing a pro-gun advocate can do in attempting to persuade an ego-involved opponent of gun ownership is tailor the message to what remains of the listener's latitude of neutrality. Perhaps the advocate can chip away at the listener's opposition in a manner akin to the foot-in-the-door technique, discussed in Chapter 7. But of course, this takes patience; it is unlikely to work on the basis of a single message and could backfire in any case. A more promising use of incremental persuasion begins with audiences that are already somewhat receptive to your point of view. Suppose you are an advocate of a total ban on gun ownership by private citizens, and you are talking with a group that was moved by the events at Columbine but is thus far willing to endorse only requiring safety locks on guns. This is a group you can probably move by increments, from, say, mandatory gun registration in one persuasive campaign to gun prohibition in the next.

When a speaker is uncertain how far to push an audience, it is often a good idea to provide a range of acceptable options. This has the added advantage of increasing the receiver's feeling of decisional freedom. "We're asking you to give $1,000 to the gun control effort. But if that's more than you can afford, we'd be happy with a $100 gift or even a $10 donation. The choice is yours."

Fear Appeals

Communicators may claim that adoption of their proposals will help audiences "get a good" (money, fame, good looks, good sex) or "keep a good" (the money you've saved, the reputation you've earned). They can also claim an ability to help them get rid of something bad (pimples, nagging headaches, sagging breasts). Or they can claim their proposal will help them avoid a bad (a bad marriage, a bad hangover, a badly bruised ego; Rank, 1982).

Sooner or later, one way or another, these arguments are likely to play on the emotion of fear. For example, communicators who predict that good (weight loss) will come from adoption of their proposal or remedy (low-calorie cereal) may combine projection of a rosier future (weight loss) with fear appeals warning of the dangers of inaction (clothes that don't fit). Communicators who offer assurances that adoption of their plan (security system) will allow audiences to keep a good (their valuables) may begin with fear appeals warning of threats to that good (reenactment of burglary).

Not all fear appeals are successful in achieving their objectives. It is extremely difficult, for example, to convince teenagers not to experiment with cigarettes and college students not to engage in binge drinking. Yet some health and safety campaigns have worked. For example, adult smoking and teenage pregnancies are down in the United States. Information campaigns (to be discussed in Chapter 10) have probably helped.

Fear appeals don't always generate fears in audiences; the relationship between fear appeal messages and perceived fear by audiences from a meta-analysis of 45 studies is described by Mongeau (1998) as "moderate" (p. 59). Overall, the impact of fear appeals on attitude change is surprisingly small, with postcollege-age participants more responsive than college students. The same holds true with the effects of fear appeals on overt behavior.

Still, fear appeals can be effective. They should be put forward vividly and forcefully to increase the likelihood that what gets communicated actually reverberates in the minds of the audience. There is apparently no evidence from meta-analysis that fear appeals arouse defensive avoidance (Mongeau, 1998). Perhaps that happens only in extreme cases and with people who have low self-esteem. But if even these people are given clear, specific, and optimistic instructions about how to cope with their fears, they, too, are apt to climb out from under the covers and take the recommended action (Leventhal, 1970).

In general, suggest Pratkanis and Aronson (1991), a fear appeal is likely to be most effective under the following four conditions: (1) it "scares the hell out of people," (2) it provides concrete recommendations for overcoming the aroused threat, (3) the action recommended is perceived as effective for reducing the threat, and (4) receivers are convinced that they can perform the recommended action (p. 165). Before presenting your fear appeal message, you should see to it that these four factors are addressed.

Adapting to Different Audiences

As this chapter has observed repeatedly, what works with one audience may fail miserably with another. The following pulls together much of what has been said about audience adaptation and adds some additional principles. (See also Appendix II.) But these are rules of thumb for broadly defined audience types. They may not apply to the particular audience and situation you confront. For example, with a *mixed* audience—some listeners sympathetic, some indifferent, some conflicted or in flat out disagreement, some even hostile to the speaker and the speaker's view—whom should you target? Whom should you ignore? Should you choose to provide "different strokes to different folks" in the same listening audience? If so, how do you win over one audience segment while not alienating another? For example, in a speech promoting use of RU-486, a new and relatively easy method for early abortions, do you concede to pro-lifers in the audience that second- and third-trimester abortions are harder to justify on moral grounds? If so, are you prepared to risk the displeasure of pro-choice audience members? Alternatively, should you risk losing the already indifferent and uninformed members of your audience by advancing the more nuanced position that although abortions even in the third trimester can be justified, first-trimester abortions are preferable? These are decisions that no textbook can make for the person behind the podium.

Nor can a textbook decide for the speaker whether to have one substantive goal or many for a single-message presentation, and what those goals should be. It is conventionally assumed that persuaders should have but one specific purpose for any given speech or essay, but a speaker may have two or more goals for the audience as a whole or different goals for different audience segments. Not uncommonly, political eulogies have been used both to memorialize a deceased leader and to press home an agenda for the future. Vice President Lyndon Johnson did this on the occasion of John F. Kennedy's memorial, for example (Jamieson & Campbell, 1982). In 1965, a speaker at Temple University used the occasion of a Temple-affiliated civil rights leader's brutal killing in Selma, Alabama, both to intensify the audience's already strong commitments to racial equality in the South and to engage in some response shaping (the *molding* of attitudes) about what needed to be done closer to home—at Temple and in Philadelphia generally. The sympathy evoked by the civil rights leader's death made the case for facing up to problems of racial discrimination in the North more palatable to the Temple audience.

The first rule, then, in constructing any message is *to formulate both substantive and relational goals and think strategically about how to achieve these goals in tandem.* Recall the case of Mike, the student who defended vengeance as a legitimate reason for capital punishment. In addition to winning a reasonably receptive hearing for his substantive goal, he was able, in the process, to enhance his personal credibility with the audience. Buller and Hall (1998) even suggest *distracting* audience attention away from the person of the persuader if the persuader's competence and trustworthiness are low. On the other hand, a speaker regarded as a *superrepresentative* of the audience (seen as highly attractive, trustworthy, *and* competent) might *distract* the audience from potential objections to the substantive proposal while highlighting his or her personal commitment to it (Buller & Hall, 1998).

The second rule is to be situationally sensitive. For example, although humor tends to be a great disarmer of hostility, there are clearly occasions (e.g., moments of crisis such as the Columbine shootings) when humor is inappropriate.

Summary

Sometimes, a public speech must be put through multiple drafts until it comes as close as possible to meeting the multiple demands that are placed on it. But for most of us, most of the time, needed are the freshness and spontaneity that come from preparing well, revising as needed, but then *not* writing out the speech or memorizing it, and instead deliberately altering its wording during rehearsal so that the speaker is best prepared to communicate *with* audience members, rather than *at* them.

The speech or other public presentation should combine genuine commitment with the necessary craft skills. Preparation for a 10-minute persuasive speech, for example, will generally require strategic adaptation of goals and materials to audience and situation. For this, a three-step process for strategy analysis was recommended. In preparing the message, the speaker should review the many resources identified in the book for exploiting strategic opportunities and overcoming obstacles. Message preparation can benefit from bringing psychological principles to bear on the case at hand. It can exploit framing and "languaging" strategies. The arguments selected should contain a "psycho-dash-logic," providing audiences with both psychological income and the appearance of reason.

Preparation begins by deciding on a general topic, gathering materials, coming to judgment, and formulating substantive and relational goals for the audience as a whole and perhaps for different audience segments. The next step is to organize the message, being sure to make provision in the introduction for building rapport with the audience, gaining their attention, and orienting them as needed to topic, thesis, background information, and the like. The body of the message should build around main points that are clearly tied to the thesis, each point named, explained, supported, and concluded (NESC). The conclusion should be brief if the only purpose is to sway opinion, longer to mobilize the audience for action.

The speech (or other public presentation) should ordinarily be explicit and up-front about its thesis, but there are times for building logically to a conclusion, rather than stating it at the outset. Generally, too, the message should both advance the speaker's side while refuting the opposition's, but there are times to concede what cannot be denied (yes-but) or, in the interests of time, to dwell only on one's own case. The more extreme the position in relation to the audience, the more credible the speaker (or possibly the speaker's sources of testimony) needs to be. Alternatively, the speaker should probably advance a more moderate position (falling within the audience's latitude of neutrality), especially if those in opposition are highly ego in-volved in the topic. When fear appeals are used, they should be combined with spe-cific, doable recommendations for action and assurances that the action recom-mended will overcome or at least reduce the problem.

These generalizations about message design may have to be amended in adapt-ing to particular audiences and particular situations, as must the principles here identified for adapting to different types of audience.

A final comment is in order on the value of combining the behavioral and criti-cal studies traditions. This chapter's advice to those "going public" as persuaders would have been impoverished without the research findings and meta-analyses of social scientists and the insights of rhetorical critics such as John Campbell.

Questions and Projects for Further Study

1. What do you think John Campbell meant when he said that "the fun happens when mind happens"? Does this mean that there are no rules of persuasion? What do you think of his description of the beginning public speaking class and especially of the tendency of many students to go through the motions, rather than expressing genuine commitments? Is it only slightly exaggerated? Have you ever seen a class come to life when a student's "second" speech got real with the audience?

2. How can you best combine expressing genuine commitments with the craft skills of message preparation and self-presentation? In your experience, which re-sources discussed in this book are most useful for exploiting the opportunities and overcoming the obstacles persuaders confront? Is it possible, in your opinion, to strategize, organize, and still appear authentic?

3. Try practicing a speech aloud *without* deliberately altering your wording. Do you experience a tendency to overmemorize? On the other hand, have you experi-enced the benefits of talking a speech through conversationally with a friend, per-haps relying only on a key word outline? Try keeping the key word outline for a 10-minute speech to no more than 10 words or phrases, plus the quotations or complex statistics that you might find it necessary to type out verbatim and then read to your audience.

4. Try experimenting with different message designs, for example, an explicit up-front statement of thesis versus a message that builds logically to a conclusion, or a one-sided message versus a both-sided message that is either refutational or nonrefutational. Test-market these alternative designs with people similar to those you will ultimately attempt to persuade.

5. In your view, which type of audience is hardest to adapt to: a hostile or highly critical audience, an indifferent and uninformed audience, a conflicted audience, a sympathetic audience, or an audience containing a mix of all these audience segments?

6. This chapter has focused on persuasive speaking. What, in your opinion, are the chief differences with persuasive writing?

7. Plan and execute a 60-second guest radio editorial for a fictitious radio station on Main Campus (WOWL). Submit an audiotape plus a two- to three-page strategic plan. Be sure to include the test-marketing stage.

Note

1. Note how Mike had used a source, Simon Wiesenthal, whom the audience could accept. This is one of the principles to be emphasized in dealing with hostile audiences.

References

Allen, M. (1991). Meta-analysis comparing the persuasiveness of one-sided and two-sided messages. *Western Journal of Speech Communication, 55,* 390-404.

Allen, M., Hale, J., Mongeau, P., Berkowitz-Stafford, S., Stafford, R. S., Shanahan, W., Agee, P., Dillon, K., Jackson, R., & Ray, C. (1990). Testing a model of message sidedness: Three replications. *Communication Monographs, 57,* 274-291.

Allen, M., & Preiss, R. W. (Eds.). (1998). *Persuasion: Advances through meta-analysis.* Cresskill, NJ: Hampton.

Aronson, E., Turner, J., & Carlsmith, J. M. (1963). Communication credibility and communication discrepancy as determinants of opinion change. *Journal of Abnormal and Social Psychology, 67,* 31-36.

Buller, D. B., & Hall, J. R. (1998). The effects of distraction during persuasion. In M. Allen & R. W. Preiss (Eds.), *Persuasion: Advances through meta-analysis.* Cresskill, NJ: Hampton.

Campbell, J. A. (1996). Oratory, democracy, and the classroom. In R. Soder (Ed.), *Democracy, education, and the school.* San Francisco: Jossey-Bass.

Cruz, M. G. (1998). Explicit and implicit conclusions in persuasive messages. In M. Allen & R. W. Preiss (Eds.), *Persuasion: Advances through meta-analysis.* Cresskill, NJ: Hampton.

Douglass, F. (1968). *Narrative of the life of Frederick Douglass: An American slave.* New York: Signet. (Original work published 1845)

Garrison, W. L. (1968). Preface. In F. Douglass, *Narrative of the life of Frederick Douglass: An American slave.* New York: Signet. (Original work published 1845)

Hamlin, S. (1998). *What makes juries listen today.* Little Falls, NJ: Glasser LegalWorks.

Hart, R. P., Friedrich, G. W., & Brooks, W. D. (1975). *Public communication.* New York: Harper & Row.

Jamieson, K. H., & Campbell, K. K. (1982). Rhetorical hybrids: Fusions of generic elements. *Quarterly Journal of Speech, 68,* 146-157.

Kardes, F. (1988). Spontaneous inference processes in advertising: The effects of conclusion omission and involvement on persuasion. *Journal of Consumer Research, 15,* 225-233.

Leventhal, H. (1970). Findings and theory in the study of fear appeals. In L. Berkowitz (Ed.), *Advances in experimental social psychology* (Vol. 5, pp. 119-186). New York: Academic Press.

Mongeau, P. A. (1998). Another look at fear-arousing persuasive appeals. In M. Allen & R. W. Preiss (Eds.), *Persuasion: Advances through meta-analysis.* Cresskill, NJ: Hampton.

Morris, D. (1997). *Behind the Oval Office.* New York: Random House.

Petty, R. E., & Cacioppo, J. T. (1996). *Attitudes and persuasion: Classic and contemporary approaches.* Boulder, CO: Westview. (Original work published 1981)

Pratkanis, A., & Aronson, E. (1991). *Age of propaganda: The everyday use and abuse of persuasion.* New York: Freeman.

Rank, H. (1982). The thirty-second spot quiz. *The pitch* (pp. 1-2). Urbana, IL: National Council of Teachers of English.

Reinard, J. C. (1998). The persuasive effects of testimonial assertion evidence. In M. Allen & R. W. Preiss (Eds.), *Persuasion: Advances through meta-analysis.* Cresskill, NJ: Hampton.

Sawyer, A., & Howard, D. (1991). Effects of omitting conclusions in advertisements to involved and uninvolved audiences. *Journal of Marketing Research, 28,* 467-474.

Sherif, C. W., Sherif, M., & Nebergall, R. E. (1965). *Attitudes and attitude change: The social judgment-involvement approach.* Philadelphia: W. B. Saunders.

Zimbardo, P. G., Ebbeson, E. B., & Maslach, C. (1977). *Influencing attitudes and changing behavior* (2nd ed.). Reading, MA: Addison-Wesley.

Planning Campaigns

For as long as the villagers of Diabougou, Senegal, could remember, it had been custom for the young girls of the community to submit to the extremely painful and often dangerous process of female circumcision. Each year during the rainy season, the ritual circumciser of Diabougou would use a razor blade to remove the clitoris, and sometimes the inner and outer vaginal lips, of 200 children. The process was not unique to Senegal; indeed, according to Vivienne Walt (1998), about 130 million African women in 28 countries are circumcised, and thousands die as a result. Thus, it is all the more remarkable that one educational campaign was able to turn public opinion around in much of Senegal. Since July 1997, 29 Senegalese communities have declared an end to female circumcision and begun pressing other villages to join them.

The single speech or other one-shot communication described in Chapter 9 is important, but seldom does it achieve a significant, enduring impact on its own. That job is left to persuasive campaigns—organized, sustained attempts at influencing groups or masses of people through a series of messages. Campaigns take many forms—political campaigns (discussed in Chapter 11), product advertising campaigns (Chapter 12), and various issue-oriented campaigns (Chapters 10 and 14). This chapter introduces campaigning as a multistage, multimessage process and then explores in more detail two particular types of campaigns: indoctrination campaigns and public relations campaigns.

Campaign Planning

Campaigns proceed through stages, each stage building on the last yet exhibiting a life of its own (Figure 10.1). All of them should be anticipated in the initial planning, but plans will also need to be modified from time to time as new information is received. The following summary of factors to consider in the planning process is intended to be quite general to encompass a wide variety of campaign types.

Setting Campaign Goals

Campaigns arise from a sense that interests (e.g., a corporation's profits) or values (e.g., a people's safety or survival) held dear by an organization must be protected or advanced (Salmon, 1989). But to succeed, a campaign must have specific goals. The goal might be to elicit specific behaviors: enough votes to win election as student council president, enough raffle sales to enable the college orchestra to make an overseas trip, or enough support from local townspeople to get city council approval for a bicycle-only lane on Main Street. Other campaigns are less concerned with specific behavioral payoffs than with influencing beliefs and values. They vary from public relations campaigns that aim at fostering more favorable images of a group or organization, such as a fraternity or sorority, or church or synagogue, to indoctrination campaigns that seek to socialize or resocialize individuals with the aim of getting them to endorse entire ideologies and lifestyles. Religious cults stage indoctrination campaigns of this sort, but although far-out worship groups might be accused of brainwashing or thought control, mainstream organizations such as the military and the U.S. Immigration and Naturalization Service often get by using similar persuasive tactics under far more acceptable labels such as "re-education" (Pratkanis & Aronson, 1991). Varying degrees of legitimacy are also conferred on reform-oriented social movements (discussed in Chapter 14). Their efforts at institutional change might target personnel (e.g., hiring more black police officers and firing the police chief), practices (e.g., stricter enforcement of housing codes), policies (e.g., university policies of "publish or perish"), or institutional values and priorities (rewarding research by faculty over quality of teaching).

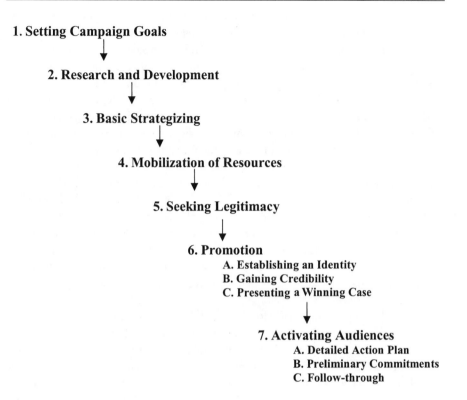

Figure 10.1. Stages and Components in Campaign Planning

Audience and situation also should be taken into account in formulating subsidiary goals. For example, a fund-raising campaign in behalf of a college orchestra should not be so aggressive that it garners the orchestra an overseas trip at the price of reduced attendance at home events. Other secondary goals in situations primarily designed to elicit specific behaviors (e.g., lottery sales) might revolve around issues of personal identity. Will those who volunteer for this fund-raising effort feel good about themselves when it's been completed? Will they have made friends rather than lost them, honored their consciences rather than betrayed them? Can people commit to the cause without feeling utterly consumed by it (Dillard, 1988)?

Situations are seldom ideal for the fulfillment of campaign goals. Thus, it is a good idea to formulate primary goals at several levels: (a) what the campaign would ideally like to achieve, (b) what it expects to achieve, and (c) the bare minimum that would still make the campaign worthwhile. Often, the large-scale information campaign is of questionable value when measured against the time, effort, and money expended to conduct the campaign. For example, it has proved far more effective—and cheaper—to mandate installation of air bags in automobiles than to educate and convince consumers that air bags are an option they should purchase.

An example of flexible goal setting involves efforts by the Temple Issues Forum (TIF) to place issues of higher education higher on the agenda in Philadelphia city politics. TIF's official mission is to promote public debate and discussion at Temple University on issues of potential interest to the university community. Its main purpose has been to stimulate civic and intellectual engagement by students, not to influence city politics. But having run a televised mayoral forum at Temple on the topic of "Higher Education and the City," TIF's planning group identified a number of issues that fairly begged to be addressed through the long term and not just by way of a one-time-only mayoral forum. These included issues of marketing the city as a world-class center for higher education and of encouraging its college and university graduates to remain in the city and perhaps start businesses in the area. It included as well issues of urban education: how better to prepare urban high school graduates to do college-level work.

TIF's planning group toyed with the possibility of promoting action on all these fronts, and it even talked with a foundation representative about organizing a consortium of colleges and universities in the Philadelphia area to be called "Greater Collegiate Philadelphia." But group members knew that this goal was remote, although the other goals were difficult to realize but not completely beyond the group's capacity to make a difference. Minimally speaking, TIF's planning group was confident it could succeed at its agenda-setting goal, and it anticipated that everyone, including TIF itself, would benefit from the mayoral forum. So, in keeping with the principles of goal seeking, TIF had short- and long-term goals, as well as optimal, realistic, and minimal goals.

Undertaking Research and Development

What management experts refer to as the R&D function of business organizations has its counterpart in persuasive campaigns. It involves the gathering of arguments and evidence to be used in building persuasive messages, as well as the development of know-how for implementation. The failure to take these necessary steps is common among amateur campaigners. One well-intentioned student attempted to launch a campaign to require bicycle safety education in the public schools. Intuitively, he decided that the best way to get action was to testify at a meeting of the city school board. Unfortunately, he had not yet come up with a plan for such a program, discovered how and where decisions of this type are made in the school system, sought to determine whether any groups might have been interested in aiding his campaign, or even developed documented proof of the existence of a problem.

TIF's planning group began with faculty and administrators inexperienced at urban affairs, but it expanded to include urban specialists. Still, its top leadership was inexpert at managing the more ambitious aspects of its campaign plan. They therefore sought out consultants, including city representatives who had been working on some of these issues for quite some time.

Formulating a Basic Strategy

Although campaign strategies must frequently be revised in light of new developments, it is nevertheless possible at the outset to formulate global strategies. A basic, coactive rule of basic strategizing is that to get what you want, you must help those you're trying to influence get what they want. Advertisers for Eastman Kodak once ran a camera-purchasing campaign aimed at families with expectant mothers; they did so on the basis of evidence that these families were least likely to own cameras and most likely to want them when the baby arrived. A Midas Muffler campaign zeroed in on the inadequacies of ordinary repair shops; it did so on the basis of evidence that these shops were their stiffest competition and were vulnerable to attack. The National Communication Association targeted alumni of graduate programs in communication for a major fund-raising effort. The campaign's organizers strategized that these alums would want to give generously if invited to contribute in the name of a valued graduate school mentor.

Some campaigns persuade indirectly. Safe sex and prosocial sexual attitudes have been promoted indirectly in a late-night radio talk show beamed at teenagers that mixes nine parts entertainment with one part serious instruction. Use of a designated driver after parties has been promoted via planted dialogue in television sitcoms (Rothenberg, 1988). Products are promoted in entertainment programming, as are corporate images—all this for a price. Some corporate public relations efforts proceed by way of low-visibility campaigns—a news report favorable to the company planted in one news outlet, an editorial planted in another.

Basic strategizing often involves selecting an appropriate frame. Affirmative action, for example, sells poorly as "preference" but well under the rubric of "fairness." Some health maintenance campaigns do well stressing the benefits associated with performing healthy behaviors; others do well stressing the costs associated with not doing so (Rothman & Salovey, 1997). Abortion can be framed as murder or as a woman's choice. But advocates of legalized abortion have found it increasingly difficult to frame their arguments for choice as threats to the mother's life. The days of illegal and dangerous back-alley abortions have faded from public memory; abortion has been legal since 1973 (Hitt, 1998).

Reform-minded groups often combine persuasion with coercion (e.g., threats) and material inducements (e.g., promises of benefits) in campaigning for social change. Campaigns for environmental protection, tobacco regulation, consumer protection, and auto safety requirements have combined agitation with litigation. Even when change advocates have lost in the courts, the publicity given their court challenges has succeeded in whipping up public fervor, especially when children were shown to be among the primary victims. Recently, the gun control lobby has had success with a "divide and conquer" strategy, splitting off gun manufacturers from the more entrenched National Rifle Association by way of incentives to the manufacturers to okay mandatory safety locks on guns (Boyer, 1999).

Normative influence can also alter behavior. For example, social ostracism is increasingly being used in place of imprisonment in campaigns to rid inner-city communities of drug dealers. Humiliating rather than incarcerating is also becoming the strategy of choice in curbing pornography in cyberspace, shoplifting, and child abuse. For example, a California judge ordered a shoplifter to wear a T-shirt that said in bold letters: "I Am a Thief."

Some reformers believe that it may be possible to effect sweeping changes in social norms, for example, making it uncool for teenagers to use drugs, keep guns, practice unsafe sex, and smoke tobacco. A privately sponsored ad campaign targeted to African Americans showed a skeleton dressed as the Marlboro man lighting a cigarette for a black child. The ad read, "They used to make us pick it. Now they want us to smoke it." The implications of this ad are (a) "Smoking Kills," and (b) "We blacks shouldn't allow ourselves to be victimized once more by the white establishment" (Rosen, 1997, p. 176).

In devising basic strategies, as in formulating campaign goals, planners need to be alert to the possibilities of unintended, undesired effects (Pollay, 1989; Warwick & Kelman, 1973). A well-intentioned campaign to reduce infant mortality and disease may succeed only too well in an impoverished country, depleting the system's meager resources and causing unemployment, poverty, and civil disorder (Salmon, 1989). A health education program encouraging weight control may exacerbate problems of anorexia and bulimia (Pollay, 1989). Public service advertisements such as the one depicting black smokers as victims of the white establishment may, by their use of "us versus them" appeals, further polarize the races.

Social activists need also to balance what they perceive to be the good of the community against threats to the assumed beneficiary's autonomy. What could be better, asks the social engineer, than to substantially reduce self-destructive teenage practices by way of normative pressure from peer groups to conform to prosocial norms or face rejection? Certainly this is preferable to incarceration on the one hand or no influence on the other. Yet libertarians have long echoed John Stuart Mill's (1859) conclusion that normative control represents "a social tyranny more formidable than many kinds of political oppression, since, though not usually upheld by such extreme penalties, it leaves fewer means of escape, penetrating more deeply into the details of life, and enslaving the soul itself" (p. 220).

The strategies identified in this section can be ordered on a continuum from most controlling to least controlling. Zaltman and Duncan (1977) identify *power* strategies as the most controlling. Examples include legal mandates and control over financial resources. These fall under what are labeled in this book as coercion and material inducements. Next comes *persuasion,* as in commercial advertising and campaign speeches. These strategies, so necessary in motivating individuals and in overcoming their resistance, are nevertheless considered manipulative by Zaltman and Duncan, and more repressive than their third category, which they call *normative-reeducative.* Campaigns described as "public information" fall solidly within this category, especially when the issue in question is how best to solve an ac- knowledged problem (e.g., drunk driving) and the presentation is relatively unbi- ased. Yet as illustrated in Chapter 3, messages presented as informational or nonpar- tisan can deceptively and powerfully persuade in the guise of objectivity. For example, informational campaigns about how to get help for drug addictions seldom mention addictions to legal drugs such as Valium; thus, by their omissions, they im- plicitly legitimate some drug habits. Finally, Zaltman and Duncan list *facilitation,* a strategy by which foundations and government agencies seek to promote the arts or aid communities by providing them with additional resources, "no strings attached." This strategy assumes that the beneficiary is capable of rationally committing those resources to useful ends.

Choosing less controlling strategies can be problematic. A small-scale, short- term, media-only information campaign directed at a widespread, long-standing, systemic social problem is bound to fail. Are drug addicts "freer" for not having given up their self-destructive habits because some well-meaning health officials believed that ineffectual public information campaigns were ethically more preferable than more potent but more controlling power and persuasion strategies? Who gets to de- cide which aid beneficiaries are so rational that they can be offered resources with no restrictions attached? If a community leader pockets the money rather than using it to assist the community, was the resource strategy truly freedom enhancing or free- dom restricting? (Salmon, 1989).

Mobilizing for a Campaign

Mobilization consists of locating, acquiring, developing, and exploiting the ma- terial and human resources necessary to run the campaign. Money is one obvious re- source, but many campaigns also depend on volunteer support and free publicity.

A clever group can work toward fulfilling several campaign requirements simul- taneously. At a metropolitan university, several students sought to organize a consumer action group. The leaders recognized that they would need money—lots of it—to build and maintain the organization and advance its goals. Conceivably, a foundation grant might have been forthcoming, but they sought another fund-raising approach, one that would help legitimize the group and promote its values at the same time. A minicampaign was launched for a campus referendum on whether money should be raised for the group by means of a voluntary dues checkoff on student tuition bills. The vote was favorable, and the group went next to the administration with a strongly worded request that it execute the checkoff—or be in the embarrassing situation of opposing an organization that had widespread student support. Not surprisingly, the administration proved anxious to please.

Other resources may include access to channels of influence and to the mass media, as well as basic information and know-how needed to communicate effectively. A student body leader used her acquaintance with the mayor's daughter as a way of gaining access to the mayor, who proved to be a valuable supporter. Another student gained access to his university's donor list; this too proved valuable to his community action group's efforts, but less as a source of funding than as a source of expertise. The alums included a retired trial lawyer and an accountant who wound up volunteering their expertise to the campus organization. Commercial organizations have long purchased market analyses, mailing lists, media expertise, and media time. Indeed, television advertising alone can easily take up 70% or more of a political campaign budget.

Seeking Legitimacy for a Campaign

Legitimacy is something conferred by others. Implicitly or explicitly, they grant the right to be heard and be taken seriously and perhaps even the right to issue binding directives. If a campaign organization lacks legitimacy at the outset, its leadership needs to be anointed with legitimacy—if only for purposes of the campaign—by those who already possess it. Hence, the importance of what Bettinghaus and Cody (1994) call "checking in with the power base" (p. 273). This may include not only those in official positions of power but also informal opinion leaders:

> The role of the legitimizer is a peculiar one. He is seldom active in the early stages of a social-action campaign. He does not make speeches in favor of the proposal. He does not write letters to the newspaper, and he frequently will ask that his name not be associated with the new idea. He may not want to give a formal approval to a new proposal. But he can effectively block the adoption of a new idea by saying, "No!" If he simply agrees that a proposal is a desirable one he may well clear the way for future operations by the change agent and eventual adoption of the proposal. (p. 273)

The more popular one's cause, the easier it is to acquire authority and to gain endorsements from power brokers. Those seeking minor reforms may well be granted the blessings of key legitimizers. But those seeking more widespread changes are likely to threaten the institution or community's interests in preserving the status quo; they can therefore expect to be threatened by opponents of change. Still, the change-minded group may use coactive persuasion to establish its legitimacy by representing its cause as one that any virtuous individual must endorse. Programs may be defended in the name of God or the Founding Fathers or the Constitution or the legitimizers' pocketbook interests. Here the promotion of a cause and the legitimacy of its campaign are joined.

Promoting a Cause

Once a campaign group has taken effective steps to plan, mobilize resources, and secure legitimacy, it is in a powerful position to promote its cause before a wider audience. Effective promotion, in turn, should open doors for the group that may have previously been closed to personnel, material, and communication resources, as well as endorsements by key influentials. The ideal persuasive campaign has continuity from beginning to end of the promotion process. An advertising campaign may go public with messages somewhat mysteriously alluding to a new product that is soon to appear on supermarket shelves. Mystery may continue as a theme once its identity is revealed, the product somewhat humorously being described as having magical qualities, its label and packaging reinforcing that concept. Rather than the usual endorsements by attractive celebrities or "just plain folks," subsequent ads may feature testimonials by actors associated with suspense theater. Should the product become an established competitor in its field, later ads may tone down the mystery theme, playing now, perhaps, on its reputation for dependability.

Four elements are key to promotion for social activists: identity, credibility, a winning case, and continued support from key decision makers. Some of these figure importantly in other campaigns as well.

Identity. Political candidates are nowhere without name recognition. Commercial advertisements do better getting negative attention than no attention. Worthy charities must somehow stand out from others making a claim on the public's generosity. So it is that campaign managers work assiduously at formulating memorable slogans, devising labels and catchy jingles, and finding clever ways to build repetition of the same campaign themes.

Effective identification symbols are those that serve members of the campaign organization (giving them an identity), as well as the larger public. Some groups choose identification symbols mostly to promote in-group solidarity. These may include special songs, handshakes, flags, ceremonies, hair styles, and speech patterns. But although once the Democrats and Republicans featured in-group images at their party conventions (party emblems and pictures of party heroes), now, with the conventions televised, the emphasis is on identification symbols such as the American flag that link the party with the people and that even make a pitch for members of the opposition.

Credibility. Moving beyond the creation of a favorable and memorable identity, the campaign leadership must establish its own believability as well as the credibility of the group as a whole. The first step for leaders is to promote respect, trust, and attraction from their own followers. Here, especially, deeds, not just words, are important. Occasionally, followers will be taken in by a charismatic firebrand, but for the most part, they will want concrete evidence that this individual has their interests at heart, is capable of delivering, and possesses such qualities as intelligence and expertise, honesty and dependability, and maturity and good judgment.

Establishing personal or group credibility to the satisfaction of suspicious outsiders may be considerably more difficult. On this score, Zimbardo, Ebbesen, and Maslach (1977) have offered a number of suggestions to college students canvassing door-to-door. These include such staples of coactive persuasion as impressing the target with your expertise, concern, and dedication; minimizing your manipulative intent; and using the yes-but approach. The authors also suggest indicating the sacrifices you have made, having a respected person introduce you, avoiding group situations where the majority are known or expected to be against you, and listening attentively to what the target persons have to say.

A Winning Case. Campaigners generally attempt to build a case within the framework of the need-plan approach discussed in Chapter 8. A need is established, and the candidate, product, charity, or self-help program claims itself to be capable of filling that need. In campaigns, of course, persuaders have the advantage of being able to pound home the same message repeatedly (using the principle of repetition with variation) or to stretch out a suspicion-arousing case through a series of stages— focusing on problems and principles in the beginning, for example, and pushing their own favorite solution in subsequent messages.

Support of Key Decision Makers. Locating those with real power or influence in organizations is not always easy. Groups seeking institutional change are often referred to minor functionaries with fancy titles who are assigned to hear out complainants and, if possible, to soothe their ruffled feelings. Unless change-oriented groups understand how influence flows and where the buck stops in a given institution, they are liable to be given the runaround. Often, moreover, key decision makers are not identifiable by their titles. One such person at a large corporation, for example, held the modest title of administrative assistant. Another was secretary to the president. Both exerted more influence than several corporate vice presidents.

Activating Campaign Audiences

Building a compelling case is not enough. Unless the campaigner seeks only to communicate information or to modify attitudes, it is necessary to make special provisions for the action stage.

Detailed Action Plans

Campaigns often fail because the campaign target lacks specific information on how to act. Voters must be told where to vote and how to vote. People with problems must learn how to get help. In the case of campaigns for institutional change, there are bound to be misinterpretations unless plans for action are made concrete. Bettinghaus and Cody (1987) have enumerated the detail needed in a proposal for a community innovation such as a new recreation center:

> The formal plan of work will include decisions about financing, operational steps to be taken in implementation, the time sequence that has to be followed, and most important, the specific tasks which each individual associated with the implementation will have to perform. (p. 279)

They add that making these decisions will result in an organizational structure charged with actually carrying out the operations. This structure will provide for appropriate lines of authority, a detailed task description for each individual, and the relation of the operational group to other community groups and institutions.

Preliminary Commitments

Professional campaigners have learned that it is wise to secure partial, preliminary commitments from people before the final action is taken. Short of obtaining cash donations, charity solicitors may work toward obtaining campaign pledges. Realtors may offer rentals of homes with options to buy. Sales organizations may allow free home trials for the price of a refundable deposit. If at all possible, the preliminary commitment should be of a public nature and should entail some effort by the individual. The attitude of the individual should be strengthened by the act of overt commitment.

Follow-Through

On election day, each major party mobilizes a large campaign organization for poll watching, telephoning, chauffeuring, baby-sitting, and so on. Advertisers seek to make buying a habit among those who have made initial commitments. Revivalist campaigns work at translating instant "conversions" into weekly church attendance.

Social activists may be granted authority and resources to put programs into operation themselves (at least on a trial basis), or they may get promises of action from an institution. In the latter case, more than one externally initiated program has failed for lack of administrative follow-through. The campaign organizations have been at least partially to blame for not maintaining the pressure. A good rule of institutions is that institutional policies are what their administrators do about them. Often, it is precious little.

In the case of programs administered initially by the campaign organization itself, there is a similar danger that once the innovation has been effectively sold, campaign activists will become lazy or indifferent or begin caring more about their reputations than about the persons they claim to be serving. At some point, the new innovation must be institutionalized, and this is another juncture fraught with potential problems. Several years ago, a group of students at an urban university helped form a voluntary organization that successfully ran a day camp for disadvantaged children. For three summers, the organization endured, even thrived on, its poverty, its dearth of trained leaders, and its lack of formal ties to the university. Then, with the members' consent, the university began providing large amounts of money, facilities, and technical assistance. The support was now there, but the spirit was gone. The appropriate socioemotional adjustments for institutionalization had not been made.

Penetration

In the ideal campaign, those reached directly become persuaders themselves. Advertisers dance for joy when radio listeners begin humming aloud the jingle they have heard in the commercial. New converts to a religious group are often asked to proselytize in its behalf. Political campaigners often rely on opinion leaders to carry their television messages to others. In each case, there is penetration beyond the initial receivers to their own interpersonal networks.

The effective conclusion to a campaign for institutional change occurs not simply when the change is put into practice but when others begin hearing about it, speaking favorably about it, and even attempting to emulate it. Serving as a model for others is often a small campaign group's most important accomplishment.

Social activism finds some of its most difficult challenges in communities wedded to health-endangering traditions. Campaign planners have identified five components of the change process: (1) identifying community leaders willing and able to bestow legitimacy on campaign messages and activities, (2) identifying leaders and organizations most effective in sustaining long-term coordinative activity, (3) generating media and other education campaign strategies geared to the community's social and cultural traditions, (4) dealing with potential conflict in the community over the campaign's goals and activities, and (5) creating long-term impact on the community's allocation of resources (Finnegan, Bracht, & Viswanath, 1989). Coactive strategies of persuasion are widely used in promotion of the campaign's objectives.

Recall this chapter's opening story about a campaign in Senegal to end female circumcision. By Walt's (1998) account, the conversion process began in 1975 when an American exchange student named Molly Melching came to Senegal and launched an intensive literacy and skills training program under the auspices of UNICEF. Melching intended to change health practices in Senegal, but she first took pains to find out what arguments and appeals would work with the villagers. "We never spoke about sexuality," she said (p. 11). Indeed, the education programs waited several months before broaching the subject of health, let alone the highly sensitive topic of clitoral removal. Other well-intentioned outsiders had wanted to make a political issue of genital mutilation, declaring it a barbaric act, but this, in Melching's view, would be counterproductive.

Key to Melching's campaign was altering the attitudes and subjective norms of the villagers (Ajzen & Fishbein, 1980). The latter would prove especially resistant to change. Melching's expertise and obvious dedication to the Senegalese gave her enormous credibility. She used it to recruit villagers similar in most respects to the people she was seeking to influence. With these opinion leaders, she focused repeatedly on the dangers of female circumcision to the health of the children, and this proved to be the winning argument. Still, there was considerable resistance, especially among the men of the communities. But when they voiced objection to breaking with tradition, Melching's recruits were ready with normative arguments the men could understand. Said one, "When the drumbeat changes, the dance has to change, too" (Walt, 1998, p. 11).

Types of Campaigns

Campaigns take many forms. Some are multimillion-dollar efforts by *Fortune* 500 companies. Others are grassroots undertakings by fledgling social movements that must rely exclusively on volunteers. Health education campaigns typically have the weight of public opinion behind them, but not, as in Senegal, where modern notions threatened centuries-old traditions of female circumcision. Campaigns by social movements (see Chapter 14) typically lack legitimacy; schools have so much legitimacy that their efforts at indoctrinating young children aren't usually thought of as persuasive campaigns at all (Chapter 10). Convincing people to embrace a new doctrine, or ideology, or lifestyle (i.e., indoctrination) is different from selling a product or promoting a candidate or corporate image.

Consider, for example, the differences between product advertising campaigns (see Chapter 12) and political campaigns (see Chapter 11). Both are generally well-organized, carefully planned activities, extending through long periods. Yet in a political campaign, said Republican consultant John Deardourff,

> All of the sales take place on the same day. The timing is important. You deliver on election day or it doesn't make a difference. In political advertising you are not interested in small market shares. The political advertiser can't be satisfied until he has 51% of the market. The political salesman—I hate that term—has got to find ways to communicate with all kinds of people. The commercial advertiser knows how much money he will spend. But in a political campaign you almost never know. You improvise. (quoted in Blumenthal, 1980, p. 188)

Even sharper contrasts may be drawn between advertising campaigns and indoctrination campaigns. In the latter, there is generally no equivalent of a product to purchase or a place such as a supermarket at which to purchase it. Ideologies and lifestyles can be experimented with but at much greater cost than in trying out most products. Conversions to new ways of thinking and doing involve much greater commitments, and, of course, there are no money-back guarantees.

Indoctrination Campaigns

Indoctrination campaigns are called many things. Some are called "informational" or "educational;" others get called "propaganda." The difference is often one of who gets to define what is socially acceptable and what is self-serving, biased, and of dubious value to society (Ellul, 1965; Hogan & Olsen, 1989; Jowett & O'Donnell, 1986; Sproule, 1997). Is a high school social studies unit on the virtues of patriotism education or propaganda? What if the unit celebrates the doctrine of "my country right or wrong?" Is it then education or propaganda? Suppose, on the other hand, that the unit celebrates America's constitutionally protected rights to free speech, extending even to flag burning? Education or propaganda? Suppose that it is not our patriotism being celebrated in a social studies course but our enemy's? In the business of labeling, it seems to matter little who the "we" and the "they" are; all nations "educate" self-servingly in relation to their supposed enemies, and powerful nations such as our own get to make their labels stick (Alinsky, 1971). We are peace loving; they are aggressors. We train commandos; they train guerrillas and terrorists. We obey the rule of law; they use violence. They brutally murder innocent citizens; our misdirected firepower causes collateral damage—and so on.

Significantly, the social studies unit on patriotism will not ordinarily be thought of as campaigning of any type. Nor will the preachments in celebration of authority by parents, religious leaders, government, or the Cub Scouts. All have a role in indoctrinating—or some might say "socializing" or "acculturating"—children and newly arrived immigrants. A traditional function of socialization has been to promote hierarchical identification—the parent, the teacher, the minister, the Almighty, the Founding Fathers, the current leaders—forming in unformed minds a seamless web of perceived beneficence. This brings benefits to all authority figures while simultaneously adjusting those indoctrinated to the social order. Learning that "our" leaders are trustworthy is a part of the process of socially constructing reality, discussed in Chapter 3. Not by accident is George Washington's portrait a fixture in elementary school classrooms.

The socialization of young children has historically involved the passing on of a tradition, uncontested and unopposed. Campaigns not labeled as such that have uncontested control over communication channels of every sort, from the family to the mass media, tend to be powerful indeed.

Against the backdrop of early socialization come efforts by some groups to alter people's fundamental equations: their sense of what equals what, what opposes what, what leads to what, what follows what, what stands above what, what is good, and what is bad (Griffin, 1969). Some of these groups are called "revolutionary;" others are called "religious cults;" still others are branded as "reactionary" or as "just plain wacko."

These "deviant" groups are often forced to campaign in nonconventional ways. By use of advertising, a well-heeled product manufacturer or political candidate can control the content, placement, and timing of a message, in this way enhancing the likelihood of reaching the intended target with the intended message. Well-respected groups such as the League of Women Voters and the United Way can also count on generous dollops of free publicity. But groups out of the mainstream are likely to be denied media attention or given negative attention by the news media and rarely have sufficient resources for paid advertising (Baxter, 1981; Gitlin, 1980; Salmon, 1989).

Moreover, successfully advancing programs markedly at odds with the prevailing wisdom would be far more difficult than, say, encouraging allegiance to the flag, even if the "deviant" group had ample resources and equal media access. Imagine, if you will, the selling task of the Chinese communist leadership at the time of their decision in 1937 to join forces with their former deadly enemy, the nationalist Kuomintang, in a united front against China's Japanese invaders. One moment, the communist guerrillas are ordered to kill anyone wearing the uniform of the Kuomintang; the next moment, they must be persuaded to take off the Red Star insignias that they had worn proudly on the shoulders of their uniforms and replace them with the emblems of their former enemy.

The words *brainwashing* and *thought control* are often used in accounts of *resocialization* efforts by far-out groups (Allen, 1999). Common to efforts at resocialization, says clinical psychologist Patrick Pentony (1981), is the undermining of a belief system or ideology. Schein (1961) labels the process of undermining belief systems as *demolition* and identifies three components of this *unfreezing* stage: (1) invalidation, (2) induction of guilt-anxiety, and (3) the provision of psychological safety. In the attempted resocialization of American prisoners during the Korean War, invalidation involved a gradual chipping away of basic beliefs under highly controlled conditions, with sleep, social contact, exercise, and the like made contingent on "progress" at giving up long-held convictions. In less constricted environments where, for example, a college student might come to a meeting of a religious group "just to see what it's all about," the guiding ideology of the student is likely to be more ripe for attack. Lofland (1977) characterizes the most susceptible targets for religious conversion as persons experiencing enduring, acutely felt tensions, usually during a crisis or turning point in their lives, who tend in any case to see the world from a religious perspective.

The induction of guilt-anxiety is an adjunct to the process of invalidation. However troubled we are by apparent inadequacies in the ideologies we hold dear, we are much more likely to attempt to patch them up than to give them up. Thus, the change agent tends to tread lightly in challenging the target's beliefs, lest the target ignore these challenges or reject them and derogate the change agent as well. Said Zimbardo et al. (1977), in their description of recruiting efforts by the Unification Church of Sun Myung Moon (commonly known as the Moonies), which had gained notoriety in the 1970s, "Nonacceptable responses elicit an immediate uniform reaction from all members of the group; they are saddened, never angered, by deviant acts or thoughts. The consequence is the arousal of guilt for upsetting them by your disagreement" (p. 184).

Some sense of psychological safety seems to be essential to the demolition process if the target is to internalize the recommended beliefs, rather than merely feign commitment. Thus, groups bent on resocialization may emphasize the positive aspects of the conversion experience and point to the group itself as a source of psychological safety.

When the targets' belief systems have been invalidated, they are ripe for the acquisition of a new structure of beliefs. This takes place during what Schein (1961) refers to as the *transitional* stage. By this time, resistance is largely gone, and the targets are anxious to replace the logics that have failed them. This process involves (a) new definitions of terms, (b) broadened or altered perceptions, and (c) new standards of evaluation and judgment.

A *refreezing* stage completes the resocialization process, according to Schein (1961). Here the props that supported the old belief system—self-confidence, group support, and belief consistency—are restored to be made serviceable for the new. When the refreezing effort is successful, the new belief structure is incorporated into the larger personality pattern and into the individual's way of relating to others. Efforts are made at this stage to discourage backsliding and to encourage active, overt commitment to the new way of thinking. Converts are often urged to engage in activities that will advertise and simultaneously reinforce their newly acquired beliefs.

Compare the resocialization efforts of groups outside the mainstream with those of more mainstream organizations—the military, the Scouts, the campus fraternity or sorority at pledge time, a church on summer retreat, and self-help organizations such as Alcoholics Anonymous. Pratkanis and Aronson (1991) have observed that all such groups are cultlike to one degree or another. Perhaps they don't deprive members of food and sleep or force them to give up their belongings and identity, as the Reverend Jim Jones reportedly did in Jonestown, Guyana, before ordering his followers to give up their lives. Maybe individuals aren't "love-bombed" at a church retreat in the same way that the Moonie leaders bestowed hugs and kisses on new recruits rather than heaping scorn on those who hadn't "gotten it yet." Still, these groups seem to share with religious cults some or all of the following characteristics:

Closed System of Thought. Providing recruits with a new version of reality while eliminating all other sources of information is commonplace. Ideological isolation can happen through imposed censorship or, even more powerfully, through induced self-censorship. The resocialized recruit will develop a closed system of thinking into which news good and bad can be filtered and fitted. Thus, for example, efforts to separate the recruit from the cult or cultlike group can be dismissed as the work of the devil. Orders from on high to lie or steal for the group may likewise be assimilated to the newly acquired belief system. New language and new jargon endlessly repeated (e.g., "Krishna consciousness," "Victory for Jesus") may make fiction sound like fact, say Pratkanis and Aronson (1991).

Us–Them Mentality. Pratkanis and Aronson (1991) speak of the creation of a *granfalloon.* The recruits are the chosen; others are the unredeemed. Having been chosen imposes a responsibility on recruits to embrace the group and break from the "other" world. Initiation into the group may involve ritual sacrifices, for example, surrender of material possessions or submission to a hazing, physical scarring, or other baptism of fire. With pride in "us" comes hatred of "them": perhaps parents, or greedy capitalists, or all nonbelievers.

Escalating Commitment. Having persuaded recruits to become converts to the group and its closed system of thinking, leaders of the cult or cultlike group may make increased demands, requiring more savings, more labor, more expressions of affection for the leader, and attachment to the group as signs of continued commitment. Recall from Chapter 2 the principle of insufficient justification. If recruits can be convinced that their sacrifices are voluntary, this brings psychological pressure on them to "purify" their thinking, eliminating all doubts—all dissonance—about the worthiness of the group and its mission.

Hero Worship. The group's leader is special, perhaps mythically so. Stories may be circulated within the cult or cultlike group about exceptional deeds and powers—perhaps a direct pipeline to the Almighty. This is the original meaning of *charisma;* only the group's leader can offer divine guidance—or, even more stunning: Only the group's leader *is* God.

Proselytizing the Unredeemed. Whether the group's ideology is religious or secular, its members are sent out to do missionary work—to convert the unconverted. As they attempt to persuade others, they further persuade themselves—another manifestation of the principle of insufficient justification.

Disruption of Counterarguing. Recruits are not given time to think for themselves. When they are not distracted by a blaring loudspeaker or diverted by scheduled events such as morning prayers, afternoon lectures, and evening songfests, they may be kept constantly in the company of group enthusiasts—even during trips to the bathroom. Once on board, the group members will be kept busy doing proselytizing or performing assigned chores. Should (perish the thought) group members begin thinking for themselves, their doubts or disagreements may be explained away as the work of a satanic force.

Vision of a Better World. For Heaven's Gate, another group that succumbed to mass suicide, it was the opportunity to shed "their earthly containers." For members of L. Ron Hubbard's Church of Scientology, it is the chance to achieve a state of "clear" in this world. This is the great prize: a glorious life after death or of a heaven on earth, made possible by attachment to the group and adherence to its teachings. The prize becomes all the more attractive in contrast to the misery of the unclear, the unsaved—those fated for an afterlife of fire and brimstone or of a hell on earth.

Public Relations Campaigns

Depending on which author you read, public relations (PR) campaigns are either the scourge of modern society or the source of much of its progress. Stuart Ewen (1996), author of *PR! A Social History of Spin,* describes PR executives as hired hacks who will do virtually anything to make malodorous clients smell sweet. Says Robert Jackall (1995), "In the world of public relations, there is no such thing as a notion of truth;

there are only stories, perspectives, or opinions" (p. 365). PR proponents deny the charge of ethical indifference, pointing with pride to the code of ethics and accreditation program of the Public Relations Society of America (Wilcox, Ault, & Agee, 1995). They insist, in any case, that their clients, like defendants in a criminal trial, have a right to the best possible representation. PR critics respond that the courtroom is inherently adversarial: This entitles each side to place its best possible case before the judge and jury. PR firms, by contrast, offer their services to one side only, and that side tends to be richer and more powerful. PR proponents deny that they operate in noncompetitive environments—sometimes yes, more commonly no. Moreover, the tactics of persuasion they use in making a corporate client look good are not much different from those any one of us uses on a day-to-day basis in making ourselves look good. PR critics respond that this is just PR about PR (Ewen, 1996; Jackall, 1995).

Public relations campaigns address issues with a view toward heading off problems, managing crises, sometimes going on the offensive, but in all cases attempting to make their clients look good (Newsom, Scott, & Turk, 1989). Looking good can in turn translate into increased sales, new clients, stock popularity, political access, respect within the industry, and much more. Two types of PR efforts are singled out for attention here: corporate issue advocacy and crisis management campaigns.

Corporate Issue Advocacy

Many organizations take public stands on controversial issues: industry lobbies, social movements, opinion magazines, professional organizations such as the American Medical Association, political action committees, and political parties are among them. Until relatively recently, large corporations were reluctant to get into the fray lest, in pleasing some consumers, they offended others. But times have changed, and corporate America, led by the Mobil Corporation (now merged with Exxon), has led the way.

Mobil's issue advocacy campaign began in 1970. Since then, it has placed editorial ads, known as *advertorials,* in major newspapers, magazines, and service club magazines. From time to time, it has also sought access to the television airwaves. This proved difficult in the 1970s because of network restrictions and federal regulations, but Mobil managed nonetheless to piece together the equivalent of its own network for an award-winning ad series called "Fables for Now." The network consisted of independent outlets and network affiliates from which Mobil purchased 30 minutes of airtime for high-class entertainment programming comparable with its Masterpiece Theater series on PBS. Into this aristocratic fictional environment Mobil placed its semifictional "Fables"—all cleverly mounted "lessons for now" performed by leading arts companies. These ads, it was assumed, would reap image ben-

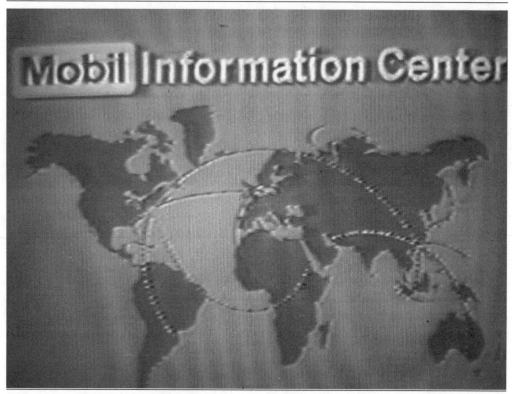

Picture 10.1. Still From a Mobil "Information Center" Television Ad

efits for Mobil even if its arguments weren't convincing. But Mobil's arguments were convincing, in part because they were framed in a disarming entertainment context.

Less effective—and pulled off the air—was an ad series commingling Mobil editorializing with the appearance of television news reporting. Many viewers objected to these ads as deceptive even as they were pulled in by "fables" editorializing in the guise of entertainment (see Picture 10.1).

Still, the most enduring of Mobil's advocacy campaigns has been its print advertorial series. Like other large corporations, Mobil has focused on environmental issues, public health and safety, and what it took to be excessive taxation and regulation by government (Smith & Heath, 1990). Mobil's Herb Schmertz believed corporate America had a story to tell, one that might reach the intellectual establishment with correctives to what he and his colleagues at Mobil took to be antibusiness editorializing and reporting by the mainstream press. The need for the petrochemical industry to tell its side of the story seemed especially pressing. Mobil and the other big oil companies had been accused during the 1970s of creating artificial oil shortages, exerting monopoly control of oil resources, reaping windfall profits, polluting air and water, colluding with oil-producing nations, bribing politicians in other lands, making illegal campaign contributions, and withholding information. But Mobil was also at this time riding the winds of change toward political conservatism in America, a trend manifested in part by shifts among some leading liberals toward the conservative camp. There was already a movement in Washington toward lower corporate taxes and deregulation—a movement, by the way, that Mobil executives claimed to have helped propel by Mobil's advertorials. Let's pause for an analy- sis of one Mobil advertorial (Picture 10.2).

Any analysis of individual campaign messages is often enhanced by placing them within their larger campaign contexts. The advertorial reproduced in Picture 10.2 appeared early in Mobil's efforts to answer industry critics while attempting to win support for its probusiness philosophy. Before pronouncing judgment on this message, consider where Mobil is coming from and where it is heading. A clue to its image management objectives is to be found in the title: Liberals are *logical* allies of business. Mobil is surrounding itself here with the aura of objectivity.

The key rhetorical strategy in the Mobil ad is one of divide and conquer. Although liberals are typically identified with one another by way of a single cultural stereotype, they are here divided into two types, the better to vilify the "unthinking" liberals, while permitting Mobil the opportunity to woo "thinking" liberals. Grouped in a "favorable" cluster of terms, along with business (including Mobil), rationality, help for the needy, and democracy are thinking liberals. Grouped in the "unfavorable" cluster, along with progovernment, antibusiness attitudes, are reflex- ive, knee-jerk, unthinking liberals. The latter group is also identified with help for the needy and democracy, but its members' inability to realize these values places them at odds with themselves.

Recall from Chapter 5 how language choices may be used to elevate or degrade. Then consider how Mobil frames business and government. Business is represented in paragraph 6 as a company's "management," while government is represented by city hall and by "government bureaucrats." Imagine, by contrast, if government had been represented by a popular governmental building ("When the White House calls . . ."), while business had been represented as "corporate bureaucrats."

Note also Mobil's use of caricature. To caricature someone is to exaggerate or distort their distinctive features, usually for comic effect. Often, a complex figure is made into a recognizable stock character from literature or the arts. The "profes- sional liberal" is consistently caricatured in the Mobil ad as an unthinking fool and is likened in paragraph 5 to another stock character in our culture, the haughty dowa- ger type who scoffs condescendingly at anything new or different. Who but such a snob would use such phrases as "impossibly vulgar," "aesthetically offensive," and "unbearably plebeian"? Mobil achieves something of a rhetorical coup by these lan-

Business and the rational mind

Liberals, logical allies of business•The snobbery factor•A plea for independent thinking

We cannot, for the life of us, understand why so many liberals in this country are so hostile to private business, when in our opinion they should be working with business to achieve what should be their basic objectives.

Liberals have been among the prime movers in the enactment of much of this country's social legislation—Aid to Dependent Children, Social Security, housing for the poor and the elderly, school lunches, and other programs. All of these programs have to be financed by revenues derived mainly from taxes on individual and corporate income.

The greater these incomes—which is to say, the more prosperous American business is—the greater the tax revenues. When incomes drop, as in a recession, so do tax revenues. Social programs then have to be reduced accordingly or supported by deficit financing, which over any extended period means inflation. For the poor and for people living on fixed incomes, inflation is the cruelest tyranny of all.

It therefore would seem to us that in all logic liberals should be as pro-business as they are pro-social progress. And we believe many more of them would be if it were not so fashionable intellectually to be part of the "trendy left." Too many of them respond unthinkingly to social and academic pressures rather than engaging in clear, independent analysis.

Part of the problem appears to be snobbery, pure and simple. To many of what might be called the professional liberals, business—indeed, our whole industrial society—is impossibly vulgar. To some it is esthetically offensive. And because business can prosper only by serving the masses of people, some consider it unbearably plebeian.

Yet one of the continuing threads in the mainstream of liberal thought has long been a dedication to the democratic process and to the right of the masses of people to make their voice heard—and heard effectively. If people stop buying a company's goods or services on any large scale—or just make a credible threat to stop—that company's management tends to listen, and listen attentively. But if you think government is anywhere near as responsive, just recall your last encounter with your City Hall, or your maddening correspondence with a government agency.

Government can become so pervasive that it becomes virtually impossible for the citizenry to turn it around and change its course, indeed, ours may already have become so. But it's doubtful that business could ever get so big or so unresponsive, because it is subject to reaction in the marketplace and to public opinion generally, and to legislation that can curb an entire industry overnight.

What should be a tip-off to any thinking liberal is that an anti-business posture, complete with the cliches that too often substitute for thinking, is mandatory in many liberal circles and is not to be subjected to rigorous intellectual examination. It is a knee-jerk reaction, arising largely from conditions that ceased to exist many years ago and to some that never existed at all.

Lionel Trilling wrote: "It has for some time seemed to me that a criticism which has at heart the interest of liberalism might find its most useful work not in confirming liberalism in its sense of self-righteousness but rather in putting under some degree of pressure the liberal ideas and assumptions of the times."(*The Liberal Imagination Essays on Literature and Society*. Charles Scribner's Sons, 1976.)

We find puzzling the extent to which liberals often seem impelled to weaken the economic structure on which not just social progress, but indeed our national livelihood depends. To them we suggest the following, oversimplified but nevertheless pointing up the heart of the matter:

Without adequate profits, no businesses.

Without businesses, no jobs.

Without jobs, no social programs.

Mobil

Picture 10.2. Mobil's "Liberals, Logical Allies of Business" guage choices. Government, conventionally viewed as on the side of the people, is now to be seen as distant and uncaring, whereas government's liberal supporters emerge as false friends of ordinary folk.

Who, asks Mobil in subsequent paragraphs, is truly responsive to the people? Not those foolish, snobbish, antibusiness liberals, and certainly not those government bureaucrats. No, it is business that cares; indeed, it is business that is truly democratic. By Mobil's rational way of thinking, democracy *is* responsive customer service. Missing from Mobil's argument is the full sense of democracy, not just customer service but government "of the people, by the people and for the people." Still, Mobil's brief for business is a powerful one, and in helping make that case, it helped itself.

Crisis Management Campaigns

When President Bill Clinton's affair with Monica Lewinsky had become clear beyond the point of possible evasion or outright denial, he and his team of public relations experts faced a crisis—indeed, the greatest presidential crisis since Nixon and Watergate. Virtually all public relations professionals face emergencies of one type or another—unexpected events or circumstances that demand urgent action. Some emergencies result in temporary disruptions but little long-term damage. Others immediately threaten the life of the organization or escalate into crises. Either way, a comprehensive crisis management campaign is necessary. In an age of instant telecommunications, public thirst for scandal, and competition among the media for news that sells, any disaster—an oil spill, a train wreck, an industrial explosion—is apt to become a public relations crisis. So, too, may allegations of wrongdoing require crisis management campaigns: a product recall combined with charges of negligence, complaints of inappropriate business practices, rumors of corruption in political office, or complaints in the Clinton case of abuse of office and of a subsequent cover-up.

In the early stages of a crisis, facts are in doubt, rumors abound, and all opinions are equally valid. The news goes through cycles: first reports, then expert analyses, then call-in shows and in-depth investigations. As the story gathers legs, interest builds. Blame is likely to be assigned along with demands for corrective action.

Into this firestorm the crisis management team must step—quickly yet carefully. Mistakes made early in the crisis management campaign may come back to haunt the organization, as happened when Clinton and his lawyers stonewalled at first, then sought, for several months, to shift blame and then distract the public from the Lewinsky affair while playing "gotcha" with inquiring reporters.

As in the Lewinsky case, public relations professionals must be in constant contact with key decision makers, and they in turn are almost always unwise to rely on their own counsel. Even as suspicion drives out trust within the organization, lines of internal communication must be kept open and a facade of optimism and togetherness presented to the general public. To whatever extent possible, the crisis management team should line up support from authority figures outside the organization, looking especially for sympathetic media coverage.

However competent the public relations team, it must expect that its damage control efforts will be less than fully successful. Even routine rhetorical situations are dilemma-laden, and crisis management is especially problematic. As organizational crises deepen, enemies pounce, competitors look to exploit weaknesses, and erstwhile friends crawl into the woodwork or go public with their disappointments. In pressure cooker environments, mistakes are made, adding to the crisis management team's rhetorical dilemmas. Yet some organizations weather these problems, whereas others fold.

Chapter 2 used the Clinton-Lewinsky scandal to illustrate the psychological principles of persuasion. Chapter 4 presented guidelines-in-theory for the political apologia but also illustrated why Clinton's unique rhetorical situation on August 17, 1998, made those guidelines difficult to apply. These sections of Chapters 2 and 4 provide the context for the dilemma-centered analysis that follows.

The dilemmas Clinton confronted in his speech to the American people on August 17 were not entirely unique. They included ethical dilemmas (e.g., truth telling versus evasiveness of a sort that might enable him to continue doing his job as president); conflicting role requirements (the temptation to attack, the need to express contrition); the need to balance the conflicting logics of law, politics, and psychology; and the problems familiar to every politician of needing to appeal to multiple and conflicting audiences. An analysis of three excerpts from Clinton's apologia will illustrate how rhetorical dilemmas can be successfully managed in times of crisis.

Excerpt 1: Opening Comments

> Good evening. This afternoon in this room, from this chair, I testified before the Office of Independent Counsel and the grand jury. I answered their questions truthfully, including questions about my private life, questions no American citizen would ever want to answer.
>
> Still, I must take complete responsibility for all my actions, both public and private. And that is why I am speaking to you tonight.[1]

President Clinton spoke carefully here, attempting to make each word just right. Yet David Maraniss (1998), his biographer, found these opening paragraphs self-contradictory, their key terms, such as "truthfully," "private life," and "complete responsibility," vague or ambiguous. Maraniss probably has Clinton about right in his readings of these opening comments. Maraniss might have added that in taking "complete responsibility for all my actions" without specifying *what* actions, if any, he was apologizing for, Clinton was again being misleading and perhaps hypocritical. The question remains, however, whether the opening remarks worked for or against Clinton's interests. No doubt many Clinton haters saw through the duplicities and now hated Clinton all the more. But for the mass of Americans who disapproved of Clinton's transgressions but who approved of his job performance, the opening chords of supplication mixed with gritty determination, of paradoxically untruthful truthfulness and irresponsible responsibility, might well have been the right chords.

Excerpt 2: The "Confession"

> As you know, in a deposition in January, I was asked questions about my relationship with Monica Lewinsky. While my answers were legally accurate, I did not volunteer information. Indeed, I did have a relationship with Miss Lewinsky that was not appropriate. In fact, it was wrong. It constituted a critical lapse in judgment and a personal failure on my part for which I am solely and completely responsible. But I told the grand jury today and I say to you now that at no time did I ask anyone to lie, to hide or destroy evidence or to take any other unlawful action. I know that my public comments and my silence about this matter gave a false impression. I misled people, including even my wife. I deeply regret that.

The chief criticism of the August 17 speech is that Clinton appeared insufficiently contrite. Politicians, pundits, and the general public repeatedly expressed anger, or at least regret, at Clinton's failure "to say I'm sorry to the American people." Some journalists remarked on the gap between Beltway opinion and public opinion, but the *New York Times,* in an editorial on August 19 ("Betrayal," 1998), bolstered its charge of "betrayal and embarrassment" (p. A30) at the hands of the president with Gallup poll data indicating that 58% of those questioned believed Clinton should have made an outright apology. Clinton's insincerity, it was argued, came through in the flatness of his tone and the anger on his face but also in his words. Why a "critical lapse" in judgment when the affair had been long-standing? Why "misled people" rather than "repeatedly lied"? Why the passive note: "gave a false impression"? Why not "deliberately deceived"?

Clinton's confession does seem rather hollow. One critic defended the choice of words "because Presidents ought not grovel" (McGee, 1998). "'It was wrong' should be as good as 'I am sorry' in the apology department, and a lot preferable in the Presidential dignity department." But Clinton could have appeared more repentant without groveling, and on subsequent occasions, he expressed more remorse for his wrongdoing. To account for Clinton's persistent unwillingness to acknowledge fully the dimensions and depth of his wrongdoing will require examining further the dilemmas he faced.

Excerpt 3: The Attack

> I can only tell you I was motivated by many factors. First, . . . by a desire to protect myself from the embarrassment of my own conduct. I was also very concerned about protecting my family. The fact that these questions were being asked in a politically inspired lawsuit, which has since been dismissed, was a consideration, too.
>
> In addition, I had real and serious concerns about an independent counsel investigation that began with private business dealings 20 years ago, dealings I might add about which an independent federal agency found no evidence of any wrongdoing by me or my wife over two years ago. The independent counsel investigation moved on to my staff and friends, then into my private life. And now the investigation itself is under investigation. This has gone on too long, cost too much and hurt too many innocent people.

The appearance of insufficient remorse was reinforced by Clinton's retreat to legalisms in this excerpt and by his continued attack on the Starr investigation. Yet Clinton's insistence (in the previous excerpt) on legal accuracy and on his innocence as regards suborning of perjury or other possible obstruction of justice is eminently understandable given the directions the independent counsel investigation had taken and the real possibilities that charges would be brought before the House Judiciary Committee, that Clinton would then be impeached or be forced to resign, and that, at the least, he would be rendered more vulnerable to conviction for civil and criminal offenses once he left office.

Had Clinton the luxury of dealing only with those among his hearers who were raised permissively, a confession of addiction to sex or to risk might have been in order, complete with a tear-filled narrative about the difficulties he and his mother faced at the hands of an abusive husband and stepfather. But although millions of Americans seek treatment for addictions, they tend not to vote for politicians who confess to needing psychological treatment, especially not for addictions. As Francis X. Clines (1998) put it, "For many veterans of the political wars, the merest hint of any psychological flaw is the ultimate taboo for a candidate and especially for the man occupying the patriarchal office of the presidency" (p. A22).

Were this a purely political or moral crisis, Clinton could have confessed more forthrightly to the dimensions and depth of his wrongdoing while reminding Americans by word and by deed of the good that he had done. Republicans such as Orrin Hatch who were eager to get on with the nation's business had pleaded with the president to come clean and express complete remorse in return for some measure of forgiveness from them. But in this context (and in the subsequent impeachment inquiry in the House and trial by the Senate), the offer had something of the quality of a double bind. Clinton would truly be damned if he did and damned if he didn't.

Instead, Clinton opted for vagueness, ambiguity, and equivocation. Days later, the news media carried stories of Clinton's political advisers complaining of having been "dissed" by Clinton in the preparation of the speech and dismayed by the president's continued legal hairsplitting. Yet the legal team's prevailing logic ultimately proved correct: Clinton could eventually earn the forgiveness of most Americans, but the independent counsel, the Republican-dominated House and Senate, and the courts would prove more demanding.

As for Clinton's decision to press ahead with yet another attack on Kenneth Starr, this, too, was criticized by Clinton's political advisers and by the media. Psychologically, if not logically, it seemed inconsistent with his earlier expressions of remorse.

Arguably, then, the attack on Starr with its reminder of monies wasted on 5 years of fruitless investigations into the Clintons' affairs should have been omitted from the speech. Perhaps it was time to leave that job to supporters, as has frequently been done in the past.

But another approach suggests itself, one exemplified by retired Senator Dale Bumpers's (1999) memorable oration during the Senate impeachment trial. Conceding horrible wrongdoing by Clinton, of a sort that his good friend would never be able to live down, Bumpers was able in the same speech to deplore the excesses of the independent counsel's investigation. "The President suffered a terrible moral lapse," said Bumpers. His conduct was "indefensible, outrageous, unforgivable, shameless." But the president was also a victim of a "relentless, unending investigation" that had brought financial ruin to completely innocent associates of the Clintons as well. Like Bumpers, Clinton could have turned the either-or of contrition versus attack into an acceptable both-and, but to do so he needed to find words and visible expressions of remorse far more powerful than those he employed.

Thus did Clinton and his crisis management team attempt to handle the president's rhetorical dilemmas. In the rest of the speech, Clinton sought to win sympathy by continuing to insist that this was a private matter, of no business to anyone except his wife, their daughter, and "our God." He also sought closure on the matter. It is time, he said "to move on."

What "grade" should be given Clinton's effort at crisis management? Did Clinton do as well as could be expected given his difficult rhetorical situation? Were his remarks appropriate not only to the immediate situation but to the challenges that lay ahead?

Judged solely on the basis of Clinton's resourcefulness in addressing the dilemmas he confronted, Clinton earns for his August 17 apologia a B+. This is probably a much higher grade than most experts and politicians would have given him (Simons,

2000). In retrospect, we know that the roughly two thirds of Americans who opposed a protracted investigation by the independent counsel into the president's sex life held steady in objecting to a long investigation by the House Judiciary Committee, to impeachment of Clinton by the House, and to a full-scale trial in the Senate (Kolbert, 1999). These were probably the same Americans who would have been predisposed toward closure on August 17, with perhaps a reprimand from the Congress as a precondition for ritual termination of the case. Numbered among them were long-standing supporters of Clinton, but they probably also included Americans who had become tired of the whole affair, others who found the sex talk embarrassing or bad for their children to hear, and still others of varying political persuasions who never believed that the affair and subsequent cover-up were the big deal that the independent counsel's office had made of it and who saw Starr and the religious right as the greater threat to America's well-being.

One final comment concerns the difference a frame makes in the management of dilemmas. Kathleen Jamieson (personal communication, October 1998) suggested that Clinton should have not just apologized but defined the terms of his possible redemption. Needed was a pledge of corrective action consistent with Clinton's high approval rating as president. Said Jamieson, Clinton should have said (in words to this effect): "I let you down, and for that I'm deeply sorry. That's why I intend to spend the rest of my term as president making it up to you."

That sounds exactly right.

Summary

A persuasive campaign is an organized, sustained attempt at influencing groups or organizations through a series of messages. Some campaigns are product oriented, others image oriented, and still others issue oriented. In the last category are campaigns aimed at eliciting specific behaviors and others aimed at hearts and minds.

This chapter presented a general introduction to campaign planning by way of a model that covered goal setting, research and development, basic strategy, mobilization, legitimacy, promotion, and activation. Having read this section, you should be in a better position to analyze persuasive campaigns and to plan and administer small-scale campaigns of your own.

One broad category of campaigns gets labeled "education" by friends and "propaganda" by enemies. It involves efforts at socializing unformed minds and, more controversially, resocialization of a sort practiced by organizations bent on converting people to new lifestyles and ideologies. Socialization campaigns typically indoctrinate under some benign label such as education or entertainment, whereas resocialization campaigns are often alleged to involve brainwashing or thought control. There are important differences between the methods of influence used by far-out groups such as religious cults and those of culturally approved groups such as mainstream denominations, but there are also similarities. This chapter has attended to both.

The field of public relations occasions bitter debate between proponents and opponents. At its most benign, public relations is information giving—for example, a news release announcing IBM's appointment of a new CEO. But public relations is also sophisticated issue advocacy, and sometimes it involves no-holds-barred crisis management. By way of illustration, the chapter offered analyses of a Mobil advertisement and of President Clinton's August 17, 1998, apologia.

Questions and Projects for Further Study

1. Why do persuasive campaigns tend to be so much more influential than one-shot speeches or essays?
2. Why is goal setting a never-ending part of the campaign process?
3. Design a campaign that you or perhaps a group of you can reasonably hope to accomplish in a month or less. Be sure to go over the seven components discussed in this chapter, considering audience and situation in goal setting and opportunities as well as obstacles in basic strategizing. Then, if there is time, try to implement your plan.
4. How, if at all, do you distinguish between education and propaganda? In your view, is all persuasion propaganda? Be sure to test your view against difficult cases. Would you say that Molly Melching propagandized, for example?
5. More than any previous chapter, this one raised profoundly disturbing questions of ethics. What would you do if you knew that your efforts at reducing infant mortality in an impoverished community would lead to malnutrition and civil strive among its inhabitants? Would you have been willing to use deliberate ambiguity in ghostwriting President Clinton's August 17 apologia? How about outright deception? Would you approve of instilling healthy nutritional habits in teenagers through campaigns that deliberately attempt persuasion in the guise of information giving or entertainment? Would you attempt to shame people into good health, even in the face of John Stuart Mill's critique of normative controls? In light of your answer to the foregoing question, would you bestow a prize or criticism on Molly Melching for her efforts in Senegal? How would you evaluate the ethics of the Mobil advertorial and of Clinton's speech?

Note

1. This and following excerpts from President Clinton's speech were from www.cnn/AllPolitics1998/08/17/speech/transcript/html

References

Ajzen, I., & Fishbein, M. (1980). *Understanding attitudes and predicting social behavior.* Englewood Cliffs, NJ: Prentice Hall.

Alinsky, S. (1971). *Rules for radicals.* New York: Random House.

Allen, C. (1999, December/January). Scholars of cults accuse each other of bad faith. *Lingua Franca,* 26-35.

Baxter, W. L. (1981). The news release: An idea whose time is gone? *Public Relations Review, 7,* 27-31.

Betrayal and embarrassment [Editorial]. (1998, August 19). *New York Times,* p. A30.

Bettinghaus, E. P., & Cody, M. J. (1987). *Persuasive communication* (4th ed.). New York: Holt, Rinehart & Winston.

Bettinghaus, E. P., & Cody, M. J. (1994). *Persuasive communication* (6th ed.). Fort Worth, TX: Harcourt Brace.

Blumenthal, S. (1980). *The permanent campaign.* Boston: Beacon.

Boyer, P. J. (1999, May 17). Big guns. *New Yorker, 75,* 54-67.

Bumpers, D. (1999). Retired Senator Bumpers's speech [Transcript]. Available at http://www.cnn/stories/1999/01/21/transcripts/bumpers/html

Clines, F. X. (1998, September 30). The therapy question: Does Clinton need to turn to ministers or a psychotherapist, too? *New York Times,* p. A22.

Dillard, J. P. (1988). Compliance-gaining message selection: What is our dependent variable? *Communication Monographs, 55,* 162-183.

Ellul, J. (1965). *Propaganda.* New York: Knopf.

Ewen, S. (1996). *PR! A social history of spin.* New York: Basic Books.

Finnegan, J. R., Jr., Bracht, N., & Viswanath, K. (1989). Community power and leadership analysis in lifestyle campaigns. In C. T. Salmon (Ed.), *Information campaigns: Balancing social values and social change.* Newbury Park, CA: Sage.

Gitlin, T. (1980). *The whole world is watching: Mass media in the making and unmaking of the new left.* Berkeley: University of California Press.

Griffin, L. (1969). A dramatistic theory of social movements. In W. Rueckert (Ed.), *Critical responses to Kenneth Burke.* Minneapolis: University of Minnesota Press.

Hitt, J. (1998, January 18). Who will do abortions here? *New York Times,* pp. 20-27, 54, 56.

Hogan, J. M., & Olsen, D. (1989). The rhetoric of "nuclear" education. In T. J. Smith III (Ed.), *Propaganda: A pluralistic perspective* (pp. 165-180). New York: Praeger.

Jackall, R. (1995). The magic lantern: The world of public relations. In R. Jackall (Ed.), *Propaganda* (pp. 351-399). New York: New York University Press.

Jowett, G. S., & O'Donnell, V. (1986). *Propaganda and persuasion.* Newbury Park, CA: Sage.

Kolbert, K. (1999, January 25). Those poll-defying Republicans. *New Yorker, 74,* 25.

Lofland, J. (1977). *Doomsday cult.* New York: Irvington.

Maraniss, D. (1998). *The Clinton enigma.* New York: Simon & Schuster.

McGee, M. (1998, August 19). A rhetorical criticism of Clinton's speech. *CRTNET.* (CRTNET is the official listserv of the National Communication Association. See www.natcomm.org)

Mill, J. S. (1859). On liberty. In J. M. Robson (Ed.), *Collected works of John Stuart Mill* (Vol. 18). Toronto, Ontario, Canada: University of Toronto Press.

Newsom, D., Scott, A., & Turk, J. (1989). *This is PR: The realities of public relations* (4th ed.). Belmont, CA: Wadsworth.

Pentony, P. (1981). *Models of influence in psychotherapy.* New York: Free Press.

Pollay, R. W. (1989). Campaigns, change and culture: On the polluting potential of persuasion. In C. T. Salmon (Ed.), *Information campaigns: Balancing social values and social change.* Newbury Park, CA: Sage.

Pratkanis, A. R., & Aronson, E. (1991). *Age of propaganda: The everyday use and abuse of persuasion.* New York: Freeman.

Rosen, J. (1997, October 20/October 27). The social police. *New Yorker, 73,* 170-179.

Rothenberg, R. (1988, September 7). Social engineering: How far should TV go? *Wisconsin State Journal,* p. JC.

Rothman, A., & Salovey, P. (1997). Shaping perceptions to motivate healthy behavior: The role of message framing. *Psychological Bulletin, 121,* 3-19.

Salmon, C. T. (Ed.). (1989). *Information campaigns: Balancing social values and social change.* Newbury Park, CA: Sage.

Schein, C. H. (1961). *Coercive persuasion: A sociopsychological analysis of the "brainwashing" of American civilian prisoners of the Chinese Communists.* New York: Norton.

Simons, H. W. (2000). A dilemma-centered analysis of William Clinton's August 17th apologia: Implications for theory and method. *Quarterly Journal of Speech, 86,* 438-453.

Smith, G., & Heath, R. (1990). Moral appeals in Mobil's op-ed campaign. *Public Relations Review, 16,* 48-54.

Sproule, J. M. (1997). *Propaganda and democracy: The American experience of media and mass persuasion.* New York: Cambridge University Press.

Walt, V. (1998, June 23). Female circumcision: A village issue. *International Herald Tribune,* p. 11.

Warwick, D. P., & Kelman, H. C. (1973). Ethical issues in social intervention. In G. Zaltman (Ed.), *Processes and phenomena of social change* (pp. 377-417). Huntington, NY: Robert Krieger.

Wilcox, D., Ault, P., & Agee, W. (1995). *Public relations: Strategies and tactics* (4th ed.). New York: HarperCollins.

Zaltman, G., & Duncan, R. (1977). *Strategies for planned change.* New York: John Wiley.

Zimbardo, P. G., Ebbesen, E. B., & Maslach, C. (1977). *Influencing attitudes and changing behavior* (Rev. ed.). Reading, MA: Addison-Wesley.

Staging Political Campaigns

Several years ago, the *New Yorker* ran a story on tactics used by campaign organizations in visual character assassinations of opponents (Stengel, 1998). Frank Luntz, a Republican campaign consultant, is reported as saying that black-and-white photos are used to resemble police mug shots. Small, fuzzy photos of the opponent are selected to force the television viewer's attention. According to the reporter, the visual grammar of the images is fairly standard. "Your opponent's face should have some combination of the following elements: a five-o'clock shadow, half-closed eye or eyes (or that attractive deer-caught-in-the-headlights look), and an open mouth" (p. 52). Democratic consultant Henry Sheinkopf gives testimony of the lengths to which ordinary color shots of Republican opponents are "grayed up," decolorized, to add to the opponent's sinister look. Another Democratic consultant is quoted as warning that the picture shouldn't be too awful, lest the viewer lose trust in the candidate running the ad: "Ugly, but not nauseating—that's the standard" (p. 53).

The United States is a republic of words and images. Its institutions of power are increasingly dependent on the media, its power holders and power seekers increasingly dependent on money and technological know-how to purchase and effectively use media resources.

The mass media—including television entertainment programming and not just news—are forces of influence in their own right. For example, in running its story, the *New Yorker* could have chosen from a number of available news frames. (The one thing it could not have done was avoid a frame.) It could have presented itself as a watchdog for the public, ever alert to the misdeeds of those nasty candidates and their even nastier spin doctors. It could have written an admiring piece—aren't those folks clever? It could have been—and perhaps it was—faintly ironic: Many Americans naively believe that pictures don't lie, that seeing is believing. This magazine and its sophisticated readers surely know better. But here's some news on how the game is played. Interesting, isn't it?

When Americans "think politics," they usually have in mind political campaigns, especially contests for high office. Some people, perhaps most, then utter a collective groan and pronounce them boring. To be sure, political campaigns have boring *elements:* the same dull speeches given week after week, the same hoopla at party convention after party convention. But they are important. If you pick up on the strategizing behind political campaigns, they are endlessly fascinating and immensely instructive about the art of persuasion. The campaign managers will assure you that in getting out their candidate's story, they are merely telling it like it is, but that is just part of the hype of political campaigns.

Way back in 1924, Calvin Coolidge's brain trust produced a silent film for movie house distribution showing "Silent Cal," as he was called, to be a man of great energy and vigor. The hyping of political candidates in Campaign 2000 has not changed much since that day, but it has become a good deal more sophisticated. The Clinton years provided a textbook's worth of lessons in how to capture the ideological middle, steal the opponent's thunder, and weather scandal after scandal through two elections. But it was the Republicans—advising first Nixon, then Reagan—who fashioned today's technologies for fine-tuning the electorate, targeting swing voters with market-tested, custom-tailored appeals, and, above all, raising the enormous sums of money necessary to run extravagant television campaigns. No industry—not the soap or the beer or the car manufacturers—spends as much for mass persuasion on an annualized basis in the United States as do the organizations that seek to get their candidates elected to high office. American political campaigning is now being imitated worldwide, complete with sound bites, photo opportunities, quick responses, nightly tracking polls, focus groups, opposition research, and devastating attack ads (Nagourney, 1999).

These accoutrements of the "new politics," as they've been called, are overlaid on the old in the United States. The new politics is never ending; no sooner has an election been won (or lost) than the next election's hopefuls begin plotting strategy, lining up supporters, and gathering funds. First-term presidents may govern more or less independently, but they always need people near them who'll answer the question, "How will this affect the chances for reelection?" The pollsters and the media consultants are seldom far away from the Oval Office.

The "old" politics is confined to a period marked out as "electing time," a time and a place for the type of persuasion called "campaigning." It's often marked visually by flags, balloons, bunting done in patriotic colors, posters, bumper stickers, perky music, and campaign slogans—"America must get moving again!" Electing time is a special time and place separate from political business as usual. It is a time for assessing where we've been as a political people, where we are, and where we think we ought to be going—a break in the usual debates over ways and means, war and peace. Sometimes, as in the days of Lincoln and Douglas, it involves long speeches in stuffy auditoriums or long harangues at outdoor rallies, but increasingly it is marked by sound bite politics and the visual politics of television ads and photo ops.

This chapter examines political campaign persuasion as visual spectacle and verbal argument. In particular, it will take note of the strategies and tactics of contemporary presidential campaigns, some of them so Machiavellian as to place the interests of the campaigner in competition with those of the society as a whole.

Persuasion in the Four Stages of Presidential Campaigning

Political campaigning in this country has become an extended operation even for local and county offices. Presidential campaigning, in particular, proceeds actively for more than 2 years. At different stages are specialized forms of persuasion.

Pre-Primary Period (Surfacing)

The ideal presidential candidate is an ideal president—a statesman able to transcend politics in the nation's and the world's interests. But to become president, one must be a politician in the narrow sense: able first to wrest the party nomination, then to be the superior competitor for election in November. Few among the nation's leaders possess all these attributes, and those who do may choose not to run. The prospect of having to solicit enormous sums of money deters some potential candidates. Those who do run tend to be fabulously rich or well connected. To be taken seriously, they will need organization, endorsements from party influentials, and name recognition. Of course, some candidates declare themselves candidates from a faint hope that their candidacies will "catch on" because they want the chance to exercise influence in the campaign or because realization of their ambitions for the future requires that they enter what they know in advance will be a losing battle.

"Serious" contenders—those with a real chance at their party's nomination—must be recognized as such. First, they must get party members, the news organizations, and a critical mass of citizens to think of them as a contender. Then they must be outfitted and positioned for the journey ahead. Experienced organizers will be needed in every state to get the candidate's name on the ballot and to build a campaign infrastructure. The news outlets must quote the candidates and label them as genuine contenders before the general public sees them as such. Enough citizens must come to believe in them so that they get a significant percentage of positive responses on polls asking the question, "If the presidential election were held today, for whom would you vote?"

Early money, and plenty of it, plays a crucial role in winning press attention, earning the respect of party regulars, and garnering additional funding from organizations and individuals that literally invest in politicians, hoping to get access and more. Lewis and the Center for Public Integrity (1996) reported that in every presidential election from 1976 to 1996, the candidate who had amassed the largest campaign bankroll at the end of the year preceding the election became his party's nominee in that election. This held true in Campaign 2000 as well, and it raises important questions about the ethics of today's political campaigns. If candidates are preselected by wealthy campaign contributors, is the electoral process truly democratic?

Primary Period (Winnowing)

To win their party's nomination, candidates need a majority of the convention delegates behind them. These days, that convention vote is nearly always a formality. Because most delegates are elected in state presidential primaries and a number of primaries have been moved up, by April 1 of the election year nearly all convention delegates have been selected and pledged to one or another of the candidates. In the pivotal month of March, competitors for their party's nomination must wage primary battles in several states at once. Little wonder that some drop out at this point for want of money, press interest, energy, or significant public support.

The voting populations in primaries are different from those in general elections. Relatively few people exercise their options to vote in primaries, and they tend to be party loyalists except in the few states that permit persons not registered with a party to vote in that party's primary. Not only are they loyalists, but they tend to be ideologically committed: more conservative than the typical Republican in Republican primaries, more liberal than the typical Democrat in Democratic primaries. In Campaign 2000, George W. Bush piled up impressive margins in states that restricted Republican primaries to registered Republicans, whereas John McCain garnered the votes of Democrats and Independents in states that allowed them to vote in a Republican primary.

Sometimes, a candidate runs unopposed or enjoys an early lock on the party's nomination. But most candidates are not so fortunate. Instead, they must court the ideological extremes of their party, in the process striking chords that might prove to be sources of embarrassment in the general election.

Not only must competitors for their party's nomination play to its ideological extremes, they must adapt their campaigns to state and regional interests. Bill Bradley learned early on in his campaign for the Democratic nomination, for example, that ethanol (made from corn) matters a great deal in Iowa; it matters not a whole lot in his home state of New Jersey.

Styles differ from state to state as well. New York City dwellers tend to go for a confrontational style of politics that is anathema in Minnesota. New Hampshirites expect candidates to address them face-to-face and to campaign in New Hampshire early and often. California requires an altogether different style of politics, built around heavy television advertising in the state's costly media markets. Local experience is increasingly necessary to know how to run multiple minicampaigns simultaneously in the different states.

Primaries offer lessons to candidates. For example, Bill Clinton began his run for the nomination in 1992 by stressing his gubernatorial experience and success in turning around the economy of Arkansas. By the end, his themes of hopefulness and "reinventing government" had taken over. He stressed economic programs at the beginning and medical reform and crime programs at the end. What happened? He found so-so responses in the early primaries, and therefore changed his emphases until he was getting more positive reactions from his audiences.

Convention Period (Legitimating)

The official role of political party conventions is to formalize the party's presidential ticket and its platform—the positions it expects the candidates to run on. With presidential primaries stealing all the suspense of who the eventual nominee will be, the major television networks no longer provide gavel-to-gavel coverage, as in the good old days, when party conventions provided much more drama and excitement.

Still, the conventions have important functions to perform. Well-orchestrated conventions can give a candidate a 10- to 15-point bump in the polls, and small wonder. Millions of voters watch who might not otherwise have paid much attention to the candidates. They do so, moreover, under conditions close to ideal for displaying adulation by the faithful, celebrity endorsements, a closing of ranks among party factions, and most important, the presidential candidate on film and then live, presenting a nomination acceptance speech that has been carefully crafted and market tested for maximum impact on the undecided voter. The convention experience is designed to energize the party faithful and prepare them for the upcoming struggle, but the audience that matters most is outside the arena. Both George W. Bush and Al Gore enjoyed sizable bumps in the polls following their acceptance speeches in 2000.

Convention planners work particularly hard to nail down early commitments to their party's candidate—this at a time when increasing numbers of voters are postponing their decisions until October. The planners hope that a sizable proportion of those watching will find some issue or aspect of the candidate compelling. Will an African American vote for a Democratic candidate because Jesse Jackson was on the schedule to speak on his issues, or will a member of the Christian Coalition vote for a Republican candidate because its leader was extended the same courtesy at that party's gathering? Does the platform statement on the death penalty convince some single-issue voters to go with one side or the other? Did the candidate's film capture qualities in the candidate that some viewers will find well nigh irresistible?

The centerpiece of the convention is the nomination ritual. It begins with a film about the candidate, reviewing his life and accomplishments. As in the Reagan film, discussed earlier, the campaign film personalizes the candidate while at the same time demonstrating the candidate's extraordinary leadership qualities. The film provides contexts for understanding and assessing the candidate as someone larger-than-life, so that when the acceptance speech is given, it seems as if the delegates are applauding not just the person who won the primaries but a full-fledged political visionary. The speech then is broken by applause to create as much of a sense of political interaction—candidate statement-positive public endorsement—as is possible through speech. Plenty of one-liners are offered so that the speech can later be chopped up into 10-, 20-, and 30-second ads for broadcast in the fall. Then, the unity demonstrations follow, as friend and foe alike gather to congratulate the candidate before the candidate goes off to do head-to-head battle with the opponent from the other party.

General Election Period (Contesting)

Traditionally, the general election campaign began on Labor Day of the election year, although today, serious campaigning is already well under way by August or before. Voters decide on a candidate for a number of reasons, not all of them directly related to the campaigns being waged by the opposing candidates. Party identification (i.e., voting the party rather than the candidate) used to be highly determinative of election outcomes and remains important but is less a factor today. The principle of social proof is operative with other Americans; they vote for candidates who are ahead in the polls. Here the news media may play a role. Jamieson's (1992) study of network coverage revealed a disturbing pattern: The candidate ahead in the polls tended to be taken at face value in reports on day-to-day campaigning; the candidate(s) behind in the polls was more likely to be second-guessed as having said or done something for effect, not from sincere belief. The news media strive to remain evenhanded and, in recent years, have engaged in greater public self-scrutiny (Kurtz, 1993), but the issues and events they choose to cover and the way they cover them remain influential (Cappella & Jamieson, 1997).

What, then, is the influence exerted by the candidates themselves? Do they have "minimal effects," as some have argued? Is their influence minimal but in close races decisive—sufficient to turn the tide or to mobilize the active support of those already inclined in their direction? Are they highly influential, able to win converts from among substantial percentages of the electorate? This controversy continues to engage researchers on political campaigns (Cappella & Jamieson, 1997; Perloff, 1998).

There seems little question that campaigning can be decisive in close races and can contribute to the large margin of victory in landslide elections. Campaigns are better able to shape and reinforce responses than to change them outright, but this seems to be true of persuasion generally. Three types of campaign-related factors weigh on voter decisions: (1) candidates' positions on issues, (2) their perceived "habits of mind" (Jamieson, 1992), and (3) perceived attractiveness.

Positions on Issues. Candidates provide reasons why voters should elect them and not their opponents. On hot-button issues such as crime, gun control, capital punishment, abortion, and social security, these reasons alone may be sufficient to secure commitments from some voting blocks—for example "soccer moms," blue-collar workers, and senior citizens. Occasionally, candidates introduce issues that had not been on anyone's radar screen. For example, in 1960, John F. Kennedy accused then Vice President Nixon of partial responsibility for what he alleged was the nation's missile gap with the Soviet Union. The charge was false, but it effectively stole Nixon's thunder as a champion of military preparedness. The Massachusetts program of furloughing prisoners became an issue in 1988 after the Republicans introduced it in some highly effective attack advertising (to be featured later in the chapter). In any given election year, some issues are on virtually everyone's radar screen, and these, especially, require candidates to align themselves with swing voters.

Habits of Mind. Voters form general perceptions of candidates' trustworthiness and competence and perceptions as well of more specific habits of mind, such as whether this candidate is genuinely a good listener, that one able to make tough decisions, this one disorganized, that one unintelligent or badly informed. These perceptions are less the result of what candidates say about themselves than of what they exhibit under fire, as in debates and press conferences. Of course, advertising plays a role as well—the candidate's and that of the opponent. Opposition research provides the basis for many an attack ad or comparison ad that contrasts one candidate's shin- ing qualities to the other's objectionable qualities. Habits of mind are important—as important as candidate's positions on issues. The winning candidate may not live up to campaign promises once in office, but it is unlikely that the candidate's habits of mind will change.

Attractiveness. Candidates who appear likable, who appear to like the public (recall Cialdini, 1993, on cognitive shorthands), and who seem physically more attractive have a decided edge over their less attractive counterparts. Are these factors the most relevant to a president's capacity to govern? Probably not, but they weigh heavily on many voters' decisions. Bill Clinton outcharmed George Bush (1992) and Bob Dole (1996), and Republicans counted on George W. Bush to do the same to Al Gore when they filled his campaign coffers to the brim in 1999, all but sealing his nomination. Reacting to Republican primary candidate Steve Forbes's presentations in 1999, a focus group could not disattend his pockmarked face. "It's hard to get by his looks with me," said one woman. "He has some skin problems," said another. Focus group members also thought Forbes needed to smile more. A man chimed in, "When he's got a serious look on his face, it's not as appealing" (Berke, 1999, p. wk3).

Candidates work hard during the contesting phase, particularly with a view to- ward generating favorable media coverage. Issue speeches are given at strategically se- lected spots: perhaps a labor and jobs speech in Detroit, a farm program speech in Des Moines, a Social Security speech in Miami or Phoenix, and an urban recovery program speech in Los Angeles or New York. The background serves as much of an incentive to believe the candidate as do the words; as well, the carefully selected site will give the news media a "good shoot," which means the speech more likely will get TV coverage. Press conferences are regularly called, whether or not the candidates are present; releases can be offered even if they're not around. Some candidates attempt to control press coverage by releasing statements on different subjects on different days; the "issue-of-the-day" strategy has not worked spectacularly through time, al- though Ronald Reagan had some success with it in 1984 (Covington, Kroeger, & Richards, 1994). In all this, the candidates' staffs are trying to get them positive "free" (unpaid) coverage that's in sync with their paid coverage—ads, phone calls, and pamphlets.

Joint appearances (debates) are among the most dramatic events of the general election. Having the candidates go head-to-head can pull more than a 100 million viewers to their TV sets, making such debates mega-events by American broadcast- ing standards. Candidates work doubly hard on these occasions to avoid mistakes and to look "presidential," with facts at their fingertips and valuative visions crafted in metaphors and verbal images.

Machiavellianism in Political Campaigns:
A Guide to Getting Elected to High Office

The term *Machiavellianism* derives from Niccolo Machiavelli (1469-1527), author of *The Prince* (1513/1977), a renowned guide to political strategy and power. Today, the term refers to communication strategies that appear to be serving audience members but rather are tools to maximize the gains of the person using them. They're the tools of persons who believe that winning is all. They're embedded in slogans in the advertisements of campaign media experts and consultants: "You can't govern if you don't win," "When you win, nothing hurts. But you don't have to suffer to win," and "Do you want to win this election? If you answered YES the next few sentences can make the difference between an election night acceptance speech and one of concession" (ads in *Campaigns & Elections,* April 1996 issue).

This chapter has described the sorts of persuasive messages that permeate campaigns. But how candidates execute those messages—whether they manipulate their own positions, doctor those of their opponents, or deceive voters with impunity—is another matter. As you read these rules, be aware that the strategies here identified are not necessarily those that I or other political communication scholars (e.g., Jamieson, 1992, 2000; Perloff, 1998) personally endorse. The rules typically serve candidates, but the degree to which they serve society is another matter. Think about the ethics of persuasion as you read through the following suggestions for making it in American politics. Here's a Machiavellian guide to campaign success for the 21st-century candidate.

General Strategies

1. Run a permanent campaign. Whenever you face a political decision, at election time or not, ask yourself, "Will this help or harm my reelection campaign?"

2. Practice political cybernetics. Reflect voters' opinions back directly in what you say and propose. Use focus groups to try out themes and one-liners.

3. Romance the voter. Celebrate what they already believe, and never try to change them too much. Practice eating tacos with Mexican Americans, spaghetti with Italian Americans, and a little goulash in the Hungarian part of town.

4. Appear as a superrepresentative of the people you are seeking to influence. Be as much like your constituents as you can be, but always sprinkle your

talks with quotations from Plato or Lincoln or Elvis to appear more elevated than they are.

5. Subordinate issues to imagistic considerations. Use issues and talk about issues to position yourself strategically in relationship to your opponents. Consider where you stand relative to how that stand will contribute to the public's perception of your competence, your character, your good intentions, and your personal attractiveness. Remember that the ultimate campaign issue is who should get elected.

Fundraising

1. Raise as much as you can, however you can, as early as you can. Use money to raise money, for example, by buying some direct mail mailing lists.

2. Let it be known that you will listen to funding sources for a stiff price, but only on certain matters and in discreet ways. First, work from sources consistent with your values and issue positions. Avoid obviously tainted money. Try to avoid "late" money because it almost always comes with strings attached.

3. Get around the limitations on contributions by organizing political action committees, by accepting nonmonetary gifts and low-interest loans, and by funneling so-called soft money contributions to your party. These unlimited contributions can legally be used in only limited ways, for example, in voter registration drives. Increasingly, however, campaign managers have been discovering loopholes in the law permitting "creative diversions" to a candidate's campaign, such as issue advertising (see Case 11.4).

4. Deplore the reliance of contemporary election campaigns on fat-cat contributions even as you seek them out.

Physical Appearance

1. Look the part. Although female and African American candidates have done better in recent years than in previous years, voters still seem to prefer physically attractive, healthy, and athletic-looking white males. Males: cut the beards, trim the eyebrows, and go for some hair replacement when needed.

2. Dress the part. Men should spend most of their days in conservative suits and sportswear, long-sleeved shirts, and dark shoes. Women somehow have to avoid looking either soft and demure or tough and aggressive. But they can

take comfort in knowing that many women before them have moved "be-yond the double bind" (Jamieson, 1995).

3. Work on your photographic poses. Look serious but friendly; tilt your head for dynamic angles; avoid looking straight into the camera. Wear a winning smile, and be photographed in gracious conversation with both beloved old politicians (legitimacy) and eager voters from various demographic groups (bandwagon appeal).

Choosing Arguments and Appeals

1. Pick a memorable slogan. Kennedy's "New Frontier," Johnson's "Great Society," Nixon's "Peace With Honor," Carter's "A Government as Good as Its People," and Reagan's "A New Beginning"—these were easily remembered and could be used by voters to recall other themes. Watch out for troublesome ones, as were some of these from 1988: Robert Dole's "What's the difference?" could be interpreted either as a way to define his special features or as a type of political cynicism. Richard Gephardt's "It's your fight. Vote. Volunteer. Contribute" stressed only process, not visions and issues. Paul Simon's "Isn't it time to believe again?" came off as soft and Peter Pannish, not firm and determined (see Stewart, Smith, & Denton, 1994, Chap. 10).

2. Stand for patriotism, free-market economics, family values, destruction of the drug cartel, and other noncontroversial positions. Never forget to attack government waste, even while protecting the defense contracts in your own state and area.

3. Always appear upbeat about the future. Even the gloomiest statistics can be pitched as "the darkness before the dawn." Michael Dukakis's 1988 slogan, "For a Better Tomorrow," or Bill Clinton's 1996 trips on the train he called "the 21st-Century Express" can be used effectively by every candidate.

4. Be ready to "go negative." Do your polling and opposition research to know your opponent's softest points. Particularly if you get behind in the opinion polls, take your best shots. Keep using negative ads until you've drawn even or until you seem to be losing ground again. Unless you're woefully behind, you should withdraw them before the last 2 weeks of the campaign so that you can finish on the "high ground." Then you can also attack your opponent's attack advertising.

5. Take courageous stands on controversial issues as long as the majority or plurality of the voters take the same stand or can be convinced to take the same stand. You may have to be careful about gun control, given the money that

the National Rifle Association has distributed to campaigns, and waffling on the abortion issue is wise if you're pro-choice, given that the antiabortion supporters seem more likely to vote on the basis of this issue than their in-the-majority, pro-choice counterparts. But otherwise, take to heart the political adage, "Follow me; I'm right behind you."

Video Politics

1. Adapt your campaign to the more than 80% of the voters who say that they get their political news exclusively from television, including television news, television advertising, and (increasingly these days), television entertainment. You'd better have an experienced media consultant on your team.

2. Plan on new ways of getting media exposure nearly every day. Television news caters to the here and now, the ever present today, so you'll need something new or different—an issue position, an attack, an announcement about your campaign—available daily, preferably in the morning so that it can be in the noon, 6:00 p.m., and late evening news slots.

3. Work on strategies for controlling the news information broadcast about you. Try the issue-of-the-day strategy to see if it will work; work for short sound bites, cuing your supporters to cheer loudly, so that the broadcast piece will show off both you and the adoring masses. Try the trick the Kennedys perfected in 1960. Gather a crowd at the airport and hold them back with a rope; then, as you descend from the plane, drop the rope and have them mob you—it makes for a great evening news picture.

4. Pick the right backgrounds for yourself. Announce your agricultural policy from Greenfield, Iowa (Jesse Jackson, 1988); offer your social reform plank in an East L.A. low-income neighborhood (George Bush, 1992); call for environmental reform from the Snake River in Idaho (Robert Kennedy, 1968); go on a fact-finding trip to South America to show your understanding of foreign policy (Richard Nixon, 1959); remind voters you're the incumbent by speaking from the White House Rose Garden (Bill Clinton, 1996); appear outside an auto factory if you're courting the labor vote (Gore, 2000). If your health is questioned, be shown on a horse whenever possible, as did Ronald Reagan during his presidency.

5. Control your television exposure as much as possible. The one-on-one interview program, with ground rules, is preferable to an open press conference, unless you're trying to appear as someone who doesn't have to give programmed answers (e.g., McCain in New Hampshire). Talk shows—espe-

BOX 11.1 A Test-Marketed Kiss?

SOURCE: Reuters/STR/Archive Photos. Reprinted with permission.

Vice President Al Gore sought to distance himself from Bill Clinton on the occasion of his nomination acceptance speech in August 2000 by locking lips with his wife, then holding her in a seemingly passionate embrace for what journalists calculated was at least four and perhaps seven seconds (Purdum, 2000).

The Democratic National Convention proved a turning point in the election, enabling Gore to overcome Governor Bush's double-digit lead in the polls. Political experts debated whether Gore's acceptance speech and choice of a running mate contributed to the turn-around, but few questioned the influence of the smooch, particularly among female voters (Klein, 2000; Page, 2000). Weeks later, Governor Bush would declare on the *Oprah Winfrey Show* that the gift he most liked giving was a kiss to his wife, but this verbal declaration seems to have had far less effect than Gore's visual demonstration.

cially the morning shows or MTV's "Rock the Vote" broadcasts—are easier to control than news programs.

6. Lay out your day to maximize media exposure. The morning and afternoons are times for airport hopping, the fly-around, getting out of the plane only long enough for a photo op and a brief statement. Reserve the evenings for longer interviews, mealtime conversations with constituents (with press access), and preparation for the next day's hops and for the new "ad libs" you'll be rehearsing.

7. Practice, practice, practice. All but memorize answers to questions about the news of the day, your main issues, your opponent's policies and pronouncements, and the state of politics in America. Construct pieces of talk that include some facts, some well-phrased judgments about them, a proposal for study or action, and references to particular constituencies affected by the issue; these are *opinion molecules*—"a fact, a feeling, and a following" (Abelson, 1959, p. 344).

Advertising

1. Remember that Americans now get more political information from candidate-controlled sources than from media-controlled sources (Jamieson, 2000). In part, this depends on striking ads that enthrall a voter; in part, it depends on your ads being interesting enough to be considered news. Since the 1988 election, many print, radio, and television outlets do weekly analyses of ads—commentaries, "truth boxes," and the like—so make sure your ads are prereleased for free broadcast.

2. Pictures can be worth a thousand words. As noted in Chapter 5, visual depictions can work to set ideas or propositions in people's minds. Want to attack your opponent's ethnic background? Don't say it—show it. Find pictures making your opponent look silly and yourself look grand. (See the Republican's "Dukakis Tank" ad shown later in this chapter.)

3. Always be technically accurate even if your implications are misleading. Condemn your opponent for missing the House's final vote on the Railroad Retirement Act renewal, as Roger Jepsen (Iowa) did when taking on Tom Harkin (Iowa) in their 1984 senatorial contest; never mind that the bill was unopposed in its second reading, so of course it would pass unanimously on its third and final reading, with or without any particular Congress member's vote.

4. Timing is everything. Begin with image (voter identification) ads. Move into some easy issue ads; go negative if you're behind, or stay on the high road as long as you're not losing ground. Better still, do comparative advertising: contrasting your upright stand on an issue with your opponent's bad judgment (Jamieson, 1992). Be prepared to respond quickly once you're attacked. Finish with high-ground ads and patriotic music; Bill Clinton's final ads, with pictures of his family at the 1992 and 1996 conventions and with scenes from his campaign trips on buses and trains, are exemplars.

5. If you know you're going to be hit on an issue, do *inoculation ads.* These are ads that attempt to undermine anticipated attacks before they happen, perhaps by way of forewarnings of the opponent's scurrilous plans. Knowing he would be attacked for his lack of military experience, Bill Clinton did strong prodefense ads and delivered a speech to the national convention of the American Legion. George Bush (the elder) put out ads on his social reform measures before he was attacked for his veto of a major day care bill. Bob Dole made sure he was seen working and swimming at hotels during the 1996 campaign, attempting to stop talk about his age. Al Gore moved his Campaign 2000 headquarters from Washington, D.C., to Nashville, Tennessee, so he couldn't be accused of being "inside the Beltway."

Endorsements

1. Know that low-involvement voters will judge you on such peripheral factors as the company you keep. Be pictured with veteran leaders, media personalities, and musical icons.

2. Construct endorsement teams. Get some economists to say your tax reform proposals are solid, as Clinton did in both 1992 and 1996; some retired generals to comment on your ideas on first-strike needs; and some environmentalist groups to endorse your "Save the Chickadee" campaign.

3. Travel across the demographic map. Be photographed with teenagers, health club members, social activists, African Americans, Latinos, Asian Americans, new immigrants, retired persons, and so forth. Concentrate on the 45-year-olds and up, because they've got the best voting records.

Speech Making

1. Polish a set speech. You need at least one such speech frame, with your principal vision for America and your slogans in its outline, yet one flexible

enough that you can substitute in various issues depending on where you're speaking. Clinton was able to make almost any issue "a bridge to the 21st century" in the fall of 1996. George W. Bush could do the same as a "compassionate conservative" in 2000.

2. Practice your oratorical skills for the stump and conversational skills for radio and television. Old-fashioned political oratory—us-them contrasts, spread-eagle appeals to patriotism, three-part lists ("life, liberty, and the pursuit of happiness"), and quotations from Abraham Lincoln—plays well at rallies. Intimate talk, with emotion-laden stories, pauses, and a soft face, plays well on television. Partisanship is better in the open air than under the lights (Atkinson, 1984).

3. Make the audience part of your message. A good speech gets enthusiastic response, and that enthusiastic response is important to reporters and to radio and television audiences hearing it rebroadcast.

Campaign Debates

1. Never refuse outright an invitation to debate. If you're the incumbent or far ahead in the polls, however, find ways to stall and avoid, complaining about timing, the format, your opponent's unwillingness to negotiate, the lack of neutral sponsors, and disagreements about the number and location of debates.

2. Treat debates like a press conference. Concentrate on points that you want to make, rather than in any serious give-and-take on issues. One of Bob Dole's problems in the 1996 debates was that he kept trying to correct past misperceptions rather than thinking of his answers as little political essays that could sculpt an image of him and demonstrate his political savvy.

3. Hold to your strengths; cover up your weaknesses. If you run into a difficult question on foreign policy, don't tackle it with inaccurate information, as did Gerald Ford in 1976. Retreat to your statement on general principles, perhaps with "Now I'm not going to turn this into a foreign policy seminar. Let me instead set out the principles that I believe should govern all our relations with foreign countries."

4. Treat questioners warmly. Most members of the press are well enough known to be worth having as personal friends, so create that impression. Both Clinton and Dole did an excellent job on this matter in the San Diego debate in 1996.

5. Choreograph the end of the debate. Memorize your final statement. Make sure that you're gracious to your opponent. Have your family rush the stage to hug you. Have your spin doctors—members of your staff or supporters who are good at positively interpreting what you said and negatively interpreting your opponent's remarks—ready to go backstage.

Campaign Decisions That Matter: Five Case Studies

If two opposing candidates each follow the Machiavellian rules for getting elected to high office, why is it that one wins and the other loses? Political analysts have identified a number of determinants of electoral success or failure besides campaign acumen. Sometimes, a first-term president is lucky enough to have inherited a strong economy from the previous president and to ride its waves for four more years. Sometimes, party identification is so strong that it compensates for a candidate's weak campaign.

Still, campaign strategizing *can* make an enormous difference (Jamieson, 2000), and following are five campaign decisions that mattered. These case studies illustrate the art of political campaigning—not just its science. In addition, as with so much else that has been discussed in this chapter, they also raise questions of ethics.

Case 11.1: "Furlough" Ad

Background

In 1988, Republican presidential candidate George Bush trailed his opponent, Democratic Michael Dukakis, by 17 points after that summer's party conventions. Dukakis was not a charismatic leader, but he came out of Massachusetts with a reputation as a competent and compassionate governor. Vice President Bush, on the other hand, had been tarred by the Iran-Contra scandal in President Ronald Reagan's second term of office, and Bush seemed wooden in comparison with Reagan. Still, Bush had inherited a brain trust of some of Reagan's slickest political operatives, and in late summer they decided to put their expertise to work in the form of negative ads that pictured Dukakis as soft on defense ("Tank" ad, Picture 11.2) and hypocritical about environmental protection ("Boston Harbor" ad, Picture 11.3). But potentially their biggest attack weapon was information revealing that Dukakis had been governor when Willie Horton, a black convicted murderer, had been released from prison under the terms of the state furlough program. After his release, Horton had kid-

Picture 11.1. Clip from "Tank" Ad: Dukakis smiling atop tank. The irony is that this staged event by the Democrats was supposed to display Dukakis to his advantage. But the smiling Dukakis didn't measure up to most people's idea of a president as commander-in-chief. Thus, the Republicans wisely turned the image of Dukakis into an attack ad of their own.

napped a white couple, brutally assaulting the man and repeatedly raping his girl-friend in the man's presence. Worse yet, Dukakis had failed to apologize to the couple for the tragic events that had occurred under his watch.

The Willie Horton case presented the Bush campaign with opportunities but also something of a dilemma. Linking Dukakis with Horton could play well to supporters of capital punishment (Dukakis was opposed to it) and especially to whites who associated violent crime with young blacks such as Willie Horton. But a direct attack on Dukakis for furloughing Willie Horton might seem too blatantly racist. Besides, the Massachusetts furlough law had been signed by Dukakis's predecessor, a Republican.

Fortunately for the Bush camp, an ad directly linking Dukakis and Horton had been prepared by an officially independent political action committee. It remained

Picture 11.2. Clip From Republicans' "Boston Harbor" Ad, 1988: With this ad, the Republicans succeeded in stealing the Democrats' thunder as environmentalists, making Dukakis and his supporters appear hypocritical to boot. As with the furlough ad, the facts are more complicated than the Bush campaign made them out to appear. For example, the sign that you see has no relation to Boston Harbor (Messaris, 1997).

for Bush's operatives to tar Dukakis with a broader brush, one linking him with fur-loughs for convicted murderers and, even more generally, with being soft on crime.

Decision: The Furlough Ad

The furlough ad (Picture 11.4) is considered by many to be a masterpiece of attack advertising. Its visual track opens with a slow-motion pan of a prison tower set against two mountains. The next visual, of a lone prison guard patrolling stealthily with a rifle, plays further on the viewers' preexistent fears. These fears are reinforced by the metallic drone of an electronic synthesizer in the background. Then comes a

Picture 11.3. Stills From Republicans' Furlough Ad, 1988: Democrats cried foul at what they took to be deceptive advertising, but they failed for weeks to answer the ad with one of their own. Meanwhile, the damage was done. Dukakis became linked with a furloughed convicted murderer who used his weekend pass to kidnap and rape. Many Americans found the image of prisoners being let through a "revolving door" particularly threatening.

revolving gate scene, the prisoners—silent, depersonalized, heads bowed—shown exiting the prison to the grating and rhythmic sounds of their own shuffle, as the narrator warns about the consequences of electing the permissive governor of Massachusetts as president. The ad works through the visual and auditory associations that viewers make: stark and shadowy, black-and-white depictions of the prison and revolving gate, and the menacing sounds and sights of prisoners being permitted to leave those gates to kidnap, mutilate, and rape. In addition, the ad offers startling statistics. As the narrator intones, "The Dukakis furlough program gave weekend furloughs to first-degree murderers," subtitles announce that "268 escaped" and "many are still at large."

By all accounts, the furlough ad worked well for Bush in 1988: It was a major contributor to his subsequent 30-point turnaround in the polls. Yet questions persist about the ethics of the advertisement. Because the narration and the subtitles appeared together, viewers may have been invited to make the false inference that the 268 who "escaped" were murderers. In reality, only four were murderers, and all were eventually caught and returned. Moreover, Dukakis himself did not decide who got furloughs, and prisoners who overstayed their furloughs by only 4 hours were counted as "escapees." A discerning viewer, operating by way of Petty and Cacioppo's (1981/1996) central route to persuasion, might have asked, "Just how unusual is the Massachusetts furlough program? Do other states have similar programs? What is the success rate of such programs? How many prisoners were furloughed in Massachusetts without serious incident?" But most viewers did not have the motivation or the wherewithal to view the ad critically. Moreover, the Dukakis camp was extremely slow in responding to the ad, and the news media tended to focus on strategy rather than content in their reporting of the 1988 contest—on the furlough ad's impact, say, rather than on its accuracy (Jamieson, 1992).[1]

Case 11.2: A Place Called Hope

Background

Bill Clinton had articulated several themes through Campaign 1992. He began by presenting himself as a political technocrat, someone who knew how to use government to solve people's problems. During the late primaries, he spent more time on the "change" issue, with much talk about turning America around. He also used time and space to try to rid himself of negative attacks on his morality—his sexual life and marriage, his financial dealings in Arkansas, and his apparent penchant for changing his mind. By the time the summer Democratic convention rolled around, Clinton and his staff knew that he needed to make a major statement on political morality. How could he do that without sounding defensive or preachy?

The Decision: A Place Called Hope

The Clinton campaign team opted for a mythic, biographical film. The last night of the Democratic convention, the chair of the meeting, then Texas Governor Ann Richards, assured the delegates that they did not have a "cardboard candidate" but a "real man" with a "story to tell." The film, *A Place Called Hope,* told that story. It was a personal story about a public man. Although the moral of the story never was articulated in so many words, it was suggested by implication again and again: *Bill Clinton's private virtues will become his public virtues when he's president of the United States.*

The role of *myth* is central to campaign persuasion (Osborn, 1986). Myth must be understood broadly here to include falsehood. Richard Nixon used myth in trying to construct his hometown of Whittier, California, as a value-rich environment (Black, 1970). Ronald Reagan did the same for Dixon, Illinois, and Bill Clinton, for Hope, Arkansas. But the concept of myth also refers to our understanding of life as a whole, our place in the universe, our past-present-future; understood in this way, myth becomes what Ernest Bormann (1972) calls a *rhetorical vision,* that is, our ways of seeing social life and using that way of seeing as an orientation to the world.

A Place Called Hope offered a vision of the future, but it was mostly concerned with creating a mythic past. The film was divided into four episodes. The first episode shows that Clinton came from a special place, like a true hero. Even the name, Hope, Arkansas, foretold of Clinton's greatness in this story, as did the grandparents who raised him while his mother was in school; they knew education was the way out of poverty and that segregation was wrong.

The heart of the film, however, is Episode 2, offering stories of Bill's youth. Mythic markers—signs that he was predestined to greatness—appear regularly in this segment: (a) He was born the day after his mother saw a film called *Tomorrow Is Forever;* (b) even as a youth, he confronted his drunken stepfather and protected his mother from him; (c) as a little boy, he said to his mother that "if Arkansas will let me, one day I'm going to get us off the bottom;" and (d) when he was sent to Boy's Nation in Washington, D.C., he shook hands with John F. Kennedy, who seemingly anointed him as a successor (Picture 11.5). Each of those experiences displays virtues—a vision for tomorrow, strength and protectiveness, political ambition, and achievement—that could become the grounds for his public values.

Similarly, Episode 3 has stories from Clinton's adult life. Viewers see him meeting Hillary and learn why she married him; his impulsiveness is illustrated in a story about his marriage proposal; his daughter shows us his supportive and compassionate side.

Personal knowledge of Bill Clinton is added in Episode 4 with a couple of stories from the campaign. A *60 Minutes* program during which he and Hillary talked about their marriage is reviewed through the eyes of their daughter, Chelsea, and then he is

Picture 11.4. A Mythic Moment: Bill Clinton Meets John F. Kennedy

shown saying in a speech that "the hits I've taken in this campaign are nothing com-pared to the hits that the people of this state and this country are taking every day." The film finishes with Bill reminiscing about his youth, with home movies of a swimming hole, a small-town parade, and Chelsea doing ballet. His final line is, "I still believe in a place called Hope."

In an era when the issues—economics, health care, crime—are beyond the understanding and control of the average citizen, voters often put their faith in right-minded individuals who, they hope, act in their best interests when wrestling with those issues. *Characterological persuasion*—persuasive appeals built around "trust me" stories about the persuader's virtues—has become popular in American politics. *A Place Called Hope* is powerful as a story of Bill Clinton's virtues—virtues that the 43% of the electorate that voted for him hoped would become his public values, his measures for guiding the country.

Case 11.3: Should Dole Have Attacked Clinton's Character in 1996?

Background

By 1996, doubts about Bill Clinton's character had escalated with additional news about his prior business dealings and alleged past sexual peccadillos back home in Arkansas and with new allegations of improprieties in the White House. Bob Dole, by contrast, seemed a model of rectitude. Disabled by his service in World War II, he had come back a war hero and served for years as Senate majority leader, earning plaudits for statesmanship from Democrats and Republicans alike. Dole, when pushed, had a rapierlike sense of humor. Shouldn't he have used it to destroy the Man from Hope's continuing claims to virtue?

The Decision: Waffling

The Dole campaign team was wary of attacking Clinton's character. When Bush had questioned Clinton's patriotism in one of their 1992 campaign debates, Clinton had "gone meta" to Bush, questioning the propriety of the attack and intimating that Bush's father, the distinguished Prescott Bush, had fought against just such "McCarthy-like" tactics during his tenure as senator. Then, in his 1996 campaign film, Clinton had preempted a character attack by congratulating Dole on his high-mindedness and predicting that he and his worthy opponent would stick to the "real" issues of the campaign in the fall. Thus did Clinton protect himself from attack.

Still, many Republicans believed that with the nation at peace and the economy strong, they would have to make Clinton's character the central issue of the fall 1996 campaign. Repeated attempts were made to inject Clinton's ethical problems into the campaign but to little avail. Rather than responding to the personal attacks, the Clinton campaign countered with substantive proposals on issues such as the economy, jobs, and environment that swing voters cared about. The Clinton team's "values" agenda, as it was called, was designed to position Clinton as a caring man, one who knew best what was good for the country. Dole's honesty, his reliability, and his feel for traditional values dominated the Republican convention and was set in contrast to Clinton's perfidy. But, said Morris (1997), "Voters see through adjectives; they want action; they want results; they want specifics. They want verbs" (p. 270). Morris added that by 1996, Clinton was a known quantity, his record in office counting far more for most voters than his character defects.

Attacks by Dole on Clinton's character trailed off in the fall but were not dropped entirely from the Dole campaign. But calling Clinton "Bozo" or reminding audiences about his alleged dalliance with Gennifer Flowers and Paula Jones didn't seem to lower his approval ratings. Voters seemed to be more concerned with issue position than with character (Morris, 1997, 1999).

Case 11.4: Clinton's Early
Issue Advocacy Advertising

Background

It is illegal as of this writing for candidates to funnel contributions to their political party for use in their own campaigns. But it is not illegal for the parties themselves (or anyone else, for that matter) to run so-called issue advocacy ads that just happen to dovetail with the candidate's message (Jamieson, 2000). This is just one of the loopholes in the current campaign financing laws.

With this loophole in mind, Dick Morris went to his fellow Clinton advisers with a proposal to have the Democratic Party take out issue advocacy ads as early as 16 months before the general election of November 1996. Issue advocacy advertising was something of an innovation for political campaigns, but early advertising—16 months early—was practically unheard of. It was therefore not surprising that Morris's proposal met with resistance in the White House.

Still, the idea of starting early with ads that might indirectly bolster Clinton's candidacy had a certain logic going for it. After winning both houses of Congress in 1994, the Republicans had apparently become overconfident—daring, for example, to shut down the government when their budget proposal wasn't signed into law by the president and threatening reductions in scheduled rates of increase for Medicare. Why not take out ads ridiculing these unpopular views? Why not link them directly to the Republican leaders of the House and Senate, one of whom, Senator Dole was the likely Republican nominee for president, the other the much discredited Speaker of the House, Newt Gingrich?

The Decision: Early Issue Advocacy Advertising

The issue advocacy blitz began in early July 1995 and continued until near election day. Its cost exceeded by far the $40 million spent by the Clinton-Gore campaign for television advertising, but because it issued forth from the Democratic Party and was financed independently, it imposed no economic burden on the Clinton candidacy. The ad campaign focused was on legislative issues—no mention of the Clinton-Gore reelection bid in these ads—but it had the effect of bolstering the Democratic candidacies dramatically. A typical ad showed Dole creeping around

Picture 11.5. Still from one in a series of ads by the Democrats linking Dole with House Speaker Newt Gingrich: Note the Democrats' unflattering photo selections. The Democrats justified their use of soft money to pay for this ad by insisting that it engaged in issue advocacy, not promotion of the Clinton-Gore ticket. Republicans cried foul but used similar ads themselves to get around spending limits on presidential campaigning imposed by federal law as a condition for receiving government matching funds. Ads of this type proliferated in Campaign 2000, often paid for by unidentified sources.

behind Gingrich at a press conference, or Gingrich waving his hand in support, as one or another Republican leader intoned about the need for cuts in educational spending or other popular programs (Picture 11.6). Morris's advertising plan had gone "outside the dots," but in so doing, it gave Clinton a huge early lead that he never relinquished. Was it ethical? The Republicans claimed that it was dirty pool, that the president's hands were all over it, that it wasn't truly about legislative issues but about reelecting Clinton. Yet they probably regretted most that they hadn't done to Clinton what he had done to them.

Case 11.5: George W. Bush
Campaign in South Carolina

Background

In the contest for the 2000 Republican nomination, George W. Bush faced a do-or-die battle against challenger John McCain. Senator McCain had surprised nearly everyone by clobbering Bush in the New Hampshire primary. McCain had come on as a maverick, a crusader, a populist—challenging his fellow Republicans to join in outlawing soft money campaign contributions and also insinuating that far from re-forming, Bush's tax reduction plan gave every indication that he favored the rich. McCain had become a media darling, in no small measure because he had made himself fully available to reporters. He had also captured the hearts of New Hampshire voters who liked their candidates up close and personal; McCain had worn these voters out with his willingness to answer their questions long into the night. McCain was also a certified war hero, having remained true to his principles through 5½ years of captivity in Vietnam.

Going into New Hampshire, Bush had seemed the odds-on favorite to capture the Republican nomination. But McCain's 18-point victory in New Hampshire destroyed George W's aura of invincibility while reinforcing doubts about his competence and even his enthusiasm for the job. Now Bush was chastised as the establishment candidate, the prepackaged candidate, the mistake-ridden candidate. Articles appeared suggesting that he was not too bright and that his rise to the top as the son of a well-respected and well-connected former president had been unearned.

Like New Hampshire, South Carolina is an open primary state, meaning that anyone—Democrats and Independents, not just Republicans—were able to vote in the Republican primary. Thousands did; nearly twice as many South Carolinians turned out in the 2000 primary than in the 1996 Republican primary. Not surprisingly, the Independent and Democrat votes went 2:1 for McCain.

But Bush triumphed in South Carolina by an 11-point margin, winning 2:1 over McCain with registered Republicans and 3:1 among "Christian conservatives." How did he achieve his great victory?

The Decision: Taking It to McCain

The Bush campaign in South Carolina used many of the techniques of persuasion already discussed in this book. Drawing on his financial reserves and on impressive organizational support from the religious right, Bush tilted toward his conservative Republican base in this highly conservative state, even launching his campaign at Bob Jones University—so conservative that it forbade interracial dating. Among Bush's rhetorical stratagems were reframing, going meta, and persuasion in the guise of objectivity.

Reframing. Bush campaigned aggressively against McCain, refusing to concede to him the mantle of reformer. Were not his demonstrated successes at improving the quality of K-12 education in Texas during his reign as governor proof that he was the genuine "Reformer With Results," whereas McCain, despite his rhetoric, was the consummate Washington insider? Conceding that he had allowed McCain to define him in New Hampshire, Bush vowed that this would not happen again. He succeeded in South Carolina in recapturing the mantle of reformer.

Going Meta. In 2000, Bush, McCain, Gore, and Bradley all had attempted to seize the high ground in their respective contests, each accusing his respective rival of unfair attacks. This had led in New Hampshire to an escalating spiral of metamoves, consisting in sometimes childlike attacks on attacks of attacks, and so on, coupled with complaints that the opponent had initiated the attack cycle. In South Carolina, McCain got his comeuppance for having launched an attack ad likening Bush's character to Clinton's. Bush responded with credible indignation in a state whose Republicans (and many Democrats) greatly respected Bush's father and despised Clinton. The attack on McCain's attack was all the more powerful because McCain had claimed the high road but had seemingly taken the low. Subsequently, he vowed to remain on the high road of strictly positive advertising, but the damage had been done. Bush emerged in South Carolina exit polls as the "victim of unfair advertising" even as some of his own advertising misleadingly suggested that he was the more principled pro-life candidate.

Persuasion in the Guise of Objectivity. Supporters of Bush used *push polls* to discredit McCain. A push poll is a survey that injects damaging information about the opponent while giving the appearance of merely eliciting opinions about the candidates for research purposes. Bush supporters used it to implicate McCain in personal scandal and political corruption. Other supporters, whom Bush expressly disowned, used innuendo to suggest that McCain had sired illegitimate children.

Stealing the Opponent's Thunder. With McCain having scored well in New Hampshire by calling for campaign reform, Bush decided in South Carolina to borrow a page from the McCain book, promoting a scaled-down campaign reform plan of his own.

Summary

The modern political campaign is a combination of the old and the new—of balloons and buntings and hour-long orations but also of nightly polling and expensive advertising. Fine-tuning the electorate—targeting swing voters, determining what they want, devising messages tailored to those wants, testing those messages on focus groups and other sample voters before sending them out on a mass basis, surveying again to determine message effects, then using the information in devising new messages—is how the newer part of the game is played. But the game keeps changing (e.g., early issue advocacy advertising) even as the basic Machiavellian rules remain the same.

This chapter has focused on the rules by which many, many candidates run for the presidency and other offices. But should these rules be the measuring rods against which the morality of politicians, even the morality built into American democratic electoral politics, is to be judged? Or are they the problem, rather than the solution? If ours is a republic of words and images, who is to protect us from the empty verbiage and twisted images of self-serving campaigners? Active voters assessing the total candidate and the total campaigner protect themselves, of course, and passive voters and nonvoters get what they deserve. But is that enough?

Probably not. The only institutions with enough resources to countermand and correct the moral errors of politicians are those of the Fourth Estate—the press. The *watchdog function* of the press is discussed in every first-year journalism class in the country, and it would be wonderful if we could go to sleep at night assured that the watchdogs were awake and alert. But the problem, of course, is that most—that is, well over half—of the money spent on political campaigns at the national level is given to the media for newspaper and television ads, for airtime for biographical films, even for editing facilities and some personnel who can be rented by a campaign for part of a year. So, is it in the press's best interest to blow the whistle on the candidates buying ads on the 10 o'clock news or representing the political (and economic) interests of the publisher of the newspaper?

In the long run, the answer is yes. Journalists, too, depend on good government. In the short run, however, the answer is no better than maybe. Most members of the press corps knew that the furlough ad was a piece of dirty politics, but they played it on news programs and rated it as if it were a blockbuster movie. The press corps also looked the other way as the Democrats used monies legally allotted to the party to promote the Clinton reelection bid in 1996. Apparently, the watchdogs aren't always ready to bite the hands that feed them.

In recent presidential campaigns, however, there have been signs of hope:

▶ CNN, as well as public radio and television, has monitored the factual claims of the candidate.

▶ C-Span's "Road to the White House" segments played and discussed advertisements, speeches, and news releases from campaigns, with public call-in time added for good measure.

▶ Many newspapers during the 1992, 1996, and 2000 campaigns printed "truth boxes" evaluating those same claims.

▶ Starting in 1992, many local television news operations spent part of Sunday night previewing that week's political ads, warning viewers about some of the claims about to be made.

The press periodically remembers that it, too, is a public servant. Just as citizens must demand higher ethical standards from candidates, so must citizens remind journalists of one of the prices of freedom of the press—the responsibility to serve the public interest.

Questions and Projects for Further Study

1. If you were running a major political campaign, how would you visually represent your candidate's opponent? "Ugly, but not nauseatingly so"?
2. Recall the discussion of news frames in this chapter's opening story. What should be the media's dominant news frame in reporting on practices such as these? Disapproval? Admiration? Ironic detachment? A fourth alternative?
3. What if the reporter were to have found one political party more prone to "uglifying" opponents than its competitors? Should the reporter "tell it like it is"? Or should the reporter remain evenhanded, providing a report that favors neither one side nor the other? Is there any way that a reporter could *not* function as a persuader in a situation of this type?
4. Is today's style of political campaigning serving the interests of democracy in the United States or in other countries where it is being imitated? What, if anything, would you do to reform it?
5. How would you characterize this chapter's framing of Machiavellianism in American political campaigning? Should it have been more admiring? More critical?
6. Compare the role of the visual and the verbal in today's politics. In your view, which is more important in getting elected?

Note

1. In several preelection issues, for example, *Newsweek* rated new political spots as they might movies—on a range of 1 for poor to 3 for excellent. But they based their rating on slickness, rather than accuracy or fairness (Jamieson, 1992). Occasionally, very occasionally, the media did report research bearing on these questions. For example, on October 12, 1988, Tom Brokaw of NBC reported a new study finding that more than 200,000 furloughs were granted in 1987 to 53,000 prisoners and that there were few problems. Indeed, Massachusetts reported a success rate of 99.9% (Jamieson, 1992, p. 27). Brokaw might have added that the number of prisoners who escaped during Dukakis's 10-year reign was about the same as the number who escaped in the preceding 3 years when the program was run by Dukakis's Republican predecessor (Jamieson, 1992, p. 20).

References

Abelson, H. (1959). Modes of resolution of belief dilemmas. *Journal of Conflict Resolution, 3,* 343-352.

Atkinson, M. (1984). *Our masters' voices: The language and body language of politics.* London: Methuen.

Berke, R. L. (1999, November 21). Focus groups sometimes emphasize the trivial. *New York Times,* Week in Review, p. 3.

Black, E. (1970). The second persona. *Quarterly Journal of Speech, 56,* 109-119.

Bormann, E. G. (1972). Fantasy and rhetorical vision: The rhetorical criticism of social reality. *Quarterly Journal of Speech, 58,* 396-407.

Cappella, J. N., & Jamieson, K. H. (1997). *The spiral of cynicism.* New York: Oxford University Press.

Cialdini, R. B. (1993). *Influence: Science and practice* (3rd ed.). New York: HarperCollins.

Covington, C. R., Kroeger, K., & Richards, G. (1994). Shaping a candidate's image in the press. In A. H. Miller & B. E. Gronbeck (Eds.), *Press campaigns and American self-images* (pp. 89-108). Boulder, CO: Westview.

Jamieson, K. H. (1992). *Dirty politics: Deception, distraction, and democracy.* Oxford, UK: Oxford University Press.

Jamieson, K. H. (1995). *Beyond the double bind.* New York: Oxford University Press.

Jamieson, K. H. (2000). *Everything you think you know about politics—and why you're wrong.* New York: Basic Books.

Kurtz, H. (1993). *Media circus.* New York: Times Books.

Lewis, C., & Center for Public Integrity. (1996). *The buying of the president.* New York: Avon.

Machiavelli, N. (1977). *The prince* (R. M. Adams, Ed. and Trans.). New York: Norton. (Original work written 1513)

Messaris, P. (1997). *Visual persuasion: The role of images in advertising.* Thousand Oaks, CA: Sage.

Morris, D. (1997). *Behind the Oval Office.* New York: Random House.

Morris, D. (1999). *The new prince: Machiavelli updated for the twenty-first century.* Los Angeles: Renaissance Books.

Nagourney, A. (1999, April 25). The Israeli war room. *New York Times Magazine,* pp. 42-47, 61, 70.

Osborn, M. (1986). Rhetoric depiction. In H. W. Simons & A. A. Aghazarian (Eds.), *Form, genre, and the study of political discourse.* Columbia: University of South Carolina Press.

Perloff, R. (1998). *Political communication: Politics, press, and public in America.* Mahwah, NJ: Lawrence Erlbaum.

Petty, R. E., & Cacioppo, J. T. (1996). *Attitudes and persuasion: Classic and contemporary approaches.* Boulder, CO: Westview. (Original work published 1981)

Stengel, R. (1998, October 26/November 2). Dept. of nyah-nyahs. *New Yorker, 74,* 52-53.

Stewart, C. J., Smith, C. A., & Denton, R. E., Jr. (1994). *Persuasion and social movements* (3rd ed.). Prospect Heights, IL: Waveland.

CHAPTER **12**

Analyzing Product Advertising

The Changing Character of Advertising Campaigns

Today's Advertising: The Pantheistic Phase

Misdirection in the Language of Advertising

Visual Deception in Product Advertising

Subliminal Advertising

Summary

Questions and Projects for Further Study

References

The first global advertisement, "Drink Coke," was broadcast simultaneously in every inhabited part of the globe in January 1992. In another case, only vigorous opposition from environmental groups prevented a firm called Space Marketing Inc. from launching an inflatable, milelong billboard into space, bearing corporate logos for various companies. The "space ad" would have appeared to be about the size of the moon, and people from every corner of the globe would have been able to view it as it circled the earth.

Advertising is one of the most prevalent forms of persuasion in contemporary American society and, indeed, around the world. Americans remain the most advertised-to people on earth. Most Americans are exposed to 3,000 commercial messages a day, and American children and teenagers sit through about 3 hours of television commercials a week (Durning, 1993, pp. 13-14). Prime-time commercials take up more airtime in the United States than in any other nation. In addition to television

▶ 275

spot advertisements, infomercials, home shopping channels, and music videos advertising CDs and tapes regularly receive high ratings.

Advertisements even pervade media perceived to be commercial-free. Companies pay filmmakers exorbitant fees to have characters use their products. Films and home videos are preceded by trailers that promote other films, and many cinemas are broadcasting ads for products in addition to spots that promote the theater chain or the delectables available at the concession stand. Companies sponsor concerts in exchange for the prominent display of product logos. Sporting events are littered with advertising—around the baseball diamond, around the hockey rink, on race cars and drivers, even glowing from the scoreboard. Books frequently contain inserts that are ads for other books, and newspapers and magazines contain more advertisements for goods and services than they do "informative" articles. In fashion magazines, articles that offer beauty tips are often thinly disguised advertisements for products. Even the clothes we wear sport labels that advertise for designers or manufacturers such as Nike or Reebok.

Advertisements are everywhere. Billboards, bumper stickers, signs, posters, and numerous other forms of publicity for persons, places, and products line our route as we travel to school or work. Most of us receive junk mail or are subjected to telephone marketing at one time or another. Advertising has even commingled with education. College classroom bulletin boards are frequently decorated with pamphlets offering vacations, test preparation courses, and self-improvement guides. In recent years, Whittle Communications' Channel One has been beamed into high school classrooms. Students are forced to watch advertisements as part of their education. Whittle even opened a clothing line that prominently displayed the Channel One logo (Whittle Update, 1993).

Advertisements have become so integral to the fabric of our lives that we may believe that we hardly notice them, and therefore, we downplay their ability to influence us. "I never pay attention to ads," is a common claim. But it is difficult, if not impossible, to escape ads, and the billions of dollars spent by advertisers each year suggest that advertisements are doing *something*. Most important, as Chapter 3 argued, advertising shapes and reinforces ideologies. Michael Schudson (1984) called advertising's dominant ideology *capitalist realism*. Says Jonathan Dee (1999), capitalist realism's central value is the "fetishism of commodities. . . . [It] amounts to an insistent portrait of the world as a garden of consumption in which any need . . . can be satisfied by buying the right things" (p. 63). Even the most "informative" advertisement reinforces the central ideological conviction that we are what we own.

Advertisements also sell us images of our ideal selves and of the world in which we live. In attempting to position us as consumers and dispose us favorably toward a product by linking it to our most cherished beliefs and values, advertisements also reinforce those beliefs and values, sometimes to our own detriment. Although we may not like to admit it, we often do believe that using a certain product will make us particular types of people, will bring us happiness, or will offer us a social identity. Advertisements work when we "buy" the images they offer: images of who we are, what kind of life we should lead, how we should spend our time and money. Thus, all ads, even the most "objective," use psychological and cultural appeals to create and reinforce social meanings and identities for their users.

The Changing Character of Advertising Campaigns

Product advertising campaigns change with new technologies and with increased knowledge about consumer psychology. Today's television advertisements are far more sophisticated than the ads of decades past. But so, too, are consumers more adept at tuning out. Increasingly, consumers are being given the technologies to skip past advertisements entirely—at least those that are not embedded within regular programming (Lewis, 2000).

As Leiss, Kline, and Jhally (1986) note, commodities have always served twin functions: to satisfy immediate needs, such as for food or shelter, and to "mark" interpersonal distinctions, such as status, power, or rank, in social groups (p. 47). Commodities, then, have both material functions to satisfy needs and symbolic or ideological functions to convey social meanings.

In traditional societies such as the United States, before the industrial revolution, whatever advertising existed occurred in a realm in which both material and symbolic meanings of commodities were familiar and commonly understood. But the coming of the industrial society in the late 19th century altered the entire social context and social significance of advertising. For the first time, people were surrounded by mass-produced goods made by unfamiliar people in unfamiliar settings; moreover, the purposes and benefits of these goods were not always immediately obvious. As a result, advertising became necessary to connect commodities to culturally approved means of satisfying needs.

Throughout the 20th century, consumption and the advertising of commodities became increasingly integral to American life. Leiss et al. (1986) distinguish four phases in the development of consumer culture that are explored in this section: *idolatry, iconology, narcissism,* and *totemism* (pp. 277-295). A fifth new stage of consumer culture is the *pantheistic* phase. These stages do not supplant one another. New modes of advertising are added to the old, as the techniques that mark each stage are periodically revived and discarded in accordance with a particular product's requirements and the advertiser's ever present need to engage the consumer.

Idolatry (1890-1925)

Advertising assumed its modern form in this period, as goods manufactured in industrial settings began to replace the familiar, locally produced and individually crafted goods of traditional societies. Factories were churning out goods at unprecedented levels, so manufacturers hired advertisers to extol the virtues of products, primarily through print media. In this idolatrous phase of advertising, the ads' messages had a tone of veneration about products and were designed to show that products would meet consumers' material needs.

The advertising technique now known as the *hard sell* was product oriented and largely heralded the benefits of products by focusing on their specific attributes. Because ads appeared in newspapers and magazines, advertisers tended to devise informative, descriptive narratives, not images, to explain product advantages. Using such rational selling strategies, they provided the "reasons-why" consumers should use a product, and they associated goods with practical characteristics such as utility, advanced technology, low price, and efficiency. Little emphasis was placed on understanding the psychology of consumers, and little time or money was spent on researching the characteristics of target audiences.

Iconology (1925-1945)

Leiss et al. (1986) describe this as the initial phase of the consumer society. Advertisers found that focus on products' attributes was inadequate for the newly emerging consumer society. The rise in real income, discretionary spending, and leisure time meant that more time could be devoted to human wants that were not connected to bare necessities. Advertisers began to serve a more important function than simply promoting goods and services: They began to manipulate social values and attitudes by stressing symbolic qualities and values of goods, rather than utilitarian aspects. Moreover, the increase in mass-produced magazines meant that advertisements began to be image based. Advertisers shifted to the nonrational, symbolic ground of consumption and adopted connotative discourse rooted in association, suggestion, metaphor, analogy, and inference.

During this period, advertising agencies became professionalized and began research into the nature of their target audiences. Through market research, advertisers discovered the positives and negatives associated with a product, and they learned as well how different target groups perceive these image attributes in relation to themselves. They used primitive polling techniques and analyzed *demographics*—characteristics such as age, sex, family status, education, occupation, income, religious affiliation, ethnicity, and geographical location—on a broad level. The focal point became the person as user of a product, rather than the product itself. Advertising agencies hired psychologists such as behaviorist John Watson, who worked for the J. Walter Thompson Agency. Watson believed that effective ads evoked basic emotions. One technique used to do so was the *consumer testimonial*. Although this ploy had been used deceptively in patent medicine scams of the 19th century, the J. Walter Thompson agency began to use celebrities instead of ordinary people to endorse products. According to Watson, these ads worked because they relied on "the spirit of emulation: we want to copy those we deem superior in taste or knowledge or experience" (Fox, 1985, p. 90). Products were increasingly associated with qualities desired by consumers: status, glamor, reduction of anxiety, and happy families (Leiss et al., 1986, p. 124).

The techniques developed during the iconistic stage of advertising continue to have relevance for product advertising today. One of the most fascinating aspects of contemporary product advertising is the exploitation of images, real or imagined, associated with the product, and linking the product with its potential purchasers. Some image projection techniques are rather obvious. They include flattery, snob appeal, plain folks devices, appeals to fears, wishes, and common concerns. Less obvious are appeals to self-concepts, including fantasies about the self called self-ideals. The reasoning goes something such as this: I have (or like, or wish to have) qualities *a, b, c, d, n;* product X has these same qualities; therefore, I like product X. Sometimes, the advertiser must first get you to *want* to have qualities *a* through *n;* more often, the task is simply one of convincing you that product X has these qualities, and perhaps they can be made to rub off on you. We see this a great deal in advertisements for luxury products such as wines or cosmetics.

Narcissism (1945-1965)

From the post-World War II period to the mid-1960s, advertising's focus shifted closer to the person, and emotion was brought clearly into the foreground. Increased industrialization and technological development led to increased prosperity and a proliferation of consumer goods. Leiss et al. (1986) refer to this period as narcissistic because consumers were asked to consider what products could do for them as individuals, and they were offered idealized images of satisfied consumers as "mirrors" with whom to identify. Products promised to transform their users by providing personal change, satisfaction, and the ability to control other people's judgments with the assistance of a product. This development was facilitated by the arrival of television in 1948, a medium that lent itself to such symbolic appeals.

As advertisers became more consumer oriented, *motivational research*, or depth psychology, began to assume a prominent role. Motivational researchers assumed that people were driven more by unconscious motives than by rational thought. To determine these motives, researchers used a variety of psychological techniques.

Projective tests, lie detectors, and even hypnosis were used to determine why people were attracted to particular products. In a *depth interview,* a consumer (or group of consumers) was simply asked to freely recall all the associations that a product brought to mind. The modern version of this is the *focus group,* where selected representatives of targeted consumers discuss topics at length, often as researchers watch them from behind a two-way mirror. Their discussions help identify "hot buttons"—positive or negative ideas, often unarticulated prior to the focus group, that excite a particular group of consumers. Ads are then created that link a product or person to an identified hot button. The ads may be further tested by asking people to evaluate storyboards or to use a dialometer—a device whereby people move a dial to indicate what they like or dislike while viewing an ad. In some cases, members of target groups are hooked up to devices that measure heartbeat, pupil dilation, or sweat glands.

Ads may also be tested after they are aired by phoning listeners or viewers to hear their responses. As a result of audience research, advertisers began to shift to *soft sell* advertising techniques such as fantasy, music, aesthetic imagery, and emotional appeals that became part of a product's meaning. A product's image became "a total set of attitudes, a halo of psychological meanings, associations of feeling, and aesthetic messages over a product's physical qualities" (Martineau, 1957, p. 146). Advertisers were attempting to persuade consumers by reaching into their psyches and promising to fulfill some deep-seated desire or to alleviate a long-held fear. In a critique of advertising first written in the late 1950s, Vance Packard (1970) revealed *hidden needs* addressed by advertisers, among them emotional security, reassurance of worth, ego gratification, creative outlets, love objects, power, and immortality (pp. 61-70). For example, Packard wrote that a study of the reasons that people first bought freezers in the post-World War II period led to the widespread use by advertisers of appeals to consumers' emotional security. At the time, freezers were popular, although not necessarily economical. Depth interviews revealed that people felt uncertain and anxious about their futures and were nostalgic for the safety and security they associated with their childhood, and particularly with the mother who always provided love and food. Researchers concluded, "The freezer represents to many the assurance that there is always food in the house, and food in the home represents security, warmth, and safety" (p. 62).

Totemism (1965-1985)

During this period, advertisers made products representative of lifestyle. Product-related images became symbols of social groups, as new computer technologies helped advertisers locate and identify the needs and desires of particular groups of consumers. Product images became totems, or badges of group membership. Ads invited consumers into a "consumption community" by emphasizing the community's attractiveness, rather than the product's desirability. Consumers are induced to adopt the sociocultural identity associated with those who use the product. Simply put, in modern consumer culture, people communicate what types of people they are through their consumption patterns.

The sophisticated use of demographic and psychographic research distinguished the totemistic phase of advertising. Demographic variables explain many consumer choices; for example, they make it easy to understand why young mothers buy diapers whereas older persons do not. Demographics alone, however, cannot explain why some mothers may use disposable diapers and others choose cloth. *Psychographics* link psychology to demographics to help understand consumer behavior. Psychographic analysis explains the values, interests, activities, and opinions of different segments of the population.

One popular psychographic measurement technique that has gained widespread acceptance among advertisers is the values and lifestyles survey (VALS; Atlas, 1984). VALS was the result of a Stanford Research Institute report on the relationship of social values and buying habits. In 1978, the VALS service became commercially available to advertisers and proceeded to revolutionize market research. VALS initially divided the American population into three types of lifestyles: inner-directed (innovative, contemporary), outer-directed (traditional, conservative), and need-driven (those with little discretionary income). Inner-directed consumers were driven by their convictions, passions, and need for self-expression, rather than by social norms and conventions. Outer-directed consumers, which made up a whopping 67% of the population, were more traditional and conservative. They responded to cues from other people in the world around them. Need-driven consumers, made up of survivors and sustainers, had little purchasing power and thus were not typically targeted by advertisers. Because different lifestyle groups buy different products, the VALS tells whom to target with what products.

In 1989, the Stanford Research Institute created VALS2. The new system placed more emphasis on the psychological underpinnings of consumer behavior than on values and lifestyle (Graham, 1989). VALS2 divides people into three self-orientations: principle-oriented, status-oriented, and action-oriented (Farnsworth, 1989). Principle-oriented consumers are guided by their views of how the world should be. Status-oriented consumers are guided by the actions and opinions of others. Action-oriented consumers like to affect their environment in tangible ways. They include "experiencers," with a median age of 25, who have a lot of energy, which they direct into physical exercise and social activities. They are also avid consumers who spend a great deal of money on clothes, food, music, and any innovative products and services. "Makers," composing the other subcategory of action-oriented consumers, are practical and self-sufficient. They devote their time to family, work, and physical recreation. They have little interest in the broader world, and their main interest in material possessions involves those with a practical or functional purpose.

Case Study: The Best Beer

Let's examine one psychographically based advertising campaign in detail—Miller Lite Beer, partly because beer companies commonly associate their product with a lifestyle, partly because Miller Lite was the first light beer marketed to men, and partly because the 15-year "Tastes Great/Less Filling" campaign was one of the longest-running, best-liked campaigns ever on radio or television. *Advertising Age* readers rated it as one of the most powerful ad campaigns in U.S. history.

Before Miller began to target males, reduced-calorie beer was marketed primarily to diet-conscious consumers (read women). According to Bob Lenz, creative director of Backer, Spielvogel, and Bates, who originated Miller Lite's "Tastes Great/ Less Filling" campaign, "Low cal was considered a sissy product, and it turned off the heavy beer drinker. And a national beer can't exist without the heavy drinker, the guy who downs 6 or 7 a night" (Morreale, 1991, p. 27).

So Lenz got the idea to market the beer to heavy beer consumers through the vehicle of professional sports. They pitched Miller Lite as a macho product that enabled men to drink more of it because it was less filling. The ads were populated by aging ex-sports figures, most of whom played themselves. They were over the hill, often known for being self-deprecating—so they were "ordinary" guys with whom the average male viewer could identify. The ads also largely excluded women—so the men who identified with the figures in the ads were defined and positioned as members of an exclusively male beer-drinking community.

The social context of the ad campaign was particularly important. By 1975, the women's movement was in full swing, and women were making gains—albeit minuscule—in achieving equality both in the home and workplace. As more women became visible in traditionally male spheres, more middle- and working-class men were losing economic power. Because many men define masculinity as the ability to be sole providers for their families (Faludi, 1991, p. 65), losing this ability created tension. There was a cultural sense of male anxiety around the loss of authority and power, an anxiety that was both evoked and allayed by the Miller Lite beer commercials. The ads reasserted male authority and allayed anxiety about loss of power through the mediation of a product, Miller Lite. For example, "The Case of the Missing Case" starred comedian Rodney Dangerfield, an "emasculated" male known by the refrain, "I don't get no respect."

By 1992, Miller Lite was losing ground to other light beers. National health consciousness led to a decrease in drinking, especially among the middle-aged men targeted by the Miller Lite campaign. Miller Lite decided to change its image and hired a new advertising agency, Leo Burnett. The resultant "Best Beer" campaign followed Bud, Michelob, and Coors Light and targeted a group that *was* increasing its drinking—male college students. The ads' style changed to appeal to a younger audience: fasts cuts, close-ups, and dissolves, rather than the slow narrative form favored in the "Tastes Great/Less Filling" ads. Most important, the ads did not express fear of women or loss of power so much as they equated "possessing" a beer with "possessing" a woman. The young men in the ads went seeking beer/women—and both were readily available. Although women did appear in the ads, they were always approached by men, were serving men, or were smiling at them. In one ad, beer and sex were symbolically equated, as the fast-cut images showed a beer bottle poised between a young man's legs, followed by a close-up of beer spurting out of an open bottle. Even the language in the ad disacknowledged women. In one scene, bartender Bob Uecker asked, "What are you *guys* having?" although a young man and woman stand at the bar. Instead of allaying male anxiety, these ads suggested that a product would fulfill and make them "real men."

Today's Advertising: The Pantheistic Phase

As consumer culture continues to proliferate, advertising has adapted accordingly. Market researchers now know far more about you than they did before and are better able to target messages specifically to you. While continuing to use tried-and-true advertising techniques such as the celebrity testimonial, advertisers have also discovered new ways to differentiate products, sometimes by use of *anti-ads* that comment on and even mock traditional advertising forms. Advances in telecommunications technology have assisted in both the construction of ads and in their dissemination.

Narrowcasting

Cable television, the Internet, and more sophisticated market research tools permit *narrowcasting,* directing specialized appeals to narrowly defined target audiences. The purchase of computerized lists enables marketers to learn much more about their customers. Any time we buy a product, or even inquire into a product, give our phone number to a cashier in a store, respond to a survey, fill in a warranty, or call an 800 or 900 number, our names may be put on a list that can be sold to other marketers. There are lists of millionaires, persons with hypertension, gay people, heart attack survivors, compulsive gamblers, newlyweds, divorcées—you name it (Tye, 1993).

In addition to asking who you are and what you like, market researchers now ask when is the most likely time for you to buy something. Called *syncographics,* this investigative tool presupposes that when consumers are anticipating an event—from a marriage or baby to a vacation or graduation—they must buy certain things.

Another branch of market research is *sociographics,* used to determine how, why, and where people cluster together, as in neighborhoods, malls, and entertainment centers. Researchers might identify promising neighborhoods for direct mail advertising by zip codes, then survey a representative sampling of neighborhood residents, then invite some of them to form focus groups for more in-depth research on what it will take to make customers of them. All this information is turned over to the advertising agency's creative staff.

As advertisers learn more about their customers, they also learn more about their products—or, more accurately, about what their products "mean" to would-be purchasers. Recall from Chapter 2 the early research on connotations of oranges and grapefruit. Research of this sort continues, as reflected, for example, in a months-long study that culminated in the identification of six key adjectives that best expressed the "brand personality" of Converse athletic shoes. These were *confident, genuine, hard-working, tough, selfish,* and *passionate.* The adjectives became the basis for a new Converse campaign (Savan, 1994).

Breaking With Tradition: Anti-Ads

A distinctive feature of the pantheistic phase is the widespread use of ads that break with conventional advertising frames. Some ads are constructed to appear to be "telling it like it is" rather than trying to persuade us. Others "go meta" to consumers' assumed awareness of the distinction between advertising images and reality, perhaps appealing to cynical consumers by mocking advertising gimmicks, all the while using mockery as a gimmick in its own right.

One type of anti-ad attempts to downplay or conceal that it is an advertisement by mimicking the codes and conventions associated with nonadvertising forms. Handheld cameras may appear to be used, as in John Hancock's "Real Life, Real Answers" series, or an ad may be constructed to appear to have been made "live," unedited, unconstructed. In an ad for Wang, the lighting is dim, workers are in shadow, and the conversation is unclear, all to give the appearance that a hidden camera has been recording natural conversations about the virtues of Wang products. In a recent ad for Saturn automobiles, a black Saturn dealer recalls the day his father bought a new car. "I don't think he was treated fairly," the man says over what appears to be actual home movies of his family at an earlier time. "Those were the times we lived in," he says. In contrast, he suggested, Saturn treats all its customers the same way. "Had Saturn been around then, it would have been entirely different. I think Dad would have come home smiling" (Dee, 1999, p. 63).

Many anti-ads transgress the codes by which we have learned to "read" advertising. Although traditional ads link their product with some desirable trait (beauty, success, etc.) and then invite consumers to identify with this idealized image, these anti-ads appeal to people who "know better" than to identify with such idealized images (Moog, 1990). See the Cole Haan ad in Picture 12.1. Besides getting attention, the ad's ambiguities permit and perhaps encourage multiple projections by viewers, all the while suggesting something basically chic about the product line.

In the "Romance" being staged by Ralph Lauren, there is the hint of a dance—a tango, perhaps—and the beginning of something more. Viewers are left to project themselves into the story (Picture 12.2).

Jonathan Dee (1999) observes that "the connection between a given advertisement and the product it ostensibly promotes has been stretched thinner and thinner, and now seems finally to have given way entirely" (p. 64). Dee's favorite example is a Volkswagen ad called "Sunday Afternoon" in which two men pick up a discarded chair, find out that it smells, then put it back again. Says Dee, "How exactly does this commercial hawk Volkswagen? . . . Is there anything, in theory, to prevent this vignette from serving as an ad for any car, or indeed any product at all?" (p. 64).

Another anti-ad strategy has involved absorbing the mass media's increasingly prevalent criticism of advertising by incorporating the criticisms into the ads themselves. One of the best known is the Isuzu car campaign, in which "Joe Isuzu," a character playing the cultural stereotype of the untrustworthy used car salesman, makes outrageous claims about the Isuzu car. As he speaks, graphics on screen proclaim, "He's lying." Viewers skeptical about slick ads are shocked into paying attention. In other cases, ads make reference to the ad-making process. Ads for General Electric promise that GE refrigerators will enable viewers to have more time to watch GE ads. New England Honda ads promise to find better announcers for New England Honda ads. Levi's 501 jeans ads appear to critique conformity and consumer culture while inducing conformity and consumption of Levi's jeans. Yet all this self-referentiality is simply another form of persuasion. Grunwald (1993) suggests,

> This is the essence of '90s self-reference: heavy on faux-irreverent irony, light on substance. We are given a knowing wink: *Aren't advertisements stupid?* But we are manipulated all the same. Even the legions of ads poking fun at the mindless jingles and hyperactive announcers and buxom blondes that advertisers use to sell us products are trying to sell us products. (p. 13)

The knowing wink continues to be a hallmark of anti-ads, and it sometimes evokes gut-splitting laughter. "How do you keep a rhino from charging?" asks an

www.colehaan.com//New York/Chicago/San Francisco/Beverly Hills/1 800 201 8001

Picture 12.1. Anti-Ad for Cole Haan

Picture 12.2. Ralph Lauren's "Romance"

African "native" in one such spot. Answer: Give it an American Express card. Another ad features a skydiver sporting with a Pepsi-drinking Canadian goose. Yet another features actual black-and-white footage of German autoworkers, race-car drivers, housewives, and so on, with their faces computer altered in such a way that they all appear to be singing "Falling in Love Again" in unison (Dee, 1999). The ad is funny, but the digital alteration serves as a reminder of Mercedes Benz's technical virtuosity.

Misdirection in the Language of Advertising

Product advertisers often mislead consumers by using the vague but suggestive language of implication rather than direct, easily verifiable claims. At other times, they protect themselves against charges of outright falsehood while still leading consumers on. The following are potentially deceptive claims. Although the examples used here to illustrate these claims are relatively clear-cut, consumers will find in magazine ads that product descriptions often fit multiple categories.

The "Nothing Is Better" Claim. "Bring out the Hellman's. Bring out *the best.*" Many advertisements for brands that are almost identical, such as mayonnaise, create the illusion of superiority by claiming to be "best." But the word *best* could mean nothing more than "equal to." If brands are identical, they are equally good, so "best" means only that products are as good as the other products in their category.

"*Nothing is proven* to *work better* or *last longer* than Advil. Nothing." But this doesn't mean that there aren't other pain relief products that work just as well and last just as long as Advil.

"Unsurpassed in speed—no other brand works faster." But this extremely expensive aspirin works no faster than regular aspirin.

The "We're Better" Claim. The ad claims superiority of some sort but does not complete the comparison.

"Preference—*Better* conditioning for *better* color."

"Scott makes *it better* for you." Makes what better? How?

"A1 Bold Steak Sauce. It's *spicier!*" Spicier than what?

The "We're Unique" Claim. This type of claim says that there is nothing quite like the product being advertised. The claim to uniqueness is supposed to be interpreted as a claim to superiority. Here are some examples.

"The *1 and only* Cheerios," or "Not just Raisin Bran. Post Premium Raisin Bran." Why should this make us buy the product? Studies repeatedly show that there is no substantial difference between brand-name and generic cereals other than cost. The brand-name cereals are more expensive, primarily because so much of their profit goes into packaging and advertising.

Clairol: "Try new Natural Instincts. The *first and only* haircolor with a *rare* blend of 3 natural ingredients, including aloe, chamomile and ginseng." Does this make the product better than its competitors? Also, why is it "rare"? Is rare necessarily better?

"Only Aquafresh Whitening has its patented whitening formula with the special ingredient *Triclene.*" What is Triclene, and what makes it special?

"There are wigs. And then there are Revlon wigs." So?

The "Trivially True" Claim. This type of claim says something about the product that is true for any product in the product category. The claim is factual but presents no real advantage over the competition.

"Tidy Cat. It freshens every minute of the day." How is this (whatever it is) different from what any other kitty litter would do?

"Great Lash greatly increases the diameter of every lash." As does any mascara.

"Rolling Rock: The Natural Beer." Rolling Rock is made from grains and water, the same as any beer.

"Palmolive—cleans the first time through." One hopes that all dishwashing liquids do the same.

The "Studies Show" Claim. This type of ad uses specific numbers or other intimations that its claims to superiority are based on some sort of scientific proof.

"Wonder Bread *helps* build strong bodies *12 ways.*" Even the word "helps" did not prevent the Federal Trade Commission from demanding that the ad be changed. Note how the use of the number 12 strengthens the claim. Now Wonder Bread simply claims that the bread helps build strong bodies.

"Easy-Off has *33% more cleaning power* than another *popular brand.*" Another "popular brand" often means some other type of oven cleaner sold somewhere. Also, the claim is not that Easy-Off works 33% better.

"Dimetapp: The brand recommended by doctors over *200 million times.*" Who's counting?

"Degree. Body-Heat Activated for an Extra Degree of Protection." This makes Degree sound like it works more scientifically than other deodorants.

"Geritol has more than twice the iron of ordinary supplements." But is it twice as beneficial to the body?

The "Poetic" Claim. This claim uses feel-good words that are colorful but literally meaningless. Still, they call forth positive associations.

"Quaker Toasted Oats: Yes, it's cold. But it warms your soul."

Post Blueberry Morning cereal: "A little taste of summer." What does summer taste like?

Count Chocula: "Chocolate taste so big, it's scary." What exactly is a big, scary chocolate taste?

"Gallo: because the wine remembers." Remembers what?

"Purina Mainstay dog food has flavor you can actually see." Who can see flavor?

"Clairol Herbal Essence Shampoo. Your hair will get very, very excited!" How will this excitement manifest itself?

"Trust is Tampax Tampons." Despite the alliteration, this one defies logic.

The Rhetorical Question. This technique demands a response from its audience. A question is asked, and the receiver is supposed to answer in a way that affirms the product's goodness.

"What would you do for a Klondike Bar?"

"Shouldn't your family be drinking Hawaiian Punch?"

"Bread du jour—Can't you just taste it?"

"Tired of dull floors? Armstrong Floor Cleaner leaves no dulling or sticky residue."

"Touch of Sweden. Could your hands use a small miracle?"

"Why settle for a cheap imitation when the real thing is now so affordable?" (for Nordic Track).

The Product Endorsement. A celebrity or authority appears in the ad to lend his or her qualities to the product. Sometimes, the person will actually claim to use the product but often does not. There are agencies that survive on providing products with testimonials.

Some of the better known celebrity testimonials involve sports figures. Athletes such as Michael Jordan and Shaquille O'Neal have endorsed products from breakfast cereal to sneakers. Tiger Woods won lucrative endorsements contracts from Nike, Buick, and others. Advertisers may even use groups as well as individuals. For example, Yoplait yogurt was endorsed by the first All Women's Cup team in one advertising campaign. Public scandals can affect celebrity endorsements, however. When Madonna released a sacrilegious music video that coincided with her appearance in a Pepsi commercial, the ad was promptly dropped.

Visual Deception in Product Advertising

Advertisers often show visually what they would be at risk to say verbally. In the case of attack ads, discussed in Chapter 11, doctored photographs may be used to malign a political opponent, or images may be juxtaposed, as in the furlough ad, to invite false inferences. Photojournalists may also editorialize, as in the two photos of George Bush the elder on the covers of *Newsweek,* discussed in Chapter 3. As in the first of these covers, the verbal ("The Wimp Factor") may reinforce the visual.

Recall the photograph of the senator between the model and the priest, discussed in Chapter 5. In a cropped photo showing Senator Jones with either the priest or the beautiful model, the viewer would get the appearance of authenticity—of the real thing. This is one of the ironies of photography (and of film and video): It can distort reality although, by virtue of its *indexicality,* it impresses us with its apparent truthfulness.

Indexicality is present, said Charles Peirce (1991), when a sign (e.g., a photo) has some physical connection to the object or event to which it refers. Examples include fingerprints, footprints, weather vanes, and thermostats. Photography is yet another example. By dint of its physical connection, it is conventionally regarded as proof that the scenes depicted in it really did occur (Messaris, 1997). Compare an ad for a laundry detergent providing before and after photographic proof of the product's cleansing powers with an ad merely asserting by way of a diagram or drawing how the chemical agents in the detergent work. The diagram might clarify, but it could not prove. The photograph, however doctored to misrepresent reality, would probably appear authentic.

Paul Messaris (1997) has identified a number of ways that visuals may create false but persuasive appearances of the real in product advertising. The following are among the most common.

Staged to Look Real. A Volvo 240 appears to have survived intact after a "monster truck" runs over a row of cars, crushing all of them but the Volvo. An investigation revealed that the Volvo was strengthened by specially added steel supports and the other cars were correspondingly weakened (Messaris, 1997, p. 143).

In another case, the soup that is served looks to be thick with vegetables. Not shown are the objects below the surface that push the vegetables to the top.

Photographic Alteration. Physical appearance is enhanced by use of computer imaging. Says Messaris (1997),

> Computers are routinely used to accomplish such tasks as making hair shinier and adding highlights; removing strands of hair that are falling in the wrong place; removing wrinkles, sun damage, pimples, and other skin blemishes; imparting an overall glow to the skin; whitening the whites of eyes and enlarging the pupils; reducing the size of hips and increasing the length of legs; and, of course, increasing the size of breasts. (p. 153)

Just as bodily appearance can be enhanced, so can grass be made to appear greener, water bluer, and skies brighter. In 1990, roughly 1 in 20 ads was digitally altered; 5 years later, according to Cooper (1995), the figure was closer to 90%.

Selection. Recall that communicators of all types have to make choices and that every selection—of a word, a photographic angle, a video sequence, and so on—is also a deflection. Understandably, product advertisers select images that will make their products look good. This can be done by shot selection, by arrangement as in a magazine ad, and by sequencing as in a television ad.

Implied Selling Propositions. Literally speaking, visuals are not a language. But an arrangement of visuals—for example, a video showing a person standing near television sets falling dangerously close to him from above, then apparently catching in his arms, first HBO1, then HBO2, then HBO3—needs little in the way of verbal explanation. The metaphors of being bombarded by bad television, then being able to catch good shows on three HBO channels, are easy to decipher (Picture 12.3).

Visuals contain no verbs or adjectives, but the familiar grammar of visual juxtaposition serves in their place to offer contrasts and analogies, causal claims and generalizations. An ad for a laundry detergent shows the advertised product removing a stain that a more expensive brand cannot handle. Here the visuals alone suggest contrast and causation; what's more, they evoke images of science—of the scientific demonstration.

Automobiles have long been likened by analogy to animals, such as lions (Toyota), cougars (Mercury), and cheetahs (BMW). Messaris (1997) regards these as partial substitutes for adverbs and adjectives. But of course the verbal can reinforce the visual with words such as *dynamic, breathtaking,* and *supercharged* (p. 193).

Television ads for familiar products such as Pepsi may display an array of smiling faces under a banner of the "Pepsi Generation." Likewise, half a globe may be shown in a magazine ad for Johnny Walker whiskey, suggesting that people everywhere enjoy this brand of Scotch. Better yet, the whiskey can be celebrated as a drink for sophisticated people by way of an ad showing—in one digitally altered cityscape—landmarks from sophisticated places such as Paris, London, Kyoto, and New York. Generalizations such as these are the stuff of fantasy and myth, not science, but they are powerful nonetheless.

Subliminal Advertising

Throughout the history of advertising, debate has raged about its power to persuade. There are those, such as Michael Schudson (1984), who believe that advertising's

Picture 12.3. Still From Television Ad for HBO Channels

power over us is greatly overrated, whereas others believe that advertising constantly massages and manipulates us subliminally—that is, beyond the level of conscious awareness. Belief in the power of subliminal advertising stems from James Vicary's 1957 research experiment conducted at a drive-in movie theater. Movie screens project 26 frames per second. Vicary flashed one-frame images of Coca-Cola and popcorn too quickly to be perceived by the naked eye. Yet Vicary reported that Coca-Cola sales increased 18% and popcorn sales, 57.8%. When Vicary repeated his study under controlled conditions, however, the results did not bear his original research out (Weir, 1984, p. 46).

Nevertheless, theorists continue to advance the theory of subliminal persuasion. Most well known is Wilson Bryan Key (1973, 1976, 1989), author of *Subliminal Seduction* and other books filled with dire warnings about the pervasiveness of hidden messages in advertising. He presents examples of the word *sex* embedded in the ice cubes of an ad for Gilbey's Gin or baked into Ritz crackers. He argues that these ads trigger subconscious emotional responses, so that people remember the ad and product when they are in the marketplace. Although he cites numerous studies to support his claims, most of the experiments that he cites had no control or comparison groups, nor was he ever able to show that subliminal techniques made people behave in ways that they would not ordinarily do. Key does not cite a single case of an advertiser admitting to using subliminal tactics. Pratkanis and Aronson (1991) note,

> Finding that 62% of the subjects feel sexual, romantic, or satisfied when they see a gin ad with the word *sex* embedded in the ice cubes tells us nothing about the effectiveness of the *sex* implant. What would happen if the word *sex* was removed from the cubes? Perhaps 62% of the subjects would still feel sexy, romantic, or satisfied. Perhaps more, perhaps less would feel this way. Without such a comparison, we do not know. (p. 202)

Pratkanis and Aronson (1991) suggest that people's beliefs and expectations play a strong role in the "effect" of subliminal persuasion. In a 1958 study conducted by the Canadian Broadcasting network, the words *phone now* flashed on screen 352 times during a popular Sunday evening program. Telephone use did not increase, and 500 respondents who tried to guess the message failed. Yet people reported feeling hungry or thirsty, probably because they thought the message was aimed at getting them to eat or drink (p. 202). This also explains the current popularity of self-help tapes, on which subliminal messages meant to build self-esteem or to aid in memory retention are embedded beneath soft music or the soothing sounds of the ocean. In another study, participants were given tapes that they thought were meant to build self-esteem, but which really contained messages concerning memory retention. Although tests 5 weeks later revealed no change in self-esteem, they were convinced that their self-esteem had improved—even though the subliminal messages were about memory retention.

Advertisements presented subliminally probably have no effect, but what about ads whose subtle enticements to buy are barely noticed? Some critics of advertising maintain that this is when advertising has its greatest effects (Miller, 1981; Postman, 1985). Says Miller, the effect of being inundated with commercials is precisely what allows them to succeed. "'It's only a commercial,' we say to ourselves, then settle back, watching without really watching, thereby letting each image make its deep impressions" (p. 29). Commenting on subliminal advertising theory, Miller adds,

> We are accustomed to think of these subtleties in quasi-Pavlovian terms, as hidden stimuli that "turn us on" without our knowing it: nipples airbrushed into sunsets, lewd words traced into some ice cubes, etc. But this conception of the way ads work and of the way we apprehend them, is much too crude. They

function, not mechanically, but poetically, through metaphor, association, repetition, and other devices that suggest a variety of possible meanings. The viewer, therefore, does not just watch once and start salivating, but senses gradually, half-consciously, the commercial's welter of related messages.

And just as the viewer needn't recognize these subtleties in order to take them in, so, perhaps, the advertisers themselves may not know their every implication, any more than a poet or filmmaker is fully aware of all that his work implies. (p. 29)

Summary

Robert Goldman (1992) has said that the "fundamental work accomplished within an advertising space is the connection and exchange of meanings between an object (a named product) and an image (another referent system)" (p. 71). This chapter has charted changes in that connection and exchange of meanings, beginning with the idolatry phase, then moving through stages of iconology, narcissism, and totemism to today's pantheistic stage. Today's product advertising uses new technologies and sophisticated market research in targeting narrowly segmented markets. Although some advertisers continue to rely on techniques of persuasion developed in bygone years, others are exploring new ways of getting the attention of consumers and their money. Some ads mock traditional conventions, others are made to look fresh and spontaneous or newslike, as in documentaries. Still others traffic in deliberate verbal and visual ambiguities, inviting consumers to project their own meanings onto the ads.

Advertisers do not tell you the good and the bad about their products; instead, they play up their good, play down their bad, while denigrating competitors' products, if they mention them at all. Broadly speaking, then, virtually all product advertising is not about truth but about persuasion, and this chapter has illustrated the myriad ways that product advertising may deceive, or at least attempt to deceive.

Product advertising can be deceptive, but does that necessarily mean that it is dangerous? What if the viewer knows that the claims made in behalf of the expensive perfume have been exaggerated and that the model's beauty has been visually enhanced? What if that same viewer enjoys the verbal misdirection and has no problem with the digital enhancement? What if she experiences even greater pleasure from imagining herself being like this perfect woman and perhaps being seen by others as similar to the model—this by virtue of her having purchased and put on the same perfume that the model wore?

Similar questions can be asked about today's anti-ads. So what if there's a disconnect between the ad's narrative and the product being advertised? So what if another ad mocks an earlier generation's advertising conventions? So what if an ad pulls us in by getting us to laugh or prompting us to believe that it has been recorded live when it wasn't?

Product advertising has a goodly share of critics. Their list of alleged harms from particular types of advertisements is large. Beauty products promote an unattainable beauty ideal, thus causing reduced self-esteem and sometimes severe problems such as anorexia and bulimia. Women are fetishized as sexual commodities in ads of many types targeted to men. Adolescents' inclination to rebel is fueled by ads encouraging nonconformity and sometimes destructiveness. Ads for alcohol products contribute to alcoholism, ads for tobacco products cause addiction, and so on.

A concern of some ad researchers is that students trained to be critical of ads such as these may not be measurably superior to those not so trained (Tatlow, 1992). Yet society as a whole has taken steps to curb or control some of these forms of advertising—for example, bans on liquor and cigarette advertising on television. Defenders of even these products insist they can be taken in moderation—that, in general, consumers must assume some responsibility for their purchasing decisions. At the least, it can be said that not everyone is harmed by product advertising that deceives or promotes antisocial values. First, there must be a predisposition to diet to excess (or eat to excess), argue those who refuse to assign full responsibility to advertisers for food disorders. They have a point.

A more general charge, that the cumulative effects of product advertising can be dangerous, was taken up in Chapter 3. Schudson's (1984) capitalist realism captures in a phrase the commodification of consumer culture in which practically everything—including antimaterialist, anticonsumerist objects—can be bought for a price. The alleged dangers of consumerism are many: a dependence on store-bought things, rather than on ourselves; a devaluing of what enriches the society but doesn't lend itself to mass marketing; excessive materialism—you are what you own; and a narcissistic society, given over to selfish pleasures. Still, as defenders of capitalism maintain, imagine how costly the truly useful and necessary things in life would be without commercial advertising. Moreover, advertising need not appeal to the worst in us to be successful. Those who carp at commercial advertising haven't found a suitable alternative.

The debate about product advertising continues, and it takes on greater significance as politicians emulate the product advertisers. Perhaps the greatest danger in a nation raised on 30-second spots of every type is that the daily deluge dulls the critical senses, prompting us increasingly to process messages mindlessly, and prompting message makers to address us in sound bites rather than with arguments and in entertaining little playlets rather than with solid evidence. Commenting on ads in which a Converse sneaker is promoted as "unselfish" or a Volkswagen promoted by way of a story that has nothing to do with cars, Dee (1999) laments that "the real condition of advertising speech is not falsehood as much as kind of truthlessness" (p. 66).

In a medium designed primarily to entertain, television advertising must entertain, and it is doing that better and better. But as Neil Postman (1985) warns us in a book aptly named *Amusing Ourselves to Death,* there are dangers in taking everything unseriously. Postman sees Aldous Huxley's *Brave New World* as prophetic. As Huxley saw it, "People will come to love their oppression, to adore the technologies that undo their capacities to think" (cited in Postman, 1985, p. vi).

Questions and Projects for Further Study

1. Do an inventory of products that you purchased in the last month: clothing, food items, and so on. How many did you learn about through commercials?
2. Find examples of ads that use traditional advertising conventions. Then find anti-ads that mock those conventions, play off of them humorously, traffic in deliberate ambiguities, or blur the line between the real and the rhetorical.
3. Find examples of your own of the various types of deceptive advertising language. In your view, are any of these potentially harmful to consumers?
4. Find examples of visual deception in advertising. Again, ask yourself whether any of these forms of deception are potentially dangerous.
5. Large retail manufacturers such as Anheuser-Busch, Procter & Gamble, Revlon, and Philip Morris provide an excellent opportunity to study narrowcasting at work because they market different brands of the same product (e.g., beers, detergents, perfumes, and cigarettes) differently, each for a different target audience. Find examples of narrowcasting by comparing a retail manufacturer's ads for different brands of the same product type.

References

Atlas, J. (1984, October). Beyond demographics: How Madison Ave knows who you are and what you want. *The Atlantic, 254,* 49-58.

Cooper, A. (1995, September 11). Eminent domain. *Adweek,* pp. 26-29.

Dee, J. (1999, January). But is it advertising? *Harper's, 298,* 61-72.

Durning, A. T. (1993, May-June). Can't live without it. *World Watch,* pp. 10-18.

Faludi, S. (1991). *Backlash: The undeclared war against American women.* New York: Anchor.

Farnsworth, M. R. (1989, July). Psychographics for the 1990's. *American Demographics, 11,* 24-31.

Fox, S. (1985). *The mirror makers: A history of American advertising and its creators.* New York: Vintage.

Goldman, R. (1992). *Reading ads socially.* New York: Routledge.

Graham, J. (1989, February 13). New VALS2 takes psychological route. *Advertising Age,* p. 24.

Grunwald, M. (1993, August 29). Metamorphosis. *Boston Globe Magazine,* pp. 1, 13.

Key, W. B. (1973). *Subliminal seduction.* New York: New American Library.

Key, W. B. (1976). *Media sexploitation.* New York: Signet.

Key, W. B. (1989). *The clam-plate orgy and other subliminal techniques for manipulating your psyches.* New York: Signet.

Leiss, W., Kline, S., & Jhally, S. (1986). *Social communication in advertising: Persons, products, and images of well-being.* New York: Methuen.

Lewis, M. (2000, August 13). Boom box. *New York Times Magazine,* pp. 36, 38-41, 51, 65-67.

Martineau, P. (1957). *Motivation in advertising: Motives that make people buy.* New York: McGraw-Hill.

Messaris, P. (1997). *Visual persuasion: The role of images in advertising.* Thousand Oaks, CA: Sage.

Miller, M. C. (1981, September 16). Massa come home. *New Republic, 185,* 29-32.

Moog, C. (1990). *Are they selling her lips? Advertising and identity.* New York: William Morrow.

Morreale, J. (1991, May). Gender and Miller Lite: The case of the missing case. *Studies in Popular Culture, 13*(2), 27-37.

Packard, V. (1970). *The hidden persuaders* (Reprint). New York: Pocket.

Peirce, C. S. (1991). Indexicality. In J. Hoopes (Ed.), *Peirce on signs: Writings on semiotics by Charles Sanders Peirce.* Chapel Hill: University of North Carolina Press.

Postman, N. (1985). *Amusing ourselves to death.* New York: Viking.

Pratkanis, A., & Aronson, E. (1991). *The age of propaganda: The everyday use and abuse of persuasion.* New York: Freeman.

Savan, L. (1994). *The sponsored life: Ads, TV, and American culture.* Philadelphia: Temple University Press.

Schudson, M. (1984). *Advertising: The uneasy persuasion.* New York: Basic Books.

Tatlow, R. E. (1992). *Media literacy vs. critical thinking: Which is the better predictor of critical viewing skills?* Unpublished master's thesis, University of Pennsylvania, Annenberg School of Communication, Philadelphia.

Tye, L. (1993, September 6). List makers draw a bead on many. *Boston Globe,* pp. 1, 17.

Weir, W. (1984, October 15). Another look at subliminal "facts." *Advertising Age,* p. 46.

Whittle Update. (1993, Summer). *Big Noise,* p. 18.

Talking Through Differences

"Sue, is that you? Hi, it's Jake. Jake Edelman. I was wondering if you'd be willing to sell one of your demo rackets—you know, the Wilson 6.4? I've been trying it out the last few weeks and I kinda like it. What with the end of the indoor tennis season, I figure you might be willing to part with it for 60 bucks."

"No way, Jake. It would cost me $140 to replace it."

"Well, it *is* used, Sue, and this is its second season. How about $75?"

"Make it $80."

"Deal. I'll bring a check this Sunday."

In an oft-quoted passage from *A Rhetoric of Motives,* Kenneth Burke (1950/1969) reminds us that "the *Rhetoric* must lead us through the Scramble, the flurries and flare-ups of the Human Barnyard, the Give and Take, the wavering line of pres-

sure and counterpressure . . . the War of Nerves, the War" (p. 23). Burke's list is a reminder that persuasion is not always cooperative; indeed, the situations that give rise
to it are often conflictual, or at least partially so. Thus, as Jake and Sue successfully
talk through their differences in this chapter's opening example, they do so by bargaining for personal advantage. Burke adds that rhetoric does have its peaceful moments: "At times its endless competition can add up to the transcending of itself. In
ways of its own it can move from the factional to the universal" (p. 23). But Burke
says that universality often becomes "transformed into a partisan weapon" (p. 23).
Burke is suggesting here that humankind's noblest sentiments both grow from factional strife and often serve as partisan tools in subsequent conflicts. Still, he argues
that the mouths of persuaders are nearly always preferable to the mouths of guns.

If this chapter had a subtitle, it might be, "From Destructive Conflicts to Productive Dialogues." The chapter explores different types of talk in the face of differences, all involving persuasive interactions. The interactions may be private, as in the
bargaining over the Wilson 6.4, or public, as in a campaign debate. They may consist
of dialogues between friends or nasty confrontations between enemies, but all involve the give-and-take of conversation. That makes them different from prepared
speeches and different again from persuasive campaigns and protest demonstrations.
A good deal of planning may take place, to be sure, but at the point of conversation,
there is an element of unpredictability. All parties to the interaction must pattern
planned remarks flexibly, listen carefully and critically, and adjust responses to the
messages of the other. Here, too, good questions may be as persuasive as good answers.

Persuasion in Social Conflicts

A *social conflict* is a clash over at least partially incompatible interests. For several reasons, the techniques of persuasion prescribed for nonconflict situations are not always applicable to conflict situations.

First, social conflicts are not simply misunderstandings, semantic confusions, or
communication breakdowns, although they sometimes begin that way. Situation
comedies are rife with apparent crises between husband and wife or boss and employee in which the source of tension is an error of fact or interpretation that is easily
correctable with a bit of dialogue. These might more accurately be labeled pseudo-
conflicts.

Second, the notion of a clash of incompatible interests presupposes something
more than a disagreement, difference of opinion, or academic controversy. This
point is important because people tend to minimize or wish away conflicts by treating them as if they were mere disagreements. For example, consider the difference

between a newspaper columnist arguing that the autoworkers deserve higher wages and the same argument coming from the head of the United Auto Workers in the midst of a collective bargaining session. The columnist would have been arguing a controversial position, it is true, but it is questionable whether he or she would have had anything more than an academic and passing interest in the matter. The union leader, by contrast, is quite clearly involved in a social conflict, evidenced by a clash over incompatible interests. Similarly, two persons—even two intimates—may subscribe to divergent religious principles without necessarily being in conflict. Their interests might well become incompatible, however, if one felt morally compelled to convert the other or if, as in a marriage, both had to decide how to rear their offspring. Conflicts over principles arise whenever one party makes unacceptable claims on the other or when, in the face of divergent goals, their activities must be coordinated.

To have an interest in something, then, is to covet or value it personally, whether it is one's personal reputation, an item of scarcity such as money, or a principle such as equal pay for equal work. For two persons or groups to have incompatible interests, each must stand as an obstacle to maximum realization of the other's interests. This includes business competitions and other contests for power or control, such as electoral contests. Two persons may disagree on the market value of a house that is up for sale without necessarily being in conflict. But should the disputants be seller and potential buyer, they would indeed be in conflict. (As in the case of the tennis racket negotiations, they might well reach an amicable compromise and still have been in conflict. In any such bargaining situation, each party's relative gain over what he or she could have paid or received is the other party's relative loss.)

Third, the same persons may be embroiled in a conflict on one level and in a controversy or disagreement on another level. Consider the case of two undergraduates engaged in a classroom debate about Israel's relationship to the Palestinians. To the extent that either party may receive a poor grade or suffer loss of reputation from being put down by the other, they are indeed engaged in a conflict. But the conflict is not about Israel's relationship with its Arab neighbors. That remains a disagreement or difference of opinion. A conflict may involve value differences or personal animosities or competition for scarce resources, but once again, the personal interests of one party must be threatened by the other party.

It should be clear by now that appeals to reason or common ground may not be sufficient to resolve social conflicts; indeed, in such conflicts as between labor and management, buyer and seller, husband and wife, and Israel and the Palestinians, the combatants might well have reason to remain antagonistic. The fourth point, then, is that attitudes in conflict situations are often linked to beliefs about relative power capacities. In a classroom discussion, one has the luxury to decide what two conflicting parties ought to do, whatever the nature of the context and of each side's willingness and capacity to reward or punish the other. The realities of conflict situations generally militate against agreement on ideal solutions. Trust levels tend to be low, ego involvements high, and channels of communication closed or restricted; neither side may be able to enforce its conception of an ideal outcome. Hence, "peace with honor" may be a truce agreement following a military stalemate. What is considered "honorable" or "desirable" is necessarily what one can hope to get under the circum- stances. Correspondingly, the conflicting parties may struggle to alter the other's cir- cumstances as a way of modifying the other's beliefs and attitudes. Here, coercion and persuasion go hand in hand. What emerges most often is an implicit or explicit compromise.

Cooperation and Competition in Mixed-Motive Conflicts

One of the paradoxical features of practically all social conflicts is that the adversaries are motivated simultaneously to cooperate and compete with each other. Seldom is either party served by annihilating the enemy, taking all the opponent's money, or totally incapacitating the adversary. Real-life conflicts, in this sense, are not like footraces or games of chess or poker. Instead, they are of the mixed-motive variety. To understand this fact of social conflicts is to understand why purely combative strategies of influence seldom make sense.

Consider, once again, the case of a labor-management conflict about wages. In theory, it is in the interests of labor to get as much as possible, and it is likewise in the interests of management to give as little as possible. Each, moreover, has combative weapons available (prolonged strikes, layoffs, and so on) by which to punish or crip- ple the enemy. Why don't they use them more often?

The obvious answer is that they have much to lose by acting combatively and much to gain through cooperation. Morality aside, let us examine the interests of la- bor and management in the potential costs and benefits exchanged by acting com- batively or cooperatively.

First, purely coercive influence entails relatively high costs. To punish another, or even to threaten effectively, one must mount an offensive capability. For example, the union that decides to go out on strike forfeits employee paychecks during the strike period. Coactive persuasion, on the other hand, may cost little or nothing. Second, because conflicts involve reciprocal influence, each side must calculate the repercussions of its actions in possible retaliation costs. The use of force may carry the day but only at the price of incurring the wrath of the adversary, who may strike back with even greater fury. For example, company management may hire nonunion labor during the strike in an effort to break the union. Third, the use of purely combative strategies over an issue such as wages may block the resolution of other subsidiary issues such as questions of worker health and safety. The ensuing buildup of antagonisms may so impede communication and reduce trust as to make what once were considered trivial questions into significant and unresolvable matters of principle. Fourth, strategies of a purely combative nature often enrage nonadversaries, who then bring their own influence to bear on the situation. Some combative acts are punished by law, others are vilified by the press, and still others cause backlash reactions from the public. Teaching assistants at Yale University experienced all these problems when they tried to organize themselves into a union. Threatening to hold back reports of undergraduate student grades until the Yale administration granted them collective bargaining rights turned out to be immensely counterproductive. Not only did the administrators turn on them; so did the undergraduates (Duhl, 1996).

Thus, the parties in a conflict will incur costs if they employ purely combative strategies, and benefits will more likely accompany the use of cooperative, coactive means of influence. Conflict theorists like to speak of benefits as a hypothetical benefits pie (Figure 13.1), and they are fond of pointing out that the size of the pie is by no means finite. Should a labor-management conflict escalate beyond control, the size of the pie is reduced. But should the two sides find a way to increase productivity and profits, the size of the pie is increased. Cooperation on one issue can breed a spirit of harmony on other issues and reduce the need for offensive capabilities.

Symmetrical Versus Asymmetrical Conflicts

A conflict between persons or groups with relatively equal power to reward or punish the other is called a *symmetrical* conflict. A conflict between antagonists having unequal power is an *asymmetrical* conflict. There are, of course, degrees of asymmetry, and relative power may vary as well from one situation to another. Parents have the upper hand in most families most of the time, but children are not without their own resources, including the capacity to withhold love at precisely the moments when their parents are most in need of it. Employers tend to be "one-up" on their employees, but the imbalance is usually reduced and sometimes reversed by a variety of factors, including government regulations restricting employer prerogatives.

How one feels about conflict and how one deals with it once it arises are partly a function of one's role in an organization. Within large-scale social systems such as universities and business organizations, symmetrical conflicts routinely develop between competing members of the system, *actor-actor conflicts,* and asymmetrical conflicts take place between rank-and-file members of the system and representatives of

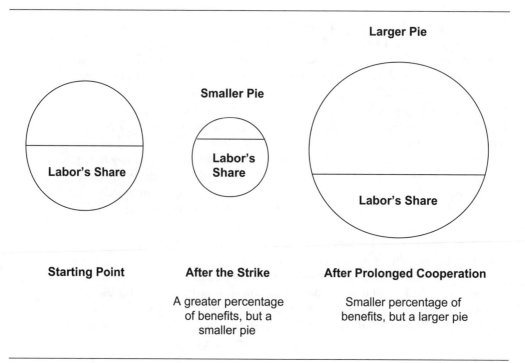

Figure 13.1. Hypothetical Benefit Pie

the system as a whole, *actor-system conflicts*. For example, student organizations often engage in actor-actor competitions for new members, and they occasionally become embroiled in actor-system conflicts with university administrators about issues of student rights.

Within their spheres of authority, administrators of every type tend to be system oriented. For these system representatives, there is an understandable preference for preventing conflict and resolving conflicts quickly once they arise. For example, college deans try to discourage competition for funds among the departments they supervise. The deans tend to identify more with the need for order and stability in the college as a whole than with the interests of any one component of the system. Likewise, the president of the United States tends to look askance on strikes that disrupt the economy. Like the dean of a college, the president tends to be system oriented rather than actor oriented.

These orientations are manifested in recurring patterns of talk about conflict, that is, in genres of conflict rhetoric. Those with system orientations tend to downplay the need for conflict within their organizations and to label conflicts as mere disagreements or misunderstandings. Their emphasis in public statements is on the benefits that can accrue to all from cooperation. Of course, they tend to reserve their harshest criticisms for the "troublemakers" who initiate actor-system conflicts. From an actor orientation, on the other hand, conflict is necessary, natural, and in any case inevitable—not something to be prevented or wished away. From the perspectives of those who lead movements in behalf of students' rights, for example, protests may be necessary even if disruptive because they call attention to injustices. A good deal more will be said about protests in Chapter 14.

Productive and Destructive Conflicts

Conflicts can be productive for both sides. When the two parties each seek to win at the other's expense (*win-lose*), rather than work cooperatively for mutually satisfactory outcomes (*win-win*), however, the result is often a destructive, *lose-lose* conflict.

Have you ever been in a really bad relationship? Consider here not just soured relationships between lovers but also between friends, family members, housemates, or coworkers. Because these are the people with whom we are most interdependent, these are also the people with whom we are most prone to experience conflict, whether productive or destructive.

Morton Deutsch (1969) has identified a number of recurrent patterns in destructive conflicts. In these lose-lose conflicts, says Deutsch, there is an increase in the size and number of principles and precedents believed to be at stake. Participants are willing to bear greater costs (both material and psychological) to "win." Each side exempts itself from norms of ethical conduct that they impose on the other. Hostility intensifies. Cooperation is driven out by suspiciousness and combativeness. There is increasing reliance on power and on tactics of threat, coercion, and deception. There is a corresponding shift away from persuasion and tactics of conciliation and rapport building. Communication becomes impoverished and unreliable. Channels are either not used or used to mislead and intimidate. Reliance is placed on espionage or on other circuitous routes for gathering information.

As a consequence, says Deutsch (1969), little confidence is placed in information provided directly from the other, and opportunities for error and selective perception are enhanced. The range of perceived alternatives is reduced. There is a reduced time perspective, a focus on the immediate. Thought is polarized, reduced to either-ors and stereotyped responses. There is greater susceptibility to fear- or hope-inspired rumors. One's own behavior is seen as more benevolent and legitimate, and there is a corresponding assumption that this "better" behavior should be more appreciated by conflict opponents. Once committed to winning at the expense of the other, there is a tendency to justify past actions and to mobilize further with each successive response by the adversary.

Dealing With Conflicts Productively

One reason that conflicts escalate beyond the intentions of either party is that neither knows how to cope with the resistance and hostility displayed by the other. Antagonists play the blame game. (Joe: "Everybody knows you're a liar." Chris: "Oh yeah? When did you start telling the truth?") Or they shift to a passively aggressive style of placating the other. ("Am I in the way, dear? I hate to be a pest. Have I said something or done something to offend you?") Or they engage in tactless candor. ("I've never liked you, Rasheed. Neither do most of your so-called friends.") (See Elgin, 1995.)

Often, attempted solutions to conflicts only exacerbate the problem as, for example, when we suggest to others that the conflict could easily be resolved if only they would be more reasonable. When students are presented with Deutsch's characterization of the process of conflict escalation, they have had no difficulty finding examples from their own experiences when, try as they might, they could not reverse a pattern of destructive conflict. Consider this typical case.

After months of nagging at her apartment mate to share equally in the performance of household chores, Chris thought she had hit on a perfect solution: a contract with Becky that would specify who would do what, when, and with what penalties for nonperformance. But Chris failed to realize that the conflict had long since expanded into a fight for control over the rules of the relationship. It was no longer exclusively about sharing in the household chores. Thus, when Becky was presented with the proposal, she rejected it outright as another of Chris's efforts at imposing her way of doing things. This of course confirmed Chris's view that Becky was impossible to reason with. A wiser Chris might have put the problem to Becky: What can *we* do to reach a mutually satisfactory solution?

In conflict situations, it is all too easy to see matters solely from one's own viewpoint. A former student complained, for example, that his impending marriage was placed in jeopardy even before it had begun. This, as he saw it, was because his fiancée constantly invoked her father's "dumb opinions" to back up her own. Little did he realize how difficult he had been making it for his fiancée to separate from her parents. His tendency to respond to her exclusively on an intellectual level was a contributing factor, because in doing so he was holding back the affection she most needed. Recognizing that individuals communicate relationally at the same time they communicate substantively was helpful for this student.

"He gets my back up." "She makes my blood boil." "That makes my hair stand on edge." Expressions such as these attest to the intense visceral reactions that conflicts can generate. Yet precisely when our bodies tell us to strike back by any means, we need to be most coolheaded. Does this sound unreasonable? Probably not. But is it easy to do? No way!

Decide *why* to fight, *whether* to fight, *when* to fight, and *how* to fight. These are the four cardinal rules of self-management in conflict situations, according to psychologist Cynthia Shar (personal communication, 1999). The important word is *decide*. Take control over what your body is telling you by making self-aware strategic thinking in conflict situations a habit.

Decide Why to Fight. Think carefully about the conflict situation motivating your desire for a fight. Is there a principle or objective worth fighting for? A wrong that clearly needs to be corrected? An obstacle that stands in the way of your legitimate interests? Think carefully on these matters before taking action lest you discover afterward that you'd been too impulsive, too carried away, or too eager to see your conflict opponents as mad and/or bad while ignoring your own contribution to a destructive pattern of escalation. Be aware that that ignorance—denial, as psychologists often refer to it—is normal and natural but not necessarily serviceable in the long run. Before you act, think about the long run.

Decide Whether to Fight. Even if your cause is just, it may not be in your interests to express your opposition, let alone to act on it confrontationally. Calculate the advantages and disadvantages. Is this your fight? Is it worth your commitment of time, energy, and resources? Are you prepared for the costs of expressed conflict—for its downsides? Have you a winning strategy for achieving your ends? What would happen if you chose *not* to fight?

Decide When to Fight. Is this the best time to fight? Would your interests be best served by postponing overt conflict action until you've had a chance to think on it, to talk it over with valued associates, to gain pledges of support from potential allies, and perhaps to wait for the conflict to simmer down? What would be the benefits and costs of delaying action?

Decide How to Fight. Conflict avoidance is often as damaging as aggressive, self-destructive conflict behavior. Sometimes we need to fight. Sometimes coercive behavior is the only action possible. But is coercion truly necessary? Can the same ends be achieved by coactive persuasion, perhaps combined with positive inducements? Can you think of creative ways to turn a win-lose conflict into a win-win conflict? Before moving toward conflict escalation, consider the alternatives.

Nearly always helpful in conflict situations is showing that you understand the other's way of looking at things. Alternatively, you may need to ask for clarification from the other person as to what the problem is. Wanda, a 35-year-old graduate student, was afraid that Judy, her live-in partner, was going to leave her for a younger woman. But not even Wanda fully realized that this was what had been making her persistently angry with Judy until Judy coaxed it out of her.

On being subjected to criticism, asking for clarification rather than becoming immediately defensive is especially important. At a large university, the dean of one of the divisions initiated a process of calling each of the department heads in for unscheduled private conferences, during which he made known a long list of criticisms that he had been accumulating. Finally, Shirley was called in. When the boss mentioned that "people weren't getting all the work done, and they were spending too much time on coffee breaks," Shirley asked for more information. She said, "Have you been unhappy with some part of my work?" The boss said he could not think of anything right then. The boss, who was really not angry or upset at Shirley at all, mentioned a few things, which Shirley accepted, and then they turned their attention to other matters in the office (Frost & Wilmot, 1978, p. 138).

Recall the discussion of framing and reframing in Chapter 6. Often, the size and severity of the conflict can be reframed to make it easier to deal with. What had been labeled a racial conflict can be relabeled a conflict between two persons who happen to be of different races. "Being treated unfairly" can become "being treated unfairly on a particular occasion." An issue of principle might be reframed as a question of how best to apply a principle.

Many of the techniques for overcoming resistance and hostility were discussed in Chapter 4. Differences can be bridged coactively by reaching out to the other, emphasizing common bonds and shared experiences as well as areas of agreement on the matter in question. Humor, too, can defuse hostility.

Several years ago, a university president and a young upstart faculty member found themselves at adjacent urinals during a break in a meeting of faculty and administrators. The meeting had been extremely tense. During the meeting, the faculty member had been a constant irritant to the president, who hoped to win faculty support on a highly sensitive plan that he and his coadministrators had formulated. Many cups of coffee had been imbibed, making bladder control difficult. But now, as they stood before their adjacent urinals, neither could get anything out. After more than a minute had gone by, each seemingly attentive to his own task, yet obviously aware of the other's presence, the two adversaries looked at each other, smiled, then broke up in uncontrollable laughter. The second half of the meeting went far better than the first.

The techniques of coactive persuasion described in Chapter 4 and elaborated on in subsequent chapters are not unlike those recommended by conflict theorists Frost and Wilmot (1978) to reduce defensiveness. These include (a) neutral descriptions of the situation, without an implied need for anyone to change; (b) a problem orientation—expressing a desire to work on a mutual problem without predetermined opinions; (c) empathy for the feelings and attitudes of the other; and (d) minimization of differences in skill, position, or intelligence.

When two or more persons get past their initial suspicions and begin to approach a conflict as their problem, noted Deutsch (1969), their talk is often lively, intense, and impassioned but at the same time creative, engaging, satisfying, and even entertaining. In productive conflicts, he observes, positions are stated directly, and there is allowance for expressions of anger as something normal and expected, even helpful. There are likely to be expressions of warm feelings as well, but care is taken to avoid premature agreement, because this only masks the underlying problem. Often, it helps to divide the conflict into parts and begin discussion of the more easily resolvable issues. Success in solving these problems breeds success with others. It also serves as a reminder of positive qualities in the other party and of common bonds. It may also lead to the realization that there is room for compromise. In breaking the conflict into parts, the two parties may even discover that their different values make trade-offs possible, each party "giving" on one issue so as to "get" on another.

Getting to Yes in Business Negotiations

Suppose that you are representing your company in its business dealings with another. Suppose that instead of selling (or buying) one Wilson 6.4, you are selling an entire brand of tennis rackets to a chain of department stores. Most of the examples presented in this chapter thus far have been of the interpersonal, close-to-home variety, but the principles apply to business relationships as well. The major differences are in scope of conflict and degree of authority. In selling a brand of tennis rackets to a department store chain (rather than bargaining over one Wilson 6.4), the stakes are higher, each side's clout is greater, and you, as the company's representative, have less freedom to act on your own authority. Still, the two sides must work to realize their common interests while at the same time pursuing their individual interests (Fisher & Ury, 1991).

This is well illustrated in William Stiles's *Tactics of Persuasion* (1994). This pull-no-punches manual for sales trainees at times reads more like a manual for war. "Stay in control." "Dominate customers." "Be the authority." "Be prepared to kill the competitor's deal." "Use sudden action." "Use the penalty close." These are some of the tactics recommended by Stiles.

Yet *Tactics of Persuasion* comes back to the need for coactive persuasion introduced in Chapter 4 combined with material inducements. "Go for the yeses." "Use empathy." "Know when to stop talking." "Get and use new information." "Work on establishing credibility." Advice of this sort attests to the importance of bridging differences coactively. As for the material inducements that might go with the sales pitch, Stiles lists lures, concessions, giving the customer something for nothing (recall the norm of reciprocity), providing demonstrator samples, and, if all else fails, explaining that you supply cheaper products, too.

Most impressive is Stiles's (1994) receiver orientation. Stiles's readers are repeatedly counseled to learn from customers what they want, how they view the initial sales proposal, what objections they have or might have, and what it will take to persuade them to close the deal. Learning from the customer requires asking questions and may require a good deal of listening to objections. But these objections often contain useful information, says Stiles. Thus, rather than being put off by them, the sales representative might reframe objections as serving an intelligence function and possibly as a plea for help in solving a problem. Says Stiles, "Welcome objections." Don't argue with customers or attempt to wear down their resistance. "Assume that the customer has a desire for what you have to sell . . . and that you are looked upon as someone who is there to help that customer get what is wanted" (p. 56).

Stiles (1994) also recommends anticipating objections and addressing the most obvious of them in advance of their being asked. These include such predictable arenas for objections as price, quality, and competitiveness. But Stiles also suggests possible responses to the many objections a customer can raise, for example: "Your line is too extensive. I can't handle it." "I'm too busy." "I want an exclusive on your line in this territory." "I don't like to take risks." "Your company is too new." "I have to talk to my boss." The potential objections to a sales proposal are nearly limitless, as they are to proposed ways of resolving interpersonal conflicts. But if there is a lesson here for those of us not engaged in business sales, it is that in our mixed-motive relationships with those close to us, we ought to be equally well prepared to anticipate and respond to their concerns.

Public Debates

A debate, says Robert Branham (1991), is a process of advancing, supporting, disputing, and defending opinions, ideally conducted by different parties who are committed to their respective positions. Debates are not always formal, and neither must they be adjudicated, as in the courtroom or in an intercollegiate debate competition. "We engage in debate when we argue with friends about the meaning or merit of a movie we have seen, or with an employer about some matter of company policy" (p. 1).

Much has been written about the value of debate in a democratic society. Said playwright George Bernard Shaw, "The way to get at the merits of a case is not to listen to the fool who imagines himself impartial, but to get it argued with reckless bias for and against" (quoted in Jamieson & Birdsell, 1988, p. 13). Said economist John Stuart Mill (1859/1949),

Complete liberty of contradicting and disproving our opinion, is the very condition which justifies us in assuming its truth for purposes of action; and on no other terms can a being with human faculties have any rational assurance of being right. (p. 19)

Said columnist Walter Lippmann (1982),

In the absence of debate, unrestricted utterance leads to the degradation of opinion. By a kind of Gresham's law the more rational is overcome by the less rational, and the opinions that prevail will be those that are held most ardently by those with the most passionate will. (p. 196)

Branham (1991) and Jamieson (1992) speak eloquently of the need not just for *clash* but also for *extension*. A clash occurs when arguments are properly disputed. Suppose that Senator Davis, a proponent of capital punishment, argues that it is a deterrent to crime, is morally justified, and is less costly than life imprisonment. Davis produces evidence in support of these arguments. Senator Mervin clashes with Senator Davis by challenging Davis's evidence as well as the premises on which Davis built her case. Mervin adds evidence and arguments of his own to further refute Davis's claims:

Is Senator Davis aware that murder rates are higher in states with capital punishment than in states where capital punishment is forbidden? How can Davis as a Christian support "an eye for an eye" as a moral basis for capital punishment when Jesus demanded that we love all humankind, including its greatest sinners?

Senator Mervin adds that the costs of keeping a prisoner on death row through years of repeated court challenges greatly exceeds the costs of life imprisonment.

Now it is Davis's turn to rebut each of Mervin's refutations. This is what Branham and Jamieson mean by *extension*. For example, Davis argues that the states permitting capital punishment are states with many violent criminals. As a counter to Mervin's refutation of the deterrence argument, Davis now asserts that the murder rates in these states would have been even higher without capital punishment.

Just as Davis has introduced arguments for capital punishment, so Mervin will have introduced arguments against it—for example, that many innocent victims of capital punishment are, in effect, murdered by the state, their innocence established too late for it do them any good. In a good debate, Davis will attempt to counter Mervin's "many innocent victims" argument (clash), and Mervin will respond to Davis's rebuttal (extension).[1]

A *public debate* is one held before an audience, whether of one person or, as in the case of presidential debates, of millions. The great advantage of public debate is the opportunity it affords to educate its audiences. The introduction of arguments by each side, together with their respective efforts at clash (initial refutations) and extension (rebuttals of refutations), enables audiences to get a reasonably complete picture of the controversy. Far more than the television ads and stump speeches and visual displays in electoral campaigns, televised political debates provide opportunities to test candidates' competing ideas, to learn valuable information pertinent to the issues, and to compare the habits of mind of the rival candidates, including their competence and trustworthiness (Jamieson & Birdsell, 1988).

Are public debates merely clashes of opinion, or are they also conflict situations—clashes over at least partially incompatible interests? The answer to this question begins with the observation that public debates are *displays,* not just disputes. As such, they place reputations on the line, inviting assessments of persons and not just of the positions they are defending.

In their book on presidential debates, Jamieson and Birdsell (1988) maintain that these exchanges should not be viewed by the media or the public as win-lose contests.

> The point of debate is not to win but to let the truth emerge and prevail. By defining them as games and assessing their outcomes as a win for one side or the other, we make of debates something they were not originally intended to be. By focusing on gaffes, appearance, and strategy but not the logic of the argument or the cogency of the evidence, we reduce debates to contests. By dismissing good argument as a mere rehash of old stump speeches, we deny that the end of debate is advancing a sense of which case is stronger and educating the audience in the process of making that determination. (p. 13)

Jamieson and Birdsell allow wish to become reality in suggesting that the point of campaign debates is not to win. Campaign debates *are* competitions over scarce commodities—the votes of the electorate. As the authors freely acknowledge, these debates can have decisive effects on voting decisions.

Much the same thing can be said about public policy debates. On November 9, 1993, Vice President Al Gore debated Ross Perot on the subject of the North American Free Trade Agreement (NAFTA). They met on CNN's *Larry King Live* before the largest television audience in the United States ever to watch a cable offering (*New York Times,* November 11, 1993, p. A22). In just 8 days, the Senate and House of Representatives were going to vote.

There seems little question that Al Gore trounced Ross Perot in their debate on NAFTA (Picture 13.1). The *Wall Street Journal* (November 11, 1993, p. A14) reported that respondents to a *USA Today*-CNN-Gallup poll made Gore a 59-32 winner. Of greater significance, support for NAFTA grew 34% to 57%, whereas opposition to NAFTA barely budged. The following week, NAFTA passed with the

Picture 13.1. Still From Gore-Perot Debate on NAFTA, November 9, 1993
SOURCE: Courtesy of Cable News Network.

support of previously wavering Congress members, some of whom credited the debate with having made a vote for NAFTA politically popular (Simons, 1996).

To be sure, public debates of all types offer many benefits to their audiences, especially when they are structured for genuine clash and extension, as Branham (1991) and Jamieson (1992) recommend. Indeed, both sides do so well at defending their respective positions, at times, that everybody wins, not least the audience. But debate is inherently adversarial, and public debate is inherently a spectacle. Under the circumstances, political candidates can be expected to seize opportunities for sloganizing, glib put-downs of opponents, and other such crowd-pleasing devices no matter what the structure. The best defense against demagogic tactics in political debates is not injunctions to view winning as irrelevant but rather opposing candidates able to rebuke them (while holding themselves to a higher standard), a public able to discount them, and a news media willing and able to assist the public in seeing through these devices.

What, then, of public debate as a vehicle for interpersonal conflict resolution? Would those who live together, work together, or otherwise coordinate their lives together be well-advised to air their differences in something akin to a public debate?

Regrettably, debates of this type are sometimes necessary. They happen, for example, in divorce courts, child custody hearings, and labor-management arbitrations. They happen, in other words, when more informal, less contentious modes of exchange fail to bring resolution. But debate is often ineffective in resolving interpersonal conflicts. The major disadvantage—especially when debates go public—is that positions tend to become entrenched. The price of clarity and crisp logic is a hardening of the emotional arteries. Whoever wins the bitter custody fight or labor-management arbitration tends to lose something in the process: the chance for reconciliation. It is better, if at all possible, to talk through differences by way of dialogue or discussion.

The Persuasion Dialogue

In Plato's *Phaedrus* (n.d./1956), his mentor, Socrates, invited fellow Athenians to consider what an ideal rhetoric might be like, as opposed to the manipulative, exploitative discourse that too often substituted for thoughtful discussion in Greek society. Some have viewed Plato's *Dialogues* themselves as models of rhetoric, but as Craig R. Smith (1998) has observed, these conversations were stacked by Plato in favor of his mentor and were hardly free of rhetorical sleight of hand.

In *Phaedrus,* Socrates is sitting by a stream when he is approached by Phaedrus, an impressionable young man who has just been duped by Lysias, a well-known speechwriter whom Socrates believes tends to speak from ignorance. Having warned of the ruses of rhetoric, Socrates then proceeds to address young Phaedrus on the subject of love. Again Phaedrus is won over, but Socrates then confesses that his own speech was insincere. Socrates' point was that persuasive effectiveness, even in a noble cause, ought not to be the standard for judging rhetoric.

What, then, are the characteristics of the ideal rhetoric? Through the centuries, that question has beguiled philosophers. Many have agreed that the ideal rhetoric is dialogic, not monologic, placing the conversants on an equal footing. But what is the nature of that rhetorical conversation? Pulling together the writings of recent philosophers, I present my own version of what Walton (1989) calls the *persuasion dialogue.*

Two (or more) persons get together to puzzle out an issue. They may have strong opinions on the matter, which they are free to express. Indeed, the fact of difference is expected and welcomed. Falsely minimizing differences or pretending to even-handed objectivity is disingenuous and will not do.

The conversants see matters differently, but their object really isn't to win anything at the expense of the other. This is key. Perhaps you have been in conversations in which the demands of the subject matter literally took over. One sign of that is a willingness to consider matters afresh, without clinging to previously entrenched positions. "Well, Jim, I know I usually complain when America plays the role of global police officer, but the ethnic cleansing of Albanians in Kosovo really got to me. I don't think our country could have stood by any longer and let that continue." "Funny that you say that, Wilma, because I usually favor military intervention where American interests are at stake, but as former Secretary of State Baker put it, I don't think we had a dog in that fight."

Persuasion dialogues may have many goals, not least of which are the pleasures of mutual exploration of a topic and possible edification. Consensus is not a required outcome of such dialogues. Occasionally, they bring closure to an issue, but more often, they advance its consideration by raising as many questions as they answer. What are America's interests? Who defines them, and how? What humanitarian principles justify military intervention in some cases but not in others? Often, as in this conversation, the talk spins out to related issues, without loss, it is hoped, of the initial thread.

In persuasion dialogues, positions are presented skillfully but not manipulatively. As one person speaks, the others listen carefully, trying at once to see things from the speaker's perspective while at the same time resisting the temptation to take everything that's been said at face value. Managing to combine empathic listening with critical listening isn't easy; it's part of the art of the persuasion dialogue. Competent conversationalists learn to retrieve in memory what's been said at a substantive level while also attending to what's been metacommunicated, perhaps unintentionally. Wilma might restate Jim's argument, then ask whether she's understood him. But she might follow with an objection to his likening of the conflict between the Serbs and Albanians to a dog fight. "Isn't that choice of metaphor itself a problem, Jim? Notice how it positions you as a gambler at the track. I find it emotionally distancing."

Still, the persuasion dialogue remains a cooperative exchange. Perhaps the conversational partners ask questions of clarification, perhaps they raise objections, but no one seeks to dominate or to put the others down. Indeed, the opposite may happen. I put forward my case, you try to improve it, perhaps even to perfect it; I do the same for you if I can. "You know, Wilma, I can really see your point. Maybe we can't be global police officers, but it sure is in America's interests to promote international human rights. So, by that standard, maybe we do have military obligations in Kosovo."

Moving to Dialogue in Interpersonal Conflicts

The example just given is one of a difference of opinion, not a conflict of interests. This should not be surprising. Indeed, it is hard to imagine two or more persons in serious conflict approaching the rigorous demands of the persuasion dialogue without the help of someone—a professional mediator or facilitator, perhaps, or just a mutual friend.

The cases to be presented next illustrate the potential for assisted dialogue to help conflicting parties advance consideration of the issues dividing them. Neither models completely the ideal of the persuasion dialogue. The first exhibits the types of resistance common to those charged with ethical wrongdoing in a conflict situation (Simons, 1995). Still, some defenses are relinquished in the company of friends, and the four participants seem genuinely at times to give in to the demands of the subject matter. The second case is a highly structured dialogue, made necessary, perhaps, by the polarized topic of abortion (Chasin et al., 1996; Roth & Becker, 1992). Here the give-and-take of the persuasion dialogue is replaced initially by strategic questioning by the facilitators, designed to get pro-choice and pro-life activists to dig deeply into their psyches for possible sources of intrapersonal ambivalence and interpersonal common ground.

Case 1: A Taped Conversation About a Taped Conversation[2]

Frank, a college professor, and Laura, a former student, had been living together off and on for 6 months and were considering getting married. Then Frank secretly audiotaped a conversation between the two of them. Laura, on learning about it, was furious, but Frank thought she was overreacting. Their quarrel about the surreptitious taping was put before Dave and Jane, Frank's long-term friends who had come to know and like Laura through Frank. At Dave's suggestion, the conversation about the conversation was audiotaped, this time with everyone's permission. The conversation was initially between Frank and Dave, but when Laura and Jean overheard Frank's defense of himself, they came in from an adjoining room.

Excerpt A

Laura: Frank, what's your conclusion? Do you think it was unethical for you to do that?

Frank: I was explaining . . . that . . . the only parties whom I imagined would ever hear this were the parties who made the tape, that it was merely a record and not a means of exposure. It was not at all meant for public consumption.

Laura: There are . . . there are other issues to be considered.

Frank: What's the big deal?

Laura: Namely that, namely that I was deceived . . . and it was a conversation that required trust, and . . . [voice trails off].

Frank: But how were you deceived?

Laura: Because I was being vulnerable and really sort of . . .

Frank: So you would be the only one to hear it besides me.

Laura: Wait a minute. Wait! . . . And really reaching in and pulling out things which were very difficult for me to say because I thought and was under the impression that we were resolving something between us, things that potentially were . . .

Frank: We were, for all times.

Laura: Under the circumstances you're less willing to be vulnerable and to stumble and to face up to things difficult.

Frank: Well, you're assuming that I'm somehow . . .

Laura: Your intentions were totally different than mine.

Frank: . . . totally natural when I'm speaking without a tape recorder, or anyone is totally natural.

Laura: Except that it imposes another level of being unnatural when the tape is on.

Frank: If it's just the character of what we're talking about, that makes us both unnatural; then we're equal.

Dave: You're absolutely right.

Laura: But then the tape is on and then it's more unequal.

Jean: Right! It's knowing something that the other person doesn't know. It gives you a sense of power, or . . .

Dave: Suppose you wanted to prove to Laura that she was stupid or . . .

Jean: It doesn't matter if you're going to use it or not, you know, or if no one else hears it.

[Frank is defensive in this portion of the conversation, but now he has friends Dave and Jean to contend with as well as Laura. Note how the process of dialogue helps not just Frank but also Laura to discover why she has been so upset by his taping.] (p. 238)

Excerpt B

Laura: Frank, are you maintaining that it wasn't unethical?

Frank: I'm maintaining that it was . . .

Jean: Borderline?

Frank: I'll tell you something. If it were done to me in similar circumstances, I would not be pissed.

Dave: I agree with that. You wouldn't be.

Frank: If you did it to me; if Dave did it to me; if Jean did it to me . . . If, on the other hand, someone I didn't know well did it to me, I would be very pissed and that's what's so disturbing about all of this—that you're sort of applying standards as if I'm a stranger.

Laura: No.

Dave: Laura wouldn't do it to you, though.

Laura: I wouldn't do it to you.

Frank: But if you did it to me, I wouldn't mind.

Laura: But I wouldn't do it.

Dave: See, there are two parts to the "Do unto others as others would have done unto you." What does that mean? Well, it could mean, "Do to others what you'd find acceptable if done to you." Another one is "Do unto others what the other would do." And they really are two different things.

Frank: Or the third, "Do unto others as you would like them to do unto you." Which is really what it means.

[Excerpt B finds Frank still defending himself, this time on grounds that had Laura taped him without his knowledge, he would not be offended. This raises for all four participants the meaning and applicability of the Golden Rule: "Do unto others as you would have them do unto you." The group senses here that the principle is relevant to

Frank's surreptitious taping of Laura, but does it exonerate him or demonstrate his wrongdoing? The group fumbles toward some sort of understanding, but they do so together. This segment of the conversation helps them move toward closure.] (p. 241)

Excerpt C [After a 30-second interlude]

Frank: The other thing is, though, we each have a different borderline. We draw the lines at different points, at different angles. . . .

Laura: That's very true, Frank.

Frank: And where I draw the line is not where you do it, and where you do it is not where I do it, so we're probably not going to agree on all of this.

Laura: But you got to the root of the problem, the problem of the tapes. You did know and that's why you didn't tell me. . . . that I would not have liked that, and you didn't respect the fact that I didn't.

Dave: That's probably true.

Frank: I don't think that's true.

Laura: I think it's true.

Frank: Because I don't mind, I didn't have the imagination to think you would.

Laura: Then why didn't you tell me?

Dave: Because telling you would have been no good. It would have denied the opportunity to get a spontaneous, candid statement on tape.

Frank: Right.

Jean: I think Dave's right. I think there are two different questions.

Laura: What are the questions?

Jean: Well, whether or not it's ethical is different than whether or not, as he said, that you would be upset by it. They're two different things.

Laura: Yeah, I agree with you that he didn't think it through.

Dave: You were stupid, you weren't unethical.

Laura: No, inconsiderate, inconsiderate.

Frank: [Laughs] I did not think it through, that's for sure.

[Excerpt C ends inconclusively. Was Frank stupid, insensitive, or downright
unethical? Yet the conversation has clearly advanced consideration of
the question. Laura has been wronged; even Frank now understands
that. Meanwhile, Laura and Frank have enjoyed the support of Frank's
longtime friends. All have learned something through the process of
exploration.] (p. 243)

Case 2: A Structured Conversation About Abortion

Christine and Pat grew up together and had always been friends, but now they
were activists on opposite sides of the abortion issue. The last time they saw each
other was outside an abortion clinic. Christine was holding up a sign saying "Abortion is murder." Pat waved a sign in Chris's face that said "Choice: A Woman's
Right." Neither of them spoke. (An example of a demonstration is shown in Picture
13.2.)

It is hard to imagine the Christines and Pats of the world finding common
ground on the abortion issue. Surely, it is among the most divisive issues facing
Americans. Yet recently, a pro-life activist and a pro-choice leader tried to bring their
two groups together on the basis of common interests. Through a process of dialogue, they discovered that (a) neither favored abortion as a means of birth control,
(b) both preferred adoption to abortion in cases in which that option was truly available, and (c) each saw abortion as preferable to having the child in cases of rape and
incest. This is but one of many success stories in efforts to bridge differences between
opposing interests on matters of public controversy. Columnist Ellen Goodman cites
the Public Conversation Project as on the leading edge of these efforts (cited in
Chasin et al., 1996; Web site is www.PublicConversations.org).

What type of communication is needed to get pro-choice and pro-life activists
to understand and respect each other, let alone to find common ground? On divisive
public issues such as abortion, attempts at direct persuasive communication between
antagonists are often destructive, rather than productive (Deutsch, 1969; Roth &
Becker, 1992); they virtually preclude any possibility for agreement by reinforcing
us-them attitudes.

Recognizing this, a group of therapists from the Public Conversations Project
decided to try a different tack (Chasin et al., 1996; Roth & Becker, 1992). Rather
than encouraging a free flow of communication between pro-choice and pro-life advocates, they set out to provide a controlled but supportive context for talk. On any
given evening, four to six recruits from each side would be seated in an alternated
pattern around a dinner table. A light buffet dinner was made available, during

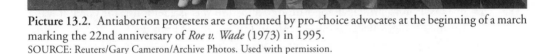

Picture 13.2. Antiabortion protesters are confronted by pro-choice advocates at the beginning of a march marking the 22nd anniversary of *Roe v. Wade* (1973) in 1995.
SOURCE: Reuters/Gary Cameron/Archive Photos. Used with permission.

which time no one was to reveal his or her stance on abortion. Instead, they were encouraged to get acquainted informally while avoiding the issue of abortion.

After dinner, the facilitators proposed several rules for the conduct of talk about abortion. The conversants' talk would be treated confidentially. There would be no interrupting. The conversants would use respectful language (for example, using *pro-choice* and *pro-life,* rather than "anti" terms to refer to the positions of others). They would each be permitted to decline to answer any questions asked of them.

The facilitators assumed a principle that deserves considerable emphasis: *If given a chance to be explored open-mindedly, people's expressed attitudes on any given controversial issue tend to soften and to exhibit signs of greater complexity, even ambivalence.* This is a principle that all persuaders need to keep in mind. The converse of this principle is that if egos are attacked, attitudes harden; psychologists call this the principle of *reactivity* (Brehm, 1966; Cialdini, 1993). In these sessions, conversants were encouraged to depoliticize the abortion issue and to address it instead in personal terms. They were encouraged, in effect, to function expressively, rather than persuasively. Initially, the facilitators asked all the participants the same three questions. Then the participants were invited to question each other.

The first of the facilitators' questions, asking the participants to say something about their own life experiences in relation to the issue of abortion, elicited revelations of far greater ambivalence on the topic of abortion than these activists had previously expressed publicly (or perhaps even to themselves). For example, Andrea talked of working at a church-related organization for children with a pregnant teenager and her boyfriend, both from abusive backgrounds. As she watched them struggle with the issue of abortion, her own attitudes were formed. Said Andrea,

> I felt that in all fairness, I certainly had to lay out all of the alternatives that were available to them. And she said, "You know, if I have this baby, I will never have the strength to give it up for adoption, and I will sentence it to the same hell that I have lived through." . . . I feel very pro-life, but I am very strongly pro-choice, because I felt like . . . I could never have made that decision for that child and she did choose to abort that baby. (Roth & Becker, 1992, p. 8)[3]

The second question asked of everyone was "What is at the heart of the matter for you, as an individual?" One effect of asking this question was that each "camp" discovered almost as many differences in their own group as they did between groups. Linda's principal opposition to abortion was as a feminist; for Gina, it was a spiritual thing, a belief about what God intended for her to do.

Having asked the first two questions, neither of which was terribly threatening, the facilitators set the stage for their third and final question, one that invited participants to comment on dilemmas, struggles, conflicts, pockets of uncertainty, times when one value bumps up against some other value, or other murky areas within their prevailing views. Their answers suggested that even on the polarizing issue of abortion, which often generates expressions of certainty, people also experience uncertainty.

> Linda (pro-life): One time I was discussing this issue with a friend and said I was pro-life, and he said, "Obviously you never grew up an unwanted child." And he was right, they wanted me. I think of the children that suffer and think to myself, would it be better if they had been aborted? But then I think, they have life. But it's really hard to watch children in pain and sometimes it's hard to be pro-life, but at the same time, I'm so pro-life. So that's something I really struggle with.

Arlene (pro-choice): The very idea of someone having an abortion on the basis of the gender of the fetus just really sends me into orbit.

Carolyn (pro-life): I think I could live with a political settlement which said there were some exceptions for criminal rape, incest, things like that. I wouldn't be happy, I wouldn't think it was still right to kill the unborn who after all was not at fault, didn't kill the rapist. But, Tay-Sachs again . . . if a baby's going to die a horrible death by age three, you know. These are awful hard cases. (Roth & Becker, 1992, p. 11)

As Roth and Becker (1992) observe, the third question not only reveals differences within groups but also calls forth similarities in beliefs and attitudes of those on opposing sides. Furthermore, it honors each other's experience and the emotional and intellectual meanings attached to those experiences. By now, the participants "have usually dropped most or all of the demonizing stereotypes they may have brought to the meeting" (p. 12), and they are ready to question and answer each other nondefensively and nonjudgmentally.

Summary

This chapter began with Kenneth Burke's (1969) reminder that rhetoric, the art of persuasion, is not always friendly, not always concerned with matters of a purely academic nature, and frequently occasioned by social conflicts. The chapter explored a variety of types of persuasive interaction, looking especially at how talk between antagonists could be made more productive. Although the focus of the chapter was on the sorts of everyday interpersonal conflicts that occur at work or in the home, it also examined other mixed-motive conflicts such as those involved in business negotiations and campaign debates. Also introduced was the persuasion dialogue, an ideal of conversational interaction more often achievable in academic controversies than in social conflicts but still worth aiming toward in conflict situations.

A social conflict was defined as a clash over at least partially incompatible interests. Conflicts are not simply misunderstandings, semantic confusions, or communication breakdowns; nor are they only disagreements, differences of opinion, or controversies—they are always something more than that. Divergent interests are at stake, interests important to one or both parties.

At the same time that antagonists are prompted to oppose each other, however, they also find it necessary to cooperate with each other, if only for purposes of coordinating their behavior. Hence, the use of coactive persuasion in these mixed-motive conflicts, combined with the marshaling and occasional deployment of power resources.

Questions and Projects for Further Study

1. Do a case study of persuasion in a social conflict of your own choosing. Drawing on concepts introduced in this chapter, characterize the conflict by type, nature of participants, patterns of escalation, and possibilities for productive dialogue. How was persuasion different in this conflict than it would have been had the conflicting parties been engaged in a mere difference of opinion? Had you been one (or both) of the interactants, what would you have done differently?

2. Practice applying the techniques suggested here for turning potentially destructive conflicts into more productive ones. Do the same for conflicts that have already moved through vicious cycles of unwanted escalation. Recalling Shar's questions, decide why to fight, whether to fight, when to fight, and how to fight. Keep a diary of your efforts at dealing with interpersonal conflicts in productive ways. Consider discussing one or more of these experiences with others in your class.

3. Divide into pairs for a mock sales negotiation. Better yet, try applying the techniques you have learned here and in Part 2 to a real sales negotiation.

4. With classmates or friends, try approximating the ideal of the persuasion dialogue. Begin with a difference of opinion over values or policy, then move, if the opportunity presents itself, to the more difficult terrain of interpersonal conflict. Compare your efforts at dialogue with those of Frank, Laura, Dave, and Jean.

5. On a polarizing issue such as abortion, try playing the role of the facilitator, in a manner similar to that suggested by Roth and Becker (1992).

6. The following case study, presented by novelist Lois Gould (1973), first appeared in *Ms. Magazine*. On the surface, it concerns a problem of bed making. Ms. Gould's husband gets up after she does and hastily tosses the covers back on the bed—a practice she finds extremely annoying.

   The immediate question for Ms. Gould is how to get her husband to make the bed unlumpily. She realizes, however, that lumpily made beds are often symptomatic of the larger question of who is to have what power in the relationship. Her "rhetorical analysis" of her husband's behavior is summarized here in outline form as follows:

   I. My husband's habitual act is symbolic in nature.
      A. He is competent to make the bed unlumpily.
         1. He made his own bed in the army.
         2. He made his own bed in camp.
         3. He taught his children to make their beds neatly.
         4. Skills like these do not rust from disuse.

B. He has as much time to make unlumpy beds as I do.

C. He, as much as I, cares that the house is kept neat.

D. Only with great reluctance did he begin making the bed at all.

II. The act symbolizes an interest in perpetuating power and privilege.

   A. Before acceding with great fanfare to my request that he make the bed at all, he offered the following arguments:

      1. Who makes the bed is unimportant.

      2. Making the bed would make me late for work.

      3. You do it faster and more efficiently.

      4. Why don't you hire a maid?

   B. Once he gave in, he played the injured martyr.

   C. If confronted over the bed's lumpiness:

      1. He would ask for a precise definition of a decent bed.

      2. He would allude to my being hung up on household sociology.

      3. He would suggest that I had far better things to do than carp at him over the bed, now that I didn't have to make it.

   D. These arguments give contextual meaning to the lumpy bed. Viewed in context, the lumpy bed is a way of saying:

      1. I'm a very important person.

      2. You're not a very important person.

      3. I, therefore, have a right to dominate in this relationship.

What strategies of influence are most appropriate in situations such as this? Discuss this case with others and ask yourself what Gould should have done. Suppose, as she reports, she had already tried a variety of strategies, including reviewing with her husband how beds ought to be made, demonstrating with ironclad logic why her husband ought to make the bed properly, and outright pleading. What should she do next?

No doubt you have been in situations similar to this one. Write a brief description of the conflict and indicate how, in retrospect, you think you should have handled it.

Notes

1. It is useful to chart the clash of opinions in protracted value conflicts, such as those between progay and antigay forces. Careful analysis will reveal where the adversar-

ies talk past each other, where each is intractable, and where, on the other hand, there is potential for compromise (Smith & Windes, 2000).

2. This section is excerpted from Simons, 1995. Simons, H. W. (1995). Arguing about the ethics of past actions: An analysis of a taped conversation about a taped conversation. *Argumentation, 9,* 225-250. Copyright © 1995. Used with kind permission from Kluwer Academic Publishers.

3. Excerpts and material from Public Conversations Project from S. Roth and C. Becker (1992, August 15), *From Debate to Dialogue: The Public Conversations Project.* Paper presented at the annual meeting of the American Psychological Association, Peace Division, Washington, DC. Used by permission.

References

Branham, R. J. (1991). *Debate and critical analysis.* Hillsdale, NJ: Lawrence Erlbaum.

Brehm, J. W. (1966). *A theory of psychological reactance.* New York: Academic Press.

Burke, K. (1969). *A rhetoric of motives.* Berkeley: University of California Press. (Original work published 1950)

Chasin, R., Herzig, M., Roth, S., Chasin, L., Becker, C., & Stains, C. R. (1996). From diatribe to dialogue. *Mediation Quarterly, 13,* 323-344.

Cialdini, R. B. (1993). *Influence: Science and practice.* New York: Simon & Schuster.

Deutsch, M. (1969). Conflicts: Productive and destructive. *Journal of Social Issues, 25,* 7-41.

Duhl, G. A. (1996, December 12). A graduate assistant union at Yale? [Commentary]. *Connecticut Law Tribune,* p. 4.

Elgin, S. H. (1995). *BusinessSpeak.* New York: McGraw-Hill.

Fisher, R., & Ury, W. (1991). *Getting to yes: Negotiating agreement without giving in* (2nd ed.). Boston: Houghton Mifflin.

Frost, J. H., & Wilmot, W. H. (1978). *Interpersonal conflict.* Dubuque, IA: William C. Brown.

Gould, L. (1973). If your husband makes the bed, must you lie in it? *Ms., 1,* 92-95.

Jamieson, K. H. (1992). *Dirty politics.* New York: Oxford University Press.

Jamieson, K. H., & Birdsell, D. S. (1988). *Presidential debates.* New York: Oxford University Press.

Lippmann, W. (1982). *The essential Lippmann: A political philosophy for liberal democracy* (P. Rossiter & J. Lare, Eds.). Cambridge, MA: Harvard University Press.

Mill, J. S. (1947). *On liberty.* Arlington Heights, IL: AHM. (Original work published 1859)

Plato. (1956). *Phaedrus* (W. C. Helmbold & W. G. Rabinowitz, Trans.). New York: Liberal Arts Press. (Original work n.d.)

Roe v. Wade, 410 U.S. 113 (1973).

Roth, S., & Becker, C. (1992, August 15). *From debate to dialogue: The Public Conversations Project.* Paper presented at the annual meeting of the American Psychological Association, Peace Division, Washington, DC.

Simons, H. W. (1995). Arguing about the ethics of past actions: An analysis of a taped conversation about a taped conversation. *Argumentation, 9,* 225-250.

Simons, H. W. (1996). Judging a policy proposal by the company it keeps: The Gore-Perot NAFTA debate. *Quarterly Journal of Speech, 82,* 274-287.

Smith, C. R. (1998). *Rhetoric and human consciousness.* Prospect Heights, IL: Waveland.

Smith, R. R., & Windes, R. R. (2000). *Progay/antigay: The rhetorical war over sexuality.* Thousand Oaks, CA: Sage.

Stiles, W. H. (1994). *Tactics of persuasion.* Dubuque, IA: Kendall-Hunt.

Walton, D. (1989). *Informal logic: A handbook for critical argumentation.* New York: Cambridge University Press.

Leading Social Movements

It is April 23, 1989—early on in a sustained student protest that will eventuate in a bloody massacre on June 3 and 4 of that year. The place is Beijing's Tiananmen Square, symbolic for its history of ritual celebrations of Chinese culture and political governance; symbolic, too, because from the government buildings adjoining Tiananmen issue forth the decrees that radiate from the capital to all of China.

Beijing is to China what Washington, D.C., is to the United States, and the Chinese university students have done what even American students would be forbidden to do. In direct violation of orders from the Chinese police, they have occupied the square on a continuous basis—equivalent to American students taking over the Mall surrounding the Washington monument and adjoining the Capitol building.

Quite apart, then, from what the speakers will be saying to the assembled multitudes at Tiananmen, the act of takeover sends a powerful message. Although nonviolent, it is an act of massive defiance—hence, far more militant, say, than a visit to one's congressional representative armed with signatures on a petition.

One of the speakers on April 23 is a professor from Beijing University named Chen Mingyuan.[1] "*We* are the masters of our country," he says. The *we* is important because it signals a joining of professors and students. This alone is noteworthy in a country in which professors traditionally stood well above their students in the status hierarchy and generally kept their distance from them.

"We are the *masters* of our country," says Chen. Is the professor suggesting something on the order of a takeover of the country by the educated elite? Or perhaps the *we* refers more generally and more ambiguously to "the people." In either case, the *we* is incendiary in a country not known for heeding the wishes of the intelligentsia or for Western democratic ideals.

"We are the masters of *our* country," says Chen. Is this a way of saying that Tiananmen is a grassroots protest, not something imported from foreigners; furthermore, that the protesters are expressing identification with the country, even as they are disidentifying with the government's policies? On this occasion, every word takes on potential significance. Never mind that thousands, perhaps tens of thousands of those assembled at Tiananmen, are probably out of earshot of the speech. Word of the speech is distilled through the crowd.

Professor Chen Mingyuan mentions the death of Hu Yaobang, a reformer who had been removed 2 years earlier as party secretary. Every major social movement has its list of heroes and legends, enemies and unmitigated evils. In the oblique language of Chinese politics, Hu had signaled his commitment to Chinese democratization and his opposition to government-tolerated corruption. Thus, the very mention of Hu Yaobang's death is a unifying expression of ideology.

Professor Chen then compliments the crowd on an earlier demonstration. "The demonstration was spontaneous, the petition peaceful, and the mourning of Comrade Yaobang very orderly. I think the students from Beijing University should feel very proud of themselves."

The takeover of Tiananmen square was a decidedly militant act. Yet it is important that protest be construed as peaceful and orderly, if at all possible. Those who witness it, or hear about it, must be convinced that the protesters are not wildly deviant or unjustifiably rebellious. They must be seen, rather, as a habitually law-abiding aggrieved group of persons who have been unable to achieve their ends by lesser means. Thus Professor Chen's compliment to the students takes on significance, and they erupt in a chant: "Long live the students! Long live democracy! Long live freedom!" The chanting at Tiananmen is reminiscent of American protests of the 1960s for civil rights ("Freedom now! Freedom now!") and against the war in Vietnam ("Hey, hey, LBJ, how many kids have you killed today?"). There is a ritual quality to chantings of this sort, as if the crowd were speaking as one, with what Gustave Le Bon (1896) long ago called the "group mind."

Chen Mingyuan then speaks of freedom:

> When I pronounced the word "freedom," some people became nervous. Some would say, "Freedom is a bad word." But I feel that freedom is the most beautiful word in the world. Why should only other people be allowed to use it? Why is it that this beautiful word is not in the vocabulary of our great motherland and our great people?
>
> Yes, we are poor. We are backward. We are uneducated. We are living a bitter life. But we do have this ideal of freedom and democracy.

To those accustomed to Western conceptions of freedom, Professor Chen's pronouncement on the beauty of the word *freedom* may sound a bit trite. But in a country barely cutting its teeth on democratization, freedom, and especially press freedom, it must have appeared to those assembled as truly revolutionary.

Yet it would be a mistake to assume that the students wanted exactly what we in the West have and enjoy. This is an assumption that the Western news media may have helped popularize, in part because the students and professors they talked with tended to be those whose English was especially good, and who, in general, were more Western-minded. It may come as a surprise that between chantings for freedom and democracy, the demonstrators would stand and sing the anthem of the Communist government, the "Internationale."

Indeed, much of the remainder of the speech is bland by American standards. It calls for a reduction in inflation, then at 18%. It demands that education be made a top priority on the list of government expenditures. It insists, in strident terms, that government corruption and government-tolerated corruption be ended and severely punished.

Then Professor Chen closes:

> Maybe someone will say, "You students should return [to your universities] and study quietly. You professors should simply teach your courses." But all these problems constantly wear us down. We can't accept this. We shall never accept it!

Note once again, the we-they opposition, characteristic of social movement rhetorics. Note as well the histrionic prediction: "We shall *never* accept it." This, too, is characteristic of what movement agitators the world over pledge to their followers.

Not only do these leaders prophesy continued unity and resistance, whatever the sacrifices, but also they insist that collective action is urgently needed, that victory is likely (or at least possible) if they band together, and that their personal interests are linked with the group's interests.

The rhetoric of protest issues not just from the microphone or the bullhorn but from the crowd itself—a rhetoric of symbolic acts, not just of words. Those at Tiananmen who repeatedly weathered the rain in flimsy sleeping bags were fortified by each other and by the support of friends, relatives, and strangers who braved the police to provide the students with food and drink and emotional support. Word spread of old ladies who stood in the way of trucks full of soldiers entering the city and lectured them to turn around and go back where they came from. Some city officials, not only in Beijing but in other cities where demonstrations erupted, apparently turned a blind eye to the events around them, or at least held back from the use of physical force. This, too, moved the protesters at Tiananmen, as it did Chinese and Western journalists. Having been moved, Chinese journalists provided inspiration in their own right. Timorous at first, they eventually defied censorship orders and provided a fuller accounting of what they had seen and heard. Western journalists, for their part, not only covered the events at Tiananmen and surroundings but also fed back to the protesters news of the sympathetic responses they were getting round the world.

What Are Social Movements?

The demonstrators at Tiananmen Square were part of a *social movement,* that is, it was *uninstitutionalized* or outside the mainstream. In extreme cases, as at Tiananmen, the ideas guiding members of social movements, their methods of action, and their core organizations (social movement organizations; SMOs) are all considered suspect or downright illegitimate in the larger society of which they are a part. Moreover, social movements are *cause-oriented* collectivities; they exist primarily to promote an ideology (e.g., democratization) and/or a program of action (e.g., petitioning the government to lower the rate of inflation). This is their *cause,* and they promote it through extended periods. Finally, unlike self-help organizations such as Alcoholics Anonymous, social movements see as their mission to exert influence outside their own SMOs. Formally, then, *a social movement is an uninstitutionalized collectivity that operates on a sustained basis to exert external influence in behalf of a cause.*[2] The civil rights movement in the United States provides another example.

In the 1960s, the SMOs supporting civil rights included the Southern Christian Leadership Conference (SCLC), headed by the Reverend Martin Luther King Jr., the Student Nonviolent Coordinating Committee (SNCC), the Congress on Racial Equality (CORE), and the National Association for the Advancement of Colored

People (NAACP). Not everyone who identified with the civil rights movement belonged to one or another of these core organizations, but without them, there could not have been a movement. The cause of the civil rights movement was, minimally, the abolition of racial discrimination in law and, beyond that, the elimination of all discriminatory practices. Some might say that the ultimate goal of the civil rights movement was equality. If so, the movement is still a long way from full accomplishment.

The civil rights movement of the 1960s was uninstitutionalized in all three respects: guiding ideas, modes of action, and core organizations. Its detractors in the South viewed the movement's opposition to segregation as nothing less than an assault on their traditional way of life. Its confrontational tactics, such as sit-ins at segregated lunch counters, were subjected to scorn and disapproval; even many in the North who approved of the movement's goals deplored these tactics as illegal or unnecessarily provocative. Its SMOs had varying degrees of legitimacy, with NAACP enjoying a measure of respectability because of its relatively conservative style and long tenure as an organization. By contrast, the SNCC members seemed to revel in their "upstart" status within the white South.[3]

A collectivity may be partially institutionalized and still be a movement. For example, the National Organization of Women enjoys a good measure of respectability in the larger society. Although it seldom if ever engages in practices considered deviant or outside the mainstream, its feminist agenda is far from being fully institutionalized. Likewise, the National Rifle Association is widely accepted in the larger society, but it also spearheads an anti-gun control effort that is highly controversial in American society and, in that sense, is part of a social movement. Examples of social movements from the 1960s are the movement for drug legalization, the animal rights movement, women's liberation, various people's right movements (e.g., Chicano rights, gay and lesbian rights, and Native American rights), Black Power, the environmental movement, the gun control movement, disarmament, antinuclear power, feminism, pro-choice, pro-life, and various *countermovements* to the right of the political spectrum, including anti-drug legalization, anti-gun control, and pronuclear power.

Types of Social Movements

The goals that movements seek to realize vary considerably, and so, too, is there great variation in their means for achieving them. *Reformist* movements generally seek passage of particular laws, better enforcement of particular laws, replacement of corrupt or incompetent officials, and so on. The gun control and civil rights movements are examples. *Revolutionary* movements go even further by seeking to replace guiding ideologies, institutions, and sometimes entire regimes, on the basis of new governing principles. They are also associated with the threat or use of force (e.g., American Revolution), but there have been largely peaceful revolutions (e.g., Poland, 1989).

Resistance movements, rather than advocating change, seek to hold it back and keep the status quo, for example, the anti-gun control movement. Given the Supreme Court's decision in *Roe v. Wade* (1973), the pro-life movement is generally reformist, whereas pro-choice is a resistance movement. But pro-choice seeks federal funding of abortions for the poor, whereas pro-life resists such funding. In this respect, pro-choice is reformist, pro-life a resistance movement. *Restorative* movements seek a return to an older and supposedly better way of life. The cause of today's Christian Identity movement echoes the rhetoric of hate toward minorities in the United States, preached in earlier days by White Citizens Councils and by the John Birch Society (Bennett, 1995). Marcus Garvey's "Back to Africa" was also a restorative movement.

Finally, *expressivist* movements try to change individuals, rather than directly trying to change institutions or laws. Religious cults such as Heaven's Gate and the Hare Krishnas are examples. Expressivists believe that just as institutions are created by people, so they can be changed only by changes in people. Common to the ideologies of movements for personal transformation are the themes of sin and personal responsibility and of possible self-improvement and enlightenment.

It is not always easy to classify movements based on this or any other typology because of internal disputes about goals and methods within the movement, as well as changes in goals and strategies. For example, a conference of 1960s-style Marxist activists hit on a decidedly expressivist note when they concluded at a recent conference that "new social movements" such as feminism and environmentalism have demonstrated that large-scale social change "is accomplished in face-to-face relations, at the level of personal identity and consciousness . . . , whether or not such change is enunciated in public policy" (Darnovsky, Epstein, & Flacks, 1995, p. xiv). Reports varied widely on what the students at Tiananmen Square wanted, although it became clear as time went on that they did *not* want the existing, hard-line regime in China. From all accounts, their demands were initially modest, but they became more radical through time.

Tactics of Social Movements

Movements select from a repertoire of possibilities available to them at any given time and place (Tilly, 1979). Some tactics, such as mass demonstrations against administrative practices, are rare in autocratic societies but common in democracies. Other tactics, such as hangings in effigy, were popular for centuries in England and the United States but have largely gone out of style. Some movements rely on verbal appeals, others on a combination of exhortations and demonstrations; still others add the threat and use of force. To advance their cause, movements have characteristically relied on *confrontational tactics,* still the method of choice for street protests. But movements seeking both ideological change and resistance to ideological change are increasingly turning to *cultural politics.*

Confrontation

Consider once again the demonstrators at Tiananmen Square, some of them on hunger strikes, none of them knowing at what point the government would strike back. When it comes to making a statement, there is nothing quite like putting one's body on the line. Schelling (1960), in this connection, makes a distinction between speech and moves:

> Talk is not a substitute for moves. Moves can in some way alter the game, by incurring manifest costs, risks, or a reduced range of subsequent choice; they have an information content, or *evidence* content, of a different character from that of speech. Talk can be cheap when moves are not. (p. 117)

The moves made by the protesters at Tiananmen were forms of confrontation. They were reminiscent of the campus sit-ins and demonstrations at colleges and universities across the United States in the late 1960s. Some of the campus confrontations were fairly mild, whereas others were quite disruptive, but all of them sought to perform attention-getting, radicalizing, and delegitimizing functions through actions that combined verbal exhortations and pressure tactics.

The confronters joined in a deliberate violation of the institution's written and unwritten code of conduct, fastening on those taboos that symbolized what the protesters took to be the institution's false ideals and inequitable practices. Representatives of these institutions were thus presented with a king-sized dilemma. Suppression of the confrontation would belie the institution's appearance of liberality and feed the flames of protest. Yet permitting violations of the code would, in effect, sanction other violations and undermine the offices of authority and discipline in the institution. And so, after promising a fair hearing and pleading in vain for a return to more moderate tactics, the institution acted to check or suppress the violations and punish the violators, frequently breaking its own rules in the process. In this way, its representatives were able, temporarily, to contain the confrontation, but in doing so, they "completed" the rhetorical act by revealing their own "ugliness" (Scott & Smith, 1969).

Cultural Politics

Brief attention was given in Chapter 3 to the role of the schools and the mass media in the shaping of ideologies. These, together with other "culture industries" such as the arts and organized religion, have always been sources of cultural influence, but groups seeking liberalization of social values (the "cultural left") and others resisting what they see as moral decay ("social conservatives") have in recent years been engaged in what some journalists ballyhooed as the "culture wars" (e.g., Gitlin, 1995; Graff, 1992). Multiculturalists, Afrocentrists, feminists, and others on the cultural left have sought to influence educational curricula. Social conservatives have formed countermovements of their own, pressing in some cases for textbook censorship and in others for cutbacks in federal funding of the humanities. Some social conservatives have sought to restore America to what they allege was its former greatness, before school prayer was outlawed, for example, and before abortion was legalized by the Supreme Court (Bennett, 1995).

These ideological battles are fought out less in the streets than in behind-the-scenes meetings of museum boards, federal funding agencies, university administrators, mental health professionals, and network news managers and, more openly, via television and in classrooms, movie theaters, churches, mental health centers, and courts. In one women's studies classroom, for example, a concerted attempt is made to "liberate" students from the intellectual and cultural domination of patriarchal (i.e., male-oriented) ideologies (Lather, 1991). Across the hall, a socially conservative professor of philosophy declaims against postmodernism, deconstruction, cultural relativism, and other intellectual challenges to Western culture's traditional faith in logic, objectivity, meaning, and scientific method (Rorty, 1992). A conservative think tank funds a young scholar's book-length critique of left-oriented political correctness (D'Souza, 1991). An Afrocentric college professor counsels high school educators on how they can increase the self-esteem of inner-city youth by instilling pride in their African roots (Asante, 1987). These are but skirmishes in today's cultural wars, but they illustrate within an academic setting what is meant by cultural politics. It is an attempt by all sides to influence ideological thought via institutions such as the schools that are not often thought of as vehicles for propagandizing. Its methods include not just active proselytizing but control over what gets put before students in the way of textbooks, television viewers in the way of programming, and museum goers in the way of art exhibits. The fallout from the culture wars in colleges and universities has given rise to questioning about the ethics of faculty advocacy in the classroom, to be discussed in Chapter 15.

Social Protests and Mass Media

Although cultural politics is highly dependent on television entertainment and on the schools to get its message across, the more traditional confrontational politics of social movements relies principally on news coverage, and especially on television's capacity to reach a wide audience with dramatic, attention-getting footage (Gitlin, 1980).

That attention may in turn inspire new adherents to join a movement and prompt sympathizers to provide increased resources and support. The larger the movement and the bigger and more spectacular its demonstrations, the more media coverage it is likely to get, thus engendering further movement support. In this respect, at least, media attention should benefit social movements.

Moreover, the mass media may confer their blessings on a movement. In the United States, movement activity is in itself considered a "good" by the media; it confirms the impression that ours is a pluralist society, brimming with political vitality. But the mass media are selective in their attention to movements and movement concerns. They are especially likely to play up exposures of corruption and scandal and to bestow sympathetic attention on proposals for modest reform. In that same spirit, the media may even furnish their own supporting evidence of social problems requiring remediation. This is of no small consequence because as Gitlin (1980) argues, the media specialize in "orchestrating everyday consciousness" (p. 3). By statement and omission, in pictures and in words, in entertainment and news and advertisements, the media produce managed, manufactured, but nevertheless eminently credible versions of reality that by dint of their capacity to "naturalize" the news, become for their viewers reality itself.

But this same power and pervasiveness are also a central problem for contemporary movements, and especially for those movements seeking more than modest reforms. Reformist and revolutionary movements, says Gitlin (1980), must either play by the media's rules or risk rejection or inattention. These rules are also in many respects those of the dominant culture. They require that the core interests of political elites not be threatened and that the prevailing rules of governance be maintained. Thus, however much the state is implicated in the exposure of evils, it must still be looked to for the remediation of those evils. The media tend to divide movements into "legitimate main acts that play by the rules and illegitimate side shows" (p. 3). They tend also to give short shrift to movements on the quiet side— those, for example, that prefer private, one-on-one persuasion over more televisual public demonstrations. Much as they celebrate civility and decorum, they also thrive on noisy drama and display. "Mass media define the public significance of movement events, or, by blanking them out, actively deprive them of larger significance" (p. 6).

Thus, in Gitlin's (1980) dour view, contemporary social movements must either adjust their goals and behavior and even their identities to media expectations or risk oblivion. Gitlin is careful to caution against viewing these influences as automatic or determined; he recognizes that movements are not without their own resources, and he acknowledges, too, that the media may magnify and hasten manageable forms of political change (p. 292). Nevertheless, says Gitlin, movements typically succumb to media treatments of them. Leaders are transformed into celebrities, or they are replaced by those who are telegenic or perhaps more willing to submit to the implicit rules of television news making. Not only does the mediated image of the movement, then, influence the movement's self-image, it also tends to "become" the movement for wider publics and institutions, including policymakers.

This, in bare essence, is Gitlin's characterization of the interplay of influence between media and movements. Written primarily from the experience of a 1960s movement in the United States, it remains applicable in a number of interesting respects to the events in Beijing during the spring of 1989. In China, television coverage of the demonstrations swelled the size and support given to the movement organizations that sponsored them. It helped, of course, that Tiananmen Square was the perfect stage, its occupants and attackers were the perfect heroes and villains, and democracy and freedom were the perfect rallying cries. No playwright could have written a more engaging drama or adopted such well-wrought scenes as the demonstrations in support of former leader Hu Yaobang, the visit to China of the Soviet Union's Premier Gorbachev, the hunger strikes in Tiananmen Square, the defiance of martial law, the erection of the Goddess of Democracy status, and the final Beijing massacre.

Parenthetically, the drama at Tiananmen Square was extraordinary for the Western news media. It was, in Dayan and Katz's (1992) terms, a *media event,* or, more accurately, a series of media events. By definition, media events interrupt routine television programming but cannot themselves be interrupted. As such, they are presented "not only as a triumph *of* television, but as a triumph *over* television," providing "direct access to the world." Media events alter the usual patterns of viewing as well. The typically apathetic viewer is replaced by an active viewer, one who assumes a responsibility to watch and to bear witness. Thus, *not watching* becomes a form of escape.

Indeed, some media events, including those at Tiananmen Square, are presented as being "beyond history." The occasions they celebrate are said to be "unexpected" or "unheard of" or "unimaginable," and they are predicted to usher in a "new era."

Leading Social Movements: The Requirements-Problems-Strategies (RPS) Approach

The following is a framework for leading social movements or for analyzing their moves and speech as a rhetorical critic. Its basic assumptions are these: (a) Any movement must fulfill the same functional requirements as more institutionalized collectivities. These imperatives constitute *rhetorical requirements* for the leadership of a movement. (b) Conflicts among requirements create *rhetorical problems,* which in turn affect (c) decisions on *rhetorical strategy.* The primary test of leaders, and ultimately of the strategies they employ, is their capacity to fulfill the requirements of their movement by removing or reducing rhetorical problems.

Requirements

The basic functional requirements of a social movement are an ability to mobilize human and material resources, to exert external influence, and to mount resistance to counterpressures. These requirements are not unlike those facing leaders of institutionalized collectivities such as business or government. For example, the managers of General Motors must recruit, hire, train, motivate, and deploy personnel, and they must likewise acquire and deploy material resources for the manufacture of its cars and trucks. Likewise, the leadership of social movements must recruit, motivate, and deploy activists; the leaders need also to acquire material resources (e.g., money). Just as General Motors must market its vehicles (exert external influence) and beat back its competition (mount resistance to counterpressures), so must the leaders of social movements promote their movement's cause and deal with opposition from countermovements (e.g., pro-life for pro-choice) and from other groups that may regard the movement as a threat.

Problems

Social movements are severely restricted from fulfilling these requirements by dint of their internal strategies and their positions in relation to the larger society. By comparison with the heads of most formal organizations (e.g., General Motors), the leaders of social movements can expect minimal internal control and maximal external resistance. Although business corporations may induce productivity through tangible rewards and punishments, social movements, as voluntary collectivities, must rely on ideological and social commitments. Existing outside the larger society's conceptions of justice and reality, moreover, movements threaten and are threatened by the society's sanctions and taboos: its laws; its maxims; its customs governing manners, decorum, and taste; and its insignia of authority. Shorn of the controls that characterize formal organizations yet required to perform the same internal functions, harassed from without yet obligated to adapt to the external system (i.e., called here the larger society), leaders of social movement must constantly balance inherently conflicting demands on their positions and on the movements they represent.

Many of the foregoing problems pose dilemmas for leaders. Among the demands on any organization are that its leaders maintain a system of accurate communication up and down the line, that they operate an efficient organization, and that they act in a consistent and therefore predictable manner. But in a social movement, the need to speak truthfully must be balanced against the need to inspire members and to fend off attacks on the movement by outsiders. The need for organizational efficiency must be weighed against the demands of individual volunteers (few of whom can be coerced or paid) for personal gratification or for promotion of pet projects. The need for ideological consistency must be balanced against the need for pragmatic adaptations.

There is no simple way to mobilize volunteers for sustained efforts. A spirited, energized membership is the strength of many voluntary campaigns, yet morale cannot be secured through abdications of leadership or of leadership tasks. Members may feel the need to participate in decision making, to undertake pet projects on their own initiative, to put down leaders or other followers, to obstruct meetings by socializing, or to disobey directives. The leadership cannot ignore these needs—especially today, when members are likely to be well educated, independent, and given to "doing their own thing." Still, they cannot accede to all of them, either.

Movements are as susceptible to fragmentation from within as they are to suppression from without. Within movement organizations, factional conflicts invariably develop over questions of value, strategy, tactics, or implementation. Purists and pragmatists clash over the merits of compromise. Academics and activists debate the necessity of long-range planning. Others enter the campaign with personal grievances or vested interests. Preexisting groups that are known to have divergent ideological positions are nevertheless invited to join or affiliate with the campaign because of the power they can wield.

These and other differences may be reflected at the leadership level as well. Rarely can one campaign leader handle all the leadership roles and tasks of the campaign. Hence the need for a variety of leadership types: theoreticians and propagandists to launch the campaign and political or bureaucratic leaders to carry it forward. There may also be cleavages between those vested with positions of authority in the campaign, those charismatic figures who have personal followings, those who have special competencies, and those who have private sources of funds or influence outside the campaign.

These internal problems were exhibited at Tiananmen Square. Within the enormous confines of the square, said leader Chai Ling, "Anyone could form an organization and change its leaders at will. Students leaders from various organizations formed territories and proclaimed themselves commanders." By Chai's count, one organization, the Beijing Autonomous Student Union, had experienced no fewer than 182 changes in its leadership (Human Rights in China, 1990; Schell, 1989).

Strategies

Because any strategy represents an attempt to meet incompatible requirements, none is ever fully satisfactory. Each, moreover, creates new rhetorical problems in the process of resolving old ones. This section first distinguishes between *moderate* and *militant* strategies, then identifies an *intermediate* strategy, and concludes with a brief examination of the *expressivist* approach.

Moderates and Militants

As applied to protests against institutional policies or practices, moderates are the embodiment of reason, civility, and decorum. They collect petitions, send telegrams to their congressional representatives, write books, picket and march peacefully, organize voting blocs, and file lawsuits. Exuding earnestness, charm, and an aura of competence, they get angry but do not shout, issue pamphlets but never manifestos, and inveigh against social mores but always in the value language of the social order. Their "devil" is a condition or a set of behaviors or an outcast group, never the persons they are seeking to influence. Those persons are assumed to be capable of "listening to reason."

To the extent that moderates are successful at garnering mass support for their positions, their actions might well threaten those in power and might thus constitute a type of combative persuasion, but their threats are generally muted or implied, and they always operate within limits prescribed by the system. For the most part, moderates seek to reduce the psychological distance between the movement and those outside it by speaking the listeners' language, adjusting to their frame of reference, and adapting to their needs, wants, and values.

If coactive persuaders assume or pretend to assume an ultimate identity of interests between the movement and its antagonists, militant combative persuaders act on the assumption of a fundamental clash of interests. In mixed-motive conflicts, each can lay claim to a part of the truth, and each can boast support from proud philosophical traditions. The moderate's commitment to coactive persuasion is rooted in the Greco-Roman democratic tradition, in Judeo-Christian conceptions of the brotherhood of man, in Emerson's faith in human educability, and in John Stuart Mill's conviction that truth will survive any open competition of ideas. Militants, by contrast, are inclined to be mistrustful of ordinary citizens or to assume that the systems they oppose are likely to be intractable. Like Karl Marx, they are apt to believe that the masses have lost sight of their "real" interests or that those in power are unlikely to surrender it willingly. Although Machiavelli wrote for princes and not for protesters, the militant is inclined to accept that writer's view of persuasion as an adjunct to force, rather than its alternative.

This is not to say that militants offer no appeals to shared values. They do, indeed, but in ways that call into question other widely held values. In general, the militant tends to express greater degrees of dissatisfaction than the moderate (Stewart, Smith, & Denton, 1994). The moderate tends to ask "how" questions, whereas the militant asks "whether" questions. The moderate sees "inefficiencies" in existing practices, whereas the militant sees "inequities." The moderate might regard authority figures as "misguided" although "legitimate," whereas the militant tends to regard these same figures as "willfully self-serving" and "illegitimate." Both might pay homage to law, but the militant is more apt to derogate human laws in the name of "higher" laws. Thus, for example, some antiabortionists have interpreted biblical writ as justification for bombings of abortion clinics.

The actions of militants are not all of a piece by any means. The practice of classic civil disobedience, for example, borders on being intermediate between militancy and moderation. To test the constitutionality of a law, that law is violated. The law in question is violated openly and nonviolently, however; no other laws are breached in the process; the rights of innocent persons are not interfered with; and, if found guilty, the law violator willingly accepts punishment.

Contrast this strategy with acts that can more clearly be labeled combative in nature: strikes, riots, political bombings, and kidnappings—all the way to organized guerrilla warfare. By means of verbal polemics and direct action techniques, protesters who practice combative persuasion threaten, harass, cajole, disrupt, provoke, intimidate, and coerce. Although the aim of pressure tactics may be to punish directly (strikes and boycotts), more frequently, they are forms of "body rhetoric," designed to dramatize issues, enlist additional sympathizers, delegitimize the established order, and—except in truly revolutionary situations—force reconsideration of existing laws and practices or pave the way for negotiated settlements.

Indeed, even the most militant acts of protesters are likely to have rhetorical elements. At the least, militants must establish the credibility of their threats and alter their target's perceptions of what is expedient under the circumstances. Beyond that, their symbolic acts of force may well engender support from those outside the movement.

So different are the rhetorical conceptions of moderate and militant strategists that it strains the imagination to believe that both approaches may work. Yet the decisive changes wrought by militant rhetorics on the left and the right in recent years give credence to the view that coactive persuasion is not the only alternative. What, then, in general terms are the strengths and limitations of moderate and militant approaches?

Militant tactics confer visibility on a movement; moderate tactics gain entry into decision centers. Because of their ethos of respectability, moderates are invited to participate in public deliberations (hearings, conferences, and negotiating sessions) even after militants have occasioned those deliberations by prolonged and self-debilitating acts of protest.

For different reasons, both militants and moderates must be ambivalent about success and failures. Militants thrive on injustice and ineptitude displayed by their targets. Should the enemy fail to implement the movement's demands, militants find themselves vindicated ideologically, yet frustrated programmatically. Should some of the demands be met, they are in the paradoxical position of having to condemn them as palliatives. Moderates, by contrast, require tangible evidence that the larger structure is tractable to hold followers in line, yet too much success belies the movement's reason for being. Not uncommonly, militants and moderates escalate their demands when faced with the prospect of success, but this makes them vulnerable to charges of bad faith. Self-proclaimed militants can avoid this problem by demanding at the outset considerably more than the system is willing to provide, but should self-proclaimed moderates do likewise, they invite charges of being "too militant."

Militant supporters are easily energized; moderate supporters are more easily controlled. Strong identification by members with the goals of a movement—however necessary to achieve esprit de corps—may foster the conviction that any means are justified and breed impatience with time-consuming tactics. The use of violence and other questionable means may be prompted further by restrictions on legitimate avenues of expression imposed by the larger structure. As a result, leaders may be required to mask the movement's true objectives, publicly disclaim the use of tactics they privately advocate, promise what they cannot deliver, exaggerate the strength of the movement, and so on. A vicious cycle develops in which militant tactics invite further suppression, which spurs the movement on to more extreme methods. Having aroused their following, however, the leaders of a militant movement may become victims of their own creation, unable to contain energies within prescribed limits or to guarantee their own tenure. Leaders of moderate groups frequently complain that their supporters are apathetic. As Turner and Killian (1957) have pointed out, "To the degree to which a movement incorporates only major sacred values its power will be diffused by a larger body of conspicuous lip-service adherents who cannot be depended upon for the work of the movement" (p. 337).

Militants are effective with *power-vulnerables;* moderates are effective with *power-invulnerables;* neither is effective with both. Targets of protest may be labeled as power-vulnerable to the degree to which (a) they hold possessions of value and therefore have something to lose (e.g., property, status, and high office); (b) they cannot escape from a source's pressure (unlike suburbanites, for example, who could escape, physically or psychologically, from the inner-city riots of the 1960s); and (c) they cannot retaliate against a source (either because of normative or physical constraints). Such targets as university presidents, church leaders, and elected government officials are highly vulnerable—especially if they profess to be "high-minded" or "liberal"—compared with the mass of citizens who may lack substantial possessions, be able to escape, or feel no constraints about retaliating. The latter are power-invulnerables.

As leaders of institutions allocate priorities in the face of conflicting pressures from other groups, they are unlikely to act on the programmatic suggestions of protest groups—even when they are sympathetic—unless pressured to do so. Hence, coactive strategies alone are likely to be ineffectual with them, whereas combative strategies should stand a better chance of modifying their attitudes. Combative strategies are likely to be less effective with power-invulnerables than are coactive strategies, and they might well invite backlash effects.

When the movement and the larger structure are already polarized, the dilemma is magnified. However much they may wish to plead reasonably, wresting changes from those in public positions requires that leaders build a sizable power base. To secure massive internal support, leaders must at least seem militant.

Intermediate Strategies

In choosing between coactive and combative strategies of persuasion, protest leaders face a series of dilemmas: neither approach is likely to meet every rhetorical requirement or resolve every rhetorical problem; indeed, the introduction of either approach may create new problems.

So it is that the leadership of a protest movement may attempt to resolve or avoid the aforementioned dilemmas by employing *intermediate* strategies, admittedly a catchall term for those efforts that combine militant and moderate patterns of influence. Leaders may alternate between appeals to common ground and threats of punishment, or speaking softly in private and stridently at mass gatherings. They may form broadly based coalitions that submerge ideological differences or use speakers with similar values but contrasting styles. They may stand as "conservative radicals" or "radical conservatives," espousing extreme demands in the value language of the social order or militant slogans in behalf of moderate proposals. In defense of moderation, they may portray themselves as putting on the brakes to hold back more militant followers.

Intermediacy can be a dangerous game. Calculated to energize supporters, win over neutrals, pressure power-vulnerables, and mollify the opposition, it may end up antagonizing everyone. The turned phrase may easily appear as a devilish trick, the rationale as a rationalization, the tactful comment as an artless dodge. To the extent that strategies of intermediacy require studied ambiguity, insincerity, and even distortion, perhaps the leaders' greatest danger is that others will find out what they really think.

Still, some strategists manage to reconcile differences between militant and moderate approaches and not simply maneuver around them. They seem able to convince the established order that bad-tasting medicine is good for it and seem capable, too, of mobilizing a diverse collectivity within the movement. The key, it appears, is the leaders' capacity to embody a higher wisdom, a more profound sense of justice: to stand above inconsistencies by articulating overarching principles. Few will contest the claim that the Reverend Martin Luther King Jr. epitomized the approach. Attracting both militants and moderates to his movement, he could win respect, even from his enemies, by reconciling the seemingly irreconcilable. The heart of the case for intermediacy was succinctly stated by Reverend King himself:

> What is needed is a realization that power without love is reckless and abusive and love without power is sentimental and anemic. Power at its best is love implementing the demands of justice, and justice at its best is power correcting everything that stands against love. (quoted in Simons, 1970, p. 10)

The major protest movements of the 1960s all seemed to require combinations of militant and moderate approaches. Militants were counted on to dramatize the Vietnam issue, moderates to plead forcefully within inner circles. Threats of confrontation prompted city and state governments to finance the building of new schools in low-income areas, but it took reasonableness and civility to get experienced teachers to volunteer for work in those facilities. Demands by revolutionary student groups for transformations of university structures helped impel administrators to heed quasi-militant demands for a redistribution of university power. Support for the cause by moderate groups helped confer respectability on the movement. Thus, however much they might have warred among themselves, militants and moderates each performed important functions.

Expressivism

As indicated earlier, many persons believe that neither militant nor moderate (nor intermediate) approaches to protest are realistic. Yet if asked whether they sought significant changes in society's institutions, they probably would respond affirmatively and might even label themselves "revolutionaries." Proponents of expressivism include many holistic health persons, gay liberationists, back-to-nature advocates, religious fundamentalists, and others concerned fundamentally with matters of lifestyle. Although the expressivist approach cannot be applied to all arenas of protest, its proponents offer a significant critique of conventional approaches to protest. Here is a summary of the position as it has been argued.

In their preoccupation with strategies of persuasion, militants and moderates are really barking up the wrong tree. Institutions do not change until people change, and people do not change as a result of the machinations of movement strategists. They change when an idea is ripe for the times, and when they have come to that idea as a result of direct personal experiences. Amitai Etzioni (1972) speaks of an "iron law of sociology that states that the fate of all popular movements is determined by forces they do not control" (p. 45). He is probably not too far from the truth.

In point of fact, moderates and militants are really cut from the same cloth, and most ironic, they are not very different from the social order they seek to change. Scratch at the source of our society's ills, and you will find a set of dehumanizing values that are also reflected in conventional protest groups. Like the society at large, moderate and militant leaders scheme, manipulate, and exploit—even their own followers. When they get caught up in their own manipulations, their only solution is to manipulate some more. Ultimately, it is a self-defeating mentality because in addition to dominating other people and the surrounding physical environment, protest leaders begin to think of their cause as a set of cold abstractions.

That is why lifestyle movements are truly revolutionary. Their target is not so much particular laws or practices but the values giving rise to society's institutions. Only when these values are changed can the institutions of society be changed. The alternative to conventional strategies, then, is an honest, unstructured, leaderless, nonmanipulative exchange of ideas and feelings among people, as exemplified by consciousness-raising sessions among women or meditation groups among Eastern religionists. It is not simply a compromise between the way of the moderate and the way of the militant but a genuine alternative.

Open- and Closed-Minded Movements

This chapter has told the story of a group with whom most readers could readily identify: the demonstrators at Tiananmen Square. Yet it is important to emphasize that social movements come in a variety of shapes and sizes and that some of them are downright ugly and more than a bit scary by most Americans' standards. Vladimir Lenin led a social movement; so did Adolf Hitler.

Protest leaders, even those of whom we approve, tend to appear most closed-minded at mass demonstrations, such as those shown in Pictures 14.1 and 14.2. Still, there is a vast difference between spewers of hate, such as Adolf Hitler, and those such as the Reverend Martin Luther King Jr., who preached a doctrine of love. Moreover, King exhibited an openness to counterarguments in his writings and in interviews with journalists—not so Adolf Hitler.

Religious cults are social movements; so is the right-wing militia movement. On the extreme right alone, one can find isolationist movements; hate groups that spew venom against blacks, Hispanics, Jews, Catholics, and immigrants of all types; and

Picture 14.1. Nazi Rally: Hitler Speaking at Dortmund, 1933
SOURCE: Archive Photos. Used with permission.

groups dedicated to bringing down government (Bennett, 1995). Timothy McVeigh, convicted in the 1995 bombing of the Alfred P. Murrah Federal Building in Oklahoma City, was one such extremist; that bombing killed 168 people and shattered the lives of hundreds more.

Depending on the examples one picks, then, it is easy enough to glorify social movements or to condemn them roundly. One's political sympathies will inevitably play a role in that as well.

Still, if there is one yardstick around which rhetoricians can unite in their judgment of social movements, it is open-versus closed-mindedness. Closed-minded movement organizations exhibit absolutistic, totalistic, and dogmatic thinking (Hart, 1984). Their ideological claims are offered as revealed truths and are thus presented impersonally and authoritatively. Rather than questioning these "truths," members are expected to swallow them whole and to compensate for gaps in their leaders' logic by supplying missing premises. Groups such as these are insular, xenophobic, and frequently paranoid. The world external to the movement is seen as sin-

Picture 14.2. Martin Luther King Jr. Speaking at the March on Washington, 1963
SOURCE: Archive Photos. Used with permission.

ister and threatening. Members, too, are seen as sinners or as prone to ideological backsliding, but there is the promise for members of redemption and salvation through acts of contrition and purification.

Clearly, not all movement groups exhibit these characteristics, not even those that one might be tempted to regard as radical or extreme. Whenever one is tempted to condemn all radicals or extremists, it is well to remember who made the American Revolution. Moderates, they were not!

The Fate of Social Movements

The fate of social movement organizations varies considerably. Some ultimately achieve legitimacy in society; the once militant labor union movement in the United States is now the highly institutionalized AFL-CIO. Some movements are successful at promoting their causes; the more moderate the goal (better enforcement of traffic laws), the better the chances of success. Some movements achieve legitimacy *and* desired gains; some achieve neither (Gamson, 1990). But even among the apparent failures, there are often long-term positive effects.

Often ignored are the effects, both symbolic and material, of one movement group on another. Militant groups help legitimize more moderate groups; Malcolm X's Nation of Islam did that for Martin Luther King Jr.'s SCLC. In other circumstances, distant movements serve as important role models; witness King's debts to Gandhi and Thoreau. Apparently, the students in Beijing were much influenced by revolutionary developments in Eastern Europe and by the freeing of the press in the Soviet Union. Great movements of the past also live on in legends and myths that are invented anew by successive generations and in institutions and forms of action that are adapted to changed circumstances (McGee, 1977). One of the most tantalizing hypotheses in recent years is Timothy Garton Ash's (1999) conjecture that the peaceful revolutions of 1989 in countries formerly dominated by the Soviet Union have provided a formula of sorts for peaceful revolution. Says Ash, the 1989 model

> combines an absolute insistence on nonviolence with the active, highly inventive use of mass civil disobedience, skillful appeals to Western media, public opinion, and governments, and a readiness to negotiate and compromise with the power-holders, while refusing to be co-opted by them. (p. 18)

He adds that although this model has not been initiated in its entirety in other countries, it has had an enormous impact on the peaceful transition in South Africa, the tactics of Burmese opposition leader Aung San Suu Kyi, and the negotiations leading to peace in Northern Ireland. (See Box 14.1.)

Summary

This chapter has examined the rhetoric of social movements, such as the movement for democratization of China centered on Tiananmen Square in 1989. Social movements were defined as uninstitutionalized collectivities that operate on a sustained basis to exert external influence in behalf of a cause.

Featured in this chapter was a Requirements, Problems, Strategies (RPS) framework for leading social movements or for analyzing its words and symbolic acts. Movements are required to perform the same essential functions as institutionalized collectivities but are severely impeded from accomplishing them. Moreover, the strategies they employ generally create new problems in the process of resolving others.

BOX 14.1 Tiananmen Square

Were the demonstrators at Tiananmen Square failures? In some respects, yes. Evidently, they were the targets of more government-initiated violence than they had bargained for. On the evening of June 3, 1989, the army moved tanks and troops onto the square and fired on demonstrators and bystanders. Hundreds, perhaps thousands, were killed.

Thus, the demonstrators at Tiananmen were crushed, although not without resistance.

One Chinese dissident against a row of tanks, outside Tiananmen Square, 1989: This photo of a citizen standing in front of a tank inspired worldwide support for the prodemocracy cause in China. The tanks eventually went around the man.
SOURCE: Reuters/Stringer/Archive Photos. Used with permission.

For a time, it appeared that in response to the massacre, the United States would deny China trade benefits. Periodically, this issue comes up, along with reports of other human rights violations. But the prevailing view among government officials in the United States seems to be that maintaining China as a close trading partner does more for democracy in China than isolating it economically.

Meanwhile, many leaders of the prodemocracy movement in China were arrested, tried, convicted, and imprisoned under harsh living conditions, while others escaped to the West and are prospering (Buruma, 1999). Demonstrations commemorating the takeover of Tiananmen Square are forbidden in China, but it remains an inspiration to people everywhere, particularly among China's educated elite. Only time will tell whether it was truly a failure.

Most strategies range on a continuum from moderate to militant. Moderates and militants differ in the degree to which they are willing to work within the system, the scope and intensity of the devils they attack, and the extent to which they rely on appeals to common ground or, on the other hand, find it necessary to bolster appeals and arguments with displays of power or delegitimizing techniques such as confrontation. Perhaps the fundamental difference between the two is in orientation. Although coactive persuaders assume or pretend to assume an ultimate identity of interests between the movement and its antagonists, militants act on the assumption of a fundamental clash of interests.

Choosing between moderate and militant approaches is far from easy. Militant tactics confer visibility on the movement and open the doors for negotiation, but it is the moderate who frequently gains entry into the actual negotiations. Militant supporters are easily energized; moderate supporters are more easily controlled. Militants are effective with power-vulnerables; moderates are effective with power-invulnerables; neither is effective with both. Some movements attempt to combine the attractive features of moderate and militant approaches by use of intermediate strategies. Other movements have looked askance at both moderate and militant approaches and have sought to develop alternative strategies that are essentially expressive in nature.

Questions and Projects for Further Study

1. Read up on the movements of the 1960s. See for example, Todd Gitlin's (1993) *The Sixties: Years of Hope, Days of Rage.* Why do you believe American campuses have been relatively free of protest demonstrations since the 1960s?

2. Search the Internet for Web pages of movement groups identified by David H. Bennett (1995) in *The Party of Fear,* Chapter 16. How do they describe themselves?

3. Analyze the rhetoric of a movement or movement leader using the RPS approach. (See Simons, 1970, for a fuller description of the approach.)

4. What are media events? Have there been any media events since Tiananmen Square? For more information on media events, see Dayan and Katz (1992).

5. Social movement groups vary from informal, grassroots undertakings to highly professionalized SMOs such as Amnesty International and the Sierra Club. Can you name other current movement organizations? Where do they fit on the continuum from grassroots to highly professionalized?

Notes

1. This record of the speech is from the Internet and is in fragments: CRTNET News #2014; June 4, 1997, entry by Dan Oetting. CRTNET is the official listserv of the National Communication Association.

2. For a similar definition and conceptualization of social movements, see McAdam and Snow (1997). They define a social movement as "a collectivity acting with some degree of organization and continuity outside of institutional channels for the purpose of promoting or resisting change in the group, society or world order of which it is a part" (p. xviii).

3. Although the civil rights movement is now favorably remembered, it met with considerable resistance at the time, even by politicians who were sympathetic to the cause. As president, John F. Kennedy knew that support for the movement would endanger his relationship with the white South, and especially with Southern chairpersons of important congressional committees. Lyndon Baines Johnson acknowledged when he signed civil rights legislation in 1964 and 1965 that this would put an end to the Democratic Party's long-term hold over the South.

References

Asante, M. K. (1987). *The Afrocentric idea.* Philadelphia: Temple University Press.

Ash, T. G. (1999, November 18). Ten years later. *New York Review of Books, 46,* 15-19.

Bennett, D. H. (1995). *The party of fear: The American far right from nativism to the militia movement* (Rev. ed.). New York: Vintage.

Buruma, I. (1999, May 31). Tiananmen, Inc. *New Yorker, 75,* 45-52.

Darnovsky, M., Epstein, B., & Flacks, R. (1995). *Cultural politics and social movements.* Philadelphia: Temple University Press.

Dayan, D., & Katz, D. (1992). *Media events: The live broadcasting of history.* Cambridge, MA: Harvard University Press.

D'Souza, D. (1991). *Illiberal education: The politics of race and sex on campus.* New York: Free Press.

Etzioni, A. (1972, June 3). Human beings are not very easy to change, after all. *Saturday Review,* 45-47.

Gamson, W. (1990). *The strategy of social protest* (2nd ed.). Belmont, CA: Wadsworth.

Gitlin, T. (1980). *The whole world is watching.* Berkeley: University of California Press.

Gitlin, T. (1993). *The sixties: Years of hope, days of rage.* New York: Bantam.

Gitlin, T. (1995). *The twilight of common dreams: Why America is wracked by culture wars.* New York: Henry Holt.

Graff, G. (1992). *Beyond the culture wars.* New York: Norton.

Hart, R. P. (1984). The functions of human communication in the maintenance of public values. In C. C. Arnold & J. W. Bowers (Eds.), *Handbook of rhetorical and communication theory* (pp. 749-791). Boston: Allyn & Bacon.

Human Rights in China. (1990). *Children of the dragon: The story of Tiananmen Square.* New York: Collier.

Lather, P. (1991). *Getting smart.* New York: Routledge.

Le Bon, G. (1896). *Psychologie des Foules* [Psychology of crowds]. Paris: Alcan.

McAdam, D., & Snow, D. A. (1997). *Social movements: Readings on their emergence, mobilization and dynamics.* Los Angeles: Roxbury.

McGee, M. C. (1977). The fall of Wellington: A case study of the relationship between theory, practice, and rhetoric in history. *Quarterly Journal of Speech, 63,* 28-42.

Roe v. Wade, 410 U.S. 113 (1973).

Rorty, R. (1992). Two cheers for the cultural left. In D. J. Gless & B. H. Smith (Eds.), *The politics of liberal education* (pp. 233-240). Durham, NC: Duke University Press.

Schell, O. (1989, June 29). China's spring. *New York Review of Books, 36,* 3-7.

Schelling, T. C. (1960). *The strategy of conflict.* Cambridge: Harvard University Press.

Scott, R. L., & Smith, D. K. (1969). The rhetoric of confrontation. *Quarterly Journal of Speech, 55,* 1-8.

Simons, H. W. (1970). Requirements, problems, strategies: A theory of persuasion for social movements. *Quarterly Journal of Speech, 56,* 1-11.

Stewart, C. J., Smith, C. A., & Denton, R. E., Jr. (1994). *Persuasion and social movements* (3rd ed.). Prospect Heights, IL: Waveland.

Tilly, C. (1979). Repertoires of contention in America and Britain, 1750-1830. In M. N. Zald & J. D. McCarthy (Eds.), *The dynamics of social movements.* Cambridge, MA: Winthrop.

Turner, R. H., & Killian, L. W. (1957). *Collective behavior.* Englewood Cliffs, NJ: Prentice Hall.

CHAPTER **15**

More About Ethics

Indelibly stamped on the pages of this book is the news of the Clinton-Lewinsky affair. Perhaps by the time you read these words, it will be a faint memory. Monica who? Yet in addition to having had an illicit sexual relationship in the White House with Monica Lewinsky, the president repeatedly lied about it to the American people, was impeached by the House, then nearly convicted by the Senate. Impeachment of an American president happened only once before in history; it was not your everyday occurrence.

Yet most Americans seem to have forgiven President Clinton, if ever they were outraged. The speech analyzed in Chapter 10 that nearly everyone of importance in Washington condemned at the time apparently did no long-term damage to the president's approval ratings; so long as economic prosperity held steady, his ratings remained exceptionally high. The analysis in Chapter 10 of Clinton's August 17 apologia focuses on its effectiveness, but what of its ethics? The president, after all, appears to have ducked real responsibility for his actions even as he claimed to be taking "full responsibility." He insisted that what he had done was a purely private matter, even as he was forced to admit that he had publicly prevaricated. He seems to have expressed greater anger at what was done to him by the Kenneth Starr investigation than remorse for his own misdeeds.

So should Clinton be condemned for unethical persuasion, even as the effectiveness of the speech is grudgingly acknowledged? Should we as a society deplore its evasions, hypocrisies, and deliberate ambiguities? Or, from another perspective, should we congratulate Clinton for slipping out of a noose that was unfairly slung around his neck? Should we applaud his rhetorical dexterity as necessary to the continuation of an exceptionally competent performance in office? Should we condemn those who blew the affair all out of proportion, including not just his Republican opponents but also the news media?

Questions of ethics are complicated and frustrating—no right or wrong answers, except when *we* feel wronged or believe we have been witness to unspeakable evils committed against others. Clitorectomies in Senegal. Human rights abuses in China. Ethnic cleansing in Kosovo. Child abuse, brainwashing of cult members, and stolen elections here at home. Then ethics become crystal clear—too clear, perhaps, because our moral certainties can blind us to complexities that deserve to be taken into account.

This book has identified many such complexities, deliberately muddying the waters. Well-told stories give truths their hind legs, it was said. But they also give falsehoods their hind legs. Persuasion operates under conditions of uncertainty, time constraints, and limited information. Not surprisingly, therefore, so-called experts give contradictory advice. Highly educated people commit logical fallacies. All people—educated or not—use cognitive shortcuts. If truth is elusive—if, on some issues there seems to be no truth or no single, overriding truth—why not lie, evade, exaggerate, or simply choose language or visuals or nonverbals that will play up your version of the truth and downplay your opponent's?

All people deceive, and some professions seem to make a virtue of it. Recall Robert Jackall's (1995) take on public relations. In that world, he said, "There is no such thing as a notion of truth; there are only stories, perspectives, or opinions" (p. 365). Jackall adds that in the world of public relations,

> As long as a story is factual, it does not matter if it is "true." One can feel free to arrange these facts in a variety of ways and to put any interpretations on them that suits a client's objectives. Interpretations and judgments are always completely relative. The only canon binding this process of interpretation are those of credibility, or, more exactly, of plausibility. . . . Insofar as it has any meaning at all, truth is what is perceived. Creating the impression of truth displaces the search for truth. (p. 365)

But if Plato was right, the same could be said about rhetoric generally: Truth is held hostage to effectiveness as the persuader makes the worse argument appear to be the better argument. (See Box 15.1.)

The ancient Sophists would probably have seen themselves in Jackall's description, but being masters of rhetoric, they no doubt would have put a different spin on it. "Yes," today's sophist declares—whether lawyer, product advertiser, political candidate, or PR professional—"I put spin on my stories, but so what? Am I so different in that respect from journalists, textbook writers, teachers, scientists, or, indeed, from ordinary people doing what *they* can to look good, feel good, and perhaps do good?" Remember the defense attorney in this book's opening story? She wound up going to jail because she believed in telling but one, unvarnished truth. No such thing!

So yes again, ethical questions in persuasion are often quite complicated, and this closing chapter is not about to resolve them. What it can do—what it will do—is offer some systematic ways of thinking about the issues, then show how these approaches to ethics can be brought to bear on the sorts of cases you are likely to confront. What it will also do, once it gets through with issues facing you, is talk about *us*—we who teach college students. When, if at all, should professors profess their opinions? Is there any way of staying neutral in academic arenas of controversy such as the persuasion classroom?

Beyond that, this chapter offers a vision of the good society, one in which people are mindful as persuadees when they need to be, and in which the major institutions of society make it easy for that to happen.

Perspectives on Ethics

There are many perspectives on ethics, among them pragmatism, utilitarianism, universalism, dialogic ethics, and situationalism (Solomon, 1984). These seem particularly relevant to the ethics of persuasion.

Pragmatism

Three people respond to your newspaper ad for a used car, and you make an appointment with each to show up at roughly the same time. You apologize for having made a mistake in scheduling, although you actually wanted all three to show up at the same time to impress them that your car is a hot item, much in demand. Ethical? Unethical? Borderline?

BOX 15.1 Kenneth Burke on "Sincerity"

Plato's critique of rhetoric applies with full force to coactive persuasion. Nothing in the coactive approach requires a notion of truth, certainly not an absolute truth. Coactive persuaders deal, as all persuaders do, in appearances. Moreover, coactive persuasion builds on what Kenneth Burke (1950/1969) called the principle of *identification*. This, in essence, is what moving toward the other psychologically is all about. Said Burke, "You persuade a man only insofar as you can talk his language by speech, gesture, tonality, order, image, attitude, idea, *identifying* your ways with his" (p. 55). But as Burke was quick to point out, this symbolic "joining together" deflects attention from human differences. Said Burke, "Identification is affirmed with earnestness precisely because there is division. If men were not apart from one another, there would be no need for the [persuader] to proclaim their unity" (p. 22).

The coactive approach thus raises fundamental questions about sincerity, authenticity, integrity. Indeed, says Burke (1950/1969), "Persuasion by flattery is but a special case of persuasion in general" (p. 55). Burke (1968) himself presents a withering picture of the persuader as chameleon, in the form of a poem about a Presbyterian.

He Was a Sincere, Etc.

He was a sincere but friendly Presbyterian—and so

If he was talking to a Presbyterian,
He was for Presbyterianism.

If he was talking to a Lutheran,
He was for Protestantism.

If he was talking to a Catholic,
He was for Christianity.

If he was talking to a Jew,
He was for God.

If he was talking to a theosophist,
He was for religion.

If he was talking to an agnostic,
He was for scientific caution.

If he was talking to an atheist,
He was for mankind.

And if he was talking to a socialist, communist, labor leader, missiles expert,
  or businessman,
He was for
  PROGRESS. (p. 238)[1]

BOX 15.1 Continued

Is the coactive approach to persuasion inherently immoral? Perhaps. But look at it from another perspective. Burke's (1950/1969) chameleonlike Presbyterian can *truthfully* be many things to many people, and, in stretching himself ever farther to accommodate himself to the beliefs, values, and attitudes of other people, he is performing an essential function of language itself: that of "inducing cooperation in beings that by nature respond to symbols" (p. 43). In using identification to induce cooperation, Burke's Presbyterian is offering up what is nearly always a preferable alternative to coercion or domination. Moreover, even if his appeals to common ground are advantage seeking, Burke reminds us, they need not reap gains at the expense of the other. Both may benefit.

Think in this connection of such ordinary uses of coactive persuasion as fraternity or sorority recruitment. Lola, a promising recruit, tells you that she is interested in learning more about your sorority. You put your sorority's best foot forward, emphasizing features of Kappa Phi Zeta (KPZ) life that you think are wonderful and that you expect Lola will value as well. Lola also allows that she is from Juneau, Alaska. "Funny that you mention it," you say. Your family vacationed in Alaska last summer and had a wonderful time. Is there anything wrong with this approach?

Now suppose that Lola informs you that she is interested in pledging a high-status sorority, one that will be the envy of her friends back in Juneau. You happen to care less about KPZ's ranking in the sorority world, but you assure Lola that, yes, KPZ has a high-status reputation. You go on to mention other features, associated with status, such as the number of beauty pageant winners at KPZ, that you think will turn Lola on. This, you will recall, is an example of reasoning from the perspective of the other.

Although reasoning from the perspective of the other is sometimes judged insincere, doesn't this depend on how it is done? Isn't the key question whether persuaders are honest about their own feelings in respect to those reasons? Suppose you make clear to Lola that you were looking at matters from her perspective, and not necessarily your own. Would this place you on safer moral ground?

I believe so. Still, coactive persuasion can be ethically quite questionable. Suppose that you and your family had not vacationed in Alaska last summer. Suppose that Burke's Presbyterian chameleon despised Catholicism, even as he proclaimed himself a Christian.

Note

1. "Sincerity" reprinted from Burke, K. B. (1968). *Collected Poems 1915-1967*, p. 238. Berkeley: University of California Press. Permission to reprint granted by Michael Burke and the Kenneth Burke Literary Trust.

One way to respond to questions of ethics is to transform them into pragmatic ones, about the probable costs and benefits of taking a given action. On the one hand, what if one of the prospective customers loses patience and decides to leave? What if a second catches on to your game and expresses resentment? What if your lover hears about your ploy and decides to desert you for someone more honest? On the other hand, what if setting up a competition among prospective buyers nets you a good price? These considerations may not be irrelevant, but they should probably not form your entire judgment in the matter, either. What about your responsibility to the prospective buyers, or to agreed-on standards for doing business, or to your own conscience? If you are to focus on consequences, you might also ask yourself what the effects would be on society if practices such as these became the norm. Finally, because our self-concepts are formed from interaction with others, you might wish to consider what the effect of your deception of others is likely to have on you. Common to all these question is pragmatism's concern with consequences.

Utilitarianism

The ethical questions raised in this book have often pitted ends against means, means against ends, and both against circumstances. Recall Zaltman and Duncan's (1977) fourfold typology of influence strategies ranging from most controlling to least controlling. Nobody likes having their freedom taken away, but Zaltman and Duncan's "power" and "persuasion" strategies (at the high end of their continuum) are far more capable of accomplishing ends considered worthy in this society, such as curbing illicit drug dealing, than are "normative-reeducative" and "facilitation" strategies, at the low end of the scale. So a persistent question is whether to use means that work or means that preserve people's autonomy.

One way of squaring this circle is to conclude that you are entitled to use ethically questionable means only when your goals as a persuader are worthy beyond question. Thus, a medical doctor might feel justified in deceiving a patient for the patient's own good—for example, by exaggerating the negative consequences of what would happen if the patient does not get enough exercise. On similar grounds, a charitable organization might exaggerate its capacity to make a difference with the dollars its donors contribute. If these inflated estimates were exposed to the press, a spokesperson for the charity might respond that organizations performing a public service are exempted from responsibilities that fall on lesser entities. By the same token, if our ends are of dubious value, presumably we are obligated to refrain from using ethically questionable means. A former student reported that in his part-time job as a telemarketer to physicians, he could vastly improve his chances of getting through to them by posing as another doctor. But the student ultimately could not justify this deceit to himself and wound up getting another job.

Questions of this type arise repeatedly in the policy-making arena. During the congressional hearings in 1990 on whether the United States should take arms to combat Iraqi aggression in Kuwait, a teenager testified to Congress that she saw Iraqi soldiers tear babies from incubators. That story was repeated many times in speeches by then President George Bush and was featured in the subsequent congressional debate on whether to support U.S. military action in the Gulf. The congressional committee was not told, however, that the teenager was the Kuwaiti ambassador's daughter; moreover, there is good reason to believe that the girl had not herself witnessed these alleged atrocities. Had he known she was the Kuwaiti ambassador's daughter, said Representative John Porter, the ranking Republican on the committee, he would not have allowed her to testify. But then again, he had heard other witnesses tell similar stories, and he thought there was strong evidence to support the charges (McArthur, 1992, pp. 57-77).

As in the above example, persuaders tend to interpret the ends-justify-means principle as rationalization for achieving success by any means. The Nazi leadership believed in its ends, and this justified their use of hate campaigns, built around polarizing symbols of identification and division. Hitler was a master of exploiting popularly held fears and resentments at mass rallies.

Recall from Chapter 11 the Machiavellian rules for getting elected to high office. Politicians are not alone in seeking to win at all costs. Public relations professionals, advertising executives, trial lawyers—and, yes, even some classroom speakers—are not above fabricating evidence or using misleading arguments. Once individuals have engaged in practices such as these, it is all too easy to rationalize them—to decide, for example, that a classroom speech is only an exercise and doesn't count in the real world or that fabricating evidence is justified because they could always find evidence just like it if they had the time to dig it out of the library. Moral standards tend to be applied selectively and self-deceptively even in conflicts between close friends and associates, as shown in Chapter 13. The tendency to apply moral standards inconsistently is all the more persistent because it is often done unconsciously. By deceiving ourselves about our own tendencies to deceive others, we manage both to protect our egos and to appear sincere to others.

Once we have rationalized an ethically questionable act, it is easy and tempting to fit new acts to the rule and, if necessary, to invent more cynical new rules. Here lie the seeds of what psychologists refer to as the *Machiavellian personality* (Christie & Geis, 1970). We can decide, for example, that ethics are for the other person; that if we don't con others, someone else will; that if we don't "get" others, they'll "get" us. Because Machiavellianism feeds on mistrust, it can become contagious, infecting entire professions and institutions.

Weighing ends against means, means against ends, and both against circumstances is most closely associated with the philosophical position on ethics known as utilitarianism. Its core principle is this: *Do more good than harm.* Given two or more alternatives, do what will provide the greatest good for the greatest number of people. Lying, ordinarily, does more harm than good, and so is presumed to be unethical. But there may be "white" lies that do little harm and a lot of good, in which case utilitarians would probably approve them.

Universalism

A third approach to the ethics of persuasion assumes that some practices are intrinsically virtuous or intrinsically objectionable, no matter what the objective or the circumstances. Universalist ethics may be derived from law or tradition or religion. For example, the Bible holds that we should never lie, slander, or bear false witness. Philosopher Immanuel Kant held to the *categorical imperative,* the position that we should always act so that the principle of our actions is capable of being universalized. By that reasoning, lying is always wrong, even when it causes no harm in a particular situation, because if everyone were to lie, no one would believe anyone. Lying is wrong, in other words, because truth telling is a necessary condition of our having any meaningful verbal interaction at all (Solomon, 1984).

Dialogic Ethics

Ethical guidelines for the persuader may also be derived from a view of communication as ideally *dialogic.* According to dialogic ethics, communication between two persons is facilitated when each treats the other as a *thou,* a person, rather than an *it,* an object to manipulate. Communication is imperiled, perhaps even destroyed, when the bonds of interpersonal trust are placed in question (Solomon, 1984). A list of ethical imperatives for the dialogic persuasive speaker or writer might include the following:

1. Practice inquiry before advocacy. Be open to a variety of points of view before you embrace any one of them.

2. Know your subject. If what you say isn't based on firsthand knowledge, get the information you need from the library or from the Internet.

3. Be honest about your identity. Don't purport to be an expert if you are not.

4. Try to tell the truth as you perceive it. Don't deliberately mislead audiences about your true opinions on a matter.

5. Avoid fabrications, misrepresentations, and distortions of evidence.

6. Don't oversimplify.

7. Acknowledge possible weaknesses, if any, in your position. Be honest about your own ambivalence or uncertainty.

8. Avoid irrelevant emotional appeals or diversionary tactics.

9. Appeal to the best motives in people, not their worst motives.

10. Be prepared to lose on occasion if winning means doing psychological harm to others and demeaning yourself in the bargain.

This, you might conclude, is a reasonable list, but shouldn't there be exceptions to it? Doesn't politeness sometimes require a speaker to *not* tell an audience what he or she thinks of them? Given constraints on a speaker's time or an editorialist's space, isn't it impossible to avoid oversimplification? Few politicians routinely admit their uncertainties to potential voters. Should we blame them? Attorneys, advertisers, and public relations experts may think it unwise to disclose their ulterior motives. Should we criticize them for that? Professional advocates of every sort may insist that their true opinions on a matter are irrelevant to their tasks as persuaders. Is there something inherently unethical about the hired gun?

Situationalism

There are those who take the position that ethics should be role- or situation-specific, thus bolstering the case for exceptions to the above list of ethical imperatives. For example, the car you want to sell has a transmission problem that isn't easily detected. Do you warn prospective buyers about it? Do you admit the problem if you're asked?

Assuming that ethical decisions should be role- or situation-specific, you might reason that evasion, and possibly even misrepresentation, are legitimate tactics for private car sales and even for business in general. A dialogic ethic is fine in the classroom or between friends, you reason, but it doesn't apply to strangers and certainly not when you're selling a car to a used car dealer. You might further assume that used car transactions are a form of *game* or *contest,* which is fair because both sides know, or at least should know, the rules. Or you might refer to the related metaphor of an *implicit contract* between prospective buyer and seller, according to which the principle of caveat emptor—let the buyer beware—is understood and accepted.

Both the game and contract metaphors are consistent with the ethical position known as *situationalism.* This view of ethics enjoins us to pay particular attention to the special circumstances of a matter. Johannesen (1996) lists such contextual factors as the following:

1. Role or function of the persuader for the audience

2. Expectations held by receivers concerning such matters as appropriateness and reasonableness

3. Degree of receiver awareness of the persuader's techniques

4. Goals and values held by receivers

5. Degree of urgency for implementation of the persuader's proposal

6. Ethical standards for communication held by receivers

Situational ethics are often applied in the borderline area of communication ethics, between the poles of moral certainty on either side of it. In the case of the medical doctor who overstated the dangers of failing to comply with exercise recommendations, the situationalist might ask how dire is the situation for the patient and whether the doctor had tried a more honest and straightforward approach in the past. If the situation is dire and honesty hasn't worked, exaggeration may be justified.

Situational ethics also prompts consideration of the institutions of society: Do they place persuaders in situations where, try as they might, it is impossible for them to act honestly and forthrightly and still survive? In Japan, payoffs to politicians and from politicians have been a way of life for decades. In much of Asia, payoffs are an accepted cost of doing business. In the United States, the escalating costs for running political campaigns have made politicians ever more beholden to wealthy campaign contributors. With increased financial dependence comes decreased political independence (Lewis & Center for Public Integrity, 1996).

Institutional analyses apply equally to the situations persuadees confront. Are they placed in situations where, try as they might, it is difficult, if not impossible, to make informed, intelligent, autonomous judgments? In theory, the voter should be able to reap the benefits of an equal contest of ideas. That ideal comes close to being realized in campaign debates. But playing fields for electoral contests tend in general to get tilted in favor of candidates who have the largest campaign chests.

The same tends to be true of contests between rival camps about legislative proposals. In the first half of 1998, insurance companies and their allies fighting in opposition to new legislation regulating health care spent four times more than proponents of the legislation—a figure even greater than the $40 million spent during that same period by tobacco interests to oppose increased taxes on cigarette sales (Salant, 1998). This is not unusual. On major issues such as health care and gun control, one side typically scrounges for meager funds, whereas the other is well financed. In the early 1990s, lobbyists for managed care were far better financed than advocates for the administration-sponsored legislation. In more recent battles over gun control, the National Rifle Association outspent Handgun Control, Inc. by a factor of 17:1 in campaign contributions during a 10-year period and used its considerable reserves for direct lobbying (Goldstein, 1999). Knowing that powerful interests can command great sums to defeat recalcitrant Congress members the next time they run for office, many buckle under to lobbying pressures (Lewis & Center for Public Integrity, 1996).

A situational ethic invites attention to other institutions as well. Which among our society's cultural, religious, and educational institutions prompt independent thinking, and which of them prompt conformist, cultlike thinking? Does product advertising prompt another type of mindless conformity, in this case to the insatiable demands of the economic marketplace? To paraphrase Bernard Barber (1996), have we become enchained by our department store chains, our food service chains, and, worse yet, by the irresistible impulses inside us to buy, buy, buy?

The five perspectives reviewed here now need your own perspective on the perspectives. In choosing a metaperspective, don't just follow the crowd. Don't assume, for example, that what's commonly done *ought* to be done. Having an ethical perspective means moving beyond *description* to *prescription,* to a sense of what's right. Recognize, too, that it is possible—at least some of the time—to be ethical *and* effective. Finally, be aware that the perspectives are not mutually exclusive; hence, it is possible to borrow from each. For example, the utilitarian who seeks to do more good than harm might look to a nuanced situationalism for an idea of the good or to the universalist "Thou shalt nots" of the Ten Commandments for a conception of doing harm. Even the universalist might concede that there are circumstances justifying adultery or even murder while insisting that adultery and murder are intrinsically evil. Even the situationalist might concede that appeal to circumstances is too often an excuse for irresponsible behavior.

Which metaperspective you adopt will probably depend on whether you see yourself primarily as a persuader or as a persuadee. If as a persuader, then you will probably be more inclined to pragmatism or situationalism. If as a persuadee, then you might be more inclined toward universalism and to the respect for message recipients inherent in a dialogic ethic. But even as a persuadee, you might identify with a persuader. Clinton supporters were far more likely than his detractors to deny that he lied under oath or to exempt him from the universalist injunction against perjury in light of the circumstances. Students rarely mind when their professors advance positions they agree with, but they decry faculty advocacy in the classroom when the professor's position gives offense.

Let's give particular thought to the college classroom. When, if at all, should educators advocate?

The Ethics of Faculty Advocacy in the College Classroom

Your professors don't usually talk about it in public, but they are often confused as to whether and when to take and defend positions on controversial issues in the classroom. One concernn is *relevance.* There is general agreement that professors should *not* advance views that are irrelevant to the subjects they are hired to teach. Your biology professor should not promote Christianity in the classroom. Your professor of English literature should not support or oppose the human genome project.

But should your religion professor promote Christianity? Should your biology professor promote the human genome project? Should your English lit professor promote readings of Shakespeare?

Another concern is *power.* Instructors not only have the capacity to assign high or low grades but also can reward with high praise or punish by intimidation. "What? You didn't know that the human genome project has already yielded advances in the treatment of cancer? Haven't you been reading the newspaper?"

But this raises a third consideration: How should *controversy* be defined? Most English literature professors think extremely highly of Shakespeare. Is their saying that Shakespeare was one of England's greatest playwrights and poets legitimate? If so, what about the religion professor who promotes Christianity? After all, aren't most American religion professors believers in Christianity? By the same token, shouldn't the biology professor be able to advocate genetic engineering, given that it enjoys widespread support among biologists?

Some students, however, perhaps even a majority, believe that English departments have for too long assumed the superiority of white male European literary figures over writers from non-Western cultures, including female authors who have gone unrecognized because of past discrimination. To them, the celebration of Shakespeare may be objectionable. Some students would be offended at hearing Christianity extolled over their own religions views. A few students might, for religious or other reasons, strongly oppose genetic engineering, at least as used on human beings. Thus arises a fourth concern: Should professors refrain from knowingly *causing offense* to their students? How can concerns about causing offense be balanced against the need to provoke thought and perhaps overcome prejudices?

A fifth consideration is *manner of promotion.* For reasons to be discussed, some ethicists believe that professors should, where relevant, take and defend controversial positions in the classroom, even at the risk of causing offense. But they insist that professors should not do so in a one-sided, dogmatic manner. Rather, they should provide full and fair background on the controversy, including presentation (or assigned readings) of opposing positions. Only then should they profess, but even then they are obligated not to impose their views, not to reward conformity, and not to intimidate or otherwise coerce. Their positions need to be defended, not just pronounced from on high, and they need to subject their arguments to student criticisms (Brand, 1996; Menand, 1996).

A sixth concern is *cultural context.* Some educators maintain the right—indeed the obligation—to correct prevailing biases in a society under two conditions: (a) if the biases are oppressive to minorities or injurious to the society as a whole and (b) if the corrective view is relatively unpopular and thus isn't as likely to be heard outside the classroom. Endorsing this *liberatory* position have been activists on both sides of various ideological divides, for example, women's advocates who believe that femi-nist teachings are a necessary corrective to what they regard as our culture's domi-nant patriarchal ideology and Afrocentrists and multiculturalists who believe Eurocentrism has been a force for cultural colonialism (e.g., Bizzell, 1991; Moglen, 1996). But the liberatory, counterhegemonic position is itself highly controversial. Critics charge that universities have run amok; that they have become overly politi-cized; and that militant feminists and other left-wing professors, especially, have been using the academic classroom as a platform to spout one or another version of what they take to be "political correctness" (e.g., Himmelfarb, 1996). Some left-ori-ented professors have joined in the critique of counterhegemonic political correct-ness. Said Donald Lazere (1992),

> My own political leanings are toward democratic socialism, and I believe that college English courses have a responsibility to expose students to socialist viewpoints because these views are virtually excluded from all other realms of the American cognitive, rhetorical, semantic, and literary universe of discourse. I am firmly opposed, however, to instructors imposing socialist (or feminist, or Third-World, or gay) ideology on students as the one true faith—just as much as I am opposed to the present, generally unquestioned (and even unconscious) imposition of capitalist, white-male, heterosexual ideology that pervades American education and every other aspect of our culture. (p. 195)

The controversy over faculty advocacy in the classroom has engendered consid-erable debate among academics in recent years. Some activists argue that faculty advocacy is not only desirable but that on controversial issues, professors cannot help project their views by the readings they assign, the lectures they present, and the manner in which they conduct class discussions. Critics of this view maintain that it is at least possible to project the *appearance* of evenhandedness. Some go further and argue that objectivity is possible (Himmelfarb, 1996); moreover, it is the job of the professor, some argue, to teach students *how* to think, not *what* to think.

Given what this book has already said about persuasion in the guise of objectiv-ity, you might predict that it would raise suspicions about claims to objectivity in teaching. If so, you would be right.

Indeed, that same suspicion applies to textbook writing, this one included. One problem with objectivity as a standard is that the term itself is ambiguous. Robert Hackett (1984) has observed that objectivity in such fields as history, education, and journalism has traditionally meant different things that are often at war with one another.

One meaning of objectivity is being accurate, free from distortion, and true to the facts. The other, considered especially appropriate with regard to controversial issues, is balance, impartiality, and evenhandedness. For example, in reporting on the firing of a popular minister of state, as opposed to the reporting of a humdrum fire on Main Street, the journalist would be sure to present "both sides" (Hackett, 1984). Likewise, the evenhanded religion professor could say as many good things as bad to students about Christianity, and the English literature professor could say an equal proportion of good things as bad about Shakespeare.

The tension between these two standards of objectivity is exhibited in at least two ways, says Hackett (1984). First, a balanced account may present an inaccurate account to newspaper readers, students, or what have you, by misrepresenting an *imbalanced* state of affairs. One political party may be running a clean campaign, and the opposition party a dirty one. As many good things may not be as sayable about Saddam Hussein of Iraq as bad things. By this same reasoning, Christianity and Shakespeare may be far more (or less) reprehensible than their critics claim.

A second problem, suggests Hackett (1984), is that there is no rule for deciding what should and should not be considered controversial; hence, there is no way to determine what should be treated as a matter for matter-of-fact reporting or lecturing and what should be treated evenhandedly. Is "white privilege" a controversial issue? Many professors don't give it a second thought. Meanwhile, liberatory professors who think about white privilege a great deal assume that its being a problem is not controversial. Should the chair of the biology department treat praise of the human genome project by a member of the department as controversial? Should praise for Christianity by a member of the religion department be regarded as controversial? Who's to say?

The issues just raised deserve far more attention than they typically get *in* the college classroom. Too often, they are reserved for discussion among academics behind closed doors. Is there an alternative?

Faced with an ethical teaching dilemma of the sort just raised, the professor might turn to the students and ask, "If you were in my shoes, how would you have handled this problem?" This question tends to be highly provocative, unleashing all manner of insights about advocacy in the classroom, including insights about persuasion in the guise of objective lecture or discussion (Simons, 1995). The question is a type of reflexive reframing, inviting as it does pedagogical talk about pedagogical talk. Typically, students come up with arguments for and against faculty advocacy similar to those just presented. Yet the discussion is anything but routine because it prompts consideration of the appropriate functions of the college classroom and not just the specific issue that was initially raised. One lesson from this exercise is that sometimes the best answer to a question (e.g., "How should I have handled this problem?") is the question itself.

Surely, one function of the college classroom is to promote critical thinking, a topic already much discussed in this book. The next section examines the topic in depth.

The Mindful Society

Noted psychologist Ellen Langer has done considerable research on conditions leading to what she calls *mindlessness* and *mindfulness* by persuadees. In one study, she and her colleagues (Langer, Blank, & Chanowitz, 1978) found that people could be persuaded to surrender their turns at a copying machine if given just the semblance of a reason: "because I need to make copies." This proved about as effective as giving a real reason: "because I'm in a hurry." But mindlessness turned to mindfulness when the request was to make 20 copies or more. Then, giving the mere semblance of a reason became no more effective than a request without a reason: "Excuse me, may I use the Xerox machine?"

The Langer study further evidences what other psychologists have demonstrated as well. People act mindfully—engage in central processing—when they are motivated to think critically and have the ability to do so. People act mindlessly—engage in peripheral processing—when they are unable or unmotivated to think critically. All of us act mindlessly some of the time, and some of us seem to operate on automatic pilot—relying on cognitive shorthands—nearly all the time.

Cognitive shorthands are often serviceable. Following the crowd, for example, can get us to soccer games in foreign countries when we don't know whether to turn left or turn right after getting off the train and don't know the language well enough to ask directions.

But cognitive shorthands can be harmful to self and society, as when students blindly submit to authority, when entire communities develop lynch mob mentalities in response to threats real or imagined, or when voters jump on the proverbial bandwagon and elect popular candidates rather than their more qualified campaign rivals. Some of that knee-jerk thinking seems built into the way most of us live: fast-paced, thousands of messages coming at us every day, little time for reflection, lots of distractions.

This book was written in part to help you engage in mindful message processing as a persuader and persuadee. The advice offered in Chapter 8 on coming to judgment prior to attempting persuasion is consistent with Langer's advice. So, too, is the advice offered on practicing an art of mistrust in attending to persuasive messages. The persuasion dialogue requires mindful speaking and listening.

Langer (1989) adds to what has been said here about the differences between mindlessness and mindfulness. Repetition is identified as one of the major causes of mindlessness. Associated with mindlessness is a tendency to create premature cognitive commitments and to allow such commitments to impose "false limits" on our competence and potential. As discussed in Chapter 2, all of us rely on filters, or schemas, by which to process new information. But we need schemas that will allow contextual factors to enter into our judgments. The mindful message processor values the play of uncertainty, appreciates the potential of nonconformity, and welcomes the opportunity to take personal responsibility in making decisions. Mindfulness is also less outcome oriented than process oriented. The mindful persuadee develops "second-order mindfulness" in thinking about the process itself. Second-order mindfulness "recognizes that there is no right answer" and "no logical stopping point" on many of the issues we confront (p. 200) but assumes that gut decisions, made after specific concerns are addressed thoughtfully, will be better decisions.

Langer's (1989) insights about mindfulness are important. Yet needed are not just mindful individuals but societal institutions that facilitate mindful message processing. Faced with mounting pressures to compete for scarce resources, the news and entertainment media, the fine arts, and even higher education are becoming increasingly market oriented (Barber, 1996; McCloskey & Klamer, 1995). Although these institutions used to provide a check on the excesses of capitalism, now they are a part of the problem. Two recent revelations are illustrative.

Prime-Time Entertainment Sellout

If ever there was a wall between entertainment programming and product advertising, it has long since been broken with the advent of MTV, of kids' shows specifically designed to promote featured products, and of product displays surreptitiously inserted into feature films. But these deceptions are relatively benign when measured against news that the government has also been attempting to persuade in the guise of entertainment (Romano, 2000). The White House negotiated a deal with the television networks forgiving them an obligation to provide so many minutes of unpaid public service advertising in return for their agreement to insert the government's prosocial messages into prime-time dramas such as *Touched by an Angel, NYPD Blue, ER, Beverly Hills 90210,* and *Chicago Hope.*

Arguably, this was a good deal for the networks. Their estimated gain would be approximately $22 million worth of added time for paid advertising. The cost would be a small reduction in their once vaunted reputation for creative independence. Television writers would not be forced to change their scripts, and the government would not be asking television producers to promote its more controversial activities—only to insert into their prime-time scripts subtle messages about the dangers of street drugs and alcohol. What could be wrong with that?

Yet as Georgetown University law professor David Cole complained, the government was not supposed to favor the content of one message over another when doling out financial benefits to facilitate private speech.

They crossed the line between government speech and private speech, and basically coerced private speakers, through the public purse, into expressing government messages in a way that was designed to mislead the American public. . . . The rights it violates are the rights of viewers and listeners not to be propagandized in an underhanded way by our government." (quoted in Romano, 2000, pp. 17-18)

Newspaper Sellout

The news, like entertainment programming, is hardly exempt from promotional efforts. Network news shows promote movies, sports, and other products owned by the networks' parent corporations. Magazines promote products in the guise of objectively reporting about them, while also permitting advertorials formatted as news. These same magazines offer glowing "news" stories about the celebrities who endorse products expensively advertised in their magazines. Collusive arrangements between newspapers and the corporations and local governments they are supposed to cover at arm's length are also commonplace. For example, newspapers create sections of the paper designed to give advertisers a hospitable environment (Frankel, 2000).

None of this is new, or for many in the news business, particularly alarming. But now comes news of a ratcheting up of demands from the front office for news that yields advertising profits. The story, written by a disgruntled media critic for the *Los Angeles Times,* concerned the extent to which that venerable newspaper's reporters and editors were pressured by top management to "think corporate" as they developed their plans for news coverage. For example, the *Times* executives agreed to run a special issue of the *Los Angeles Times* Sunday magazine devoted exclusively to favorable coverage of a new downtown sports arena. Contractors and patrons were strongly encouraged to advertise. Not disclosed in the news coverage was that the *Times* was a secret partner in the arena project and that it was to share in the profits from the magazine advertising. Max Frankel (2000), a long-time distinguished journalist for the *New York Times,* eloquently expressed his concerns about the dangers of news-for-profit:

A wall is needed to insulate the gathering of news, which should be a selfless public service, from the pursuit of profit, which is needed to guarantee the independence of the business. Journalism, in other words, is a costly and paradoxical enterprise: it can flourish only when profitable, but it is most suspect when it seeks a profit at all costs. (p. 25)

The two examples just given, of television entertainment programmers and news organizations abrogating creative and journalistic integrity for the sake of the almighty dollar, are symptomatic of the threats posed by financial *dependence* to the professional *independence* of America's cultural institutions. Consider, if you will, the fate of colleges and universities, especially those unable to depend on large endowments. Will they be forced by market pressures to place increased constraints on academic freedom? To better compete, will they adopt many of the same marketing practices they used to criticize? Will they encourage students to place a high value on criticism? If not, what will serve as the counterforce to excessive marketplace manipulations? Books such as this one offer critiques of unsavory practices by public relations professionals, product advertisers, and political campaign consultants. Will tomorrow's textbooks on persuasion teach the how-to of spin, never mind the critiques, and never mind the need for genuine commitments, to students who were raised on sophisticated forms of spin from childhood on and who may even have come to enjoy being manipulated, rather than objecting to it (Postman, 1985)?

What will happen to generations hence who grow up in cyberspace? The Internet, says Shapiro (1999), will offer a wondrous bounty of information. But how reliable will this information be, and will information—sheer information—come to replace that less tangible but perhaps more valuable commodity: experienced judgment? Will we know what to make of the information as we exercise our own judgments on the sorts of iffy questions with which persuasion is concerned? Novelist and critic Umberto Eco has remarked that when he enters a bookstore and glances at the spine of a book, he can make a reliable guess at its content from a number of available signs, but he is bereft of those skills when he goes on the Net (quoted in Marshall, 1997). Eco is not alone in finding the Internet baffling as a source of reliable information. But will there be Internet intermediaries in future to help browsers distinguish the accurate from the dubious—as reference librarians do now?

Americans are rightly proud of their freedoms, but with freedom must come responsibility. What happens if the persuaders we trust abnegate their responsibilities? What happens when that freedom is further eroded in the civic arena by the power of the purse? Is government needed to facilitate mindful message processing? If so, how can we prevent government from also becoming part of the problem?

Government can facilitate mindful message processing by passing stiff consumer protection legislation, requiring, for example, that physicians make full disclosure to their patients about how they stand to benefit financially if their patients sign up for drug-testing programs (Eichenwald & Kolata, 1999). Government can also require networks to set aside free airtime for political advertisements as a substitute for paid advertising—this in exchange for the billions in government giveaways to the networks of increased bandwidth capacity (Frankel, 1999). Government can also sharply reduce soft money contributions to the political parties, again with a view toward leveling the playing field in political campaigns.

But facilitating mindful message processing should not solely be a matter of government-imposed regulations. Schools need to teach critical thinking, argumentation, and the like, and television needs to provide models of it. Teenagers, not just

---

BOX 15.2 Katie Couric's Colonoscopy Campaign

As regards the use of role models, consider Katie Couric's campaign to save the world from colon cancer. Couric's husband of many years had died of preventable colon cancer. She had genuine motivation for her campaign. Moreover, as host of NBC's *Today*, Katie Couric commanded an audience of millions. NBC was willing to give the *Today* show 5 full days to make Couric's case for colonoscopies, a procedure that makes possible early detection and removal of cancer-causing polyps. For understandable reasons, NBC wanted to maintain the show's ratings that week, and they wanted the topic handled with dignity. So did Couric. The weeklong series achieved Couric's goals and NBC's goals. Jonathan Storm (2000) attributed the campaign's success to her status as a superrepresentative (see Chapter 4). He described her as "America's next-door neighbor—chattier than some, smarter than most" (p. C1). Storm added that his suspicions about the series had been overcome:

> A critic's temptation is to lash out at such seemingly ratings-hungry, self-aggrandizing grandstanding. Maybe they should examine not her colon, but her cold, calculating heart. But Couric's behavior, and the story she has been presenting this week, parry such attacks at every turn. (p. C1)

---

college-age readers of persuasion textbooks, need to learn how to dissect messages at multiple levels and in multiple ways, seeing evidences, for example, of persuasion in the guises of entertainment and objectivity and of advertising's role in the shaping of ideologies. Teenagers, not just college students, need instruction in dialogue and conflict management. They need help as well in coping with the new world of the Internet—learning, for example, how to evaluate its many sources of information and opinion, some trustworthy, some totally unreliable.

Television remains today's primary educator, and young people especially tend to learn by example. Why not use role models, then, including peer group and celebrity models, to teach mindful message processing? (See Box 15.2.)

A generation raised on television needs also to be entertained as it is taught, and television is in a position to teach the toughest lessons. No, "we" are not perfect; no, "they" are not all mad or bad. Too often, young people are raised on *melodrama*: the forces of good arrayed simplistically against the sinister forces of evil. Adults, too, tend to get news in the form of melodrama—an extension of the childhood socialization process. How much better it would be if children and adults saw television programming that *deepened* viewers' understanding of complex social problems, rather than reinforcing simplistic us-them thinking by way of cardboard characters in melodramatic roles. Ironically, it seems to be comedy on television that is best equipping us to understand the human condition. The Simpsons, for example, are three-dimensional characters who make tough decisions, including bad decisions, while remaining lovable for all their foibles and eccentricities. On instructive entertainment programming such as the *Simpsons*, heroes display tragic flaws; villains have some redeeming characteristics. Said Kenneth Burke (1937/1961),

> The progress of humane enlightenment can go no further than in picturing people not as *vicious* but as *mistaken*. When you add that people are *necessarily* mistaken, that all people are exposed to situations in which they must act as fools, that *every* insight contains its own special kind of blindness, you complete the comic circle, returning again to the lesson of humility that underlies great tragedy. (p. 41)

The Ethics of Being Ethically Sensitive

Ever hear of the Eichmann phenomenon? Adolf Eichmann was an upper-middle-level manager of a large organization. In that capacity, he performed his job well, always doing what was technically efficient in accomplishing the organization's mission, always following orders from his superiors. It just so happened that Eichmann's organization was a Nazi death camp.

Writing on Eichmann's trial in Jerusalem (see Picture 15.1), philosopher and political theorist Hannah Arendt (1978) was struck by how ordinary Eichmann seemed. Obedience was highly valued, expected, and required in Eichmann's organization; hence he considered himself virtuous. Operating well within the range of sanity and normality, he was simply a thoughtless man doing his job. Arendt coined the term "the banality of evil" to refer to this man without an ethical frame.

From evidence presented in Richard Nielsen's (1996) writing on organizational ethics, it appears that Eichmann was by no means alone. Organizations of every type make demands on employees to surrender their autonomy—and often their sense of ethical responsibility—in service of organizational objectives. A repeated explanation for torture of American POWs by the Japanese in World War II, for concealment of tobacco company research linking cigarettes with cancer, and for price-fixing by companies has been the refrain from organizational professionals who *did* know better: "That's the way it was done in my organization." Says Gioia (1992), organizational representatives are often not aware that they are dealing with a problem that might have ethical overtones. "If the case involves a familiar class of problems or issues, it is likely to be handled via existing cognitive structures or scripts—scripts that typically include no ethical component in their cognitive content" (p. 388).

Ethical behavior, then, begins with ethical sensitivity—something that is often in short supply. In your role as communicator and recipient of persuasive messages, ask yourself: What ethical standards should guide my conduct in this particular case? What should I expect of others? Richard Johannesen (1996, pp. 17-18) suggests going further: Why these standards and not others? To whom is ethical responsibility owed? How will I feel about myself after this communicative act? Could I jus-

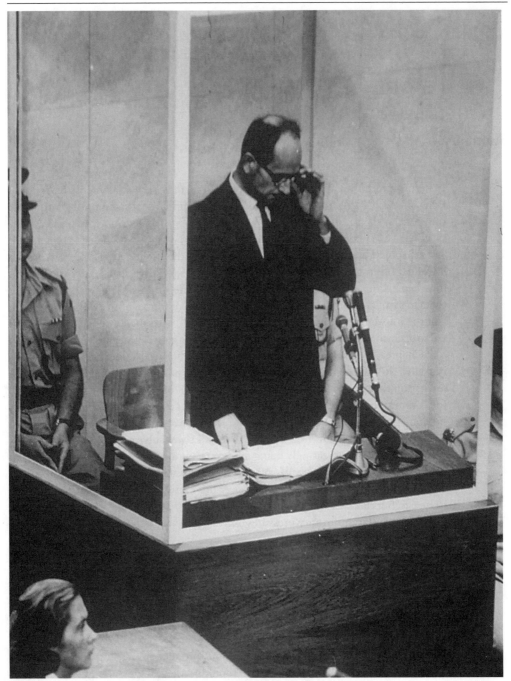

Picture 15.1. Eichmann in a Box at His Trial in Jerusalem
SOURCE: Archive Photos. Used with permission.

tify my act publicly if called on to do so? How can I judge in retrospect whether my actions were consistent with my ethical intentions? These are good questions. Appendix III provides a self-survey with specific examples for you to consider your perspectives on ethics.

Summary

In keeping with the call for a mindful society, one that is especially sensitive to questions of ethics, Part 3 of this book has traveled a difficult path, enjoining you to see things from the perspective of the persuader one moment, from the different perspective of the persuadee the next, and above all, to ask: What's best for society?

Chapter 9 brought to a head questions that had been lingering since Chapter 4's introduction to the coactive approach. How can persuasive speakers possibly combine expressions of genuine commitment with the impossible demands made on them to strategize, organize, and effectively use the resources of the verbal, the visual, and the nonverbal? Why should students "get real" with their audiences when they are so accustomed to being rewarded for performing mechanically?

Chapter 10 posed a number of the dilemmas for well-intentioned social activists. How do you balance the urgent need to accomplish short-term goals against the realization that your health campaign, for example, may result in long-term harm to the community you are trying to help? How do you choose between power and persuasion strategies that accomplish desirable ends versus education and facilitation strategies that are less controlling but also less likely to solve a serious problem? Normative influence is increasingly being used to tackle antisocial behaviors, but at what price? Who gets to decide what is antisocial and prosocial, propaganda or education? Groups at the margins of respectable society often use highly manipulative influence strategies, but should we condemn their efforts at "brainwashing" while being largely indifferent to the conformity pressures exerted by better respected, more entrenched organizations?

Chapter 11 took these and other such questions into the political campaign arena. Candidate Snodgrass is a worthy contender; her opponent is a self-serving opportunist. Does this justify Snodgrass using all manner of Machiavellian tactics to defeat her opponent, including, for example, a smear campaign based on rumor and innuendo? Should Snodgrass bend her professed beliefs to the whims of the voters, as well as to the demands of fat-cat contributors?

Chapter 12 posed ethical questions about product advertising. Advertisers use "puffery," no doubt about it. But why shouldn't they exaggerate, given that their competitors do it and their clients demand it? Product advertisers also play on our vanities, our insecurities, and our infantile urges. But why shouldn't they, if we con-sumers are foolish enough to fall for their ploys?

Chapter 13 placed us in the often ugly arena of social conflicts. Here, in the "region of the Scramble," interests are at stake, not just differences of opinion. Here, for that reason, talk can be—and often is—used to commit symbolic violence. If your roommate, your coworker, your best friend, or your spouse uses talk as a weapon against you, are you justified in responding in turn?

Chapter 14 brought us into an arena of asymmetrical conflict, that between pro-test movements and entrenched establishments. Lacking the material resources and standing in society, leaders of these social movements frequently conjure up myths of group unity, victimhood, and sacrifice, while painting their opponents as devils, fools, and puppets. Their influence strategies extend beyond peaceful petitioning to staged confrontations, civil disobedience, and guerilla warfare. Are their more mili-tant tactics justified, given the adverse circumstances they face?

Chapter 15 has brought all these ethical questions to a head. Its aims have been to consolidate, synthesize, and then raise some additional questions, this time about faculty advocacy in the classroom.

Five perspectives on ethics were introduced: (1) pragmatism, (2) utilitarianism, (3) universalism, (4) dialogic ethics, and (5) situational ethics. In the process, new questions were asked: Can persuaders be expected to act honestly and directly in sit-uations where the reigning institutions of society make that type of talk risky, even self-destructive? Can persuadees be expected to make intelligent judgments when a society's reigning institutions make that difficult, if not impossible?

Chapter 15 then took up an issue often kept under the rug in college settings: When, and under what circumstances, should instructors take and defend contro-versial positions in the classroom? The issues are complicated but readily identifi-able. They involve conditions of relevance, power, definition of what is (and is not) controversial, manner of promotion, and cultural context.

Chapter 15 concluded with a vision of the mindful society, made up not just of individuals willing and able to process messages mindfully but of institutions such as government, schools, and mass media that help make that happen. Those who man-age our society's organizations and institutions would be especially attuned to issues of ethics. Better that these leaders occasionally make bad ethical decisions than that like Adolf Eichmann, they be ethically indifferent.

Questions and Projects for Further Study

1. Evaluate the ethics of Clinton's apologia using the five perspectives intro-duced in this chapter. Then draw your own conclusions.

2. Everyone knows that advertisers make exaggerated claims about their products. So does it matter that a company selling nutritional supplements to bodybuilders displayed its product alongside an image of a champion bodybuilder, despite good scientific evidence that these supplements do no more to build muscle than an ordinary balanced diet? Does it matter that many bodybuilders expend vast sums on these products? Moreover, the ad had what some in the business call *deniability*. When confronted with charges against the product, a company spokesperson insisted that the ad was not fraudulent. Nowhere was there a verbal claim that the product could bring about extraordinary muscle growth. As for the pictures of the product next to the champion bodybuilder, the inference to be drawn from that, the spokesperson insisted, was a subjective matter (Messaris, 1997, pp. 273-274). Bring your own ethical perspective to bear on the this ad. Was it more or less ethical because of its deniability?

3. Should professors take and defend controversial positions in the college classroom? If so, under what conditions? If not, how should they treat controversial issues? Should they strive for objectivity according to one or another definition of this troublesome term? What do you think of the idea of professors posing these problems to their students?

4. Do you agree with Langer's characterization of mindful thinking?

5. In your opinion, will cyberspace technologies help make society more mindful or more mindless?

6. What role, if any, should government play in regulating the dissemination of ideas and information? Should it require the networks to provide free television time for political candidates, for example?

7. Who is more irresponsible, an ethically insensitive killer such as Eichmann or one who is sensitive to the evil he or she commits but kills anyway?

8. Hannah Arendt has observed that the relationship between ethically thoughtless people such as Eichmann and systematically corrupt environments is mutually reinforcing. That is, environments that are corrupt reward the Eichmanns of the world, and they in turn help perpetuate such environments. Do you agree? If so, how can the vicious cycle be broken?

9. What is melodrama? When are the news media most likely to resort to it? Should we attempt to learn from situation comedies such as the *Simpsons* while being critical of television news? What do you think of Burke's inclination to see humans (including ourselves) as mistaken, rather than vicious or evil? Would this philosophy, if widely adopted, advance society or inhibit good people from rising up against evil?

10. How ethical is the coactive approach to persuasion?

References

Arendt, H. (1978). *The life of the mind* (M. McCarthy, Ed.). New York: Harcourt Brace Jovanovich.

Barber, B. (1996). *Jihad vs. McWorld: How globalism and tribalism are reshaping the world.* New York: Ballantine.

Bizzell, P. (1991). Power, authority, and critical pedagogy. *Journal of Basic Writing, 10,* 54-69.

Brand, M. (1996). The professional obligations of classroom teachers. In P. M. Spacks (Ed.), *Advocacy in the classroom* (pp. 3-17). New York: St. Martin's.

Burke, K. B. (1961). *Attitudes toward history.* Boston: Beacon. (Original work published 1937)

Burke, K. B. (1968). *Collected poems 1915-1967.* Berkeley: University of California Press.

Burke, K. B. (1969). *A rhetoric of motives.* Berkeley: University of California Press. (Original work published 1950)

Christie, R., & Geis, F. (1970). *Studies in Machiavellianism.* New York: Academic Press.

Eichenwald, K., & Kolata, G. (1999, May 16). Drug trials hide conflict for doctors. *New York Times,* pp. A1, A34-A35.

Frankel, M. (1999, February 21). Save democracy first! *New York Times Magazine,* 28-29.

Frankel, M. (2000, January 9). The wall, vindicated: A sturdy barrier between news and commerce enhances both. *New York Times Magazine,* 24-25.

Gioia, D. A. (1992). Pinto fires and personal ethics: A script analysis of missed opportunities. *Journal of Business Ethics, 11,* 379-389.

Goldstein, J. (1999, June 18). Both sides in gun control debate paying to get voices heard. *Philadelphia Inquirer,* p. A10.

Hackett, R. A. (1984). Decline of a paradigm: Bias and selectivity in news media studies. *Critical Studies in Mass Communication, 1,* 1-14.

Himmelfarb, G. (1996). The new advocacy and the old. In P. M. Spacks (Ed.), *Advocacy in the classroom* (pp. 96-101). New York: St. Martin's.

Jackall, R. (1995). The magic lantern: The world of public relations. In R. Jackall (Ed.), *Propaganda* (pp. 351-399). New York: New York University Press.

Johannesen, R. L. (1996). *Ethics in human communication* (4th ed.). Prospect Heights, IL: Waveland.

Langer, E. (1989). *Mindfulness.* Reading, MA: Addison-Wesley.

Langer, E., Blank, A., & Chanowitz, B. (1978). The mindlessness of ostensibly thoughtless action: The role of placebic information in interpersonal interaction. *Journal of Personality and Social Psychology, 36,* 635-642.

Lazere, D. (1992). Teaching the political conflicts: A rhetorical schema. *College Composition and Communication, 43,* 194-203.

Lewis, C., & Center for Public Integrity. (1996). *The buying of the president.* New York: Avon.

Marshall, L. (1997, March). The world according to Eco. *Wired,* pp. 145, 148.

McArthur, J. R. (1992). *Second front: Censorship and propaganda in the Gulf War.* New York: Hill & Wang.

McCloskey, D. N., & Klamer, A. (1995). One quarter of GDP is persuasion. *American Economic Review, 85,* 191-195.

Menand, L. (1996). Culture and advocacy. In P. M. Spacks (Ed.), *Advocacy in the classroom* (pp. 116-125). New York: St. Martin's.

Messaris, P. (1997). *Visual persuasion.* Thousand Oaks, CA: Sage.

Moglen, H. (1996). Unveiling the myth of neutrality: Advocacy in the feminist classroom. In P. M. Spacks (Ed.), *Advocacy in the classroom* (pp. 204-212). New York: St. Martin's.

Nielsen, R. P. (1996). *The politics of ethics.* New York: Oxford University Press.

Postman, N. (1985). *Amusing ourselves to death.* New York: Viking.

Romano, C. (2000, January 16). Federal review of TV scripts raises constitutional questions. *Philadelphia Inquirer,* pp. A17-A18.

Salant, J. D. (1998, November 28). Foes of new HMO rules spent $60 million for lobbying in six months. *Philadelphia Inquirer,* p. A10.

Shapiro, A. L. (1999). *The control revolution.* New York: Public Affairs.

Simons, H. W. (1995). Teaching the pedagogies: A dialectical approach to an ideological dilemma. In H. W. Simons & M. Billig (Eds.), *After postmodernism: Ideological critique and beyond.* London: Sage.

Solomon, R. C. (1984). *Ethics: A brief introduction.* New York: McGraw-Hill.

Storm, J. (2000, March 6). On "Today," Katie Couric's inside story. *Washington Post,* pp. C1, C6-C7.

Zaltman, G., & Duncan, R. (1977). *Strategies for planned change.* New York: John Wiley.

Appendix I

Resources for the Persuader

Use the following as reminders of principles covered earlier in the book. Make use of the principles as needed. Refer to earlier chapters for elaboration of the principles. Keep in mind that this is but a partial list.

Theoretically Derived Resources

▶ *From Aristotelian Theory:* Combine (a) Ethos (perceived competence and trustworthiness of the speaker), (b) Pathos (the motivational/emotional appeals you can offer your audience, and (c) Logos (the perceived logic of your case).

▶ *From BVA Theory:* Influence attitudes by directing thought about audience beliefs and values: (a) Make positive beliefs and values appear more salient while downplaying the importance or relevance of beliefs and values harmful to your cause, (b) strengthen some beliefs and values and weaken others, and (c) add advantages or positives to those your audience has already thought of.

▶ *From the Theory of Reasoned Action:* (a) Convince audiences that valued others would have them act as you have recommended they act, or (b) play down the importance of what valued others think.

▶ *From the Elaboration of Likelihood Model (ELM):* (a) Encourage central processing (for more powerful, longer-lasting effects) by increasing audience ability and motivation to think long and hard about the issues, while helping them along with sound arguments and good evidence, favorable to your cause; and/or (b) encourage peripheral processing

382 PERSUASION IN SOCIETY

favorable to your cause by such triggers of relatively mindless acceptance as expressions of liking for your audience, appearing personally attractive, and naming celebrities who have endorsed your position or proposal.

▶ *From Learning Theories:* (a) Assist audiences in information processing, from reception to yielding, being mindful of the need to overcome resistance at the yielding stage by the better educated, more confident, and more intelligent members of your audience, while facilitating comprehension among their opposite numbers. (b) Present incentives to your audience by projecting rewards from adoption of the recommended action and penalties from inaction or from choosing the wrong course of action. (c) Link your proposal with all manner of favorable associations (both conscious and unconscious) while linking what you oppose with unfavorable associations.

▶ *From the Coactive Model of Persuasion:* (a) Use "different strokes for different folks." (b) Combine evidences of interpersonal similarity with an emphasis on those differences that make you appear more expert, better informed, and more reliable. (c) Build on premises acceptable to your audience, rather than proceeding expressively, or combatively, or as an objectivist. If necessary, make a case for the reasonableness of your premises. Build from common ground, possibly using a yes-yes or yes-but approach, or reason from the perspective of the other.

Framing and "Languaging" Resources

▶ *Selectivity:* Think of choice of labels, definitions, descriptions, comparisons, contrasts, contextualizations, and so on as weapons in your arsenal of persuasion. Be strategically selective.

▶ *Intensify/Downplay:* (a) Intensify through repetition, association, and composition. (b) Downplay through omission, diversion, and confusion. Choose framing metaphors with a view toward their intensifying and downplaying functions.

▶ *Creative Reframing:* Be prepared to think unconventionally and to assist your audience in dissolving or resolving problems by going "outside the nine dots." One way to go outside the dots is by use of generative metaphors.

▶ *Cultural Frames and Verbal Repertoires:* (a) Remember that our culture's notions of common sense contain seemingly opposing frames that you can exploit to advantage. (b) Practice spin control by selecting from among the range of possibilities those sayings, those lines of argument, and those word choices that work best for you.

▶ *Introductory Frames:* Take special care with the frames you will use to talk about the type of talk you are about to give. Are you here to "inform" the audience, to "explore" some ideas with them, to "sell" them on an idea, or to "advise" or "counsel" them? Remember that audience resistance can sometimes be overcome by persuading in the guise of nonpersuasion.

▶ *Going Meta:* Frame the context for the issues you are discussing as well as the opposition to your point of view by way of metamoves that make prior communications the *subject* of your communications. For example, consider commenting on the assignment your instructor has given you. (But also review Chapter 6 on the risks of going meta.)

Argumentative Resources

▶ *Stock Issues:* Consider organizing the body of your speech around stock issues. If it's a proposition of policy you're dealing with, decide first whether you want to change, repair, or retain the policy. This will determine your approach to the stock issues, including your burdens of proof and refutation.

▶ *Evidence:* Use the different forms of evidence—stories, statistics, brief examples, testimony—in combination.

▶ *Storytelling:* Tell stories that pack an emotional wallop while at the same time helping to build your case. Provide details that invite audiences to supply premises of their own, favorable to your case.

▶ *Statistics and Examples:* Be prepared to show that the factual claims are accurate, that they are relevant and representative, and that there are sufficient statistical data (or examples) to warrant the generalization.

▶ *Testimony:* Provide testimony, especially from perceived authorities and from eyewitnesses. If necessary, make a case for the credibility of your sources.

▶ *Cognitive Shorthands:* Don't neglect those in your audience who will be looking for logical shortcuts. For example, be prepared to use social proof (e.g., opinion poll evidence) in support of your case, and leave audiences with a sense that your position or proposal is psychologically consistent with the beliefs and values they hold dear.

Appendix II

 Different Strokes for Different Folks

Hostile Audiences or *Those Who Strongly Disagree With You*

1. Work hard to build rapport and to establish good will and attraction.

2. Use a yes-yes or yes-but approach. Build from areas of agreement to areas of disagreement.

3. Establish acceptance of principles before advocating specific proposals.

4. If possible, establish credibility and demonstrate the existence of a problem on one occasion; delay the specifics of a plan until the next occasion.

5. Use sources and evidence that your audience can accept.

6. Disarm the audience with humor.

7. Use the *method of residues.* That is, show why alternative solutions are not advisable as a way of suggesting that yours is the only reasonable alternative.

Critical Audiences and Conflicted Audiences

1. Use a lot of evidence. Understate, don't overstate. Document controversial evidence by citing its source.

2. Show consistency with your positions on other issues.

3. Reveal first premises or make sure they are clearly implied. Reason logically with audiences from premises to conclusions.

4. Use the both-sides-with-refutation approach.

5. Use definitions that the audience is likely to find acceptable.

6. Maintain attention and interest, even as you deal with evidence. In general, encourage central processing (see Chapter 2 on the Elaboration of Likelihood Model).

Sympathetic Audiences: Reinforcing Attitudes

1. Use extended factual illustrations. Play on the power of narratives.

2. Use vivid, intense language; don't understate.

3. Use evidence to dramatize, rather than prove. Work to intensify commitments to audience-perceived truisms.

4. Ask for specific behavioral commitments. Secure public commitments.

5. Congratulate your audience for being "right-thinking."

6. Encourage your audience to join you in formulating conclusions from premises.

Uninformed, Less Educated, or Apathetic Audiences: Molding Attitudes

1. Work especially on getting attention and achieving comprehension.

2. Introduce only a little information at one time. Repeat with variations.

3. Appear to inform, rather than persuade. Stress your expertise.

4. Use a one-sided approach if the audience hasn't the interest or time to consider both sides.

5. Don't tell your audience members why they should know and care; make them *want* to know and care.

6. Cite successful role models who agree with your position. Rely to a greater extent than with more interested audiences on cognitive shorthands.

Activating Audiences (see also Chapter 5 on compliance-gaining alternatives)

1. For the action desired, indicate who, what, when, where, and how. Be specific.

2. Secure public commitments. Perhaps encourage successful others to model the action you desire. Create bandwagon effects.

3. Encourage immediate action; stress urgency and opportunity. Perhaps capitalize on Cialdini's principle of scarcity by suggesting that the benefits are available for a limited time only.

4. Encourage active participation by your audience. Perhaps encourage audience members to role-play the position you advocate, to summarize its main arguments, or to join in a discussion of actions they could take.

5. Possibly suggest a range of behavioral alternatives.

6. Remind your audience members after they have made public commitments that they have had decisional freedom. Point out again that no one has forced them or obligated them to act.

7. Possibly encourage your audience to practice refuting others who may later offer counterarguments.

8. Arrange possibilities for future contacts with your audience.

Appendix III

 Ethical, Unethical, or Borderline? A Self-Survey

By now you're surely aware of the importance of confronting ethical issues in persuasion but also aware of their complexities. Is honesty always the best policy? If so, what about so-called white lies, those told for the purpose of benefiting others? Does the end always justify the means? If so, whose ends need to be considered? Only the persuader's? How much consideration should be given to the interests of the persuadee, or to the interest of society as a whole? Should ethics be a matter of concern only when we are the targets of persuasion, or should we strive for consistency by applying the Golden Rule—that is, by doing unto others what we would have them do unto us?

Pulled together in this appendix are more than 100 examples from the book of persuasive practices that by one standard or another might be considered ethically questionable. Are there any practices on the list that you think are highly unethical? If so, according to what standards? Are there other practices that you applaud, although others might find them objectionable? If so, are there characteristics that these cases share in common? Are there yet other practices for which insufficient information is provided, such that you might favor the practice in one context but object to it if other details were provided? If so, what is it about the details that would influence your judgments in these borderline cases?

You can use this appendix to formulate and test your own philosophy of ethics. As a first step, try rating the practices on a scale from -3 (highly unethical) to +3 (highly ethical), with the zero point reserved for the borderline cases (-3, -2, -1, 0, +1, +2, +3). Next, go back over the ratings to glean insights about the bases for your judgments. Are there consistent patterns in the ratings that reveal you to be a pragmatist, a universalist, a situationalist, or someone firmly committed to a dialogic ethic? If you judged most of the examples as borderline (0 on the scale), you're clearly a situationalist but not necessarily indifferent to ethical principles. See if you can identify the sorts of details that if added to a borderline case could swing your vote this way or that. Do they reveal you to be a utilitarian? Are you someone sympathetic to the unsophisticated persuadee but not to those who should know better? Perhaps someone who is most concerned about ethics when you yourself stand to lose? Does your self-survey reveal you to be content with adhering to society's ethical standards—or wanting to change them?

Next, go back over the list and see if there are any ratings you'd like to change. Your instructor may invite you to discuss these with the class.

List of Cases

The following examples are listed by chapter for ease of review in the text. Rate each of them on a scale from -3 to +3.

Chapter 1

1. You weave together the facts at your disposal to create a convincing case in your own defense (thus, not just letting the facts "speak for themselves").

2. A speaker impresses an audience without telling the listeners anything that they didn't know before.

3. You use fallacious (i.e., illogical) arguments to make imprudent courses of action seem wise.

4. You present yourself as an expert in giving advice without being certain as to what's best in a given situation.

5. A recruiter presents prospective graduate students with a one-sided case for applying to an Ivy League school without mentioning opposing arguments.

6. A company constructs two ads on British TV for a soccer shoe: one for white soccer players, the other for black soccer players.

7. A clothing store announces its seventh "going out of business" sale.

8. An undergraduate fabricates an excuse for turning in a late paper.

9. Female beauty is represented to children in Barbie dolls that show Barbie to be very thin, thus prompting some children to be excessively weight-conscious.

10. War propaganda presents your country's troops as freedom fighters and the enemy troops as terrorists.

11. A supermarket chain stops describing its hamburger as "20% fat" after market research shows that customers buy the same hamburger more often when it is described as "80% lean."

Chapter 2

12. Bill Clinton tried, as he said, to be "truthful but not necessarily helpful" in responding under oath to questions about the Monica Lewinsky scandal.

13. *Time* and *Newsweek* repeatedly featured the "Monicagate" scandal in their cover stories (doing so a record 26 times), not because of the scandal's newsworthiness but because it sold copies.

14. TV viewers who publicly dismissed the importance of the Clinton-Lewinsky scandal still tuned in to CNN or MSNBC each night for the latest salacious details.

15. Television ads are designed on the assumption that consumers are products of classical conditioning, much like Pavlov's salivating dogs.

16. Attempts are made to undermine an entire belief system, such as a person's belief in Catholicism or in the American way of life.

17. Recruits to a religious cult are deprived of sleep, social contact, and exercise unless they show "progress" at giving up long-held beliefs.

Chapter 3

18. Professors call students by their first names but insist on being addressed by their titles (e.g., doctor, professor) and their last names.

19. Self-deception: A student hides from herself her fear that if she wore makeup, she'd have no excuse for not looking better.

20. A mother repeatedly disguises advice on child rearing to her daughter as "merely asking a few questions."

21. A candidate plants a thought in the voters' minds by use of innuendo, for example, hinting but not saying outright that the campaign opponent may have used cocaine while in college.

22. Television ads dub in street noises and other naturalistic effects to give the false impression of interviewing unpaid respondents, rather than paid actors posing as ordinary people.

23. Hillary and Bill Clinton allegedly arrange to be "caught" by photojournalists in a seemingly spontaneous embrace at a Virgin Islands hideaway even

as the Secret Service instructs photographers that the hideaway is officially off-limits.

24. The British during World War II arrange for the Germans to discover false secrets on the corpse of a high-ranking but fictitious military officer.

25. A parent orders a 4-year-old to go right to bed on the grounds that the child is tired, when the parent is the one who is tired.

26. A news magazine uses a cover photo that casts a presidential candidate in an unfavorable light and a cover photo showing a favorable view of the opposing candidate.

27. A scientific research article in a medical journal plays up the positive findings from a study of a cholesterol-lowering drug but plays down the dangerous side effects.

28. A high school history text substitutes "Native American" for "Indian" although most Native Americans prefer to be called Indians.

29. Television sitcoms are used to promote liberal social values, for example, lesbianism on *Ellen* and having a child out of wedlock on *Murphy Brown*.

30. The advertising industry repeatedly urges more and more product consumption and, in so doing, motivates people to become increasingly materialistic.

31. World culture is Americanized, for example, Indonesians are induced to abandon their centuries-old tea-drinking rituals in favor of a quick can of Coke or Pepsi.

Chapter 4

32. Physicists do not convince Congress about a worthwhile scientific project.

33. To induce students to keep up with the readings in the course, a professor appeals to the students' desires for good grades, although the professor personally believes that students are already too grade-conscious.

34. An individual woos a would-be lover by giving each of her or his faults the name of the good quality most like it.

35. Chairs are removed from an auditorium to give the impression that it is crowded when a visiting dignitary comes to speak.

Chapter 5

36. A cigarette manufacturer attempts to play down nonsmokers' objections to secondhand smoke by representing the smoke as a perceived annoyance, not a perceived danger, to the nonsmoker.

37. The same cigarette manufacturer as in Example 36 plays up smoking as a choice, rather than an addiction.

38. An advertiser fails to indicate that the "fat-free" ice cream it is promoting has more calories than regular brands.

39. Coffee manufacturers do not say on the wrapper, "This product contains an addictive drug."

40. In a debate about whether the United States should enter into a trade agreement with Mexico and Canada (NAFTA), Al Gore repeatedly diverts attention from the issue of NAFTA's value by questioning Ross Perot's motives in opposing it.

41. Inflated language: For example, a manicurist is called a "nail technician."

42. Technospeak: For example, NATO spokespersons call the unintentional killing of Serbian civilians by NATO bombings "collateral damage."

43. Persuaders use the mirroring technique to match the looks or behavior of the person they are trying to influence, as when a sales representative with 20/20 vision puts on glasses to match the glasses worn by a prospective purchaser.

44. A server routinely makes physical and eye contact with customers to get bigger tips.

45. A parent talks one way but acts another, for example, saying "I love you" to his or her child but in a nonverbal manner that contradicts the verbal expression.

46. A Republican photojournalist for a leading newspaper edits a photo of a Democratic senator walking arm in arm with a priest and a beautiful model by cropping out the priest.

Chapter 6

47. Spin control: For example, supporters of affirmative action characterize it as "helping minorities help themselves," whereas opponents call it "reverse discrimination."

48. Indirectness: For example, Senator Fudge introduces his speech in support of an unpopular policy by dancing around the subject, then characterizing his speech as one intended to "provoke discussion of the proposed policy," rather than to persuade the audience of its value.

49. Putting one's attackers on the defensive: For example, at the Senate hearing on whether he was unfit to serve on the Supreme Court, Judge Clarence Thomas (who is black) accuses his questioners of running a "high-tech lynching."

50. Using bluntness that causes offense: For example, a male psychotherapist tells a female patient that she is masochistic, defensive, and infantile and that she unconsciously wishes to sleep with her father as well as with him.

Chapter 7

51. A textbook writer on persuasion wins the affection of his readers by characterizing himself as a "patsy."

52. Social pressure to conform is used, as when a bartender stuffs a tip jar with his own dollar bills to encouraging customers to do likewise.

53. A real estate broker takes customers through undesirable setup properties before showing them the ones she intends to truly promote.

54. Salespersons use add-ons in sales, as when a car dealer tries to sell optional extras to the customer after the price of the car itself has been agreed to.

55. Pressuring others to repay in kind: For example, a bartender provides a complimentary drink in hopes of getting a larger tip.

56. College students use the "rejection-then-retreat" technique by asking for far more money from their parents than they know they'll be willing to give on the assumption that they'll then comply with comparatively more reasonable requests.

57. The foot-in-the-door technique: For example, a protest group secures a modest commitment of support for its cause as a prelude to asking for a much bigger commitment.

58. Behavioral modeling: For example, an attractive celebrity is shown in a television ad giving blood to get viewers to consider donating their blood.

59. A salesperson uses insincere expressions of liking for a customer.

60. You make yourself appear more likable to a first date than you really are.

61. Actors who play roles as medical doctors on TV shows endorse health products in TV ads.

62. Appeals to contrived scarcity are made, as when a club keeps prospective customers waiting on the street even when tables are available to make the club seem more popular than it really is.

63. A salesperson induces gullible tourists to buy Indian jewelry by raising the price, thus appealing to their assumption that "expensive equals good."

Chapter 8

64. You use the straw man approach to refutation by presenting an opponent's arguments in weakened form so that they can more easily be knocked down.

65. A solicitor for a worthy charity deliberately presents worst cases of a problem as typical cases.

66. Propagandistic appeals to fear and hate are made, as when leaders of enemy nations are presented as more cunning and more ruthless than they really are.

Chapter 9

67. A speaker plants questions from the audience. For example, Emily arranges with the chair of the meeting for the first question to be one that Emily wants asked.

68. A speaker is deliberately vague, as when a student speaker holds back the details of a proposal that she knows her audience will find objectionable.

69. Extremely frightening images (e.g., lungs tarred by cigarette smoke) are used to discourage teenagers from taking up the habit.

Chapter 10

70. Safe sex is promoted on a late-night radio talk show that mixes nine parts entertainment with one part serious instruction.

71. Abortion is framed as murder rather than as a woman's choice.

72. Combining agitation with litigation: For example, reform-minded groups whip up sentiment against the big tobacco companies while also taking them to court.

73. The "divide and conquer" strategy is used, as in attempts to drive a wedge between gun manufacturers and the National Rifle Association by offering manufacturers financial incentives to okay mandatory safety locks on guns.

74. Campaigns to rid inner-city communities of drug dealers use social ostracism rather than imprisonment.

75. Missionaries from the West lecture Africans about the immorality of female circumcision.

76. Pictures of George Washington are placed in public school classrooms as a way of instilling patriotism in young children.

77. New pledges to a college fraternity develop an us-them mentality through initiation rituals that encourage pride in the fraternity and hostility toward outsiders.

Chapter 11

78. Visual character assassination: For example, grainy, black-and-white photos that resemble police mug shots are used in negative advertising against campaign opponents.

79. Political candidates pander to the voters by telling them what they'd like to hear.

80. Evasion: For example, political candidates duck tough issues.

81. Elected officials give preferential treatment by granting greater access to big campaign contributors.

82. Deliberate falsehoods are used, as when John F. Kennedy claimed that the Eisenhower administration had permitted the Soviets to gain missile superiority over the United States. Kennedy knew better.

83. Apparent hypocrisy: For example, Senator John McCain deplored politicians' reliance on fat-cat contributors, even as he sought them out in his own campaign.

84. A Democratic political candidate claims that the Republicans wanted to cut Medicare. The Republicans said they wanted cuts in Medicare increases.

85. Mythmaking: A campaign biography of Bill Clinton casts him as someone fated from childhood to become president of the United States.

86. Push-poll surveys are used to inject damaging information about the campaign opponent while giving the appearance of merely eliciting opinions about the opponent for research purposes.

Chapter 12

87. Miller Lite ads equate possessing a beer with possessing a woman.

88. Telemarketers call at dinnertime to catch people when they are at home but at the risk of interrupting their dinner.

89. Anti-ads transgress the codes by which we have learned to "read" advertising, for example, the Volkswagen ad called "Sunday Afternoon" in which two men pick up a discarded chair, discover that it smells, then put it back where they found it.

90. The "nothing is better" claim is used in ads designed to promote the illusion of product superiority.

91. An advertisement boasts that the product has unique features ("The one and only Cheerios"), which turn out to be no different from characteristics of comparable products.

92. Ads contain feel-good words that are colorful but literally meaningless, for example, "Gallo: because the wine remembers."

93. An ad uses visual mythmaking by displaying an array of smiling faces under a banner of the "Pepsi Generation."

94. Audiotapes are said to help build self-esteem by using subliminal messages.

Chapter 13

95. A person whose spouse has been unfaithful uses threats and deception in an effort to get revenge.

96. Rather than responding in kind to your roommate's angry accusations, you ask your roommate for clarification as to what the problem is.

97. A salesperson uses concessions in a sales negotiation to kill a competitor's deal with the prospective buyer.

98. You audiotape a conversation with your live-in partner without his or her awareness.

Chapter 14

99. Students massively defy the Chinese authorities by staging a monthlong rally for democracy in Beijing's Tiananmen Square.

100. The government puts an end to the Tiananmen Square demonstration by sending in tanks to shoot at civilians.

101. Through agitation, a charismatic protest leader gets a large crowd to shout protest slogans in unison.

102. Civil rights protesters use confrontational acts such as sit-ins at lunch counters.

103. Revolutionary movements seek to overthrow existing regimes by the use of force.

104. Expressivist groups, such as the Promise Seekers, try to effect changes in institutions by changes in people.

Chapter 15

105. Bill Clinton attempts to cover up his affair with Monica Lewinsky.

106. An individual panders to another in the guise of apparent sincerity, as in the poem on sincerity by Kenneth Burke.

107. You schedule three prospective buyers at the same time to see your used car.

108. A doctor exaggerates to a patient the negative consequences of not getting enough exercise.

109. A teenager testifies falsely to Congress that she saw Iraqi soldiers tearing newborn infants from their incubators.

110. A congressman invites the testimony in Example 109 without realizing that the teenager is the Kuwaiti ambassador's daughter.

111. You evade unconsciously, as in forgetting to tell a prospective car buyer that the car's rust has been painted over.

112. A major newspaper promotes building a new stadium in the city without explaining to its readers that it has a financial stake in the stadium project.

113. Lobbies for special interest legislation are permitted to spend 5 to 10 times more than their opponents on television advertising.

114. Professors openly take and defend controversial positions in the classroom.

115. Professors reward agreement with their views and punish disagreement.

116. Professors promote controversial positions in the classroom but do so in the guise of information giving or evenhanded discussion.

Index

Ethical sensitivity, 374, 376
Ethics:
    dialogic perspective on, 362-363
    faculty advocacy and, 365-368
    mindlessness/mindfulness, 369-370
    newspaper sellout, 371-374
    pragmatic perspective on, 361, 360
    prime-time entertainment sellout, 370-371
    self-survey, 389-403
    sensitivity in, 374, 376
    situation-specific, 363-365
    universalist perspective on, 362
    utilitarianism perspective on, 360-362
Ethos, according to Aristotle, xxiii
Etzioni, A., 351
Euphemism, 101
Evaluational consistency, 145
Evidence, for argument, 167-171, 168 (picture), 383
Ewen, S., 228, 229
Expression games, 54-55
Expressivism, 345-351
Expressivist social movement, 334
Extension, in debate, 311, 312

Facilitation strategy, 217
Fact, proposition of, 164-166, 176
Faculty advocacy, and ethics, 365-368
Fallacy, 4, 171-173
False cause fallacy, 171
False dichotomy, 171, 172
Faludi, S., 282
Farnsworth, M. R., 281
Farrell, T. B., 17
Fear appeal, 212-213
Female circumcision, 211, 223
Ferrick, T., Jr., 150, 151
Festinger, L., 43
Film:
    advertisement in, 276
    as political image maker, 18-20, 19 (picture), 263-266, 265 (picture)
    political campaign, 18-20, 19 (picture)
Finnegan, J. R., Jr., 223
First-person account, as evidence, 169

Fisch, R., 75, 116-117, 163
Fishbein, M., 28, 29, 33, 41, 145, 223
Fisher, R., 309
Fiske, J., 63
Flacks, R., 334
Flattery, 96
Focus group, 280
Foot-in-the-door (FITD) technique, 138-139, 146, 151-152
Ford, G., 117, 258
Formaldehyde Institute, 57-58
Foundation for New Era Philanthropy, 150-151
Fox, S., 279
Frame:
    introductory, 383
    metacommunicative, 124-125
Framing:
    research on, 123-124
    using cultural frames, 121-123
    using generative metaphor, 119-121
    using metacommunicative frames, 124-125, 131
    using metaphor, 117-121
    See also Reframing
Framing/language resources, for persuader, 382-383
Frankel, M., 371, 372
Fraser, S. C., 138
Frederick, J., 110
Freedman, J. L., 138
Friesen, W. V., 105
Frost, J. H., 308
Fukada, H., 52

Gaeth, G. J., 123
Gamson, W., 121, 122, 353
Garrison, H. L., 181-186
Garrison, W. L., 186
Gates, H. L., 12
Geis, F., 361
General Electric, anti-ad, 285
General Motors, 339
Generative metaphor, 119-121
Genovese, C., 139
Genre, definition of, 22 (n8)